You Just Got'ta Keep Right On'a Truckin

A memoir by Eric (Max) Odendahl

For Ruth,

May 2018 be a
Wonderful year for you
with many blessings.

Eric M. Odendahl

TABLE OF CONTENTS

ACKNOWLEDGEMENTS

My "John-Denver-Days" portrait on the cover is by Catherine Foster, a well-known San Diego painter. She was my barber for several years at the Design Center in Hillcrest, where one patron described being there as "a head trip in an antique shop." Catherine's portrait of author Henry Miller is in the Henry Miller Museum in Big Sur, a Beethoven portrait from a line drawing is in the Beethoven Museum in Germany, and a portrait of Andy Warhol scheduled for exhibition at the Warhol Museum in Pennsylvania. A fellow artist wrote that, "Every element of Catherine's life was art, from her eclectic environment to her painting, poetry, and her ability to bring people together." It was a privilege to have been one of those she gathered as a friend.

In 1994, after my fairly-mild heart attack and angioplasty, while with a Kaiser Permanente cardiologist for a follow-up visit, I noticed one of Catherine's portraits of a noted composer hanging on his office wall. "She has a great heart," I blurted out, perhaps in some sort of Freudian way. He gave me a sad look and replied, "Catherine is very kind-hearted. But she has a very, very bad heart." She died in 1995 of heart failure.

Another extremely talented artist is La Mesan Alexandra Cauldwell. Three of her paintings hang in our living room. Alexandra reviewed the final draft of the memoir, making important suggestions, and catching several glaring errors. My sister, Dorothy Voss in Houston, also examined the draft.

Special credit goes to Barbara Odendahl Fox, who grew up in the coal-mining town of Price, Utah, as the granddaughter of Uncle Walter, my father's brother. She emailed a wealth of Odendahl family history, which corrected some accounts I'd long believed. Credit also belongs to a deceased cousin, Carol Louise Odendahl Moser, the daughter of another of Dad's brothers, Uncle Ernest. Carol gathered records of nine generations of both our branch of the Odendahl family and that of our grandmother, Christine Elizabeth Schöttelkorb.

Grandmother Schöttelkorb

Much thanks is extended for a third time to leading ladies on this project, and of two earlier books—Kimberly Rotter and Robbie Adkins. Kimberly sorted through the often-garbled manuscripts and polished them into the proper format for publication as Kindle books. Robbie produced three beautiful covers. It has been such a pleasure to work with them. Thanks also to Kimberly's father, Eric Dietrich-Berryman, who proofread the manuscript and caught plenty of typos, which seem to make their way in no matter how many readings the book endures. He also ensured that German words and certain historical facts were presented correctly.

It goes without saying that I'm more than extremely indebted to my wife, Mary Johnson Odendahl, who has remained steadfast at my side for nearly 65 Years. I trust my gratitude for being with her becomes self-evident as you read through this memoir.

No doubt more than a few errors in the writing will be discovered, and disputes with "facts." For this, I take full responsibility. Please let me know what you find, that we may talk about it. Hopefully, this will lead to pleasant E-mails and/or conversations about special old times together.

The memoir mainly was written for Mary's and my children, grandchildren, and close relatives. May they, and all readers, continue to lead long, happy and productive (even sort'a Looney-Tune) lives.

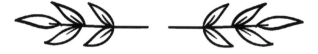

What's Up, Doc?

Many of my generation have come to the conclusion that the life they think back on more than 80 years ago was a series of Looney Tunes. Growing older, one begins to feel like Tweety Bird.

"I Tawt I Taw a Puddy Tat," is like when "I tawt I put my glasses here, but they're not here now." Seeking unobtainable answers to life's mysteries, one asks as Bugs Bunny invariably did, "What's Up, Doc?"

At an advanced age it should be okay to kid around a bit more. To laugh louder and longer about the looniness of one's life, relating to the personas of Porky Pig, Daffy Duck, Wile E. Coyote, Road Runner, and The Tasmanian Devil.

Warner Brothers gave birth to Looney Tunes in 1930, the same year I came on Earth. We'd all watch those cartoons "back in the day" before each "picture show." Theaters were filled with laughter, even when one of the characters was flattened by a safe pushed out of a second-story window. Already feeling myself a different sort of kid, that never seemed funny; I felt it moving me to the dark side. Later, found it was the sound of a different drummer.

Funny, dark, or different, I've sadly become aware that featured picture-show fantasies will never materialize. Such as the youthful dream of intimacy with my favorite fantasy woman, Ingrid Bergman. Born in 1915, *only* 15 years older than I, during my puberty she appeared ripe for my gentle plucking. Bergman became legendary starring with Humphrey Bogart and Claude Raines in the classic movie *Casablanca*. As *Casablanca* appeared for me on the silver screen, 12 years old was an age when a boy earnestly begins to appreciate such pulchritude.

Ingrid turned me on even more in the screen version of Ernest Hemingway's novel *For Whom the Bell Tolls*. Especially, you know, when she joined limbs with Gary Cooper, feeling the ground moving under her. Forty years after *Casablanca*, in 1982, cancer snatched her from our fantasies. Nevertheless Ingrid Bergman, described in one internet biography as "the most beautiful woman to ever grace the screen with her presence," has never left my mind.

Another unfulfilled fantasy involved beguiling Sophia Loren. A mere three years younger, alas, she too never shared my tender mercies. Not ever did I whisk her away from that plain-looking, director-producer-husband of hers, Carlos Ponti. In my youth I imagined giving Carlos Ponti a really hard poke in his fat little belly and driving him away from

Sophia. Yet, who knows? That feisty fellow could have been an Italian Stallion, also expert in the martial arts?

It goes without saying that during the course of my life I've experienced fantasies not only with faraway glamorous movie or TV stars, but also in closer proximity with no-less extraordinary women. Perhaps some amount of redemption came from experiencing innumerable daydreams involving other than sins of the flesh. Such as playing baseball as well as Joe DiMaggio or Mickey Mantle, listening to the roar of fans in Yankee Stadium after clubbing soaring home runs or racing back to the outfield fence to make my over-the shoulder catches.

Or writing as well as Ernest Hemingway, gazing down at an adoring crowd in Stockholm presenting me a standing ovation as I receive my Nobel Prize for Literature. Even being able to sing or play a musical instrument in Carnegie Hall. To quote New York Yankees catcher and manager Yogi Berra, "it ain't over 'til the fat lady sings"

There were occasional serious and dark sides of life to contend with–as if looking into a mirror and discovering the face of Taz, The Tasmanian Devil. With a wife who has endured my vagaries for well over 60 years, plus two daughters, two granddaughters, and a grandson, I'm working really hard here to convey the image of a fairly nice guy.

There's an advantage in "penning" one's autobiography on a computer, rather than paying through the nose for some nosy biographer to pry into one's mortal days and mortal sins. Either authorized or unauthorized, they appear to feel somewhat honor-bound to probe into incidents one would just as soon forget. Autobiographical writing allows glossing over peccadillos, twisting real or imagined sins to advantage, and jesting about most of it. As I relate my looney stories, I've chosen to sing along with the tunes of those carefree cartoon characters.

Another advantage of relating one's peculiar tale is that it can be arranged in any order, presented it in any way, and with any conclusions he or she wishes. Often knowingly or unknowingly I'll violate the King's or Queen's English. I might butcher the grammatical, relating anecdotes in the New Mexico dialect I grew up with (whatever that may be), sort'a Tex-Mex-Southern slang talk. Most certainly these stories are related in an unscientific methodology. Clichés fill the tales. Much in my life has happened to others, clichés in themselves. It's like quoting Yogi Berra once more, finding his *déjà vus* happening all over again.

We'll strive for some amount of accuracy. If journalists find truth falls as the first casualty of war, autobiographies by their very self-centered nature wound accuracy. Vague recollections are tempered with such phrases as "probably about (year)," "as I recall," "as

I remember it," "I believe maybe," or "I think it was." Stuff like that to keep a reader speculating about the veracity of any of it, or whether some sort of serious dementia already has set in.

For as my good wife keeps telling me, "The older you get, the more you embellish your stories." However, as in a stale old joke, they say three things happen as you get older, "The first is that you lose your memory...and...I can't remember the other two."

Read on, McDuff, if you wish is to learn a bit about some Looney Tune days, at least those I still am able to recall.

CHAPTER 1 – HOLDING HANDS

S he toddled over to the barbed wire fence separating our yard at 211 Romero Street from hers. We lived in Hurley, a small copper mining town in southwest New Mexico. The year 1933 found me, as I expect she might have been, three years old.

Entrance to Hurley, N.M.   6-X-89

Gloria Ann Baulsch (sp? but do remember it pronounced —BAWL-SH) squatted down on her diaper, or maybe by that time she was into training panties? She looked at me through the fence. I also sat down, gazing back into her eyes. She put her hands between the strings of barbed wire. I gripped her fingers, entwined them in mine. Our hands held for a minute or two as we gazed at one another.

A loud shriek suddenly came from her mother, who appeared on the front porch of her next-door house. "Gloria Ann Baulsch, you get away from that fence! Come back into this house! Right now!! I want you to stay away from that nasty little Odendahl boy. Do you hear me? Don't you ever go near him again! Do you understand me?"

Gloria Ann began to cry, let go of my hands, got up, turned, and ran toward her mother. My own mother came rushing out of our house, asked Mrs. Baulsch what terrible event had happened. Mrs. Baulsch's response was my mother should see to it that I stay away from her daughter. Now, let me tell you, that's about the first thing I can remember about starting a life in which, when one comes down to it, there ain't all that nothin' much has never ever happened. But what you got'ta do is just keep right on 'a truckin'.

The first nasty boy Gloria Ann encountered didn't know what he had done wrong, but could sense it wasn't good. It was a first of lifelong sermons with messages for nasty boys and men. (1) Life can be a dangerous business; be careful about touching any girl or woman when a loved one might be watching. (2) You're very naughty if you touch a female and you ought'a feel real guilty about it. (3) If you get caught, you'll pay the consequences, which often can be quite painful.

Whatever happened to Gloria Ann Baulsch, or to her parents? I can't tell you, only mention her as one of my first memories. I don't even know where she was born. My own birth date was May 28, 1930. Most of us kids living in Hurley arrived on this Special Earth in a hospital about 10 miles away. The hospital sat next to a Santa Rita's giant open pit copper mine, proudly then declared to be the third largest such in the world.

Like my family, Gloria Ann's lived in Hurley Company housing, next to the mill and smelter. Her father worked for The Company we simply called Chino, a moniker for the Chinese who had toiled in the Santa Rita mine during earlier days. It probably was Nevada Consolidated Copper Co. in 1930, later became Kennecott Copper, and finally Phelps Dodge.

Maybe there ain't all that much has never ever happened to Gloria Ann Baulsch neither? It would be mighty satisfyin' for me to learn, that she's just kept right on'a truckin', that her life turned out successful and prosperous. Besides growin' long past holdin' hands with a nasty boy, nature most probably moved her into doin' better stuff with men. For sure, Gloria Ann already claims fame if she was born in that Santa Rita Hospital perched next to that giant copper pit. As The Company continued digging closer and closer to extract more copper ore, it decided to move not only the hospital but also much of the town. And that's what Chino did, expand the pit's perimeter to haul away more copper-bearing ore. All that remains of the earlier perimeter is ethereal space over the pit.

Grown-up Gloria Ann, long gone from Hurley, likely was still living as groups of America's astronauts landed on the Moon as part of the NASA space program. Among the landers was Harrison H. (Jack) Schmitt, who later became one of New Mexico's Senators in Washington. Schmitt had been born in 1935, in the Santa Rita Hospital.

Forty years after his birth Schmitt got together with Ted Arellano, Claude Dannelley, Joyce Bradberry, and Robert Heavy to form the Society for Persons Born in Space. And with Gilbert Moore, a high school classmate of my two-year-older brother Alan. Gilbert was working in Utah on space-age stuff for Thiokol. You may recall, Thiokol once was in the news as the firm responsible for supplying the O-ring which failed on a space shuttle flight, reportedly causing the explosion which killed all aboard —including schoolteacher Christa McAuliffe. I have no idea whether Gilbert's work had anything to do with O-rings.

All of us who came into this world at the Santa Rita Hospital now were born only in that ethereal space over the giant copper pit. Ted Arellano saw his first light in the Santa Rita Hospital in 1927. Hurley boy Gilbert Moore was born in the hospital in 1928, the same birth-year as my older brother. Alan became a member of the Society of Persons Born in Space, not because he was born May 1, 1928, and not because that birth occurred in Hayden, Arizona. It was because Alan attended and was graduated by Hurley High School.

In order to broaden the membership, Born in Space eligibility began to be offered beyond those first seeing light in the Santa Rita Hospital. Additions included being born in Santa Rita or Hurley, attending Hurley High or the Sully School. Or even being invited to membership by a member of the society. At one year's annual party, attendance was estimated as high as 1,500. My "little sister," Dorothy, came into this world in the Santa Rita Hospital December 14, 1937, so she's a genuine (jen-you-wine) qualified (qual-lee-fied) Society member.

Me, Alan, Dorothy, Dad and Mom

Another of the *really famous* members of the Society of Persons Born in Space was Ralph McPherran Kiner, born in that Santa Rita hospital October 27, 1922. He was elected to baseball's Hall of Fame in 1975, by coincidence the same year the Society was formed. Playing for the Pittsburgh Pirates, Chicago Cubs, and Cleveland Indians. Kiner led the National League in home runs seven straight years 1946-52, with his best season 1949 when he smashed 54 homers, batted in 127 runs, walked 117 times and posted a .310 batting average. He had 369 career home runs, and 1015 runs-batted-in during his 10 seasons. He later became a long-time New York Mets announcer.

You certainly ought'a know by now, there ain't nothin' much like that has never ever happened to me. I mean, you know, like as far as goin' for a ride to the moon in a spaceship, or like beltin' out home runs as a major league baseball player. Really important stuff like that.

Yet now, I've got'ta wonder. I'll bet famous folks like Jack Schmitt or Ralph Kiner maybe never ever did get hollered at when they were three years old. That is, for holdin' hands and just lookin' a few moments into the eyes of a little baby girl through a barbed wire (*waar*) fence? I sure could tell them somethin', now that's a fact for sure.

"It was worth it."

CHAPTER 2 – HARD TIMES

Those days my Mom had more to worry about than Gloria Ann Baulsch, and her over-protective mother. That was partly because of my conception in 1929 during the beginning of The Great Depression, generally referred to as "Hard Times." Not a good time to be joyous about addin' another child to a relatively poor family.

Dad wanted to name me Clerk, after James Clerk Maxwell, who lived from 1831 to 1879. The British physicist created the electromagnetic theory of light, leading to the discovery of gamma rays, X-rays, ultraviolet and infrared light, and radio waves. Out of this evolved radio, television, and radar.

"Clerk Maxwell was born in Edinburgh, Scotland," Dad argued to Mom. "That's part of the Scotch-Irish roots on your side of the family, and the boy deserves to start out with a special name."

Mom disagreed. "He'd be the subject of ridicule here in New Mexico with a name like Clerk. Nobody would understand it." They compromised, dubbed me with my middle name Maxwell and decided to call me Max.

On July 30, 1931, at age 41,Dad re-applied at Silver City, New Mexico, to regain his American citizenship, as he earlier had become a Canadian citizen when taking out papers for a homestead in Canada. He was described as a white male with fair complexion, blue eyes, and light brown hair. He was 5 feet 9 inches tall and weighed 150 pounds. His occupation was listed as a machinist. Dad was 41 when I was born.

On March 30, 1933, my Canadian-born Mom became an American citizen. She was described as age 40, a white female with dark complexion, dark eyes, brown-streaked gray hair, 5 feet 3 1/2 inches tall, weighing 150 pounds (ironically the same weight as Dad). Her race was listed as Scotch-Irish, with her former nationality Great Britain (Canada). She was 36 at my birth.

Hard Times were stressful ones for the family. Such as the first time Baby Max visited El Paso, by way of a narrow two-way highway reaching about 150 miles southeast of Hurley. In 1931, 18-month-old Baby Max was nearly dead.

"The doctor told us Max was on a hunger strike," Dad said, relating the family story. "We had taken Max to the Santa Rita Hospital, and the doctor said he'd done everything he could for several days, even prescribed a special formula."

"There's nothing more I can do," the depressed doctor told Dad. "The boy's going to die. I'm sorry."

Dad refused to accept the verdict. "Isn't there somewhere we could take Max? Like maybe to a baby specialist?"

"Well, there's a pediatrician in El Paso, Harry, but I can tell you he can't help the baby. He's too far gone."

"That old doctor got mad about me questioning his ability," Dad related, "but I made him give me the name of the baby specialist in El Paso anyway." Our family immediately loaded into its 1929 Chevrolet and headed for El Paso. Alan rode in the front with Dad. Mom sat in back with the sick baby, my face drained of color with blue lips.

On the way, we stopped to heat a bottle of milk with hot water from the car's radiator. "You drank about half that bottle, Max," Dad related, "so I kept hoping: 'Maybe we can keep the boy alive until we get to El Paso'."

Our family arrived at the pediatrician's office to face a filled waiting room. The nurse at the desk took one look at me, hurried to fetch the doctor. He quickly examined me and ordered Mom, "Bring him into the office right away. You've got a mighty sick baby there." The pediatrician cleared an examining bed, immediately connected Mom and me with needles and a tube. Her blood fused with mine.

Mom broke into Dad's story, "Right away, you began to get color back in your cheeks. The blue went away from your lips." She said the pediatrician eventually told her I had been receiving the wrong formula. I began to thrive on his new one.

"It still makes me mad as hell," Dad almost shouted. "That old quack at Santa Rita would have let Max die if I hadn't had guts enough to stand up to him."

"I don't believe it was deliberate," Mom quietly chimed in. "I think the doctor was out of touch with things or he wouldn't have been working for the Company at both Santa Rita and Hurley. Also, he's mainly a surgeon, just doesn't know much about babies." Dad shook his head.

Later, after my sister Dorothy was born in 1937, another trip was made to El Paso for one of Dad's eye exams. Mom stayed home with Dorothy, while Dad, Alan and I gathered at the square in the middle of downtown El Paso, watching crocodiles being fed large chunks of meat at a fenced-in pond.

"It's scary," I muttered as the crocodiles climbed out of their pond and ravenously gobbled meat thrown over the fence of the enclosure by a man wearing blue overalls.

"It *was* scarier here the last time," Dad said, putting his arm around my shoulder. I wasn't certain, but I thought I saw Dad's eyes glazed with tears.

The Great Depression meant nothin' all that much to a young lad like me, because everyone around us sailed in the same battered boat. In late 1934 the open pit at Santa Rita, along with the mill and smelter at Hurley shut down. My parents, especially Mom, always watched our pennies, but the Great Depression came close to consigning the Hurley Odendahls to stand somewhere with those waiting in bread lines outside charities, or at soup kitchens.

Hard Times began in 1929 about the time of "Black Tuesday," October 29, the day the stock market lost $14 billion, and was worse between 1932 and 1933. There were 13 to 15 million Americans unemployed in 1933, one out of four people without work. The average family income had fallen from $2,300 to $1,500 per year. It is estimated 50 percent of children did not have adequate food, shelter, and medical care. Hard Times lasted at least until 1939.

The U.S. government provided no unemployment benefits as Dad drove around much of New Mexico in our 1929 Chevrolet looking for work. He finally found a job at Jerome, Arizona, at another copper mine. In Hurley, I'd barely begun to savor the pleasure of listening to music, which came about each time my parents inserted slotted paper rolls into the upper part of our player piano. The slots in the paper moved across a magic-like mechanism which caused keys to push down, pressing pads against the strings stretched on the rear of the piano.

Before he left for Jerome, Dad gutted the mechanical innards of the player piano, to make it lighter, "to cut down on moving costs." Dad's trashing of the mechanism may have saved money in the short run, but producing a non-mechanical-playing piano obliterated many dollars from what would have been its present-day high antique value.

Allowing Mom to ship to Arizona what was left of her player piano was one of Dad's concessions to her. Our less fortunate tall and heavy RCA Victrola was sold. Besides the player piano, I'd delighted in listening to sounds on that Victrola. From 78 RPM records played through metal needles a bit larger and stronger than those used for heavy sewing. Needles had to be constantly replaced when their tips wore down. You (Mom or Dad, never us kids) cranked up the Victrola, carefully placed the needle in the first groove of the revolving record, and tenor Enrico Caruso might begin singing for you.

Years later, while attending our niece's —Alan's daughter Nora's — wedding at Princeton, N.J., sister Dorothy told me her Republican friends in Michigan teased her about being a Yellow Dog Democrat. "What's that?" I wondered.

"They tell me," she replied, "it's a person who would vote for a yellow dog if the Democrats ran it for office." We chuckled about that one, because it's fairly close to the truth; she and I most often do vote for Democrats. We were curious what Republicans who traditionally vote close to a straight ticket ought to be called. They commonly champion what seems their distorted form of the "Free Enterprise System." Generally meaning they should be left free to do whatever they wish to do to become rich at the expense of the poor even during Hard Times. And because they wrap themselves in the flag of super-patriotism, I suggested Bald-Eagle Republicans.

How do dogmatic types like us in both parties become the way we are? Probably, most often it's like how we formed our religious beliefs. Our parents took us to a certain kind of church, or synagogue, or mosque, or other edifices, or no place at all. We listened intently to discussions about politics at the dinner table, where our parents and relatives explained who they are voting for and why. When we became of age, we generally went to the same religious centers and cast our ballots for those of the same party as our parents.

When Grandfather Carl or Karl (Charles) Odendahl came to the U.S. from Germany, he found only dangerous work in coals mines in West Virginia and Ohio. John L. Lewis and his coal miners' union were esteemed by my family, while Republican families in Hurley and Jerome saw evil in Lewis's bushy eyebrows, envisioned him as some sort of Satan controlling labor unions.

"I think we're going to make it," our mother announced near the end of the depression. "Your father's pay has been raised to $5 a day."

Dad felt President Herbert Hoover was to blame for Hard Times, while Republicans viewed Hoover as a wise man who simply wasn't allowed enough time to put into effect his ideas for ending the Great Depression. At any rate, we didn't call it Hoover Dam at our house, but Boulder Dam —the original name.

Although Hoover was in office when I was born, the first president brother Alan (and later sister Dorothy) and I were old enough to be aware of was Democrat Franklin Delano Roosevelt. We Yellow Puppies went around lauding his New Deal, while our Bald Eaglet friends blamed Roosevelt for the sad state of affairs. Some of their parents claimed family savings ($500 and less was a lot of money then) were wiped out forever during Hard Times when the banks closed. Immediately after taking the oath of office in March 1933, FDR ordered all banks across the country to lock their doors.

"Checking accounts, shoot, those were gone and they didn't pay it back," one old timer recently recalled on the Internet. "If you got money back on savings accounts, it was only a sprinkle." The way Mom explained it to me, "There was 'a run' on the banks. People lined up outside trying to withdraw their money. But, much of it had been loaned out — so all their money wasn't there. Roosevelt had to do something, so he closed the banks. You've got to remember, Hoover did nothing."

FDR's idea was to keep the doors of all banks locked while determining which ones were strong enough to reopen, and to restore bank customers' faith. Many Bald Eagles never had that faith restored, claimed they forever lost money deposited in banks, and never forgave Roosevelt for what he had done.

Nevertheless, Hard Times convinced lots of other folks to vote the Democratic ticket. As many still do, they figured only the rich benefited from being Republicans. They referred to the GOP as the party of the rich, but not yet the party of the racists. At that time Southern Democrats were openly racist. After the Civil Rights Bill was passed in 1964, many switched to the Republican Party during Richard Nixon's Southern-Strategy quest for the Presidency.

Our family had about $400 in the bank when Dad was laid off in Hurley. Mom later told us kids about the dilemma that money caused her. We needed every dollar for the Odendahl family to survive. Many Hurleyites were left penniless after spending their last paycheck. We had our meager savings in U.S. Post Office bonds, and it's possible some of our neighbors could have lost theirs in banks which President Franklin Delano Roosevelt closed? "I felt guilty as a Christian not sharing what little money we had, tried to salve my conscience by handing out items like beans and sugar to others who 'borrowed' now and then."

Hard Times were nothing new to my parents. My brother Alan was not the first child born to our parents, for an older sister had been delivered in Alberta, Canada. Mom and Dad met at a boarding house in Vancouver, British Columbia, Canada.

It would have been wise to have paid more attention at our supper table when Dad told stories. I'm not sure how he drifted from Ohio to Vancouver, except that he picked up mechanical expertise along the way. For a period, Dad worked keeping the engine going on a Coast Guard boat in the Great lakes.

"We and the Canadians were trying to keep Chinese from getting into the United States," he told us. "When we spotted a boat which looked suspicious, we'd take after it so the Coast Guard could go aboard and arrest any Chinese sneaking in from Canada to work in the U.S. Some of their boats were fast, but we were faster —had a secret fast speed they didn't know about. I'd be below deck in the engine room, get the order to shift into the speed notch and we'd catch them."

Dad also had worked to maintain engines of a fairly large fishing boat off the west coast of Canada. Fishermen in those days rowed away in smaller boats to catch salmon, probably using baited hooks and lines and pole the fish in. The smaller boats would return to the larger one, where fish were iced.

One day Dad was standing next to the large boat which was docked (probably in Vancouver, British Columbia). A man came by, and asked, "Chief, could I take a look at your engines?" Dad agreed, and after touring the engine room, the man identified himself as Zane Grey. Once a dentist and minor-league baseball player, Grey had become a famous western author and one of the first millionaire writers. His best-selling and most famous novel was the 1912 *Riders of the Purple Sage.*

"If you'd like to," Grey said, "come by and take a look at the engine room on my boat." I don't know if Dad went there immediately or later for his tour.

"That boat on the outside looked like an ordinary seagoing tug," Dad told us, "but inside were mahogany panels and the engines were of a special design."

"I can go anywhere in the world in this," Grey told Dad, and that the tugboat-look brought no attention to the presence of the famous author. Grey had a crew of at least a cook, and a "captain" steering and navigating oceans to allow the famous writer to leisurely pursue his love of fishing in places like off waters of Australia and New Zealand.

AFFIDAVIT OF BIRTH

We, the undersigned, Charles Henry Odendahl, and his wife, Christina Odendahl, of Strachan, Alberta, do solemnly swear, that our son, HARRY CHARLES ODENDAHL, was born at Shawnee, Ohio, U. S. A., the sixteenth day of September, in the year of our Lord eighteen hundred and eighty-nine.

SWORN BEFORE ME, at Strachan, Alberta, this *Eleventh* day of May, 1926.

N. Scott

A Commissioner of Oaths for the Province of Alberta.

Chas. Henry Odendahl
....
Signature

Christine Odendahl
....
Signature

SWEET GRASS, MONT.

5-20-26

Admitted for perma nent residence, Had I.V. & paid H.T.

J C Bailey,
U.S. Immt. Dept.

17

Dad had worked in Detroit for Hup Motor Car Company, which produced Hupmobiles from 1909 to 1939. The plant also made motorcycles. "One day they came by with a new motorcycle which was very quiet, and seemed to run better than anything we were making. What Hupmobile had done was buy up the patent for this motorcycle. They crushed it so no one could copy it. That brought tears to my eyes."

This practice has been common over the years. Someone invents something better and a large firm buys the patent to prevent competition. It probably was a fairly paltry sum paid for that Hubmobile motorcycle patent. Big change now in the social media, where a large firm often buys out a new, innovative, smaller one for millions of dollars.

Mom taught school in Vancouver while Dad worked as a mechanic at a large garage —she a college graduate, he with a fifth-grade education. Mom later admitted to us kids about her snobbishness about seeing grease under Dad's fingernails as they sat around a common supper table at the boarding house.

Even as she still mourned a Canadian high-school boyfriend killed during World War I, Dad turned in Mom's favor one afternoon when she glanced through the open door to his room. Several books sat on his dresser. Dad wasn't there. She cautiously entered his room and noted titles and authors, among them volumes of Robert W. Service's poetry about life in the cold Yukon. "I figured a man who read poetry must have some redeeming values," Mom told us kids. "Of course, I shouldn't have gone into a man's room without an invitation. And, the door would have had to stay open even if he had invited me in."

Mom and Dad were married June 27, 1921, in Vancouver by Rector M.H. Jackson of St. George's Church. My Aunt Helen, one of Mom's unmarried sisters, was a witness. Dad was listed on the marriage certificate as a "bachelor" and Mom as a "spinster." The newlyweds moved to their "dream" homestead in the Canadian province of Alberta. Perhaps Mom agreed to the move because a new adventure might help dull the memory of her former, deceased beau? Their dairy farm was located east of Edmonton at a place called Prairie Creek. The nearest town was Rocky Mountain House. The transition proved very difficult for Mom, who knew little about farming or the rigors of establishing a homestead.

Jean (no middle name) Robinson was a city girl born on Christmas Eve, 1892, and raised in Victoria, B.C. In 1908, Mom at 15 years old in high school had led the whole Dominion of Canada in the McGill University exams. My grandparents figured she was too young at 15 to travel alone almost all the way across the Dominion to Montreal. It was not until the next year that she attended McGill University. She came home from McGill as a junior and was graduated in the first class of the new University of British Columbia in Vancouver.

Mom's father, Alexander "Sandy" Robinson, was an educator. Holding a doctorate, an elementary school later was named after him in Vancouver. He once served as head of all the schools in British Columbia from his government office in Victoria. Mom was the eldest of eight surviving children brought into existence by my Grandmother Emma Robinson. There were eight others, who were either stillborn or died very soon. Grandmother once even was told by a doctor to keep away from my horny grandfather, to move back to be with her Nova Scotia family for a year. My kindly grandmother also raised four of her grandchildren.

Harry Charles Odendahl and his twin sister Elizabeth Christina (Aunt Elsie) were born September 16, 1889, in Shawnee, Perry County Ohio, and at 13 days old baptized into the Roman Catholic Church. His father, not only a coal miner, but also a union organizer often left his family to help strikers in other West Virginia towns.

Strachan, Alberta, Canada,
April 23, 1926.

The Probate Judge,
Probate Court Perry County,
New Lexington, Ohio.

Dear Sir:

On account of the changes in the Immigration laws I find it necessary to register my children, which I have previously omitted to do, not thinking it would be required.

Below find data. If any further are required, kindly advise. Also if official forms are needed, please send the same, with statement of fee.

Charles Henry Odendahl and Christina Elisabeth Shoettelkorb, married on March 9, 1886, at St. Mary's Catholic Church, Shawnee, Ohio, by the Rev. Father Hannon. License taken at New Lexington, Ohio.

Naturalization certificate issued on November 5, 1887, to Charles Odendahl, a native of Germany, by Frank O'Kelly, Judge and ex-officio clerk of Perry County Probate Court at New Lexington, Ohio.

Children born near Shawnee, Ohio.

1. Twins, Harry Charles and Elizabeth, born September 16, 1889, at New Straitsville, small mining town near Shawnee, Ohio. Birth attended by Dr. Axline.

2. Walter Bruno, born November 22, 1894, at Carrington, near Shawnee, Ohio. Birth attended by Mrs. E. Shoettelkorb, as nurse.

I should be glad if you would give this matter your immediate attention, and inform me if there are any other regulations,(such as my sending an affidavit from here, etc.), which must be complied with to effect the registration of these three children of mine.

Yours very truly,

Chas Henry Odendahl

Dad and Aunt Elsie spoke only German until they started school, which put them at a great disadvantage and probably subject to much ridicule and teasing from English-speaking kids. Mom told me how Dad said he needed to hunt nuts and trap squirrels in the woods to help feed his family. He, himself, was reluctant to share much of this past, memories of which must have been very painful.

My uncle Walter, one of Dad's younger brothers, at the age of 84 in 1978 described in ink to his own family about Odendahl life beginning in Turkey Knob, West Virginia: "*I can still see, in memory, the coal miners walking home in the late evening with their coal-burning mine lamps fastened to their caps. It was something resembling a candle parade as they wended their way homeward...*

"*My name was Bruno Richard Odendahl—however I heard a man call his dog Bruno. So I came storming home as a four-year-old and told my parents I would not have the name of Bruno—it was a dog's name...My parents asked what name I wanted and I said Walter. So Walter I became.*

"*Then memories of my father returning from a wage agreement. The big bonfire at the RR station—my father carried on the miners' shoulders—because he had won a 25-cent-a-ton raise in their pay. Then moving from one place to another—13 times before we finally settled again in Murray City Ohio. My father had been told to leave West Virginia because he was blacklisted by the mine operators...*

"*I knew no one personally who had less to eat than I. With our family moving 13 times and the loss of income because of it, I often had dinners consisting of one slice of bread and some coffee. Many times rendered lard with some salt substituted for butter. We seldom had milk to drink or on any cereal. I only remember having corn flakes (then called Force) once in my life until I was 14.*"

As Grandfather periodically earned $1.50 a day working a 12-hour-shift in coal mines seven days a week, the Odendahls suffered through Hard Times long before the Stock Market Crash of 1929. To help support that family, Dad left elementary school at age 13 for work in a glass bottle plant. Uncle Walter, having to leave school in the seventh grade, began working also at age 13 in a furniture factory, 10 hours a day. Hard, physical labor required by the homestead was nothing new for the Odendahl brothers.

Dad had become a Wobbly, a member of the International Workers of the World, and had supported Socialist Eugene Debs, who received close to a million votes in the Presidential elections of 1912 and 1920. Following Debs, Socialist Norman Thomas ran for President in 1932 and received 896,000 votes, although I'm almost certain both Mom and Dad voted for Franklin Delano Roosevelt that year. Thomas, also a founder of the American

Civil Liberties Union, later was quoted as mildly complaining that the victorious FDR of 1932 had stolen all his ideas.

Mom and Dad didn't begin marriage living quite by themselves, because their homestead was next to that of Grandfather Carl Heinrich Odendahl. Born November 6, 1865 in Pattscheid, Germany, Grandfather had come to the United States in 1882, apparently to avoid second-time military service in Germany. His father also had worked in an "ore mine" in Germany.

There you have it. My grandfather probably was a draft dodger when faced with German army duty for the second time. In contrast, I know a "patriotic" woman who boasts to have descended on both sides of her family from those who arrived in America on the *Mayflower*. That tiny *Mayflower* sure carried a lot of people! Nevertheless, I'll bet if she digs around enough she might also find a draft dodger, or maybe a horse thief, perhaps even worse among those ancestors. Call them Black Sheep if you wish, but they simply appear now and again in family ancestries at whatever levels you wish to perceive as wickedness.

Grandmother Odendahl's maiden name was Christina Elizabeth Schöttelkorb, and she also arrived from Germany —in 1884. She and Grandfather met in Corning, Ohio, married either March 1 or March 9, 1886, at Shawnee, Ohio. There were two sons born to my grandparents before twins Dad and Aunt Elsie arrived. Charles lived 10 months and John was stillborn. Two other children died after Dad's birth, Amy "in infancy" and Clarence at 14 months of cholera.

Also residing at the Alberta homesteads were my uncles, Dad's younger brothers — Walter Bruno, born November 20, 1894, in Shawnee, Ohio, and Ernest Ralph, born October 24, 1903, in Murray City, Ohio. My married Aunt Alma, born October 11, 1891, in Ashland County, Wisconsin, lived on a farm a few miles away.

Uncle Walter, Dad, Uncle Ernest

Mom told me she figured my old and injured Grandfather's pro-German sympathies concerning World War I might be part of the reason some of the Odendahl family had moved to Canada. Why anti-German Canada, which suffered great losses in World War I, would be more favorable to Grandfather Odendahl's political views never made sense to me. As I expect is the case for most of us, we never get to the bottom of how lines of descent came about, or exactly what our ancestors did, or why they acted how they did. Perhaps the RIP (Rest in Peace) on some gravestones is the best way to leave it.

A coal-mine accident seriously had injured Grandfather Odendahl. Dad told how he and Uncle Walter were delivering a meal to his father deep in the mine in Ohio. Uncle Walter suffered a broken back. Dad's head was badly cut; he still listed the scar on the back of his

23

head when re-applying for American citizenship. I think that emotional experience convinced Dad never to make his living working in coal mines. However, after the homestead experience, Uncle Walter became a mine inspector and owned a coal mine in Price, Utah, for a period of time. After the accident, Grandfather found himself unable to do much work.

In any event, Mom discovered homesteading life with the Odendahls to be no bed of roses, and I can imagine how with loftier expectations she probably became a bit much for them to put up with, too. Mom and Dad at first lived in a tent until Alberta's below-zero winter nights forced them to move in with the older Odendahls, in a house which Dad and my uncles Walter and Ernest earlier had built. The most notable part of the house, constructed of logs, was a circular staircase inside from the first to the second floor.

I suspect my sister Jeanie, named of course after my mother, could have been conceived in the tent. She died three days after being born at Rocky Mountain House April 14, 1922. A plot in the town cemetery would cost $35, money which Mom and Dad didn't have. The midwife lined a grocery box with cotton wool and white China silk, meant for a bassinet. Jeanie's tiny body was placed in the box, carried by sleigh to the homestead, and buried next to a tree.

Mom always contended Jeanie would have lived if adequate prenatal care had been carried through on the homestead. "I didn't get the proper food to eat," Mom said with sad eyes, although she rarely talked much about Jeanie. When she did, it always made me sad. One of the obvious joys of having an older sister is that she might have taught me how to dance, a great advantage for a boy in Hurley High School coping with shyness in dealing with girls.

After her retirement from teaching in New Mexico, Mom wrote several novels. Jeanie 's death, Mom's love for her Canadian beau killed in the First World War, and life on the Alberta homestead figured in those novels. Operating a marginal dairy farm in Alberta proved a constant struggle. One major problem was that Wisconsin farmers were able to convince the U.S. Congress to impose a quota on dairy products shipped from Canada to the United States. The U.S. was a major market for those products from Alberta farms.

In August of 1926 a heavy snowstorm hit Prairie Creek, wiping out the homesteads' oat crop raised for feeding dairy cows the next winter. With no Canadian government aid, it was the last straw. Dad reluctantly gathered his machinist's tools, headed back to the States searching for work. He found a job at the copper mining town of Hayden, Arizona, and Mom joined him there.

When the wind changed, sulfuric-acid smoke from Hayden's smelter smokestack would drift across the small community. "In that case," Mom told us, "we had to dash out and take any wet clothes off the line. If we didn't do it in time, the smoke would burn holes in our clothes and ruin them."

My brother Alan was born in Hayden May 1, 1928. After Jeanie's death, at least it always seemed to sibling me, Alan became the real joy of Mom's life. Several times she referred both to me, born two years later, and Dorothy, nine years later as "accidents."

"Two bad things happened in 1929," Mom related to me more than once. "First, the stock market crashed, and then I found out I was pregnant with you." Let me tell you this: My stoic Mom generally wasn't one to mince her words.

Me and Alan

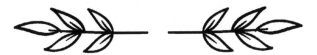

CHAPTER 3 — THE FIRE BUG

It was late 1934 or early 1935, when Mom, Alan, and I got off the bus after it arrived in Jerome, Arizona. Dad began whispering to Mom. I had learned to listen carefully, without letting on, that when Dad whispered to Mom, something serious was being discussed.

"How much money do you have left?"

"Ten dollars," she whispered back.

"Good, I don't have any. That should get us by with groceries until my next paycheck." A close one, for many others were less fortunate during Hard Times.

On a trip through Arizona a few years ago, wife Mary and I found Jerome looking like a "ghost town." Settled in were what appeared to be mostly vagabonds, sort'a like hippies. Brightly-painted Volkswagen busses were parked here and there on the main drag, alongside some dressed-up houses and other run-down buildings. Now Jerome's pegged as a bit-more-spruced-up art colony.

Bustling Jerome in 1935 sat on the side and atop a mountain. Phelps Dodge owned Jerome, and our house rested on a terrace referred to as the 500 Level. All of Hurley had been flat. So upon playing in front of the house, I immediately fell down several concrete steps. Luckily, only bruises.

One afternoon when I arrived home from kindergarten, there was a Company fire engine in the street. I rushed up the concrete stairs to see what was going on. "What's happened?" I asked Mom, who appeared very distressed, added, "I'll let you know later."

I walked around the house and there was Alan, sitting dejectedly on the back steps. "What's happened?" I asked again. Alan just pointed to the shed next to the rear fence. About half of the shed, still smoldering, was charred by fire. Obviously, Alan wasn't in the mood to communicate. Mom, who had followed me around the house, asserted curtly, "Your brother has been playing with matches. You leave him alone."

When Dad arrived home later from work, I overheard him whispering with Mom. It was determined that, overall, minor damage resulted from the shed episode, but they feared my brother might have tendencies toward pyromania. I didn't know what a pyromaniac was or did, but I'd heard of fire bugs and figured that's what they might be murmuring about.

I had mixed emotions. At first I was elated that my brother, and not me as so often happened, found himself in serious trouble with Mom and Dad. Alan always overshadowed me with his intelligence, compounded by being two years older. Yet, I felt sorry for him in this situation.

He hadn't begun speaking until the age of three, and then in complete sentences. His behavior had worried my parents, who apparently didn't know (as I didn't until about three quarters of a century later) that Albert Einstein also was slow to develop and didn't start speaking until 2 ½. The story is that Einstein's first words were that milk he was drinking was too hot.

Asked by his parents why he hadn't spoken earlier, the little genius Einstein was supposed to have replied, "Because previously everything was in order." I have no idea what Alan's first words were, or if he felt things were in order. Even if Alan also were a genius, I wasn't so sure I wanted to live with a fire bug. I thought: What if he decides to burn the house down while we are asleep and none of us can get out in time?

There was meager talk at the supper table that evening, but it was the end, as far as I know, of Alan ever showing any fire-bug-like tendencies. The closest to such activity I know about came years later on a pleasant note when he was out camping by himself in a remote spot in New Mexico with his 1936 Hudson Terraplane coupe —which we both owned at one time or another.

A cold morning and the battery would barely turn over the heavy, straight six-cylinder engine. Alan knew the car wouldn't start and the battery had almost run down. He gathered wood and built a small fire under the oil pan of the Terraplane. A few minutes later he figured the heavy oil had warmed thinner, tried the starter again and "Voila!" The engine sputtered and began running.

I wouldn't recommend Alan's method of cold-starting for modern cars with engine compartments crammed full of sensitive accessories and electronic equipment. In this case, the bottom of the old Terraplane's oil pan and lower part of the engine block were heavily smoked. Several wires also were burned; luckily none of them touched one another and shorted out anything.

After he came home and told his story, I was so surprised and marveled at my brother's atypical practical ingenuity that I helped him replace the burned wires. This sort of brotherly bonding was uncommon because of considerable sibling rivalry between us. For, simply stated, Alan always was smarter than I in "book learning," though not always in what folks referred to as "practical sense."

I recall other vivid images of living in Jerome, Arizona. While waiting for the bus to kindergarten, elementary school kids placed pennies on a railroad track so wheels of the Company's huge steam engine would flatten them. Spreading broken grass several feet along the tops of the tracks provided more excitement because that sometimes caused the engine's wheels to spin. Engineers shook fingers and heads at us; I think not so much due to irritation about spinning wheels but because they worried about the danger of us kids getting too close to the wheels.

One day a chubby, fat-faced kid, who was only an acquaintance, came by with part of a prickly pear cactus wrapped in a rag so thorns wouldn't prick him. After staring coldly at me for a few seconds he said, "Wan'na have some fun? Old Mr. and Mrs. Jackson aren't home (I don't recall the correct name. We called any adult Old Mr., Old Mrs., or Old Miss—not the university). Let's take this cactus and put it in their bed."

"What for?"

"So when they crawls in'ta bed they'll get stuck all over their legs," he laughed, partly about the prank but also at my ignorance. It certainly didn't sound very funny to me, but the kid adds, "You're too chicken-shit to do it."

"I'm not either," I lied about doing something I didn't want to, or knew wasn't right, but proving not to be chicken-shit continually dunked me in hot water during my growing years. Answering his dare, we went into the house, and the kid pressed the cactus under the top sheet next to the mattress.

"They's goin' really be surprised when they crawls in'ta that bed," the kid said, cackling again. Happiness for me was being able to leave the house undetected, and I never did learn whether the cactus performed to the fat-faced kid's expectations. I'd doubted it at five years old, and still do, because the cactus left an obvious bulge in the bed.

That experience could have been my first dealing with a "criminal mind." I remember Dad later telling a story at the supper table about an experiment into the workings of such a mind. A woman suffers from cancer or some such dreadful disease requiring an immediate operation. She takes all her money out of the bank to pay for it. On the way to the hospital, her roll of money accidently drops out of her purse.

"The people being interviewed were told her sad story," Dad related, "and asked what they would do if they found the money."

"Run and catch the lady and give it right back to her," Alan broke in. Dad nodded his head in appreciation, then grew serious, "But you know, a few of those interviewed said, 'I'd keep the money. It was the lady's own fault she dropped it. Finders keepers, losers weepers. Those were the ones with criminal minds, because they're born with no conscience."

I figured, for sure now, the fat-faced Jerome kid with his prickly pear cactus had a criminal mind. Of course, I didn't mention our little episode to Dad to heighten his awareness about *my* knowledge of the criminal mind.

While we were in Jerome, I had a series of stomach aches. Mom took me to a Company doctor, who determined the problem to be an ulcer. I was put to bed in the Phelps hospital for several days, made to eat very bland food —mainly bananas.

One day a nurse or hospital worker put in front of me a tray with real *food*–roast beef, mashed potatoes, gravy, and vegetables. A dish of dessert sat next to the main plate. As I began to dig into the food, Mom returned to the room. She stopped me from eating and called the nurse. It turned out I'd gotten some other patient's food tray. Mom was very irritated about that. "A hospital, of all places, ought to know how to take better care of a five-year-old boy." A day or so later the doctor allowed me to eat half of a baked potato, the best-tasting potato I've had in my life.

A few weeks after leaving the hospital, Mom left me under what she thought was the lifeguard's supervision at the Company swimming pool while she went "on an errand." Several boys, a year or two older with water dripping from their swimsuits, walked about four feet high on top of a concrete block wall next to the pool. Not to be outdone, I pulled myself up on the wall and also began walking. Suddenly I slipped on water left by the dripping suits, fell off the wall onto the concrete sidewalk below.

I felt a sharp pain in my left arm. When I sat up and looked at it, the bone stuck out about an inch and a half at almost a right angle —broken completely off. I later learned that such a protruding broken bone means you have a "compound fracture."

I let out a wail, kept wailing as a man volunteered to take me in his pickup to Jerome's Company hospital. As we drove along, my loud crying bugged the man.

"Shut up, kid," he finally sputtered in an exasperated voice. Glancing several times at the protruding bone, he modified his tone to, "OK, I know it hurts. Try to think about something else."

When he carried me into the hospital, there was Mom sitting in the waiting room! Her "errand" had been a visit to the doctor, probably concerning some "female problem"– something a mother wouldn't talk about with a child. "Boy, am I glad to see you," was all I could say as the Exasperated Good Samaritan transferred me to Mom's arms.

I can't recall if they put this little wailing boy out; if so, they most probably did it with chloroform. Medical personnel carefully stretched the arm and put the bone back into place, perhaps did some stitching. With that arm in a cast for several weeks, it was kind'a fun being the center of attention, letting other kids sign their names or put their initials on the cast. But it also began as the source of lifelong consternation over questions asked when one fills out medical history forms. Like, "Have you ever had on operation? If so, when?"

Was that medical work on my severely-damaged arm when I was five years old an operation, or what? Or, didn't that happen until I had my appendix removed at 16 or 17?

When we lived in Jerome, and before that during those Harder Times without a job, Dad had not only been working at any job available but also spending from our meager funds on courses in mechanical engineering from International Correspondence Schools in Scranton, Pennsylvania. His diploma, awarded February 12, 1935, which I hold in my hand at this writing, reads, "This certifies that Harry Charles Odendahl has studied and satisfactorily completed all of the subjects included in our Mechanical Engineering Course, has passed the required examinations, and is hereby awarded this Diploma as an acknowledgement of his efficiency and in recommendation of his requirements."

"I made As on all my courses," Dad told us, "except for a couple of those which as a machinist I thought I knew more than they did. So I gave them better answers than those which came out of their books. They graded me down for that." Dad undoubtedly would have excelled in college, once he had discovered that many profs want their lectures parroted on tests. Worse than that, Dad and Mom were disappointed that The Companies he worked for never recognized his correspondence-school efforts enough to give him job promotions.

They felt some of his bosses with college degrees were less proficient in knowing how to operate a copper mill than Dad, who generally read and thought ahead of his time. What else could a man with a formal fifth-grade education working full-time supporting a family do to better himself? As I look at this diploma, I swell with pride thinking about what Dad was able to accomplish.

Dad found out the copper-producing operation at Jerome, Arizona, was about to come to an end. Luckily, for the Great Depression still hung heavily over us, word drifted in that the mine at Santa Rita, New Mexico, along with the mill and smelter at Hurley, soon were reopening. We moved back to Hurley in 1936–where Dad would become a foreman, in charge of keeping about half of the copper mill's machinery and equipment repaired, and running 24 hours every day.

I was ready to begin the first grade. Unwritten rules reigned over Hurley's first grade of elementary school on opening day in the fall of 1936, a procedure not unlike my first day of United States Navy Boot Camp in the Summer of 1948. Even though Boot Camp began with a plethora of rules shouted louder, the first day of school turned into more of a surprise.

USN Boot Camp

My arrival at school showed no such mother-son trauma as depicted by modern TV shows and movies. I'm not even certain if Mom took me to school that first day. If she did, it would be to check me in or fill out necessary paperwork, not to hug me with misty eyes as if I were some departing warrior headed toward certain death. As a matter of fact, being hugged by your tearful mother in front of other kids would be quite embarrassing to a Hurley boy. With schoolhouses a few blocks away, we, except for those arriving by bus from neighboring ranches, knew how to walk there.

Living by The Rules began when teachers showed us how to line up before entering the old wooden school building. "When we call for you to line up, we don't want anybody lagging behind," a teacher cautioned in her no-nonsense voice. Lines formed according to classes, with girls in one line and boys in another. Wary teachers watched for hanky-panky, which we knew little to nothing about. Of course, I did soon learn it would seem to be fun stealthily reaching across and slightly pulling a girl's long hair while she waited in her line.

We marched into our new (pretty old) classroom, where we sat down in well-worn desks assigned by our teacher, who identified herself as Mrs. Quinlin. With red hair and a determined look on her face, she appeared pretty formidable to me. I decided right away not to give *her* any trouble. But as Bobby Burns, Scotland's national bard said, "The best laid schemes o' mice and men gang aft a-gley."[1] Something to remind oneself of when writing one's autobiography, yet we can only plunge ahead. But, I digress. We kids were listening: "First of all," Mrs. Quinlin said, "I want you to pay complete attention to me."

I heard what she said, while gazing around the room —at my classmates, at pictures on the wall, at the ceiling. Giving me a riveting stare, Mrs. Quinlin added, "We tie little monkeys up."

I had no idea what she meant by that. Was it simply an expression, like when I did or said something silly and Mom would talk about "monkey shines" or respond, "You're made out of blue mud"?

Mrs. Quinlin continued lecturing us about The Rules, like how she always should be addressed as Mrs. Quinlin or "ma'am." "When I ask you something, your answer is 'Yes, ma'am' or 'No ma'am'. You're to call me ma'am or Mrs. Quinlin. Is that understood?"

I understood, although I'd never had to address Mom or answered her questions in such a strict manner. My main, mainly ADD (Attention Deficit Disorder), focus now riveted on a print of George Washington's portrait between two blackboards. George's curly white hair hung down around his ears. I had no idea he wore a wig, had never seen any person in either Jerome or Hurley who looked anything like that. The portrait fascinated me.

"That's it," Mrs. Quinlin suddenly shouted, moving swiftly over to a closet. She opened the closet door and I noticed all sorts of school materials inside it. The learning device Mrs. Quinlin pulled out of her closet was a long rope. She marched over to my desk and began coiling the rope around me, and the seat of the desk. As she tied knots in the rope, she shouted to make certain all the other pupils heard, "We tie little monkeys up. Now, you listen to me, Max Odendahl. You look straight ahead and don't move until I tell you to."

---

[1] "Oh wad some power the giftie gie us," Robert Burns also wrote, "to see oursels as others see us! It wad frae monie a blunder free us, an' foolish notion."

I didn't, because my attention certainly had been diverted from George Washington's wig. Embarrassment from other kids snickering about my predicament, laughing at my expense, enveloped me. I don't know how long I remained tied to my desk, yet I'm almost certain that when Mrs. Quinlin untied me she got in another verbal jab about my lack of attention to her listing of The Rules. It now seems to me she must have delivered her jabs in the manner of some wild-eyed preacher cleansing sinners in church. I have no idea which church Mrs. Quinlin attended, or if she did at all.

Such absolution by the rope wasn't my cup of tea, but many of Mrs. Quinlin's students years later swore loyalty to her. As their first teacher (there was no kindergarten at Hurley), she made a lasting and favorable impression on them. And I'm pretty certain, even if Attention Deficit Disorder had been known about in 1936, the malady wouldn't have held up as an excuse for what she simply viewed as misbehavior in school. Certainly not with Dad, who told Alan and me, "If I find out you got a whipping for acting up in school, you're going to get a lot worse one when you get home."

That same sort of logic held for what we ate. If we didn't like, say fried liver, we weren't required to eat it. We Odendahls dined family-style together at a table, with bowls and serving plates passed around. "If you put it on your plate," Dad warned, "you eat it."

I'm still too much of a Hard-Times kid – especially in restaurants. Paying "good money" for food, trying to keep up the habit of leaving behind a "clean plate." This does not help one who would benefit more by dieting, leaving some food unconsumed. Or taking some home.

Food left in bowls and serving plates during the Great Depression appeared as "leftovers," usually at the next supper. We certainly never raided the refrigerator between meals. There were few things Alan and I wouldn't eat. In fact, we scrambled to get our share of food, especially any kind of meat, including fried liver, as it was passed around at suppertime.

After I was grown, I told Mom the story of being tied to my desk the first day of school and being referred to as a little monkey. Mrs. Quinlin was one of Mom's longtime teacher friends, but she was irritated, "I certainly would have had a *word* with her about *that* if I had known."

It was just as well. I don't think Dad would have seen the situation in the same light. Being tied to your desk only once and keeping your mouth shut about it worked better for me than the real possibility of a "good" spanking at home. I've also read somewhere that some of those suffering from ADD purposely look for trouble to be the center of attention. My ADD-life is a many-years-later, self-diagnosed disorder. It could just as well be, because we are part of the human race, that trouble simply comes our way, arrives in some sort of random fashion.

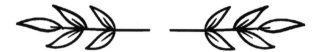

CHAPTER 4 – DOROTHY JOINS US

Somewhere deep in my possibly ADD-led mind there is a tiny vacuum cleaner slowly sucking memories away, including many of those from the first until sixth grades. Like sucked into a bag, or a deep-brain garbage can? Sort'a the same as when you move stuff into your computer's recycle bin?

Never have I been possessed with the memory of a now-deceased old friend who began his stories something like this, "It was just before dark, on a Thursday in November of 1946, when..."

Can't recall the day of the week nor the time but December 14, 1937, marked the birthday of my sister Dorothy. Although Mom talked to Alan and me about the coming arrival, I don't remember seeing Mom much pooching out her dress. Not like some women one observes in shopping malls with thin, over-large, tight T shirts stretched across their abdomens.

Mom spent 10 days in the Santa Rita Hospital after Dorothy's birth. She told us she enjoyed those days away from two small and feisty boys, one 9 and the other 7. Children under 12 years old weren't allowed to visit in the hospital.

Wonder why Mom and other women were kept in the hospital so long? And when my appendix was removed as a teenager, I was forced to spend 10 long and *boring* days in that same Santa Rita hospital? I've read stories about pioneer women getting off wagons to give birth, maybe with the train waiting overnight. As those stories go, the next day new mothers painfully climbed back into wagons to continue the journey west. Those were tough days in rough, bouncing wagons. Many of those babies, and mothers, died.

It was argued long hospital stays like Mom's were necessary as a matter of sanitation. In 1937, hospitals were viewed as more sanitary than the average home. A 10-day hospital stay was seen as more likely to insure the survival of mother and child. Sanitation also deemed that children under 12 could not visit patients in hospitals. Why kids became more sanitary after 12 wasn't explained. I expect the main consideration was the noise factor of younger visitors.

The pendulum has swung back toward covered-wagon time, with hospital stay for mothers and newborns only a day or two. With staph infections common in hospitals, most homes might be more sanitary. Or, it could simply be a matter of economics, with the skyrocketing per-day-co-charges for a hospital room out-of-reach for more than a day or so for most persons. Health-care plans, HMOs, and Medicare balk at longer stays. The

Odendahl family was lucky because The Company provided hospital and other medical care, including medicine.

Alan and I waited anxiously in Hurley when Dad went to the Santa Rita Hospital to bring Mom and the new baby home. Someone must have driven him there, as we had no car at that time. "Here is your new sister," Dad said as he proudly showed us the small bundle he held in his arms.

It was love at first sight for me. There was little sibling rivalry as Dorothy grew up–perhaps because she was a girl, and always the baby of the family. I'd lived with more than enough rivalry from Alan. Dorothy was younger and Mom stayed at home her first few years. I still regret not spending more time with my little sister while she was "raised."

I occasionally took her riding on my bike. Surviving is a picture of Dorothy holding on behind me on my burro. She is maybe about six and I 13? Can't recall how much I paid or from whom I bought the burro; probably from some other Hurley boy. By this time I was earning money delivering newspapers–at one time or another the weekly national *Grit,* the daily *Silver City Press*, the *El Paso Times* or the *El Paso Herald-Post* .

Me and Dorothy on my $3 burro

Neither Dad nor Mom were keen about my owning that donkey, which had to be kept out of town, roaming on its own for feed. The burro also had the habit, with you aboard, of loping alongside barbed-wire fences. He would brush so close to the fence that a leg could be scraped open by the barbs if you didn't quickly lift it away.

When I was forced to lift a leg and sit sideways on the burro's back, pointing away from the fence like on a chair, that burro would begin to buck. Usually he threw me off and, if I let go of the rope around his neck, the burro ran away. A boy can run a long way and finally corner a burro, but routinely catching that donkey proved a real chore. It was easier to catch the burro with his rope around its neck, yet I feared the donkey would entangle the rope on another fence or something else and choke himself. By the time the burro was caught, I often was tired out, plus not in any mood to attempt another ride and again be bucked off.

One day a Hispanic man from Central, about six miles by highway from Hurley, offered me $3 for my burro. Looking back, I should have given the man $3 of my hard-earned newspaper money to take that blasted burro off my hands! I readily accepted the man's offer. Three dollars was a good bit of change for a boy in those days.

"I'll come by and pay you when I get the money," the man said as he led my burro away with its rope. I never saw the man, the burro, or rope for several months after that. One day I resolved to hitchhike to Central to collect my $3. Hitchhiking was common for Hurley boys headed for Silver City about 16 miles away, or for stops in-between like Central. A few folks would take the time to pick up boys, and it was a sort of unwritten law that one stopped and gave any hitchhiking military serviceman in uniform a ride.

Somehow I found my way to the man's house in Central. He came to the door. I asked him about my $3. He told me he did not have the money, that times had been hard. As I looked at him, unconvinced, he said, "Just last night my wife had a baby girl. Would you like come in and see it?"

I followed him inside where his wife lay in bed, holding the smallest baby I'd ever seen. Remember, Dorothy was 10 days old when I first saw her. Something came over me as I thanked the woman for showing me her baby and went back outside. I muttered to her husband something like, "That baby of yours sure is pretty. It's going to take lots of money to take care of it and your wife now. So, forget about the $3 for the burro. It's a present for the baby."

He nodded with a smile on his face. I walked back to the highway to hitchhike home. That was a quite unusual event between a prejudiced Anglo Hurley boy and a Hispanic. Like prejudice toward Hispanics at the Hurley picture show Friday "Mexican Night." Spanish-language films drew a full house each Friday. I once heard an Anglo man complain, "Those Meskins live like animals."

"How's that?" someone asked.

"Well, just look at what those Meskin women do at their Friday picture shows. They sit there with their tits hanging out in public feeding their babies." Strange, I thought even then. What about Mother and child —Madonna and Jesus? I'd bet that guy secretly enjoyed looking at those brown breasts. He must have gone inside the movie theater to take a more than fleeting glance at them. I doubt if he understood Spanish, didn't care much about what the actors on the big screen were saying or doing.

Saturday afternoon found us boys lined up for "cowboy" picture shows, which cost 10 cents. Jerry Shinn, who lived just down the alley from us, had a big dog named Sergeant. "He can whip any other dog in town," Jerry proudly claimed.

Another boy didn't think so. He showed up with his large dog one Saturday as we lined up for the cowboy show. Jerry stood in line, Sergeant at this side. The dog fight began. The manager of the picture show rushed out and demanded the dogs be pulled apart. He wasn't about to attempt it himself. "Make those dogs stop fighting and send them home," he shouted, "or I won't let you boys in the picture show."

Jerry and the other boy pulled their dogs apart and ordered them to leave, which they did. Actually, those dogs behaved pretty well when not egged by their masters, and fights were so short that little damage was inflicted on either dog.

"This has got to stop," the manager explained in a softer voice. "If you bring either one of those dogs here next week, you can't see the picture show. That's for sure."

It didn't stop. Dogs occasionally fought, and all of us always saw the picture show. When the door to the picture show opened, we boys paraded down to the front row, even though the picture on the screen there was a bit out of focus. "We got the best seats in the house," a boy would say, as others proudly seated on the front row nodded heads.

Alan had become the entrepreneur of Odendahl paper routes in Hurley. He, like I, began in the newspaper business by delivering *Grit*, a homey publication which arrived by mail each week. When Alan moved up to delivering the *El Paso Herald-Post* and the *El Paso Times*, I took over his *Grit* route.

Before long Alan was the manager for all four El Paso newspaper routes in Hurley–two for the afternoon *Herald-Post* and two for the morning *Times.* These four routes were for the south, Anglo side of Hurley. No papers that I know of were delivered on the Hispanic part of Hurley, north across the railroad tracks. Looking back, I see clearly that most Hispanic boys needed money from newspaper routes more than Alan and I and other Anglo boys did. It could also have been that folks on that side of the tracks couldn't afford newspaper subscriptions? Many Hispanic parents, of course, spoke only Spanish and couldn't read newspapers printed in English.

It would have been a dangerous business, requiring more diplomacy than we Anglos possessed, if Hispanic boys attempted to deliver papers on the south side. At the least they would have been subjects of much taunting. The same reception would have greeted us to the north. Prejudice's ugly head reared itself on both sides of those tracks. Unfortunately, we lacked mutual respect for each other. I still hold that much prejudice could have been alleviated if we had been allowed to learn Spanish from other kids at school.

Whenever other Anglo boys dropped out of the newspaper business, Alan and I sometimes were forced to deliver all four routes of the El Paso papers, plus the weekly *Grit*. The afternoon *Herald-Post* arrived at the Post Office by bus, routinely running late. Delivering "afternoon" papers late in the evening, often after dark, resulted in unhappy customers.

The scheduled morning *Times* drop-off from a large truck occurred between 4:30 and 5 a.m., with those arrivals habitually running late. The truck driver placed the newspaper bundles into a large, metal box just inside the town gate. The entrance sign stretched across it with the letters HURLEY, next to a narrow, two-lane Highway 180 leading to Deming, then further southeast to El Paso.

There was a cover on the metal box. When the truck was late, Alan or I or other boys (most usually we were by ourselves) arrived about 5 a.m. to deliver the *Times*. We'd crawl inside the box, prop open the cover slightly for air with part of a Yucca stick, and sleep. The truck driver would bang on the box cover to awaken us when he arrived.

On cold winter mornings, you'd wrap yourself in leftover newspapers inside the box to keep warm. It was not unusual for the papers to arrive at 6:30 or later. That meant rousing yourself from sleep a second time, making a mad scramble of deliveries before a quick breakfast, and heading off for school.

When the bus arrived late, we paperboys were forced to deliver the "afternoon" *El Paso Herald-Post* in the dark. On cold, wintery nights, the wind often would howl through town. Between streets, one had to walk next to the two-lane Highway 180. You were by yourself out there by the highway, further away from the protection you felt those in

39

town always provided. This frightened me very much; I scurried along against the wind with my heavy paper bag as quickly as I could.

Lots of folks in Hurley regularly attended church. My family didn't, with organized religion not the main focus of our lives. Those who went to fundamental churches were hearing about "The Devil" and "Satan" on a regular basis. Some, if originally from Down South, feared "the Boogie Man." Evil for them was depicted as Satan or the Devil. Good was Jesus and/or God. An eternal battle supposedly raged between these forces. Fundamental ministers remained confident, regularly preached about "Hell." That place was depicted as one where you eternally roasted in fearful fires if you didn't shape up. Most obviously opted to choose the side of "good." Yet, it took great perseverance to do so, like when young girls attempted to save their virginity for husbands.

Mom or Dad never cautioned me, Alan, or Dorothy about "The Devil" or "Satan" or "Boogie Men" or frightened us about roasting in "Hell" if we didn't conform to what they believed or wanted us to do at the moment. We were told about how some people were dishonest, that there were even those ones bad or evil, capable of doing us great harm.

Mom and Dad agreed evil men and women should be put in jail or prison, just where we might find ourselves if we did great wrong. Those with mental illness needed help, often only available at very few mental institutions. Yet, be careful, Alan and Max. Stay away from them, especially the men who pick up garbage barrels in alleys behind each Hurley home.

Well-muscled men were required to lift heavy barrels into garbage trucks. "Leave those men alone and let them do their work," Mom warned us in a whisper. One she secretively pointed to, adding, "I understand he has some sort of mental problem. He could be harmless. Nevertheless, he doesn't deserve any teasing from you boys." She need not to have worried; he already scared "the Hell" out of me. I'd looked at his muscles and knew to leave good enough alone.

My fright while delivering papers and trudging on a windy night near Highway 180 wasn't from the possibility of being accosted by some strange creature, Devil or Boogie Man. It was that one of those bad/evil or mentally ill men (maybe a garbage guy?) might somehow be lurking along that highway, ready to do some unspeakable harm to me. I had no idea exactly what that might be.

Lately, I've noticed that Steven King-types of horrible creatures, or those from outer space, seem to be popular for TV watchers. They appear more awful than Frankenstein did in old black-and-white picture shows. I don't care to watch them, but these kinds of movies and TV shows make lots of money. Are these new monsters replacing the Devils and Satan as what to be most frightened of?

Grit was delivered to the door, and boys collected for each weekly issue. The El Paso papers quickly were folded into triangles, thrown onto porches, with separate weekly collections. Part of the occasional sport of morning deliveries was to aim the thrown triangles at empty milk bottles awaiting exchange for full bottles. With two or three inches of tasty cream at the top. Scattering empty milk bottles, sometimes waking folks, did not make for happy-camper customers. You had to randomize your throwing so as to be able to claim on-target hits as accidents.

One woman asked me to put her newspaper inside her screen door and I think I nodded I would. Yet, I continued to throw triangle-papers at her porch. The weekly price of the newspaper was say, 17 cents. When I came to her door to collect, she opened it and threw 17 pennies out into her yard. "That's how I've been getting my paper. So, go out there and pick up your money the same way."

I handed her a receipt and gathered the pennies I could find. Angry, I vowed to stop delivering to her, but here's how it worked: A boy ordered a certain number of newspapers for each route, for which he was charged the wholesale price. You made no profit until after you had collected the wholesale amount each week. Folks moved away and left you holding the bag, or they would not be at home when you collected. There were weeks when you barely gathered the wholesale price, were forced to go out and collect a second time to make any of your own money.

The penny-throwing lady always was at home, always paid her 17 cents. I began placing her newspapers behind the screen door. Whether she thought she deserved special treatment, or had some physical ailment she did not wish to share knowledge about, I have no way of knowing.

I also learned one of my first lessons about charity when delivering newspapers. For example, one "old" lady, probably about 60 with a husband working at some menial job in the mill, kept money for her newspaper in a special bowl–from which with a smile she paid me each week. At Christmas, she would hand me an extra dollar bill, shouting, "Merry Christmas" and thank me for delivering her paper that year.

Another woman, the Company superintendent's wife, rarely was at home when I collected. I would tell her she owed, say, for three weeks. That's 51 cents at 17 cents per week. Her husband was reputed to be making about $25,000 a year, while ordinary mill employees earned less than a fifth of that. "Oh, no," she'd exclaim, "I don't owe you that much. In fact, I'm sure I paid you last week."

Newspapers provided us with receipts books, with tiny dated stubs printed for each week. When a customer paid, you handed him or her a receipt for that week. "Well, ma'am," I'd reply politely, in the back of my mind not wanting to somehow get Dad in trouble with the superintendent, "I still have your three weeks of receipts in my book. Of course, ma'am, if you have those receipts – then you don't owe me for those weeks."

"I know I paid you," she would emphasize, with a look as if I were B.T. Barnum pulling off some scam at his circus, "and I'll find them." I'd wait several minutes in the cold; she never invited me into the largest house in town. "I can't find those receipts, right now," she'd say upon her return, "but I certainly paid you. Just this one time I'll pay you for three weeks. But, I'm going to be watching you from now on. Understand?"

"Yes ma'am." No Christmas bonuses from that lady either; never a "Thank You" for delivering to her. Was that class difference or just a range of Hurley personalities?

While making my collections, I watched another woman face death. She had cancer, probably throat or lung cancer, perhaps from smoking. She paid promptly each week, and I noticed she was getting thinner each time I collected. One day when I came to her door she had a tube in her nose which must have been inserted down her throat. From a straw, she seemed to be sipping some kind of pulverized food from a water glass. There was a strange, bad smell coming from that house.

"Thank you for doing such a good job of delivering my paper to me," she said, as she handed me 17 cents with her free hand. That's the last time I ever saw her.

But this chapter shouldn't end about death, because it began with a birth–the arrival of my sister Dorothy. In 1968, Mom wrote a story *So Many Christmases*, probably for one of her writing classes. One episode was about the Christmas of 1938 in Hurley:

"An eight-year old boy, at our Company house on Aztec Street next to the Balls proudly showed his mother the toy he'd just bought for his baby sister. 'Think she'll like it?' he asked anxiously as he pulled the wheeled thing across the floor, making music as it turned.

"And the mother, thinking he'd been reckless with his precious one dollar, reminded him that Dorothy couldn't yet even stand up, let alone walk! But how she loved that toy later on!"

How could I *ever forget* the name of another female I so loved in 1941 or early 1942? I did forget her name, but haven't *her*. One of my sixth grade teachers, she was beautiful, yet it was music that helped work her way so deeply into my heart.

"Listen closely. This is Edvard Grieg's *Peer Gynt Suite*," she told us. Her small hands fascinated me as she leaned over, her fingers gently placing the needle onto the 78rpm record. This then-modern, compact-but-still-bulky turntable operated on electricity, unlike the earlier hand-wound Victrola of our family. The turntable came alive with sounds I'd never heard before.

"There are four movements to the *Peer Gynt Suite*," she explained. "Morning Mood, Ase's Death, Anitra's Dance, and In the Hall of the Mountain King." "In the Hall of the Mountain King" became my favorite.

At the age of 11, testosterone must have begun to work its way through my system, for I still recall how, even though she was a tiny woman, sweaters showed her chest to advantage. Something unique was happening to me as we listened to Grieg, a Norwegian who had his music influenced by living for a time in Denmark. Grieg's music didn't flow from the turntable every afternoon, only when my beloved came up short on whatever else she had to teach that day.

Hurley's elementary school wasn't like college, where students take notes in competition with one another, frantically moving along with the professor's pace of lecturing. Rather, its methodology was repeat, repeat, and repeat. One simply didn't learn the alphabet in the first grade and continue from there. Ordered to the front of the room, first graders plodded as far as they could in recitations of the alphabet. Often this became so much of an ordeal that some girls and even a few boys, so embarrassed about having to stand in front of the room facing us, literally peed in their pants–the liquid puddling the flood. The rest of us youngsters, of course, giggled each time that happened.

Mrs. Quinlin's disapproval of such behavior, both the giggling and the peeing, scared those kids into urinating even more the next time they stood in front of the room. Maybe if she'd let terrified kids go to the bathroom more often, her floor would have been less puddled. Raising a hand to go outside to bathrooms in a smaller building next door was looked at with disdain.

"Recess is the time to go to the bathroom," she would say, "except in an emergency." Mrs. Quinlin didn't view a kid being so frightened of recitation that he or she peed in his or her pants as an emergency. Always having a bit of ham in me, I was not as afraid to face the class, also must have had a strong bladder because I don't remember embarrassing myself. I piddled reciting but didn't puddle.

At any rate, the class laboriously moved through the letters of the alphabet. The slowest kid in the class, lowest common denominator, set the pace. Then boring, boring, and even more boring for those just above the common denominator, or with ADD. Yet, I don't recall any real animosity against those slow to recite.

Listening to the *Peer Gynt Suite* over and over again had the opposite effect on me. The more times I heard those movements, the more I enjoyed them. I still perk up when a classical radio station plays a portion of the *Peer Gynt*.

And, unlike Mrs. Quinlin and most other teachers, I paid rapt attention to my sixth grade mentor and all she taught, besides the four movements. My eyes also followed *her* every movement. Perhaps her beauty provided a placebo effect which kept my ADD in remission those fall months. I soon became one of her favorites, called upon to help with tasks like erasing the blackboard.

The remission from grade-school boredom had begun about December 7, 1941, when the Japanese attacked the U.S. Pacific Fleet at Pearl Harbor, Hawaii. Less than two hours after the attack began, 21 ships including battleships had been sunk or damaged. American dead numbered 2,403.

"We're gon'na be at war with the Japs, now," Gilbert Moore, one of those who later initiated The Society for Persons Born in Space, told Alan as we headed toward the picture show.

"I bet we'll take on the Krauts, too," Alan said. He and Gilbert, both very bright, were in the same class. The next day, Americans across the nation huddled next to their radios as President Franklin D. Roosevelt spoke to Congress and called December 7, 1941 "a date which will live in infamy." He said later in the speech that "no matter how long it may take us to overcome this premeditated invasion, the American people in their righteous might will win through to absolute victory."

The same day, Monday, men from Hurley and from coast-to-coast lined up to enlist in the armed forces. This meant young men from around the country soon would arrive at the Army base at Deming, in Luna County 37 miles to the southeast.

It was common knowledge in Hurley that the Deming school superintendent was some sort of fundamentalist Christian. "If I catch one of my teachers in a Deming liquor store or bar, that teacher will be looking for another a job," he is supposed to have proclaimed from time to time. The result was that some of the feistier of Deming's female teachers avoided his temperate words by flocking to bars and nightclubs in Grant County near Silver City, east of Hurley.

They drank their liquor and cavorted away from the eyes of the righteous superintendent. Those young men at the Deming army base, having produced more testosterone than I, picked up the scent and followed after the feisty teachers. My beautiful sixth grade teacher was feisty enough to have me fall hopelessly in love with her. I have no idea about her drinking habits or whether she ever frequented bars or nightclubs. Nevertheless, what she said one day hit me like another Pearl Harbor attack.

"Class, I need to tell you something," she said quietly. "I'm going to have to be leaving you. I've met a man from the Deming army base and we're going to be married. I must go with him wherever he goes to help the war effort. I'm sure you understand." I understood only that she would be leaving me. Tears began to well in my eyes. She came over, patted me, then put her arm around my shoulders. Though in grief, my shoulder and back felt joy, with pleasure much exceeding that I'd first found holding hands with three-year-old Gloria Ann Baulsch.

For those few sad but still wonderful days that my sixth grade teacher remained with us I simply couldn't accept she could be leaving me. I realized only too well her man had to be larger than me in *every* way, but he couldn't possibly have loved her as much. He just couldn't have! If only she would have waited until I also was a man. Bigger. But it was too late. She was too soon gone, never to return.

Life continued in the sixth grade with a series of teachers in Hurley schools during World War II. While several other young ones quickly fell prey to handsome soldiers at Deming or young men elsewhere, the older and/or uglier usually remained. It was a fairly young and fairly pretty Ruth Bilbrey (boy, do I remember that name!) who eventually replaced the woman filling my life with love and music. Miss Bilbrey didn't play the *Peer Gynt Suite* for us, nor did I fall in love with *her*. Yet, I did learn more than I needed to about her private life, and paid the consequences for it.

We Odendahls had no car during the Second World War. The last family automobile had been the 1929 Chevy, sold in Jerome. Our garage behind the house was vacant, until we rented to a Mr. Kelly. One day I spotted Miss Bilbrey riding alongside Mr. Kelly in his car. Aha!

Impulsiveness of ADD completely out of remission, I hadn't paid the attention I should have to Miss Bilbrey's sixth-grade lecturing. One afternoon just before recess, I tore a sheet of lined paper out of a tablet with a red cover displaying the face of an Indian chief in full feathers on it. I doodled a stick figure of her and Mr. Kelly holding hands on the sheet. Below, in an ADD outburst I wrote, "Bilbrey loves Kelly." Below another stick figure of her alone I scribbled, "To hell with Bilbrey."

Big mistake!

At recess I showed my handiwork around to other boys on the playground. One of them might have fallen in love with Miss Bilbrey. He waved the sheet at me and said,

"This is terrible. I'm going to show it to her." Not believing him, not sensible enough to snatch back my crude artwork, I ADD-mocked him, "Go ahead if you've got the guts to."

He did. Miss Bilbray told me to stay after school. After the classroom cleared of students and the teacher from across the hall arrived, I knew Miss Bilbrey simply wasn't going to talk the situation over with me. Why? A witness! A Hurley teacher would not paddle you unless she had another to witness it. Miss Bilbrey began, "Max, did you write and draw this?"

"Yes, ma'am"

"Well, even though it is a very private and personal matter between Mr. Kelly and me, I could have forgiven what you wrote. But I cannot allow you to go unpunished for saying to hell with me. No sir, young man!"

While Miss Bilbrey laid out her obvious plan, out of the corner of my eye I saw the other teacher heading toward us with a wooden paddle she had taken out of a closet. About 18 inches long, it had a short handle, with the punishment part about four inches wide with four or five holes drilled along the center. The purpose of the holes was not only to inflict pain but also to leave welts.

"Bend over the desk," Miss Bilbrey ordered. Perhaps a coward, certainly not courageous like some boys who defiantly suffered "whippings" in tearless silence, I squalled a bit louder with each blow. Some teachers took pity on squallers, but this seemed to spur Miss Bilbrey to faster and harder whacking. Finally, I grew silent and she stopped.

"Stand up, Max," she barked. "I hope you have learned your lesson. You can go home now." In this day and age a student might show his parents welts and the teacher might even be removed from his or her job. No corporal punishment allowed. In my case I knew Dad meant it when he said, "If I hear you got a whipping at school, you're going to get a lot worse when you get home."

I suffered in silence at home, although a bit of a hero at school the next day among other boys besides the one who ratted me out. I didn't tell them about my tears and squalling. The fact of the matter was, I believed then and still do, that I deserved that "whipping."

But the next whipping Miss Bilbrey gave me in that sixth grade was one I didn't deserve. *Really!* Following the "to hell with Bilbrey" episode, she ordered me to move to a desk centered directly in front of hers. I knew she was "keeping an eye on me," so I watched my behavior.

She also kept a sympathetic and obviously pleasurable eye on a student nicknamed Superman, who now sat two desks behind me. Handsome, six feet tall, 16 years old, and muscularly developed like a grown man, he had been "held back" in school several times. I can't recall his real name, but Superman remained a mellow fellow when in the sight of Miss Bilbrey. Because he didn't "hit on all his cylinders," none of us sixth-grade boys knew quite what to expect from Superman and we feared to find out. We did know he was capable of doing strange things when Miss Bilbrey wasn't watching.

A fish bowl with a single goldfish swimming around in it sat in front of me on Miss Bilbrey's desk. The goldfish provided a special distraction for one with ADD. Not only did I like watching that little fish swim but I also liked it. One morning, when preparing to sit down at my desk, I noticed the water in the fish bowl was black. I got up, was peering into the bowl for the goldfish, when Miss Bilbrey screamed, "Max, you get away from my fish bowl and sit down."

"Where's the goldfish?" I asked.

"*Someone* poured ink into my fish bowl and killed my goldfish," she replied, with a combination of tears and fire in her eyes. "Max, I want you to stay after school." I knew what that meant!

During recess and at lunch time it was the consensus of all of us boys that Superman was the real culprit. "If Superman kilt that little fish by dumpin' ink in the water early in the mornin' before Old Miss Bilbrey got here," one asked, "what would he done do to us if we was to tattle on him?" None, including me, cared to find out. All of us contemplated my fate. Sure enough, after the other kids left that afternoon the teacher from across the hall came marching in.

"I know you did it," Miss Bilbrey said, fire burning even brighter in her eyes while the other teacher retrieved the paddle from the closet, "and, Max, I just want to know why. Why?"

"I didn't dump any ink in your goldfish bowl," I said.

"Well then, "she asked mockingly, "who did?"

"I don't know," I lied.

"Lying doesn't help. It just makes it worse. I just can't understand you, Max Odendahl. How could you do such a cruel thing to a poor little fish? I suppose it's because you hate me. You thought this up as some sort of mean way of getting even for your last spanking. Now, didn't you?"

She could tell by the look on my face that I was lying. And lying I *was*, because I told her I didn't know who did it. I worried more about if I told the truth, more about fellow boys' admonition that Superman surely would hurt me in some, perhaps stranger way than inking a fish. Stuck on the horns of a confusing dilemma, I had told a lie —a fishy story. I couldn't think of anything else to say to Miss Bilbrey, so I didn't.

The routine was the same. Ordered to bend over the desk, a furious Miss Bilbrey beat the tar out of me with the paddle. I squalled. Carrying my welts home, I didn't tell my parents anything.

That's about the extent of excitement I remember from the sixth grade. The seventh grade, junior high, loomed as a turning point in our lives. That's when we Anglos would have to share school with the "Meskins." I don't recall hearing their mild term for us, "Gringo," until later in my life. A railroad track used by trains hauling copper ore from the mine at Santa Rita divided Hurley, laid out with streets on one side facing "true" north and on the other "magnetic" north. Hispanic families were relegated to "The North Side" of the tracks where many lived in shacks, while Anglo families to "The South Side" were in more comfortable Company housing.

As part of such segregation, youngsters went to separate schools from the first to the sixth grades. Integration began on The South Side in Hurley's junior high and continued there through high school. Hispanic children headed south to "our" across- the-railroad-tracks schools by walking through a pedestrian underpass. The first day of junior high Anglos watched with trepidation as a stream of brown-skinned kids arrived.

It was common, though inaccurate, knowledge among Anglo boys that most of their Hispanic counterparts were dangerous, carried switchblade knives and knew how to use them. I am unaware of any Hurley Anglo, child or adult, being cut by a Hispanic-carried knife, although there were reputed to be adult male knife fights in local Hispanic bars. School boys from both sides of the tracks only occasionally matched up to fight with their fists.

The only switchblade-knife incident I know about occurred with a Hispanic seventh-grader, soon after we all had settled in. He sat in the row of desks across from me, wearing a zoot suit, which may have originated in the Los Angeles area among young Hispanic men. It was a dress, Sunday-goin'-to-church suit modified so that it was sewn with baggy trousers falling over shined black shoes. The coat, widened into padded shoulders and narrowed to the waist, stretched nearly to his knees. He wore a chain across the front of his zoot suit, to which was attached a switchblade knife hidden in a coat pocket.

Our substitute teacher that day was Mrs. Henry, a middle-aged woman who lived just two doors away from us and a good friend of Mom's. One day, as Mrs. Henry presented her lesson, the zoot-suiter took out his knife, opened it, and began waving it around for the class to see.

"Put away that knife," Mrs. Henry ordered. Playing with a knife in school was unacceptable, even though many of us boys–Hispanic and Anglo —carried ordinary pocket (often official Boy Scout) knives. She moved toward the young Hispanic, stood next to him, and repeated her order. Holding the knife by the handle, the youth jammed the blade into the wooden desk. He grinned up at her, as if saying, "What are you going to do about it?"

Mrs. Henry's right arm shot out, her fist slamming into the youth's jaw. Her blow knocked him out of the seat, into the aisle next to me. "All right now," she said, "get back in your seat and give me that knife." He rose from the floor, slid back in his desk's seat, and meekly handed his knife to Mrs. Henry. She had a serious talk with him after school, during which she returned his knife. Mrs. Henry had no more trouble with the zoot-suiter and they became friends. I soon lost my fear of him and also became friendly for the remainder of that school year. Like so many people in my life's journey, I wonder whatever happened to him.

Friendly, but not a close friend, because Hurley boys and girls on different sides of the tracks rarely socialized after school. In today's "zero tolerance" scenario, kids can be suspended or expelled from school for merely having a knife in their possession. A teacher would lose her job for striking a youth not in self-defense, and his parents could file a lawsuit against her and the school, perhaps settled out of court successfully with big bucks for them. Right or wrong, attending school now is different.

Testing substitute teachers was great sport for us boys. Substitutes held down the fort after regular teachers married servicemen or joined up themselves as WACs (Women's Army Corps) or WAVEs (Navy) during World War II. One of my ADD symptoms was being extremely shy, so I attempted to hide my insecurity by "playing the fool," putting myself in the limelight, showing off at any opportunity.

One substitute had taken roll early in the morning but discovered my desk empty after recess. Not knowing who was missing, she again took roll and discovered it was me. About that time strange noises began coming from the closet where teachers kept their instructional materials. She opened the door, looked inside, and found nothing. I screeched like a cat and scrambled down from a high shelf where I had been hiding. It scared the liver out of her, much to the delight of the rest of the boys in the class.

Not as resolute as Mrs. Henry, she simply ordered me back into my desk seat. She was so flabbergasted by my behavior that it probably didn't occur to her that I "deserved a good paddling." (None I ever got was "good.") On the other hand, maybe I escaped because of her being unaware how easy it would have been to mete out punishment simply by sending across the hall for a witness carrying a paddle.

Despite my reputation among teachers as a "problem" boy, I recited the class speech when we graduated from junior high. That first experience with the kindness of a Christian minister surprised me as much as it may have my junior high teachers. He had taught us once or twice as a substitute teacher, part of "making ends meet" with his job as minister at the non-denominational Hurley Community Church across the street from grade and high schools. The Roman-Catholic church was on the town's main street, several blocks away.

"I think you can handle giving the eighth grade graduation speech," the minister confided to me on the playground one afternoon late in the spring of 1944.

"Huh?"

"Not only can you do it, but it also will be good for you to be involved in something constructive. I've already cleared it with your teachers."

"I don' know."

"You'll have to write your own speech, Max, but I'll help you. You will do it, won't you?"

"I guess so."

My feeble effort at writing the speech, of course, turned into *his* speech. Each of his additions or heavy editing was followed with something like, "You want parents to be proud of all of you students when you read this speech, don't you, Max?" or "I know you haven't gotten along with all your teachers, Max, but we've got to thank them in some way for all their effort in putting up with you."

He grinned at me, I grinned back, and the speech progressed. After honing it to his satisfaction, he took me to the empty high school auditorium. I would stand at a podium on the stage reading the speech, while at the back of the large room he signaled by waving his hands and arms. Louder. Softer. Faster. Slower.

When I presented the speech in the filled auditorium, also a basketball court, the minister perked up my courage and kept me going with his wild signaling from the rear of the big room. After the speech, he put his arm around my shoulders and told me, "I do wish you could have paid attention a bit closer to my signals because I think it would have helped you. But you did a great job, Max."

The next day at breakfast, Dad went through his list of what he saw as my deficiencies in speech making. It was like when you worked much of the day weeding the whole back yard. Dad would come home, point, and say: "You missed those three weeds in the corner."

That's just the way it was with Dad. I think he simply was treating Alan, Dorothy and me like he remembered growing up in a rigid German family. Which is not say that Dad didn't care for or protect us. He simply didn't show much emotion, never called me "Son." At the supper table he told stories about history, either his own or from books he'd read, and discussed the news. He did his best based on the rigid and poverty-stricken German family life he had experienced as a child.

While of grade-school age, I enjoyed going to the end of our Aztec Street alley to meet Dad. He and many others of the mill workers came home for a quick lunch, which we called "dinner." When Mom wasn't teaching school, she'd cook what now would be considered a very large evening "supper." Later, when she taught school across the tracks in "Mexican town," Dad, Alan, Dorothy, and I would put together our own "dinner," usually sandwiches filled with meat,

Gene Ball, who lived next door to us, usually preceded Dad out of the mill when I went down the alley at lunchtime. Ball had been a cowboy in his younger days. "What da' ya' say, Max?" he'd call out.

I would answer, "Hello. Mr. Ball," One day I mustered up enough courage to be first in greeting, "What da' ya say, Mr. Ball?"

"I'm afraid to say it."

On cue, when he greeted me first, I used his reply. Never have figured out why we were "afraid to say it" and/or what we might have feared. I was afraid of the Collie at a house at the end of that alley. The big Collie routinely lunged at a white picket fence. He was provoked further by boys taking sticks and running them across the pickets. I know I'd run a stick on the pickets once or twice. I sure didn't one day expect to see that Collie *outside* his fence, charging toward me. I froze in terror.

I didn't see Dad, who moved quickly between me and the Collie. He gave the Collie two swift kicks with his work shoes and it slunk away. As a kid, I probably never was more proud of my dad.

There was a grapevine which grew on the barbed-wire fence which separated our yard from the Balls'. The roots of the grapevine were in the Balls' yard and they watered it. Mrs. Louisa Ball didn't like it when Alan or I picked any grapes from that vine, ripe or not, hanging on our side or not. I think she wanted all the grapes to be consumed by her two younger sons. Mom ordered Alan and I to do as Mrs. Ball said.

Gene Ball, on the other hand, would advise Alan and me, "Any time those grapes get ripe on your side of the fence, you boys eat all you want." A dilemma.

Many evenings Mr. Ball would sit on his front porch whittling. Out of one big stick of wood, he could whittle a chain, with a cage containing a ball hanging on the end of the chain. That's something we did in Hurley on long, hot summer evenings. With no air conditioning of houses, not even "swamp coolers," folks sat on front porches and parents visited with neighbors. Mom always did more visiting than Dad who, to put it mildly, didn't mingle too well with others.

Gene Ball later contracted lung cancer, probably because he was a heavy roll-your-own cigarette smoker. When the pain became too severe, he went out to his coal shed in the back yard, put the barrel of his .30-.30 deer rifle into his mouth, snapped his bare toe on the trigger, and shot off the top of his head. I was either in the U.S. Navy or at college when that happened, so not able to attend Mr. Ball's funeral service. Mom told me almost everyone in Hurley was there at the Hurley Community Church.

Gene Ball, like my first minister friend who probably performed that funeral service, was a fine man. They were like in Rudyard Kipling's poem, "You're a better man than I am, Gunga Din!"

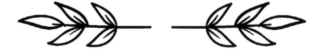

CHAPTER 5 – HURLEY WAYS

"Ya'll hear what happened?" a friend asked a group of us.

"Nope."

"The little pissant wuz climbin' up into that electric high-line tower near his house to get some little- bitty crows out'a their nest. The juice jumps across and killt ' im. Deader than a doornail."

"Jesus!" one of us exclaimed.

I tried to imagine what happened. The steel tower held high voltage lines supplying electricity to power the pumps at one of the Company's water wells. I wondered, "He musta' climbed the ladder to the crow's nest and got too close to one of those hot-juice wires?"

"That's what they tells me," proudly replied the kid who figured to be in the know. "The juice hits him in the face and fries it. Killts him right off."

"Wow!"

We boys became gloomier after our Scoutmaster found us later in the day. He explained we'd be pallbearers at the stricken boy's funeral. "The kid is barely 12, just joined the Boy Scouts," the Scoutmaster said, trying to rally us. Like most adults so often do, the Scoutmaster was telling us something we already knew.

"So, eight of you boys will be carrying the casket," the Scoutmaster continued explaining. "Wear your uniforms and be sure to put on your merit badge sashes." It all sounded a little neater then, getting to wear our uniforms in front of lots of folks.

We arrived the next day at the mortuary in Silver City, about 45 minutes before the service. The mortician greeted us. "I guess you boys would like to take a look at the deceased?"

"Sure," one of us responded for the nervous group. It was fairly certain, that like I, most of us never had seen anyone dead. The group grew silent. The mortician led us into another room, where we gathered around a closed casket resting on a gurney. The mortician lifted a half-cover off the casket as we circled in for a closer look.

Gazing into his casket, each Scout checked the tiny body to see if it moved. Would he rise and say "Hello," like characters sometimes did in picture shows to make everyone laugh?

The boy didn't move, and it wasn't funny. One side of his face was charred black, covered with white powder. The result was grotesque. After the last of the eight of us filed by, the mortician said, "What do you think, boys? I tried to do the best I could to make your friend look natural for the funeral."

"Oh, yeah," one blurted out a lie. "You did a great job, sir." We were instructed to wheel the casket into the mortuary chapel. When flowers were piled around the gurney, they created an odor overpowering my sense of smell. In the months that followed, merely being in the vicinity of flowers, either cut or growing in a field, almost sickened me. Since then, funerals have made me even more aware of my own immortality, how precarious and short life is. Attending them brings out a range of emotions, from love and sadness about never seeing the deceased again to the uncomfortableness of mechanically sitting through a service for an acquaintance.

A few persons began to be seated. The room filled by the time the boy's family slowly marched in and took seats on the front row. The preacher obviously didn't know much about "the deceased" or his family. "We're here today to celebrate the life of a wonderful boy whom God has taken to be with Him in Heaven," he said. "We shouldn't look at this as a day of sadness, although, of course as mortal beings, we're all overcome with sadness. But, really, this is a day of joy. Yes, one of joy because that boy *is* with God in heaven. God wanted him to be there with him. That's why this happened, all a part of God's glorious plan none of us is capable of understanding."

I and the other boys in uniform tried to look straight ahead, like we'd observed soldiers doing at military funerals in the picture shows. It was difficult to do when the preacher looked toward the open casket, and asserted, "This boy came from a loving family," when obviously he didn't know the family at all before the tragedy.

I didn't know what a eulogy was, that it came from a Greek word meaning "to speak well of." I just figured the preacher simply knew so little about the family that he'd resorted to plain lying. The preacher continued laying it on thick about the marvelous family when the boy's mother rose out of the front row pew and began flailing her arms in the air.

"Oh, Jesus," she wailed, "don't take my boy! Don't take my boy, Jesus! Please, Sweet Jesus, please!" Her husband rose, grabbed his wife by the arm and attempted to pull her back down. The woman, whom we Scouts had figured weighed in at least 200 pounds (she probably weighed more than that), directed her flailing at her husband and pounded him down in the pew. He covered his head with his arms to ward off her blows.

"Oh, what awful torment this poor women is going through," the preacher said, awakened from his prepared eulogy by the extent of the mother's hysteria. A quick-

54

witted fellow, he added, "We just can't put this good woman through any more torment. This service is over. The family will file out first and anyone wishing to view the body can do so after they leave."

The mother didn't buy it. "I got to look at my boy myself one last time," she wailed, pulling free from her husband and rushing to the open casket. She lifted her son by the shoulders and had wrenched his stiff body almost to the boy's chest by the time her husband firmly grasped her. She sobbed for several minutes with her son's head in her arms, suddenly lowered him in the casket, shook herself out of her husband's grip, and, with her head held high, walked out of the room.

"Thank God, that's over with," one shocked Boy Scout muttered. It wasn't over with by a long shot. A line of persons began to file by for a look at the boy, whom the mortician hurriedly had re-aligned in the casket. A few grasped the boy's hand, held it a second or two. Others softly said, "Goodbye."

The mortician, visibly shaken by the mother's outbursts and robust handling of her son, stood wary of more trouble until the last person had paid respects to the deceased and left the room. Only the mortician and eight Boy Scouts remained. Now calmer, he carefully closed the casket, like Antonio Stradivari might a case after showing off one of his precious violins.

Having regained control of the situation, the mortician ordered, "Okay, boys, let's git goin'." We pulled away the flowers, rolled the gurney through a door to the hearse. The mortician showed us which handles to hold in lifting the casket to put it into the hearse.

"Jesus Christ, this thing's heavy," one of us mumbled. We experienced what "dead weight" meant, even though the boy didn't weigh much more than 100 pounds. Besides being sickly, the boy took after his small father. "Maybe it's this casket that makes it so damn heavy," another boy mumbled back.

"Boys, you're going to have to maintain silence during the grave-side service," the mortician warned, adding, "Now listen here, any cussing is out of the question."

Struggling, we shoved our fellow Scout's casket into the hearse.

"Okay, good work," the mortician told us. "I'll drive the hearse and you boys ride in that car over there. Meet you at the cemetery." As the hearse moved out of the mortuary driveway, a black car containing the boy's family pulled in behind it. We Scouts were next in another black automobile.

Out of earshot of the mortician, we Scouts babbled about the antics of the mother. "We done knowed before this that Old Lady's nuts," one said. "This just proves it for sure." Another added, "She musta' scared the Hell right out of him, a'shakin' it out of him there in that casket. I bet he'll go to Heaven for sure, now." Although not a real belly buster, all of us giggled at that one.

At the cemetery, the hearse pulled alongside the grave site. The mortician rushed back and began escorting the family to seats in front of the open grave. While people were seated, we Scouts stood back. "Okay, boys," he whispered, "let's do 'er again."

I, still frightened, at first thought "'er" somehow meant doing something to or with the boy's freaked-out mother, then realized he meant the boy's casket. As we grappled it out of the hearse, each of us fumbled around searching for handles to hold on to. "Jesus," one exclaimed.

"Shut up," another mumbled in exasperation, now more afraid of the boy's mother than the mortician, what she might do to us if she overheard cursing., or "taking the Lord's name in vain."

Without further instructions, the mortician led us toiling Boy Scouts to the grave. If one stumbled, others had to pick up added weight. Each had a hand frozen to a handle; all feared we would drop the casket. Flashing in my mind was a vision of the boy falling out, of his mother seeing her son's blackened face as the heavy powder flaked off it. I felt afraid to look toward her; I imagined a hateful mother glowering in meanness at us Boy Scouts.

A strange apparatus covered the grave. None of us knew its purpose was to lower the casket slowly down into the hole. Silently, the mortician made weird motions for us to put the casket on wide belts stretched across the grave. When we placed the casket on the belts, the front rested precariously on the last webbing. "Lift 'er up," the mortician murmured. "Shove 'er forward. Just a bit. Stop! Stop! That's it. Let 'er down."

He motioned for us to move to empty reserved seats. One Boy Scout made a snappy military about-face, saw his error, right-faced to follow the rest of us stumbling toward our seats as if still holding the weight of the casket.

The preacher stood in front of the casket and began final rites for the boy. He didn't get as far as "ashes to ashes, and dust to dust" before the mother rose out of her seat, propelled herself toward the casket. As she threw her bulk across the casket, the webbing underneath stretched farther down. Another Scout gave my ribs a quick elbow punch. "She's a'goin' down in the hole with him," he whispered.

But the webbing somehow held, and the mother stood up, scratching on the casket with her hands in an attempt to reopen it. "Oh Jesus," she screamed, "I got to see my boy! One more time. Oh Sweet Jesus! One more time!"

Earlier, back at the church, the mortician had called for help. It had arrived at the cemetery in the form of a State Policeman and a big deputy sheriff. The two law officers pulled the mother's fingers off the casket and wrestled her toward the black mortuary car.

"Let go a'me," she screamed again and again. "I got to see my boy. Oh, Jesus. Sweet Jesus. Save him! Save him!" The large men, with great effort, forced her into the black sedan and it drove away. That was the end of the grave-side service. Others in attendance also quickly left. We Boy Scouts remained behind with the mortician.

Two Hispanic men seemed to appear from nowhere and helped the mortician with the apparatus. The casket slowly was lowered to the bottom of the grave on the wide belts, which after releasing them on one side, were pulled from underneath. On the mortician's orders, the men quickly began to shovel dirt on top of the casket.

"They's got to fill it up in a big hurry," another Boy Scout commented loud enough for all of us to hear. "They's plumb worried about that old lady comin' back and divin' in that there grave on top of her kid." He wasn't grinning. He wasn't telling one of his usual jokes. He was as scared as I and the six other Boy Scouts.

We kept glancing down the road where the mother had been taken, half expecting her to return, that she might do something even more awful. That didn't happen, but my first funeral service experience has lasted a lifetime.

What made the experience double scary was that only a few weeks before I'd also climbed one of those metal power-poles. My discovery of a crow's nest was only halfway up, easy to climb to on a metal ladder, and I didn't get close enough to the wires be "fried" like our fellow Boy Scout. Lucky, I took one of the baby crows out of its nest and climbed down.

Arriving home, I found myself covered with lice, apparently not the kind which you pick up from other kids at school. At least these washed off in a bath with no nits to laboriously pick or comb out of my hair. Thus began the job of feeding my new pet. I'd go by the Company butcher shop and ask for leftover scraps of meat.

One day, I figured my crow was big enough to learn to fly, so I climbed on the garage and gently threw it off. It did flap to the ground unhurt, but no further. A few days later he/she was missing. Don't know whether the crow flew away or Dad took it somewhere out of town and released it. I've always suspected the latter, still wonder how good a pet a grown crow might have become.

Mom was not very happy, anyway, about that crow being around our yard and my efforts to teach it to fly. She also didn't appreciate the quality of the English language, drawling slang I was learning from my Southern-Tex peers. At her urging, I signed up for Latin as a freshman in Hurley High School. "It will improve your English," she advised. "It also will be of great help should you ever study other languages."

So began a lifelong struggle with foreign languages. Searching for an excuse, I now can blame this deficiency, as I inanely do other of my shortcomings, on Attention Deficit Disorder. Study of a foreign language requires one to pay close attention in class, to take time for the drudgery of memorizing vocabulary, learning verb tenses, and unraveling baffling idiomatic phrases. Not the cup of tea for an ADD victim. I dropped Latin after less than two weeks of non-effort.

The auburn-headed Latin teacher also taught math, had begun to work us through the exigencies of algebra. One day she routinely declared, "If you multiply anything by zero, the answer is zero." I raised my hand.

"Yes, Max."

"If you had seven bottles of Coke sitting on a wall, and you multiplied those seven bottles by zero, wouldn't you still have seven bottles on that wall?"

"We heard about you in junior high school," she shouted, shaking her finger at me, "and that you were coming to Hurley High. Well, I'll tell you one thing, Max Odendahl. You won't get away with such behavior in my class. Do you understand?"

I nodded, wondering what kind of teachers' network had gotten me in such hot water, certainly not from the kindly minister who worked me through the eighth-grade graduation speech. I didn't understand that simple phenomenon of math and haven't many others since. Each time I repeat my Coke bottle story, math-competent types roll their eyes, shake their heads, and explain, "It's simple. When you multiply nothing with another figure, or your dumb Coke bottles, nothing is there."

"So those dumb Coke bottles I'm seeing are invisible? There's really only a wall there?" They continue to roll their eyes. You know now why I decided not to major in math or science in college.

My favorite high school class was English, taught by Mrs. Matthews, longtime divorced from Slim Matthews–the perennial Grant County sheriff. Just before elections, Slim would claim he closed down the three whorehouses on Hudson Street in Silver City. The *Silver City Daily Press* verified his claims by publishing front-page pictures showing him standing next to purportedly boarded-up-by-the-law windows on one of those houses of ill repute. In truth, a parking lot behind the houses remained filled with cars, and ladies of the night continued their often land-office business.

I doubted if Mrs. Matthews divorced her sheriff husband because of his mendacity concerning the closing down of whorehouses. I suspected it might have been because of lying to her about other of his personal activities. She never mentioned Slim in class and, if she did to my mother (who was a close friend), Mom didn't violate any confidence. I did know Mom didn't think much of Slim Matthews.

Mrs. Matthews's classes came alive with revelations about the writings of another of her loves, William Shakespeare. We were sent home to read part of *Macbeth*, which only baffled us. The next day she said, "Tell me some of Shakespeare's lines you enjoyed the most."

Quickly pawing through what we were supposed carefully to have read earlier, we randomly selected lines. After we pointed out our new "favorites," she somehow made us feel they must be mundane–if any of Shakespeare's words can be considered mundane.

"Well, I'm glad you enjoyed those lines but think about these," as she began to read, "*To-morrow and to-morrow, Creeps on this petty pace from day to day , To the last syllable of recorded time; And all our yesterdays have lighted fools The way to dusty death.*" Death rested far back in our young minds, but came to the forefront when she read that life "*is a Tale told by an idiot, full of sound and fury, Signifying nothing.*"

During high school days I often translated that into life in Hurley. *Signifying nothing.* Real life beckoned somewhere out there, far from Hurley, and one must get away and live it to the fullest before the certain arrival of *dusty death.* How many others over the years had come to such a realization in Mrs. Matthews's English classes?

Some of Hurley's young men, who like others in places such as the hollows of Appalachia faced a dead end for opportunity, yearned to leave. They hoped to find more prosperous lives in "the real world." The attack on Pearl Harbor afforded such an opportunity; and some servicemen who survived World War II never returned to Hurley.

Yet, as did many of my high school peers, other returning servicemen revered semi-arid Hurley as some sort of garden spot in the high New Mexico desert. With an elevation exactly a mile high, living in Hurley somehow imbedded fervent loyalty to the town.

"When you graduates from high school," one high school lad echoed another, "the Company'll hire you. What more could a guy ask for?" After young Hurley males followed their fathers' footsteps to work in the copper mill, they usually married area women, producing families. Sometimes they wedded quickly because of pregnancy.

"If you knock her up, you got to marry her," prevailed as righteous Hurley wisdom. "It's the right thing to do." Yet, others who got a girl "into trouble" were burdened only with selfishness, unconcern, or lack of being able to share affection. They couldn't face up to a life of "quiet desperation." They figured the thing to do was to enlist or re-enlist, leaving behind pregnant women to fend for themselves. In a severely limited job market for women, life as single mothers was far from an easy lot.

Some men having "scrapes with the law" also found military service provided legal escape from jail or prison time. They followed the posters still nailed to telephone poles and elsewhere. The ones with old, white-haired Uncle Sam pointing his finger and demanding, "I Want You." Honor and respect bestowed upon those going into "The Service" during and after World War II, including the few bad eggs, almost paralleled that of receiving a "Call" and becoming a minister.

I think about how wonderful Mrs. Matthews's English classes *would be now* for interested students. She'd be able to show a film or DVD of one of Shakespeare's plays, say with Richard Burton or Lawrence Olivier in lead roles. After each showing, students with more perspective than we ever had could study lines, recite them, discuss with their teacher, and use them for a glimpse into their own lives. How marvelous it must be when it all comes together, when Shakespeare fills the screen the second time.

Four "solid" classes interspersed with the same number of study halls provided the routine at Hurley High. Considered non-solid extras were such classes as wood shop, cooking, and typing. One semester I joined another youth in enrolling in typing. "Just think," he said, "we'll have all those girls to ourselves."

With possibly ADD and certainly raging testosterone, I found great difficulty striking the correct typewriter keys, with their letters hidden. We were graded on how quickly we could punch the right blank keys, averaged for each minute, with points taken off for each error. As I recall, over 50 correct words a minute placed you in the category of being an adequate typist. After many exercises, by the end of the semester my score wasn't much more than half that. The typing teacher, keenly aware I had shown more interest in ogling girls and overhearing their mysterious conversations than discovering the right blank keys, said, "I'll make a deal with you, Max. If you promise not to enroll in Typing II, I'll give you a D in this class."

It proved a bit ironic that I would spend several years of my life working for a wire service and newspapers–making my living pounding on a manual typewriter. Obviously, more proficiency in typing would have been a plus. That was especially true in my first part-time journalism job during my senior year at the University of New Mexico–with Associated Press in its Albuquerque bureau. Stories would be phoned in from newspapers around New Mexico, and AP staffers would type them verbatim. My typing was so slow that it often frustrated seasoned newsmen on the other end of the line.

I rarely took school work home from Hurley High, as there was more than enough time in study halls to complete assignments for the next day. The remainder of study halls was spent either daydreaming or surreptitiously watching girls. Not only was I very shy around girls, but also figured that if they caught me looking at them they somehow could become privy to my carnal thoughts. Now, who would date a guy like that?

Of course, I later came to understand girls knew we boys were checking them out. While at the same time watching us, many had their own carnal thoughts to contend with. While physically bothered as we boys were; some girls were aware of the effect they had on us. For, perhaps a shapely, short-skirted cheerleader in bobby sox would walk past to sharpen her pencil. Sudden "boners" were commonplace for boys anywhere in high school.

A teacher watched over us at the back of study hall, perhaps unaware of all the boners of the boneheads. To break the tension, a favorite trick was to take marbles to study hall, where silence was ordered to reign. You took a couple of marbles out of your pocket, threw them down the aisle. The study-hall teacher leaped up from her desk, dashed to where the marbles landed. If you were in luck, she chastised another boy close to where the marbles landed, bounced, and rolled away.

Luckier was when a well-endowed girl with a loose-fitting blouse headed down the aisle, dropped her pencil, leaned over, and slowly picked it up. Was that simply luck, some sort of predestination, or a girl's cleavage cleverness? More likely cleavage cleverly provided only for the benefit of the football player sitting at another desk.

As brawn generally ruled over brains in the pecking order at Hurley High School, football and basketball players dominated the male side of the mating roost. With no girls' teams, cheerleaders kept guys under their thumbs on the top of the other side of the roost. The loftiness of a girl's IQ rarely elevated her in roost-ruling. Rather, the heavy weapon was beauty. And, though often with ordinary faces, the well-roundness of cheerleaders' shaking butts, revealed by the lifting of short skirts while bending over waving pom-poms or leaping into the air, caught many a male eye and often later (sometimes sooner) resulted in marriage.

I don't recall anyone ever taking IQ tests at Hurley's schools. Perhaps somehow administered surreptitiously, none of us, including bright athletes and cheerleaders, were made privy to test results. Randiness prevailed, while if there were high IQ scores they rested hidden in files, no match for the flexing muscles of young male athletes or eye-popping resulting from near-unbosoming from clothes of cheerleaders doing cartwheels.

Nevertheless, Alan's high school class embraced an unusual number of gifted students who moved on to many accomplishments. "I don't know what to do with that class," one teacher revealed to Mom. "I have a policy never to give out more than two A's, but all of those special students deserve them."

Besides Alan, she was referring to Gilbert Moore, previously mentioned as working with the space program and a co-founder of the infamous Society of Persons Born in Space. And Lindy Haggerson, who after Hurley High was consolidated and moved four miles away to Bayard, became principal at the resulting Cobre High School. Lindy ended up with a doctorate and became a professor of education at Arizona State University.

And John "Pig" Pack who unfairly received his nickname simply because his father raised pigs, collecting "slop" from places in town where the Company dispensed food–like the Bunkhouse's café for single men. John designed radio circuits while in high school and later became a researcher for General Electric. And Jack Hailer, who as a petroleum engineer, set up oil "cracking" plants in the Odessa, Texas, area.

There also was at least one very bright woman in that class, named Lorraine Billings. I hope Lorraine became a physician, a lawyer, or found another worthy occupation and is richly enjoying her retirement. Most likely, though, she ended up as a nurse or teacher in a period when women with college degrees mainly were relegated to those positions.

Alan, as it will be discussed in due time, became an economist and worked many years for the Small Business Administration before his retirement. I don't recall any of those "egg-head" guys in Alan's class, or the bright Lorraine, as being especially "popular." The dating game at Hurley High tested Charles Darwin's theory of natural selection, and Herbert Spencer's "survival of the fittest." Because popular young women, including cheerleaders, generally preferred jocks as dates, and athletic young men usually sought out cheerleaders as "rare beauties," many of the rest found ourselves usually dateless. We, the unpopular of both sexes, were cast adrift in a sort of early "quiet desperation" which according to Henry Thoreau wasn't supposed to happen until boredom overtook marriage.

I'm sure if most had it to do all over again, those of us not deemed popular would actively seek out many of the opposite gender, anyone willing to date, and learn as much as possible. It would have been much less wasted youth. But my problem, as with so many others of both genders in that era, was that I was extremely shy.

Perhaps, I've always thought, that if my older sister born in Canada, Jeanie, had survived, she would have advised me about how to act around and talk with young women. She also could have taught me how to dance, the great ice breaker. Later, when I was at New Mexico State Teachers in Silver City, a young man from Alamogordo told me about his sister. He claimed that in high school she'd let him practice how to reach around her back to quickly unhook a bra. "When a girl's in the mood," he said he was told, "she doesn't want some jerk fumbling around like he doesn't know what he's doing." I sort'a doubt, would like to think, that Jeanie wouldn't have been quite that helpful.

Football, suspended at Hurley High during World War II, didn't resume until the time I was in Mrs. Matthews's English class. The Company constructed a lighted football field at the south edge of Anglo town. This upset Dad because the Company had charged some football field construction costs to his mill repair section. Dad felt this made it appear as if he were a spendthrift. He was proud of being frugal in holding down mill repair costs. He didn't believe in the "if it ain't broke don't fix it" adage, prided himself about "preventive maintenance," changing out parts early before machinery broke down. Shutdowns were costly in 24/7 copper production.

An almost-spent battery in the tiny device which opens door on our Toyota Camry reminded me of preventive maintenance. Purchasing a two-pack at the local Radio Shack, I replaced batteries in both wife Mary's and my "clickers." Preventive, or preventative, maintenance for the second remote.

"What the Company is doing is a tax deal," Dad told us. "That football field is new construction and taxable. But, if they charge it to mill repair, they don't pay taxes."

Besides, Dad figured football as an unhealthy game for young men.

"When they get my age, all those broken bones will be filled with arthritis." Dad felt I, at a skinny 135 pounds, would end up with some of those broken and arthritic bones if I tried out for the football team. He ordered me not to play. Yet the coach, who had observed me catching passes in touch football games in the street, thought I'd fit in as an end. There were no offensive or defensive teams. Coach only made rare substitutions, with the best players usually playing the entire game.

"Come on out for practice," Coach advised, "and we'll put some muscle and pounds on that scrawny frame." It actually wasn't so much added weight or glory on the football field which I sought, but a letterman's jacket bringing admiration on the mating roost. Maybe even from one of those well-round-butted cheerleaders.

So, in my first real defiance of one of Dad's orders which I can remember, I checked out a football suit. It was fun joining in the macho locker-room ritual of climbing into clothing with knee, hip, and shoulder pads. The first day's practice consisted mainly of attempting to learn the fundamentals of tackling.

"Make 'em squirt at both ends," Coach kept shouting. I didn't make anyone squirt, as players ran over and past me. It could be that Alan ratted me out. Nevertheless, at the supper table that evening, Dad said, "I understand you are going out for the football team even though I told you not to?" Mustering up all my courage, I replied, "That's right, and I'm going to make the team."

"Well," Dad said severely, "here's what's going to happen. I'm going to send a note to that coach telling him we're going to sue him and the high school if you get hurt." The next day at practice, I informed Coach about what Dad planned to do.

"It's too bad he feels that way," Coach said. "Football would have put some muscle and a few more pounds on your bones. I think you have good hands for catchin' the ball and would have made it as an end for us. But I can't take the chance if your dad is talkin' about suein'. I guess you better check your suit back in."

Thus was the finish of my brief football career, an ending which would become even more depressing. Hurley High lost its first post-World War II football game, maybe against our arch rival, the Silver City Colts. After the game, Mrs. Matthew's commented in her English class, "All of you boys who are on the football team, raise your hands."

Up went hands of most of the other boys in the class. "I just want to tell you boys how proud I am of you," she said." We may have lost, but you boys showed real courage in defeat."

There was my favorite teacher, lauding most of the other boys in the class and, I thought, intimating that those of us who didn't play football were cowardly. Maybe even worse. "Chickenshits." I scrunched down in my seat, figuring there certainly would be no dates for me with any cheerleaders at Hurley High School.

I was correct about that. Yet, I still feel right about suiting out to play football. Maybe I'd have broken a bone, or now, like most elderly ladies, be sleeping with old Arthur Itis. Dad simply didn't and never would understand the seriousness, the same as in Texas, with which football was taken in small New Mexico towns.

However, in retrospect, Dad was wise not allowing me to play football. At this writing, the professional National Football League is paying off retired players suffering early dementia as the result of brain concussion. For having their heads shaken too hard, too many times during those "great hits" the fans (short for fanatics) savor, Watching on TV sets while munching calorie-laden nachos and quaffing Budweiser (the heavily advertised, yet generally recognized as inferior beer to that produced by new hordes of mini-breweries).

Those in the Odendahl family and others in Hurley not already up, rudely had been awakened at 5:29:45 a.m. July 15, 1945, when they felt their homes rattling. I recall being shaken in bed almost as if tackled on the Hurley High football field. A severe earthquake or what? But, this wasn't California? We gathered around the radio, to be told that a large ammunition magazine containing high explosives and pyrotechnics at Alamogordo, New Mexico, somehow had blown up. Later that morning, I was in a summer-school class at New Mexico State Teachers' College in Silver City. Dad thought the high-school class in machine-shop work was what I needed. Of much greater interest for me was observing in the next classroom other youths taking an auto-engine-repair class.

Some of us were discussing the great explosion at Alamogordo with our machine-shop instructor when a friend of his joined us. The man said he had been piloting an ore train out of the huge open pit copper mine at Santa Rita when the earth began to shake. "I was at the top of the pit, and from there I seen a long ways at what looked as if the whole sky's lit up. Tell you what, boys, I bet'cha that weren't no ammunition explosion from in Alamogordo. No sir, it's sumpin' lots bigger than that. And to boot, sumpin' big-like was a'rising up into the air. The military is behind it; now that's for sure. We might never ever know what's a'go'in on."

Just weeks later, on August 6, 1945, a "Little Boy" atomic bomb was dropped on the Japanese city of Hiroshima and on August 9 a "Fat Man" on Nagasaki. That's when Hurleyites found out what was going on. What had awakened them in July was the first atomic explosion at the Trinity Site about 230 miles south of the Manhattan Project headquarters at Los Alamos, northwest of Santa Fe. That first atomic test bomb of 19 kilotons was detonated in the Jornada del Muerto Valley, a remote section of the Alamogordo Air Base.

I figured Hurley, as the crow flies, maybe was 150 miles away from the first atomic Trinity Site blast. And, as far as I know, no folks in our little New Mexico town suffered any ill effects. Yet, who's to tell? Maybe it ain't ADD which has been my problem over the years?

A February 11, 2017, Associated Press story reported that "the world's first atomic bomb test caused generations of southern New Mexico families to suffer from cancer and economic hardships." A group calling itself the Tularosa Basin Downwinders Consortium complained that those living close to the site weren't told about the dangers of radiation, nor were they compensated for resulting health problems. Tularosa is an historic Hispanic village a few miles north of Alamorgordo.

A woman teaching part-time in the San Diego State Journalism Department once told me how she grew up in St. George, Utah. During that time, our government was conducting atomic explosions deep underground in Nevada. Nevertheless, levels of radiation escaped into the atmosphere and apparently blew across St. George. She was married, pondering as her childbearing years approached their end. She deeply worried about whether she should become a mother because of how atomic radiation might affect her offspring.

The U.S. Navy also took part in tests where nuclear devices were detonated on remote (some nearby islanders later claimed not so remote) islands in the South Pacific. Sailors actually watched such tests without properly covering their eyes against the harmful flashes of light. It was reported that many of these service personnel later suffered ill effects, such as cancer, as a consequence.

There seems little doubt that the explosion at the New Mexico Trinity Site in 1945 when I was 15 years old changed the world as it brought us into the perilous age of atomic, hydrogen, and perhaps even worse weapons. I'd read about the pioneer research of Nobel Prize-winning Marie Curie on radioactivity, discovering two elements—polonium and radium. She died in 1934 due to aplastic anemia as the result of radiation exposure from mobile X-ray units she had set up In World War I and during her research carrying test tubes of radium in her pockets. Folks also had minor worry about the "radium" dials on their watches, but were told really bad consequences only had come to those poor souls hand-painting the dials and licking on the brushes.

Radiation took on a different meaning after 1945. The atomic bomb the United States dropped on Hiroshima in Japan was estimated to have directly killed 70,000 people, with injury and radiation increasing the number of deaths to 90,000-160.000. The second A-bomb on Nagasaki was estimated to have killed 35,000, with 60,000 wounded and 5,000 missing. Horrible radiation deaths, often lingering, and disfigurement for many who survived, followed the bombing of both cities.

We learned about Geiger counters for measuring radiation. That if you hear faster and louder clicking, it's time to get out of there pronto. As the U.S. began expanding its nuclear arsenal, uranium mines were being dug to stockpile the radioactive chemical element of the ore, with the district near Grants, New Mexico, becoming a mining center. Mary's brother-in-law, Al Cynova, became a foreman at a uranium processing plant at Shiprock, New Mexico. The family became greatly concerned that Al might somehow undergo too much radiation, even though told that unprocessed uranium ore held less danger. But, Al's plant was processing it; what did that mean? A secret, because information about the U.S. preparing for a nuclear war was prohibited.

We did learn, after the Soviet Union had acquired nuclear weapons, that we were in what Winston Churchill had dubbed as "The Cold War."

CHAPTER 6 – OTHER LOVES – INCLUDING A 1929 ESSEX

We had moved from mid-town Hurley on 5 Aztec to 112 Pattie Street on the southern edge of our little hamlet when I acquired the 1929 Essex. As either a sophomore or a junior in high school, paper route earnings burned in my pockets. Somehow, I figured, I ought'a find sufficient money for some cheap "wheels."

While out delivering papers, I spotted an old car in Mr. Canady's backyard, with wheels but without tires. His son, Bobby Joe who was graduated with my high school class, went on to become a professor of education. Here you have two Hurley boys with somewhat similar career histories. Both of us eventually received doctorates, and sort'a changed our names.

Dr. Robert J. Canady, the last I attempted to find out, was retired. He and his wife, Dr. Shirley Raines, co-authored books for the primary grades, including *Story S-t-r-e-t-c-h-e-r-s: Activities to Expand Children's Favorite Books.*

"I was finished with my doctorate and looking for my first full-time teaching position," she was quoted as saying. "He was a professor and chaired the committee that found me for the job at the University of Alabama. A year later, we were married." His wife called him Bob, the same as Hurley folks did his father. The younger Canadys had a "blended family" of four children stretching from Tennessee to California, and three grandchildren in Kentucky.

"He was the only art major on his football team at Western New Mexico University (in Silver City)," his wife again is quoted as saying. "He is now a wonderful (stained glass) artist." In 2001, Dr. Raines had the honor of becoming the first woman to become president of the University of Memphis. Congratulations to both of them.

No doubt Robert J. has a more professorial ring to it than Bobby Joe. In my case, Max, as part of Eric Maxwell, was changed to Eric M. in 1964, soon after I arrived to teach at what was then San Diego State College.

The time living in Hurley, I always thought my first given name was Eric. However, that still remains a bit of a mystery. When applying for a passport to travel to Europe in 1984, it became necessary to write to Grant County for a copy of my birth certificate. It listed me as Carl Maxwell Odendahl, the Carl probably after my grandfather's German first name of Karl and/or Dad's middle name Charles, the English equivalent of Karl.

But —-the Carl on my birth certificate had been crossed out when I was nine years old, and Eric put in its place. Dad had died July 12, 1978 and when I asked Mom, who was then 90, about why the change was made, she said she couldn't remember. Or maybe she didn't want to for some reason, hence a deeper mystery.

Years earlier Mom had revealed my being named Eric was in honor of the *best friend* of her close Canadian companion killed in World War I. Maybe Mom hadn't wanted to offend Dad and agreed to Carl?

But perhaps no stranger than some figured it was when, at the age of 34, I decided to be called Eric. My aversion to Max partly came about because of a noted middleweight boxer called Slapsy Maxie Rosenbloom, who won 210 of 300 fights with 23 knockouts. He died March 6, 1976, at the age of 71.

Sometimes laughingly called Slapsy Maxie in Hurley, I didn't care for that joke at all. Could it be Bobby Joe Canady at some point in his life came to feel his name sounded sort of countrified? Several members of both my and my wife's families still call me Max. And, if meeting Bobby Joe again after all these years, I probably would at first greet him by his Hurley name.

Bobby Joe's older brother, Raymond Canady, a star running back for our high school, graduated in 1943, served on a submarine that slipped under water through barrier nets into Tokyo harbor during World War II. Another older brother, J. D., also was known for his athletic prowess. After service in the Big War, both of the older Canady "boys" played football as Mustangs for New Mexico State Teachers College at Silver City.

The Canady boys had an attractive sister named Betty Lou, a bobby-soxed cheerleader and one of the objects of my yearning eyes during those long hours when I languished in the study hall at Hurley High. I've lost track of Betty Lou (probably now called only Betty or even Lou —hopefully aged gracefully, enjoying grandchildren).

At the 1999 H.H.S. reunion in Hanover, I chatted with her brother Ray and his wife, the former Joan Coldwell, who also was part of my 1948 graduating class. Ray and Joan retired in Deming, where he had served as a coach. J.D. coached at a high school somewhere in the southwest New Mexico area. Ray's first name, as his father's and also little brother Bobby Joe, also was Robert. Ray died December, 10, 2010.

But I digress.

Back to high school days. I proceeded to Mr. Canady's backdoor and he led me to the 1929 Essex, parked next to a fence in his backyard. "She's got a couple of rods knocked out of her," he cautioned. "That old Essex doesn't have an oil pump. Depends on the rods

69

to splash enough oil on themselves and into a little shelf to lubricate the main bearings. The design didn't work very well. You might get 500 miles out of her if you re-babbited the rods and drove real slow, maybe less than 35 miles an hour. I don't think it's worth it." A warning a young man searching for fairly "fast wheels" should have heeded.

"Why didn't you just get yourself a Model A Ford?" Austin Robbins, father of my friend Jim, asked too late. "The Model A is reliable and you still can find all the parts you need for her."

Advice I should have taken, but I already had talked the reluctant Mr. Canady out of the Essex. I think I paid him a token $10 or $15 and he went back into the house shaking his head. When new, that Essex —manufactured by the Hudson Motor Car Co. of Detroit — was advertised for $735. One source notes 277,655 Essexes were manufactured in 1929, third in sales of automobiles in the United States that year. Many of them must have run much better and longer. Was mine a lemon? Probably, but that term for a faulty-manufactured automobile came much later.

The Odendahl family didn't own a car from 1935, when Dad sold the 1929 Chevrolet in Jerome, until after the Big War. We acquired a used Hudson, a 1939 straight 6. Dad, Alan and I regarded a good reason for buying the car was the *Consumer Reports'* high rating for Hudson engines, especially their straight 8. Hudsons held the record for the number of hours their engines could run at high speeds.

One trouble was our Hudson's body rattled something fierce. Not as quiet as the later 1941 Chevrolet with knee-action shock absorbers, or the even smoother Packard owned by a family across our alley when we lived at 5 Aztec Street. Dad found our Hudson straight 6 in an ad in the *El Paso Times*. He called long distance to a dealer in El Paso and a salesman brought the used car the 150 miles to Hurley. Dad drove it around town, listened to the engine, and the other macho stuff men do when buying cars.

Mom may have written a $600 check and handed it to the salesman. More likely, the $600 already had been taken out of the Post Office–by cashing precious Postal Savings Bonds. Shaking of hands closed deals and cash was the usual medium of exchange for the title to used cars. There was no bickering about the price for the Hudson, for the salesman had quoted $600 before he drove up from El Paso. Take it or leave it. I'm not sure how the salesman returned to El Paso; quite possibly he rode the bus.

Alan and I both learned to drive in the 1939 Hudson. When Alan came of age, Dad took us to a dirt road south of town. Mom, Dorothy and I sat in the back seat as passengers. "Okay, Alan, back her up a ways. If you learn how to back up, moving forward will be much easier."

A light misty rain fell while Alan tried his hand at backing the Hudson. It was either slick mud on the road, errant clutching, wobbly backing —probably *all of which* put the car in a muddy ditch. A rear spinning wheel sank down and we were stuck. Dad remained undaunted about his method of teaching one how to drive. "That's okay, Alan. You did pretty well for a first-time drive. So, boys, you gather up some brush and I'll dig under this wheel. After we get her out, Alan can give it another try."

We always carried a short-handled shovel in the Hudson's trunk for such occasions. As I searched for brush several feet away from the stalled car, I started to step over what appeared to be a "cow chip." The middle of this cow chip moved. It was the head of a rattlesnake, coiled in striking position. I jumped back and began to shake, couldn't speak.

"What's the matter with you, Max?"

I pointed a shaking finger at the rattlesnake. Dad rushed over and killed it with the shovel. He cut off the rattlers with his pocket knife and I kept them for several years, proud of the number of rattles. Each rattle was supposed to designate a year in a snake's life. I'd say it was a medium-sized rattlesnake.

"It was a good thing for you it was rainy and cold, "Dad told me later. "On a hot day that snake would have struck right away." At the time, anti-venom wasn't in the vogue and a few persons died each year of rattler bites—which also left disfigurations, often on legs.

Another close call with a rattler, (they usually stay well-hidden) came one bright summer day as I hunted cotton-tail rabbits with Dad's .410 shotgun. I'd gotten off a shot at a moving rabbit which had disappeared. An old, overturned washtub lay several yards in front of me, so I lifted it up with the barrel of the shotgun and there appeared a coiled rattler.

Immediately, I shot the snake and dropped down the washtub. Lifting it back up with the shotgun, I also used it to raise the snake, which suddenly wrapped itself around the gun. Dropping the shotgun, I scrambled back several feet. Noticing no movement, I gingerly pulled the shotgun by its stock away from the dead snake. Learned later that snakes often curl up or around something in their death throes. Boy, that sure scared the liver out of one of those persons frightened just by the sight of snakes.

About two years after Alan received his driver's license, Dad took me out to learn to drive by first backing up. When Dad thought I was ready, he accompanied me to Hurley's Justice of the Peace. I thought I was 13, but Lindy Haggerson's recollection at the H.H.S. Reunion was that 16 was the first age we could receive our licenses.

"Is that boy ready to drive, Harry?" asked the JP.

"Yep, I've taken him out and showed him how."

"That's good enough for me." No written test. No driving test. But the deal was: Dad had vouched for Alan and me; it was a *responsibility* he had assumed.

On some pretext, I drove the 1939 Hudson over to the Canadys. Mr. Canady hooked a tow cable from the Hudson to the 10-year-older Essex to pull it away from its parking place beside the fence. Problem was, the old car's tire-less iron rims attached to wooden spokes were solidly in the ground, sunken a few inches by rains. The Hudson's clutch began to smoke.

Those 1939 Hudsons had cork clutches which were lightly lubricated by special oil, something resembling olive oil. I thought the cork on the clutch had just about burned off when the old Essex suddenly lurched out of its sunken parking place. I must have had someone with me to steer the Essex while it was towed home.

Open sage brush stretched from the back yard of our house on Pattie Street all the way to the semi-pro ballpark, and past that to the tailings about a mile further away. The at-least-a-mile-square white tailings were sandy material left over after copper had been extracted from the ore at the mill. The white sand rose many times higher than the sagebrush. It covered on the semi-arid desert.

I towed the Essex into an open spot across the alley from our house. I figured Dad, a machinist and all, would be happy to spend his leisure time after work helping me fix the thing. A sort of father-son bonding, it might even make him forget the clutch on the Hudson I figured I'd burned out. Maybe we also could fix that together.

"Where did you get that old piece of junk," were Dad's first words about the Essex.

"From Mr. Canady. I figured you could help me fix 'er up."

"What's supposed to be wrong with it?"

"Mr. Canady said it had a couple of rods knocked out."

"If they knocked all the way through the engine wall, you'll need a whole new engine."

"Gee!"

"Well, you need to jack it up, drop down the pan and I'll have a look at it." I could tell Dad wasn't overly excited about the whole project, bonding or not. What probably saved my bacon was that it turned out I hadn't completely burned out the family Hudson's clutch. I poured a little more special oil into the clutch's plug hole, hoping for a little miracle to occur before Dad drove the Hudson again. Somehow that special olive-like-oil did work its way into what was left of the cork, expanding it back to usefulness. Mum was my word to Dad about the clutch.

Although the final result never fully met my satisfaction, working on the Essex proved to be a good learning experience. It also kept me out of trouble after school. Already I knew how to change tires on cars, so jacking up the old car was no problem. Somewhere I scrounged railroad-tie-sized beams and put four of them under the axles to hold each wheel.

I took out all the screws holding up the oil pan, dropped it to the ground. When Dad came home from work, he crawled with me under the Essex, took a look at the piston rods with the beam from his metal flashlight. The verdict: "You're lucky. None of them have come completely loose. What's happened is that the babbitt is knocked out of some and the others are loose. We could shim the loose ones, but you're going to have to get the bad ones re-babbitted. Probably the best thing to do is to re-babbitt all of them while you have the pan off."

The piston rods of more modern cars had begun to have inserts of babbitt-like material available in various thousands of an inch to fit re-machined crankshafts (no more shims). The Essex's rods, pistons, and piston rings had to be pulled out of the cylinders. The rods would have to be pressed off their pistons, shipped to El Paso for re-babbitting. It was the beginning of a BIG and EXPENSIVE job.

About this time, Alan decided he also needed wheels. Wiser than I, he found an early 1930s Ford with one of their small-horse-powered V-8 engines. So Dad now oversaw two car projects at the same time.

Compounding my mistakes with the Essex, I discovered a catalog (probably J.C. Whitney) and purchased six pistons for a 12-cylinder Lincoln which would fit the Essex. These pistons, shaped to provide more compression, were just what I *didn't* need pushing against the fairly soft babbitt of piston rods of a car with no oil pump. Of course, I imagined gaining a teen-ager's common dream —-MORE SPEED!!

So, the Essex's piston rods were sent to El Paso for re-babbitting. Alan and I toiled as mechanic's helpers while Dad followed up with precision work like fitting rings to the pistons and checking our shimming of the rods. We also learned how to do such tasks as grinding valves with a contraption that looked like a hand food mixer. These days, special shops grind valves and overhaul cylinder heads for mechanics and auto agencies. Modern engines have valves stretching down as part of heads. In older cars, the valves lifted up– resting in the engine block itself.

Dad preferred to replace everything "wet" with oil in a rebuilt engine. Oil was squirted between the rods' babbitt and crankshaft, between the pistons and cylinder walls. He said some mechanics didn't worry about this, waited to let the oil splash between parts when "motors" started. "That's a good way to score your pistons walls," he contended.

Recently an RV mechanic pointed out to me that the correct designation for the main mechanism powering an automobile is an "engine." "An electric starter or alternator is a motor," he explained. At any rate, the big day arrived for Alan's and my cars when starting motors got the engines running. From the beginning Alan's V-8 ran more smoothly than my straight 6, but I remained confident the Old Essex would purr contentedly once it "broke in."

Alan's Ford continued to run well until he sold it. The Essex's fate arrived much sooner, even as I was contemplating all sorts of grandiose schemes to redesign the old car. It originally had been a two-door sedan, probably called a Super-Six Coach. Mr. Canady, or perhaps someone before him, had cut off the rear section of the sedan and made it into a pickup. The back of the car, complete with its window, had been attached behind the front seat to form a pickup cab.

Bob Canady was known not only as a successful deer hunter, but also part of a diminishing breed–the stalker and killer of mountain lions. He might have taken the Essex, with its pickup-like bed loaded with camping provisions on a few of his lion-hunting excursions deep into the Gila National Forest.

For a good look at life in that forest, read *Gila Country Legend, The Life and Times of Quentin Hulse,* by Nancy Coggeshall, University of New Mexico Press, 2009. Hulse (1926-2002) worked most of his life at the bottom of Canyon Creek in Gila River Country, where he served as a guide for hunting and fishing trips.

Probably the most-classic book about the area is *River of the Sun: Stories of the Storied Gila* by Ross Calvin, University of New Mexico Press, 1946. Ross served as Episcopal rector at the Church of the Good Shepherd in Silver City. The book I hold in my hand with its original slightly-torn cover was Mom's, who thought a lot of Ross and his writing. Perhaps not only because he was an Episcopalian Rector (she an Anglican), but also because he held a doctorate in English philology from Harvard and later was ordained at the General Theological Seminary.

Mom may have attended Ross' Silver City church, but sister Dorothy doubts it because we were without a car for so many of our Hurley years. Dorothy can't recall ever going to that church with Mom.

Ross became noted with his first book, *Sky Determines*, published in 1934 by The Macmillan Co. I have a later edition with illustrations by an old Roswell acquaintance, painter Peter Hurd, printed in 1948 by the University of New Mexico Press. The gist of that book is that climate and weather patterns, like the blue sky Ross found in Silver City rarely shedding water, influences everything man does. Biographer Ron Hamm, in *Ross Calvin: Interpreter of the American Southwest*, Sunstone Press, Santa Fe, 2016, remarks that *"his home (Silver City) was fewer than 15 miles from Hurley to the southeast with a drop in elevation of some four hundred feet, yet a world apart. There the countryside rapidly begins to take on the look of the desert—expanded vistas, tumbleweeds replacing trees, and springtime (monsoon)winds blowing dust that sometimes darkens the landscape like nighttime, forcing drivers to take special care lest they lose their way and stray into the path of an oncoming vehicle with sometimes deadly results."*

Yessiree, *that's my hometown of Hurley for you, folks.*

While hiking in the mountain area east of Hurley, I once spotted fellow teenage Bobby Joe Canady carrying a deer rifle. I don't know whether Bobby Joe, Ray or J.D. hunted in the Gila when adults; they must have been there with their father as youngsters.

I never considered restoring that Essex sedan. My dream didn't ever imply putting it into "cherry" condition. Rather, the crowning of my vehicle was to be in the form of two plexi-glass airplane turrets I had ordered by mail from some military-surplus store. I planned to cut holes in the roof of the cab of the Essex and bolt down the turrets. I and a passenger then could pop our heads up inside the turrets now and again as we drove along. Neat, huh?? Neater yet to have a female riding along, and I could observe her bobbing from seat to turret!

A fairly complicated vacuum-gravity tank fed gasoline to the Essex's carburetor. I replaced it with an electric fuel pump. The electric systems on most cars until about 1960 –my Essex, Alan's Ford, the family Hudson, etc.–were six volts rather than the present 12-volt standard. The Essex demanded all kinds of other expenses–like purchasing four new 20-inch tires and tubes. I barely kept up, with the costs eating up almost all of the paper route earnings I collected each week.

The old car did have a beautiful temperature-gauge-radiator cap, with a red mercury thermometer one could view through the windshield. There was no engine thermostat, rather louvers in front of the radiator. On cold days, I pulled a rod attached from the dashboard to the louvers to shut off the air, keeping radiator water and engine warm. On hot days, I'd push open those shutters to cool the engine. I thought this to be really "cool." (Although, we didn't yet use the word "cool" like that; we fantasized about girls becoming hot, not cool. The latest I notice in magazines is guys commenting about a woman's looks, "She's really hot." Times, and language change back and forth.)

I'm sure the Essex became a talking point for Hurleyites as I drove around town. One evening something seemed wrong with the wiring to the newer and brighter sealed-beam headlights. I had ordered these from somewhere and installed them to replace old bulbed-units. Undaunted, several of us youths started out. Someone rode with me in the cab and others behind in the pickup bed. I recall riding along were Amos Stone, Jim Robbins, George Bowman (perhaps also his younger brother Oscar), Joe Ketchum, perhaps George Hailer, and maybe even one or two more. A merry crew!

Sure enough, after it became dark, the headlights failed to operate. I asked someone to shine the way for me with the beam of a flashlight over the cab. That didn't "turn-out" too well, as I ran into a culvert, and knocked one of the wheel rims loose and had to be towed home for repair.

It wasn't much later, out on another jaunt, when the babbitt on a piston rod came loose. *Undoubtedly because with no oil pump, there wasn't proper lubrication.* Again I brought the knocking car home for repair. Old Bob Canady had been right all along. The car lasted about 500 miles for me, and I figure I'd spent as much as $500 on her–somewhere near a dollar per mile.

I never did fix the Essex after that. A restored 1929 model was offered on the Internet more than 50 years later for $1,000. I would have made a lot more money putting $500 in a bank for 50 years, but I still don't regret it at all.

After Hurley High School graduated me, I served on active duty in the U.S. Navy for a year. By the time I returned home, Dad had asked the Company to haul away what he–and no doubt Mom–viewed as an eyesore behind our house. It must have been towed to the ball-mill scrap yard. Scrap metal was melted into "iron" balls and used in the mill to grind copper ore into a fine powder. After copper was extracted in a chemical flotation process, what was left, including the grindings from the iron balls, became tailings. What's left of my Essex may still lie somewhere deep in the high mill tailings south of our town.

Dad did take off the almost-new tires from the and save them. I later gave these to Sonny Kennedy's father, who had an old car which they would fit. I suspect they never were put to use, as Mr. Kennedy already had pretty good tires on his old car and died not too long after that. One regret about the Essex is that Dad didn't save the thermometer radiator cap. It now proudly would be displayed somewhere in my office. Perhaps it was retrieved by someone before the car was crushed into scrap and melted down. Hopefully, it graces some other office desk as a paperweight now.

Nevertheless, failing to hold onto a car you've come to love is similar to grieving about the loss of a beloved woman. We men imagine ourselves to be like Mustang horses, rounding up cars and women as stallions do their mares. For whatever use can be made of them. Our hands never forget either the feel of working on beloved cars or caressing beloved women.

As lives race on, our fantasies about cars and women roar along, even though few of us ever obtain the riches to own Mercedes or Jaguars. Nor do we obtain enough money to enjoy the sauciness of rich Frenchmen —apparently with some wives' approval — keeping other beautiful women secretly lodged, fed, and pampered.

"You need to trade a car when it gets 50,000 miles on it," I once was told by a man who drove an expensive American automobile and could afford a new vehicle that often. "It'll save you a lot of trouble in the long run."

I have kept my cars, new or used for about 10 years, rarely traded before 100,000 miles. Yet, I'm certain I could handle a Mercedes or Jaguar. Our fantasies extend to beautiful or near-beautiful women. Some of us actually kid ourselves into believing that, if we could afford to round them up, kept women genuinely would want to remain with us.

It was during high school, attempting to "restore" my 1929 Essex that I discovered I couldn't round up or keep even one young woman of my dreams. Her name on the class roll at our 1948 graduation was Sara Katherine Von Tress, and she gave the Salutatorian speech.

Robert Neel, who usually sat near me in our classes because his last name began with an "N" and mine with an "O," spoke as Valedictorian. Bob Neel joined Sigma Chi at the University of New Mexico, where after my Navy time and a year at New Mexico State Teachers' College I became his fraternity brother. He flew in the Air Force during the Korean War, became an engineer at Sandia Corporation, designing and working with top-secret atomic weapons developed at Los Alamos near Santa Fe. Bob retired from Sandia, did a superb job putting on the 1999 Hurley High School Reunion at Hanover.

It was in a chemistry class at Hurley High that I gave my heart to Sara Von Tress, who lived in the Hanover-Santa Rita area. Chemistry wasn't a class which meant much to me, mainly because I didn't apply myself sufficiently to learn enough. We mixed up concoctions in test tubes and beakers and wrote down the results in workbooks. Paired with bright Sara, we switched-off concocting and recording. We chattered with each other about many other subjects during these chemical processes.

77

I simply *knew* that she liked me. One day as a ruse I told Mom that I had to go to the Hurley Garage to check the air pressure of tires on our Hudson, which I had been using weekdays to drive her across the tracks to teach school on the Hispanic side of town. Sure enough, Sara and two or three other girls remained at the high school waiting for a bus to take them about 10 miles to the Santa Rita area. I asked if they'd like a ride and they piled in.

Luck was with me. I was able to drop off the other Hanover-Santa Rita girls first. When we arrived at Sara's house, I hurried around the Hudson, opened the door on her side. After she got out and as we stood next to each other beside the car, I mustered up my courage, "Would you like to go with me to the Thanksgiving dance?"

"No, I'm sorry. I'm busy then."

"What about the Christmas dance?"

"No, I'm busy then too."

"I think there may be some dance or something for New Year's, or even after that. Maybe we could do that then?"

"No, I'm going to be busy around that time, too."

"Okay," I grunted, slinking around to the other side of the car. I waved forlornly at her as I drove off. She waved back meekly, without smiling. Crushed, I had no idea what I had done to offend her. I've come to believe (at least I'd like to) what happened was she *did* at least sort'a like me in that chemistry class but her later conversation with girl friends went like this, "I think Max Odendahl is kind of neat."

"What!! That nerd (creep, jerk, whatever)!! He's real skinny and doesn't even play football or basketball. What do you see in *him?*"

"Well, he was nice to me in our chemistry class."

So my two first real loves in high school–Sara Von Tress and the 1929 Essex —conked out on me. I like to think, given time, I could have re-babbited the rod, somehow figured out how to install an oil pump in its engine. A fairly recent web site listed a 1929 Essex fitted with a 350 cubic-centimeter Chevy engine, a 350 transmission, a Ford rear end, and Chevy brakes. That's certainly a non-virgin car, not "cherry" at all, but, it's still running.

As far as literally conking out, Sara certainly didn't overwhelm me. She lived many years after our high school days. Bob Neel emailed me just before the 1999 reunion that Sara had died some time before that. I know nothing about the circumstances of her post-

Hurley times or death and can only hope her shortened life proved to be a good, happy, and productive one.

I did take another girl to either the junior or senior prom (unsure which it was). Of course, by that time I also had a crush on her, nearly as severe as that with Sara. It ended just as sadly. Somehow I had the idea my new, perhaps not-knowing love and I would dance away that evening, even though I didn't dance well at all. "Let's go fill out our cards," she said as we arrived at the gym for the dance.

She went right over and asked a guy, already going steady with another girl, to mark his name on her card for three dances. I guess she figured him to be really handsome, although I saw him as sort'a short and skinny. I wasn't quick-witted enough to ask his pretty girlfriend, going steady or not, to initial her card with me for those three dances. That's the way it went as I stood around, except for a couple of dances with my date when she hadn't filled her card. She did save the last dance for me, but I could tell she'd rather have been dancing the light fantastic with that handsome dude then, too. No good-night- kiss for me, either.

That isn't to say all of Hurley High's young men faced such dire consequences. A few years later, at the University of New Mexico, I ran across that same handsome fellow and asked him if he still was connected with a steady high-school girlfriend. "Naw. We broke up a long time ago."

"I guess going steady in high school had some real advantages?"

"You mean, like getting into her pants?"

"Yeah."

"Of course I did; all the time. Why in hell do you think I was going steady with her?"

Whether he was bragging or not, it shows how naive I was. Scenes at Hurley duplicated many scenes in the 1971 movie *The Last Picture Show,* still one of my special favorites. The movie came out of a book written by Larry McMurtry —born in Wichita Falls, Texas, only six years after me in 1936. Hurley, with homes and other buildings painted and maintained by The Company, wasn't as rundown as that little burg in Texas. To me, though, most of our high school's girls acted much the same. Such as the hefty one McMurtry portrayed necking in the pickup truck with her steady boy-friend.

They park. She takes off her sweater, then her bra and hangs it on the rear-view mirror. He begins fondling her breasts, tries to move his hand up her thigh, and she slaps his hand. He says something like, "I thought, seeing as it's my birthday, that we could do something else tonight."

"We can do that after we get married," she answers, adding that she doesn't want to become pregnant. He tells her he doesn't want to go steady with her anymore. She angrily puts her bra and sweater back on. "That's the trouble with you boys. You don't appreciate us nice girls"

Hurley High boys joked by ourselves, long before the production of that film, about a slogan most of our young women not-very-likely were privy to, and surely wouldn't have appreciated, "Nice girls put it in for you."

While I never figured out much about what or when I could or couldn't do in cars with young women of that period, they faced an almost impossible situation. If they were to remain "nice girls," they hung onto their virginity. If they had given it up they often attempted to keep that a secret from prospective husbands. At the same time, they tried to appear "sexy," physically sensual enough to help lure young men into marrying them. It was a tough row to hoe.

In those lovelorn high school days, our Pattie Street house was a drab brown, yet cottage-like, covered on all sides with wood shingles. Next door lived a family, all of whom were bestowed with good looks either by the Good Lord, good genes, or plain good luck. A sometime resident there was a beautiful young woman just a few years older than Alan.

Her knockout beauty was like her mother's. Still holding her own well against the ravages of time, her mother in her youth must have been even more beautiful than the daughter. The daughter wasn't around next door very often, either married or off to college. I would expect it was the latter, yet each time she arrived home I observed in delight her every move. When she wasn't there, her mother remained a pleasing substitute. Both would be called "eye candy" now.

Her husband was a muscular and handsome dude who, like his wife, always greeted me with a smile and a kind word. Once, when Alan and their oldest son had run out of gas in Alan's car the night before, he told them, "Boys, it doesn't cost any more to run on a full tank of gas than an empty one."

The son had natural musical ability. He could go to a honky tonk, listen to a new song, and the next day sing all of the words or play the tune by heart on his harmonica. I sometimes tagged along with the younger teenager in that family. Filled with ideas, he was a year older and certainly more streetwise than I. One late and cold fall day he arrived at the conclusion that adequate school spirit was lacking at Hurley High.

Our arch rival, the Silver City Colts, loomed as our football opponent for the next weekend. Just after dark, he laid out his plan to me and an even younger youth, "Let's paint some school spirit on the water tank."

"Sounds great!" With little thought, we agreed.

Already prepared with a can of black paint and a brush, we moved to Hurley's tank providing water for both the Anglo and Hispanic sides of town. Made of metal, it sat on legs, rose about a hundred feet in the air. A metal ladder led to a catwalk around the base of the aluminum-painted tank. The older youth led the way up the ladder, with me in the middle, and the younger fellow a ladder-rung behind.

The problem was that moisture, perhaps from morning dew, had frozen on the circular rungs of the ladder. The higher we climbed, the more ice we encountered. All of us were scared, admitted it to one another. Carrying the paint bucket, our leader pressed on, his feet or free hand slipping on an icy rung now and then. When he did, I pushed him up, and the younger youth did the same for me. In order to keep climbing himself, he periodically had to grab on to my Levis or legs. We finally sprawled together on the catwalk.

Our leader tip-toed along the catwalk, his paint brush splashing out "Beat Colts" in black, wide letters as high as he could reach. We all clapped our hands and shouted as if we had won the World Series. The descent on the metal ladder proved not as slippery because we did not have to pull ourselves up. Our fearless leader decided the job wasn't completed because black paint was left in his can. "Let's paint something close to the high school."

We emptied our paint can by brushing "Beat Colts" again on the back of a garage across the parking lot, but facing the school, and "Beat Silver" on another. I suppose we dumped the paint can, the evidence, in someone's garbage barrel. Proudly, we headed home, savoring our handiwork and figuratively crossing ourselves for surviving the icy climb up the high tank's metal ladder.

However, the next day, the superintendent of all of Hurley's schools did not savor our handiwork. Between classes, he called a special assembly and, rather than lauding our school spirit, announced our painting adventure to be that of hooligans. I can't recall much of what he said except we had brought dishonor to our school and if identified would be suspended.

"We are going to get to the bottom of this, and those responsible will be severely punished," Mr. Wright said. I became more frightened than climbing that icy ladder the night before.

John Wright was a dapper man with an elegant flair to him. I knew Mom thought a lot of and respected him. Mr. Wright lived just down the block from us in another brown, shingled house. Mom would not hang any washing out on Sunday. "Mr. Wright might see it," she said. "I don't know how he stands with the church. Many think the Sabbath should be kept for rest, and he might think less of me for working on Sunday."

It didn't make much sense to me, but I knew Mom needed to keep her job. I also knew she was good at it, and was proud of her in a day when women were not adequately recognized for their intellectual capabilities. I wasn't worried about laundry, but paint, as I shuffled past the principal's office at the end of that school day. Mr. Wright stepped out into the hall from the principal's office and beckoned me. "Come into the office, please, Max."

I figured this was it. He told me to sit down and closed the door, with only the two of us in the office. "Max, "he said, "I'm really upset about the painting of the water tank and the garages. I checked with the Company today and it's going to cost at least $500 to cover over that black paint on the water tank alone. And, then there are those two garages to take care of."

I knew $500 was a great deal of money in 1947 or 1948, with plenty of folks getting by on $25 weekly or less. I silently doubted it would cost that much to send some Company painter up the ladder to cover new aluminum paint over what we had done.

Mr. Wright continued looking me straight in the eyes, "So, Max, I know you wouldn't want to tattle on any of your classmates, but if you should hear anything about who might be responsible for this, I'd really appreciate your letting me know. It would be in strictest confidence. Just between you and me. Do you know anyone?"

"No, sir. I'll sure ask around," the lie came through my teeth, "and let you know if I was to hear sumpin'."

"Thank you, Max, I'd really appreciate that."

To this day I don't know what Mr. Wright suspected before he talked to me. Could he tell that I was lying, that I either did know who had done what he viewed as a dastardly deed, or more likely that it was obvious I was responsible? He knew something. I never knew if he had talks with my co-conspirators. We all continued to be very frightened. We lay low, staying away from one another. We didn't tell other students. Nothing happened to us

My engaging in foolish, Looney-Tune behavior wasn't confined to the outside walls of Hurley High. One day when I was either a junior or senior, George Phillips, whom I ranked just behind Mrs. Matthews as my favorite English teacher, gave us an assignment,

"I'd like you to write down what you think of this class, and what could be done to improve it. You can either sign it or not."

My ADD erratic impulses must have risen to a manic episode. Now called ADHD for Attention-Deficit Hyperactivity Disorder, it has been described as "a neuro-behavioral condition marked by inattention, hyperactivity, and impulsivity that's predominantly seen in children." Adderall now is one of the prescription treatments, pills which I've never taken.

I took out a piece of lined notebook paper and impulsively wrote, "'Those who can do, those who can't teach'–George Bernard Shaw." I signed my name underneath the quotation, one which Dad had related to us at the supper table a few weeks before. Teacher Mom immediately had given Dad a disapproving look.

"Oh, I know there are lots of good teachers out there," Dad added as he looked back at Mom. "I think what Shaw means, is that many teachers don't have much real-life experience."

"That's true," Mom agreed, her face mellowing.

After Mr. Phillips's next English class, he asked me to come by to see him later that afternoon. It didn't take a rocket scientist to figure out that he wanted to talk about my little note to him. "I was quite disappointed by your assessment of me, Max," Mr. Phillips said, holding up and waving my notebook sheet. "Somehow, I had the feeling you enjoyed being in my class."

"Oh, I think your class is neat. I just wrote down that George Bernard Shaw thing as a sort of joke." (A Looney Tune, but I didn't say that.)

"Well, it wasn't funny to me, and a strange way of showing how you think my class is, as you say, 'neat'." Mr. Phillips grew even more serious, went on for several minutes telling me why he had decided to become a teacher.

"I could have made more income in some other profession or line of work," he concluded, "but I have found that , as they say, 'shaping young minds' to be much more rewarding."

"You're a really good teacher," I muttered, with my head bowed.

"So then, let's forget you ever wrote that note. Do you agree?"

"Sure."

"You may go now."

After I got up, was almost to the door of his classroom, Mr. Phillips added,

"Max, when I look over your assignments for this class I've come to the conclusion that you might be able to make a career as a writer. Might be, that is."

"Gee, thanks, Mr. Phillips."

"But it won't be easy. Writing is hard work. You'll have to show much more effort than you have in my class in order to be successful." He waved his hand for me to leave. As I moved outside along the hall, I realized this was the first time anyone had encouraged me to be a writer. Or complimented me for anything else at Hurley High.

I already should have learned the lesson that putting something down in writing can get one in plenty of trouble. Like being in hot water with Mr. Phillips. That "good" whipping much earlier in the sixth grade for writing an insult about Miss Bilbrey should have been enough of a lesson. It would be years later, however, before I discovered that whatever you write, there is someone who will take issue with it. You simply can't worry too much about that, but there is no reason to write mean things about people who don't deserve such treatment simply because you're trying to be a "smart ass." That's not being smart at all.

Somehow, despite not applying myself to studies, I managed to muddle my way through to the point at which I became pretty certain of being graduated. A few days before the ceremony, Mom came home with what to her appeared to be startling news.

"I just had a talk with Mr. Wright," Mom said, "and he told me something both of us had a hard time believing."

"What's that?" I wondered out loud. The painting episode still loomed in the back of my head Maybe Mr. Wright found out?

"The results of the high school tests for seniors arrived in Mr. Wright's office, and he told me you scored in the top 10 percent in the state."

"Wow! That's neat!"

I was baffled about how my high test score could have happened. Trying to figure it out later, I came to the conclusion that much of my knowledge came from reading and perusing so many magazines both at home and at the Hurley Clubhouse, a recreation building complete with an upstairs poolroom and bowling alley in the basement. The clubhouse contained a reading room with the latest magazines and newspapers. It was there I regularly looked through *Life,* and *Look,* and read most of *Time* each week. Those and other magazines and books allowed me to move vicariously out of Hurley and into a larger world.

At home we subscribed to *National Geographic, The Nation, Harper's, Scientific American, Popular Science, Consumer Reports,* and probably a couple of other magazines like *Atlantic Monthly* I've forgotten about. Scanning of these added a good deal to my knowledge. *Scientific American* baffled me, yet fascinated Dad, who had a futuristic turn of mind. "One of these days they're going to...," he would begin.

Like, when Igor Sikorsky's type of helicopter came to the forefront during World War II, Dad envisioned one in our back yard after the fighting ended. "We'll go straight up in the air, head for El Paso, which as the crow flies will be closer than driving the highway, and drop down there to do any kind of business we need to." El Paso, about 150 miles to the southeast by car, was Hurley's nearest large city.

Helicopters would prove too expensive for folks learning from Hard Times the danger of going into debt. Furthermore, worry about colliding with other aircraft relegated helicopters to never meeting Dad's expectations of replacing or complementing the family automobile. My Dad, with his fifth-grade education, in his own way was "as smart" as Mom with her college education.

I understood most of what I read in *Popular Science,* which also had a futuristic bent. Even detective Dick Tracy in the funny papers, with his wrist radio, a two-way device with which he could converse with others in law enforcement, teased Alan and I to look toward what could lie ahead.

Especially fascinating to me were *Popular Science* columns about a fictional garage mechanic named Gus. Each month someone would bring into Gus's garage his or her car with some mysterious ailment. Gus would try this and that, shaking his head, and at the end of the article always solved what was causing the automobile's engine or an accessory not to operate properly.

Since the inception of Consumer's Union in 1936, the Odendahl family had perused *Consumer Reports* before making purchases, particularly major ones such as washing machines and automobiles. Even though such occasions were few and far between during Hard Times, a boy could learn a lot reading about how large and small household appliances function, and why some were rated better than others.

"I'm proud of you, Max," Mom told me about my scoring high on the state exam, perhaps even patting me on the back. I don't recall her or Dad ever hugging me as I grew older. Can't remember either of them doing it when I was smaller, either. We, like lots of other

Hurley folks, weren't natural huggers. "But," Mom added, "of course, you only scored in the top 10 percent. Alan was in the top 100 for all of New Mexico."

At Hurley High School

Shortly before we were graduated, the Class of 1948 took its senior trip. We went to Doc Campbell's hot-springs place (still operated by Allen and Carla Campbell) near where the forks of the Gila River come together. An ordinary car couldn't make it to Doc's place in the Gila National Forest, and the Army's four-wheel drives hadn't been incorporated into civilian vehicles. Pickup trucks filled the bill. We piled in the beds of several trucks and let their "grannie" gears grind us slowly over rocks and gullies in the road.

We spent a day of our trip at the Gila Cliff Dwellings National Monument, exploring ancient Native American ruins. Deep in one of the caves I discovered several small corn cobs, two or three of which I put in my pocket. A "no-no" now.

Hurleyite John King collected more than 230 Native American ceramic bowls, ollas, other pottery pieces. Most are from the Mogollon culture of the Mimbres Indians. He also gathered metates and manos (bottoms and tops of heavy stone hand corn grinders) plus thousands of beads, along with arrowheads and axes. John had moved to Hurley in 1914. His wife, Mary Alice Riddle, whom he married in 1943, glued much of the broken pottery back together. The extensive collection now is in the King Room of the Luna Mimbres Museum in Deming.

My too-early-deceased friend Jim Robbins, who also made our 1948 high school trip to Doc Campbell's, later dug up several Native American pots at another location. Like King's, Jim's pots were found buried and, even though lifted gently out of the ground, fell apart. They had to be glued.

After daughter Terry became an anthropologist, I gave her the one Gila Cliff Dwelling corn cob still in my possession, plus a stone axe Dad found at a Mimbres Indian ruin at Cameron Creek near Hurley. I worry less now about the "no-no" of taking those corn cobs. I have a friend who taught physical education at San Diego State University. In a cave in the Anza-Borrego desert area, he and his small sons found an almost perfect Native American pot. "I tried to set a good example for my boys," he told me, "and we turned the pot over to a park ranger."

He added that later he tried to find where the pot was being displayed so he could take his sons to look at it again and appreciate their civic duty. "Rangers told me it was in a warehouse somewhere, that hundreds of pots are stored there. If I'd known that, we'd have taken our pot home. We could have displayed it for our friends to see, and it would have been handed down in the family."

The highlight of the 1948 senior trip to Doc Campbell's for me came not with the ancient, but in the present. A male classmate's present. One night during that weekend a blond, curly-haired male fellow held hands with one of the more attractive girls wearing a dress as they walked into the forest. Later, as a few of us boys who hadn't even held hands with a girl any time during the trip listened breathlessly, he told us, "When we got out there in the woods, she lays by herself down on the ground, pulled off her pants, and told me to do it to her," Silence overcame us for a few seconds while this momentous event soaked in, before someone asked, "How was it?"

"Good, real good, although I was so horny I couldn't last long. But she cum too, real quick-like. She sure did squeal a lot. So I could tell that she really liked it."

"Jesus Christ," another of us mumbled in amazement. All of us listeners identified as Christ's name was invoked. It was sort'a like a common prayer to God that the day wouldn't arrive soon enough when we also could be so fortunate.

CHAPTER 7 — SAILING THE OCEAN BLUE

As we boymen sat self-consciously on the auditorium/gym stage, wearing robes for the 1948 graduation ceremony, one of us (not me) began passing a pint of whiskey around .

In bravado I took a sip, even though I didn't like the stuff, all the time worried some school authority might spot one of us imbibing and whisk away our diplomas. Certainly someone must have seen the bottle, simply let it pass. What I feared most was that Mom would become aware of me taking a swig.

My aversion to whiskey had come about months earlier, one night when I'd gone to a honky-tonk called Casa Loma, just off the highway toward Silver City. Beer and mixed drinks (sometimes for the ladies fancy cocktails with names like Grasshoppers) flowed from the bar to those over 21. We underage high school boys shouldn't have been allowed into Casa Loma at all. Nevertheless, when you reached a certain height, especially if accompanied by someone of age, the bouncer at the door usually looked the other way.

"Just don't try to buy any drinks at the bar," was the drill. Act as if you're older and you'll get along okay. The of-age guys had to order drinks.

Some of the men dancing at the honky-tonk also brought their own booze along with them. The preference was whiskey, with bottles stashed under front seats of cars. When the band stopped playing for intermission, men went into the parking lot to light up cigarettes, and swig on their whiskey bottles.

Some of those underage who couldn't purchase drinks inside waited until the band began playing again, until the older men went inside to return to dancing, and retrieved one or more whiskey bottles from under car or pickup seats. The idea was to take such a small swig that it would go undetected. A risky business if one of those older men, most of them firm and muscular from hard work, were to catch you nipping at his booze.

I took more than a small swig that one night, must have ended up chug-a-lugging most of a stolen bottle. The next thing I remember was waking up in the morning in my bed at home, with Mom glaring down at me. Bad news, bad day, and I rarely have had a nip of Kentucky whiskey since. That's not to say I didn't guzzle more than my share of beer over the years, later wine as it became the fad in California, on to tequila-filled margaritas, and occasional Scotch on-the-rocks, maybe with water. Lately, only now and then, Jameson Irish whiskey—which tastes to me sort'a like good Scotch. Maybe better.

Another memorable event at Casa Loma came during the summer between college semesters. Some of us young men, including brother Alan, had gone to hear Lefty Frizzell, then an up-and-coming country singer. I don't think there was a cover charge. Casa Loma's management figured a large crowd for Lefty meant selling a significant amount more alcohol.

Born in 1928, about a month before Alan, two of William Orville Frizzell's most noted songs were *If You've Got the Money Honey, I've Got the Time* and *I Love You a Thousand Ways*.

Alan and I and another young Hurley man, all toiling at menial jobs (made us want to return to campuses!) for the Company that summer to save money for college, sat at a table nursing our beers at Lefty's event. Maybe old enough to drink, or because of the large crowd, our driver's licenses weren't "carded." Then, for some unknown reason, a fistfight broke out. Several men were involved. Alan suddenly stood up and remarked, "I'm going over to see what's going on." Before either of us could grab his arm, he headed across the room.

Since childhood, Alan had worn fairly-thick glasses and didn't see too well, especially in a darkened and smoke-filled honk-tonk. Like a parting of the Red Sea, Alan walked through the fighting crowd, turned around and came back. Like a Moses, returning through the expanding fray.

"Boy, they're really getting into it," he reported unscathed, and completely unaware of his miraculous journey. As the entrance to Casa Loma became blocked by the increasing number of fighting men, we, searched a way to escape. I found a window above the sink in the men's bathroom.

"Come on," I said, and the three of us scrambled into the unoccupied bathroom. A half-open window made it easy to climb onto the sink and out of Casa Loma. We piled into our car. As we pulled out of the parking lot, several police and/or sheriff's vehicles, with red lights flashing and sirens screaming, passed us going the other way. They headed for the front door of Casa Loma.

I don't have any idea how many persons were rounded up, or arrested. Some probably spent the night in jail. I expect deputies escorted Lefty Frizzell safely out of Casa Loma, even if he might have taken part in the fisticuffs. I know it was one of the few times Alan figured his little brother was pretty smart. Lefty Frizzell had high blood pressure, a problem with alcohol, and died of a stroke in 1975 at the age of 47.

Even though in a period of peacetime, the military draft had begun to blow over the heads of young American males. Mailmen (in Hurley families rented boxes at the Post

Office) presented dreaded letters with Uncle Sam's salutation, "Greetings." That official hello meant being selected, presumably at random, by the county's draft board. Drafted into uniform for 24 months of service.

After enduring hot summers on the high New Mexico desert, many of us looked askance at the possibility of marching all day with a heavy U.S. Army pack on our backs. Or "didn't cotton to" being shouted at and deprived of sleep by Marine drill sergeants, engaging in hand-to-hand combat. Maybe being horribly wounded or suffering a slow death in those two branches of "The Service." What appealed for many of us in Hurley was the U.S. Navy. Away from the desert, out on cool water in a ship. No pack on your back. No bayoneting or being bayoneted. If the ship sank, you quickly drowned—seen as a relatively painless way to go.

Flying high in the sky, perhaps at the controls of a fighter plane, also appealed as some Hurleyites dodging the draft enlisted in the Air Force. Scrawny guys like me found the Navy more alluring although Hurley's more physical types looked forward to tough service in the Marines or special Army duty such as with paratroops.

In my particular case, listening to stories of veterans of World War II, such as Ray Canady and Freddy Byrd, lured me toward the Navy. They spun yarns about the fun they had, on purpose neglecting to mention their own rigors in World War II or other details about rugged military life.

One day, an article in the *Silver City Daily Press* presented an alternative. If one acted quickly before receiving a "Greetings" letter, a young man could volunteer for a year in any of three military services —Army, Navy, Marines (I don't think the Air Force was included). After that, *just* a mandatory six years in the Reserves.

The Navy Recruiting Office was located in the Grant County Courthouse in Silver City. On the first day one could enlist in this new program, I got up at about 5:30 a.m. and drove over to the courthouse. Another young man arrived around 7. We sat together on the steps talking, waiting for the place to open. The Navy recruiter arrived a little after 8 and beckoned us into his office. "Well, boys, I hate to have to tell you this, but I've got only one opening for our Naval Enlisted Volunteers Program. That's all the Navy allotted for Grant County. Which one of you boys was out on those steps first?"

I told him I was. "Okay, then. You fill out these forms." As an example of polite regard for one another during those times, I recall the other young man shrugging, saying something like, "It's sure a disappointment to me. But he *was* here first. What's fair is fair."

And he walked away. Someone might threaten to sue now, yet it's a stretch for me to believe anyone would seek out an attorney to help him or her join a desired military branch as an enlisted person. There probably are those who would, though, especially if the draft were still in effect. I don't know if he had to be the first one at the courthouse, but my friend and member of the same high school graduating class, Jim Robbins, was able to volunteer for the one-year Army deal at about the same time.

One late evening a few days later, it wasn't Mom or Dad, but friend Sonny Kennedy who drove me to Florida (pronounced Floor-ee-duh, and I'm pretty sure it isn't even there now), between Deming and Hatch, and we said goodbye on the tiny railroad platform. I waited a couple of hours in semi-darkness for the train, slept in a chair car until morning. I used the bathroom on the train before heading for the Albuquerque Recruiting office. Wrong move. A man in a white Navy uniform handed me a paper cup and ordered, "Piss in this."

I went into the restroom, but nothing happened. Quite nervous, not only about joining the Navy but also as a Hurley boy alone in "the big city," I carried that cup around the hall for about a half hour. Finally, I performed my first unofficial duty for the U.S. Navy. After that, I joined several others in various lines as part of our physical examinations. Gave blood, was probed here and there. Passed. All who passed lined up again. We held up our right hands, pledged to protect our country, gave allegiance to the Constitution, to the United States Navy, vowed to defend against all enemies, "foreign and domestic."

"Okay," a uniformed man in charge (I couldn't tell a Naval officer from an enlisted man then) yelled at us. "You're in the Navy now. You're mine." He began to shout all sorts of obscenities about civilians and about us, how unworthy we were in his eyes. Having grown up in a copper mining town, I had become fairly comfortable around men who cussed, but not those who cursed me. I really didn't understand what was wrong with the man, and still don't. Was he mentally sick? Yet, he wasn't the only one of the few strange ones I would discover in the U.S. Navy. But, it's a big outfit.

It is my hope that, nearly three-quarters of a century later, young men going into military service immediately after pledging their lives to defend their country, don't have to put up with that sort of mindless harassment. Yelling at us at boot camp or during basic training "to shape up" is something else, a sort of initiation into military life.

From Albuquerque, we were put aboard the Santa Fe Railway. I had my first meals in a dining car, waited on by African-American porters at tables covered with white cloths. We headed for Los Angeles, switched to another train going to San Diego, then to a bus. I observed from the bus what appeared to be prisoners marching behind a tall cyclone fence. A guy in charge of the bus pointed at the "prisoners" and laughingly shouted, "You'll be sorry."

They wore light blue shirts and darker blue pants. When I noticed they all also wore white hats, it came to me. These guys are in the Navy! Yep, they were companies of recruits marching in their dungarees at the San Diego Naval Training Center. That's not the way Navy guys looked when they came home. They wore either spiffy blue or white uniforms which caught the eyes of Hurley girls, something I imagined and hoped would happen to me when I returned.

We were escorted to a mess hall line, picked up metal trays for our first Navy Boot Camp meal. On to barracks, where chief petty officers awaited four new companies. We were given sea-bags, personal items like toothbrushes and toothpaste, and enough Navy clothes which fitted us for the night and the next morning. Our chief explained about basic necessities, such as using the "head"– the bathroom and shower facilities

I had showered in the locker room with guys in high school and camped with Boy Scouts, but here many more young men lived 24/7 closer together. There was no reason to be self-conscious except, perhaps, my constantly being reminded of how much better endowed some of those men were than I. No pajamas were issued. We slept in T-shirts and skivvies, as I did my whole year's active naval service.

Everything now became Navy talk, with "decks" for floors of the barracks, "bulkheads" for walls, "hatches" for doors, "ladders" for stairs, and "overheads" for ceilings. We took off our civilian clothing and changed into Navy T-shirts, shorts ("skivvies"), and dungarees (blue work clothes). All our civilian clothes and other items, such as pocket knives and watches, plus anything else we had brought along in our bags or suitcases were set aside to be sent home.

The next day we marched to a warehouse with our seabags, which further were filled with what was figured all the items we'd need in the Navy—including a "peacoat" and a dress uniform. After we lugged the heavy sea-bags back to the barracks, the chief began barking more orders. We took items out of the bags, counting while placing them on our "racks." The idea was to make certain we had the correct number of each required item.

He next showed us how to roll our clothes, tie them with short pieces of cord (square, no granny knots). We packed the rolled clothes carefully into our bags. That was the last time I ever rolled and tied my Navy clothes, because we next took them out of sea-bags and into footlockers near our "racks." Back in saltier times, sailors probably lived out of sea-bags with rolled clothes.

93

Later in the day, our chief petty officer began to march us. Our company's "boots" included about 45 from Texas and 25 or so from North Carolina. By the completion of boot camp, several of those North Carolinians had put a few more pounds on their skinny bones. They also had extensive dental work, which I dodged because Hurley's water had quite a bit of fluoride in it. I suspect many hungry-arriving North Carolinians eventually re-enlisted and completed careers of 20 or 30 years in the Navy.

Each day outside the barracks, just before evening chow, we washed T-shirts and skivvies by hand with bar soap, scrubbing them on a wooden table. Yet it seemed as if most of our time in Boot Camp was spent marching. A few of the seaman recruits from Texas had taken R.O.T.C. (Reserve Officers Training Corps) classes in high school. They were involuntarily volunteered to help the chief march us.

The gold insignia on his right shoulder designated him as Chief Petty Officer. Our chief also had gold "hash marks" on the lower arm of the coat of his uniform signifying many years of unblemished service. Actually a real piece of work, he bent rules whenever convenient. When the floor of our "head" failed to pass inspection, the Chief sneaked in illegal sand at twilight which that night we used to scrub and grind the tiles into shininess. Nevertheless, no matter how well we cleaned and polished our barracks, he constantly referred to our whole unit as a "shit house."

One morning, our Chief lined us up at attention. "I'm going to tell you just one God-damned thing," he shouted at us. "You might think you're sailors. But, you're not!! You're nothing but God-damned boots!! Do you hear that? You won't be sailors until I say you are!! Now, fall out and go to breakfast."

None of us quite understood what precipitated that particular tirade, typical of him. Nevertheless, finally, we "passed in review" in front of Naval Training Center officers and for those relatives of boots able to attend our graduation ceremony. We had completed boot camp. Most in our company "went ashore" (although, of course, we already were ashore) on "liberty" to San Diego. Four or five of us walked together. A young man who was headed back East for a Navy school to become a hospital corpsman, said, "Let's go eat Chinese."

It first flashed across my mind that he planned to do something mean to Chinese persons, but we ended up at a Chinese restaurant. "Let's each order something and we'll share," our leader exclaimed. "I've really missed all kinds of Chinese food."

Around the table, each ordered from the menu. When it came my turn, I ordered what the last person had. "You've never eaten Chinese, have you?" our leader accused me.

"No," I answered, and he ordered something for me, although actually I'd dined on chop-suey once at a Chinese restaurant in Silver City.

Even more confusing was boarding a real ship–D.D. 731, the USS *Maddox*, a destroyer. In boot camp, the Chief shouted at us and bossed us around. Aboard ship were all ranks of enlisted men in special classifications–such as Torpedomen, etc. To whom should I pay special attention or deference? In addition, there were officers aboard.

On board the USS Maddox

Dad had advised me to become part of what he called "the black gang', those working in the engine room. "You'll learn something there you can use when you get out of the Navy." Someone at a table in boot camp once asked me what I wanted to do and I replied, "Work in the engine room." He nodded, so I figured that's where I was eventually headed. Not to be. My first job aboard DD-731 was as part of the "deck force." Each morning a boson's pipe sounded over the ship's loudspeakers, "Sweepers, man your brooms, clean and sweep down, fore and aft."

Others slept in while we swept and mopped decks. The rest of the day was taken up with such menial tasks as chipping off old paint and applying new. We also polished any brass visible. "If it doesn't move, paint or polish it. If it moves, salute it."

After about a week, an officer, probably an ensign, hailed me, "Odendahl," (they didn't call you by rank–"Seaman Odendahl" — like officers do in TV shows like *JAG* and *NCIS*). He continued, "I found out you scored pretty high on the GSD (or some such achievement test I took in boot camp), and you ought to make a pretty good Sonarman striker. If you decide to do that, report to the first class Sonarman at the sonar shack."

I did and he told me I'd learn how to work sonar gear, yet as lowest in rank would clean up the sonar shack. Analyzing quickly, I could tell that would be a lot less work than helping maintain outside decks of the whole destroyer. "You're making a big mistake," the Chief Boson's mate later told me. "Some of those guys where you're going are queer. The real Navy is right here–as part of the deck crew."

SONAR is an acronym for Sound, Navigation and Ranging. We *tried* using sonar to get our destroyer into position to drop depth charges on U.S. submarines–which one day presumably could be Soviet. The simple sonar equipment on USS *Maddox* I became acquainted with in 1948-49 - while not designated "Top Secret," reached the next lower level, "Confidential," and I'm certain now that what we worked with soon became viewed laughingly as quite primitive.

I expect anything technical I might recall about sonar more than a half century later wouldn't be useful to any enemy of the United States. Mum's still the word, because most Navy old timers, including short timers like me, still hold honor-bound to the oath we took, raising our hands, swearing to defend against those enemies "foreign and domestic." "Domestic" has always posed a problem, though. How does one determine the point at which fellow citizens in a nation dedicated to widely divergent viewpoints become "enemies"?

A FirstClass Sonarman, a SecondClass Sonarman, and a lowly Seaman just out of boot camp. We three manned the Sonar Shack of the USS *Maddox*, adjoining the main radar and radio communications room. Our ship often rested, chained to a buoy in San Diego Harbor. I kept the Sonar Shack clean and performed a bit of maintenance on sonar equipment in the bowels of the ship. It became my job to take care of a winch on the ship's fantail (rear end). Added together, this proved much easier than the boredom of day-long swabbing, painting, and polishing on the deck force.

That third USS *Maddox*, a 2200-ton *Allen M. Sumner* class destroyer, 376 feet long and 41 feet wide, had been commissioned only four years earlier in 1944. During World War II, she had been hit by a Japanese suicide plane, killing four of her crew.

After my time aboard, she saw much action in the Korean War. On August 2, 1964 the *Maddox* apparently reported that it had been attacked while it was on what the Navy described as a routine patrol off the North Vietnamese coast. Patrolling with the *C. Turner Joy* (one of the destroyer partners in our division during 1948-49 "Hunter-Killer" exercises), both ships supposedly reported further attacks Aug. 4.

This became known as the Gulf of Tonkin incident, but recently unclassified information leads to different conclusions. Either that nothing happened, or the "attacks" were of little consequence. There was neither damage to the destroyers nor casualties to their crews, but President Lyndon Johnson nevertheless ordered air strikes against North Vietnam. He also asked Congress for a joint resolution authorizing him to "take all necessary measures to repel any armed attack against the forces of the United States and to repel further aggression." Congress passed the resolution, nearly unanimously, within two days.

The main purpose of most of our 1948-49 Pacific Ocean runs several miles out of San Diego Harbor was for "Hunter-Killer" exercises. *Maddox* and two or three other destroyers would move into place in open sea around an aircraft carrier. "Enemy" (our own) submarines then would attempt to get past the destroyers, into position where they would have been able to fire torpedoes into the aircraft carrier.

If the subs got past the sonar of destroyers searching for them, they would send up a black smoke signal–meaning a figurative kill. Or, we hunters might pick up the presence of a sub on sonar and head for it. When right over a sub, a hand grenade was thrown over the fantail of the destroyer–a figurative, non-lethal depth charge which those in the sub heard. Our kill. All a peacetime cat-and-mouse game, which I figured at the time would be won by the Soviets–because there seemed to be more black smoke signals rising from the water than hand grenades going into it.

After being assigned ashore for four weeks to the Anti-Submarine Warfare School near Shelter Island, I looked forward to returning to the *Maddox* because of the quality of shipmates gathered together in our area of the ship. Besides Sonarmen, they included Radarmen, Radiomen, Electronic Technicians, and Quartermasters (those who steered the ship). All smart guys. (No smart women aboard ship then. Our loss.)

One of the men was openly gay, at least to the extent that another sailor *claimed* to once have had a rendezvous with him out at sea. Long before President Bill Clinton in 1993 tried to fulfill a campaign promise of allowing gay military personnel to come out of their closets, and Senator Sam Nunn of Georgia countered with the compromise proposal of "don't ask, don't tell."

Anyway, while a naive youth of 18 in close contact with an allegedly gay shipmate, I never was bothered by him in any manner. We women-less straights had plenty of our own problems to contend with. Like that of my best buddy in the Navy, Darrell Dean Smith of Eads, Colorado. Also a U.S. Navy Enlisted Volunteer, he sent two letters nearly every day to two separate women in that small Colorado town where he had grown up. "How are you able to do it?" I once asked him. "Nothing much different happens on this ship."

"Mainly I just tell each of them how much I love her," he said, "and how much I miss her. I write almost the same two letters every day." One day I went out on deck and my friend was leaning over the rail with a forlorn look on his face. "What's the matter?"

"I really screwed up this time," he answered, and handed me a single letter. It was from *both* of his girlfriends. They angrily agreed they wanted nothing more to do with him. "I don't know how I did it, but I switched the letters when I put them into the envelopes. They really got pissed off, got together, and wrote this Dear John letter."

"I sure don't know," I said, shaking my head, "what to tell you." Undaunted, he contended, "The main problem is being on this ship. If I was at home, I'm pretty sure I could straighten it all out."

"How?"

"Well, I guess I'd need to pick one of them and stick with her. But I doubt if I can do much good with either one by sending any more of my letters."

As young sailors, we had "Minor" stamped on our ID cards so couldn't legally enter San Diego bars. Some obtained fake ID cards. My friend and I figured carrying one of those would be too dangerous, not worth the chance of being caught. We might end up in the brig–manned by what we viewed as unfriendly Marines. So, besides movies, the main attraction for us "young salts" became the Hollywood Burlesque Theater.

What we saw at the Hollywood was billed as quite risqué, and might have been to older generations. Those shows now would be considered comical. Middle-aged men pranced out on the stage wearing trousers much too large for them. Periodically, they stretched out their pants, took a look down into them. Real funny, great for laughs, eh?

The women, some young and some middle-aged, would do partial strip or fan dances. They never removed their bikinis, would end their acts by taking off bras. Nipples were covered with "pasties"–small, round pieces of bright cloth or paper pasted on to cover them. Fan dancers waved their fans in a teasing manner, often revealing even less of their bodies than strippers. For its day, and for young men mostly unfamiliar with women's bodies, the acts appeared quite sensual.

While comradery among shipmates proved a plus, I found Navy life at sea monotonous and boring. Perhaps as an officer with many responsibilities, Navy life would have been more productive. From an old enlisted salt I learned a couple of other facets of a military career. Out to sea, one of our planes occasionally towed a wind sleeve behind it. On command, destroyers in our division fired live .45-millimeter rounds into the air at the wind sleeve–a mock enemy aircraft. Apparently, as ships were in competition, one destroyer changed course in order to make the wind sleeve a better target.

"Hit the deck," the old salt ordered, flattening himself on the metal floor. We younger sailors just looked at him with smirks on our faces. "That's live ammunition, you idiots," he shouted at us a few minutes later as he rose off the deck. "Shrapnel from that ship's rounds could have fallen and killed you."

That event provided a whole new perspective on what we were doing out there in the Pacific Ocean. We were practicing how to shoot down enemy aircraft which either would be strafing us with machine guns or dropping torpedoes into the water with our ships as targets. "Hunter-Killer" meant just that. In wartime, the purpose of our hunting would be to destroy enemy submarines and kill those riding in them. I became more aware that the Navy, like other branches of the service, was engaged in serious business. The business of kill and/or be killed.

When my year's enlistment neared its end, the same old salt inquired whether I planned to "re-up," to re-enlist. "Nope," I replied. "I'm going home to New Mexico. Maybe I'll get a job working in the copper mill, or I might even go to college."

"You're making a big mistake, son. I first joined the Navy before the war. During the Depression. Men were standing in bread lines begging for food. Those of us lucky enough to get into the Navy got $21 a month, food, clothing, and a clean place to sleep at night. It could happen again–another depression. Mark my words."

Living in security during peacetime was one factor to keep in mind while deciding whether to re-enlist, whether to make military service a 20 or 30-year career–followed by a monthly retirement check for the rest of one's life. At 19 years old, I wasn't yet worried about job security. Perhaps that's because at the time life in a Company town such as I grew up in offered young men 30 or more years of work. "I get up each morning," one copper smelter worker once told me, "If I see smoke coming out of that smokestack, I know everything is pretty much okay." And, for that matter, hoping for added job security is why most persons attend colleges or universities. I wasn't making firm plans to go to college, either.

While in the Navy, I was offered the chance to attend college at the Naval Academy at Annapolis. My immediate officer boss, an Ensign, again brought up my fairly high Navy entrance exam score. "Odendahl," he said, "I think I can get you into Annapolis."

It was the second time I had considered attending a post-high school military academy. The first was with the Coast Guard. Right after being graduated from Hurley High I sent in a form to be interviewed for entrance into the Coast Guard Academy. I don't know how, but somehow I missed that appointment. Freudian?

"What do I have to do, sir?" I asked the ensign.

"I have a form you'll need to fill out. You'd have to re-up for six years. Four years at Annapolis and two more Navy duty."

"That's it?"

"Well, you'd also have to take a fleet-wide exam."

Yeah, I thought, how do I know I'd be one of those selected? So I declined his offer, figured the ensign simply might be attempting to trick me into re-upping. At this writing, a retired Lieutenant Commander lives across the street in our mobile home park. When I told him this story, he differed, "Oh, you probably would have gone to Annapolis or the Ensign wouldn't have asked you. That fleet-wide exam was just a formality."

I did know benefits of officers much surpassed that of enlisted persons. A minor example: When we lined up along the deck for chow, platters of fried chicken would be carried past us to the officer's eating room by African-Americans. ("Negroes" in the Navy generally were limited to those jobs —cooking, cleaning, and waiting on officers.)

That carefully-coated fried chicken looked delicious. As we enlisted persons moved down the line into our mess hall, we also had fried chicken placed on our metal trays. This chicken was uncoated; just raw pieces which had been tossed into hot grease. Pin feathers showed. Our chicken tasted okay to hungry teen-agers, but its presentation didn't approach anything gourmet like that served officers.

Another major example: It was announced that *Maddox* had been selected to take some Naval Academy students on a cruise to Alaska. I was one of those who would move to another ship to make room for the Annapolis cadets. During the cruise, *Maddox* would stop at Victoria, B.C., where Mom's parents lived. I'd never seen them.

A married Second Class Sonarman was pegged to remain aboard, make the Alaska trip. "Tell you what, Odendahl. I've been to Alaska a couple of times and would rather be home with my wife during liberties. Let's turn in a chit and switch places. I'll remind the Ensign you know how to handle the sonar. Besides, the First Class Sonarman will be aboard. We aren't going to be making any Hunter-Killer runs on this cruise, anyway."

So we did, and the Ensign promptly turned us down. I went by to see him, quickly re-explained the gist of what was on the chit. "No, Odendahl! That's it! We have to have a Second-class Sonarman aboard."

End of argument. All I could say was, "Okay, sir." I can't recall anyone ever saying "Aye, aye, sir" like they do on the *JAG* TV show. Maybe they do now. I think that, if as a fellow officer, I could have talked that Ensign into letting me go along on the cruise. If not, I might have taken it to a higher level–even to the Captain (a Commander–the person of the highest rank on a Navy ship or boat is the Captain. Like, a petty officer could be captain of a tugboat).

In the long run, it's probably just as well I didn't go to Annapolis. After boot camp and time in the real Navy, I'd have resented upperclassmen hazing me—silliness like sitting at attention while eating, moving your fork from plate to mouth for "a square meal." I'd also have found much difficulty with math and science courses, because the curriculum of the Naval Academy basically was pegged toward engineering. Most of all, "I just don't see you as a military officer," the Rev. Garnett Foster told me during a trip to Greece with wife Mary and another Presbyterian minister, the Rev. Sue Berry. "By the little I've gotten to know you," Garnett said, "you seem too gentle a soul for that."

Be that as it may or may not be, the end of my enlistment approached as *Maddox* came to Mare Island Naval Shipyard, about 30 miles northeast of San Francisco. It was fun to look at the bottom of the Golden Gate Bridge as we steamed under it, then past Alcatraz. As the ship was scheduled for a major overhaul, many in the crew found themselves temporarily stationed elsewhere.

I was deployed to the Naval base at Treasure Island, found on a California map as the place where the San Francisco-Oakland Bay Bridge is supported as it crosses over. Another sailor I recall as a First Class petty officer went with a small group of us scheduled to be discharged. He was, eager to head home to be with a wife and newborn son.

"I'm going to save my money and buy him a brand new car when he's in high school. I never had a car in high school." That's the first time I'd come across the idea of a high school student being presented with his or her own car–new or old — by parents. Almost all in Hurley were one-car families. Some teenagers saved enough to buy halfway reliable cars like Model As, (One threw his hard-earned money away on a 1929 Essex.) I found out later in college that "rich kids" often drove cars given them by parents.

The petty officer had been in the Navy for a long hitch. Only a few days at Treasure Island with no duty assignments and the Navy discharged him early. Not so for me. Whether by prejudice against short-timers in the U.S. Naval Enlisted Volunteer program or simply bureaucracy, I wasn't as fortunate. I had to serve every day of my one-year enlistment.

That meant three more weeks as a "mess cook," not actually cooking but getting up very early, working long hours cleaning tables, scrubbing decks, and other such tasks. Much the same menial work I'd done in boot camp and when first boarding *Maddox*. I even became too tired to go on liberty. (Maybe I did once?) I thought, this isn't too smart of the Navy. What they could have done is let me loll around base during daytime, go into San Francisco on liberty every night. Then hit me with the question: "How about re-upping?"

Serving as a Seaman for several months, I had neared eligibility for Third Class petty officer as a Sonarman. They easily could have offered me that to re-up. Not that I necessarily would have, but it would have been something to think about. Advantages? For example, no more cleaning of the sonar shack. They didn't offer and I didn't re-up. So there. I still have it. It reads: "Honorably discharged from the United States Navy on the 26th day of July, 1949. This certificate is awarded as a testimonial of honest and faithful service."

Not that I never strayed from the straight line. Once, on liberty in San Diego with my Navy pal from Colorado, we came across some "green beer." I don't know whether it had been colored green for St. Patrick's Day, more likely dubbed as green for not completely brewed? The memory of how we acquired beer without a legal ID card also remains long irretrievable. A Navy Shore Patrolman even stopped us, told us we could go on our way if we "straightened up."

Anyway, I must have consumed more green beer than my Colorado buddy. Or, though he still may have been more consumed by worries about letters and women, could handle his liquor. We passed by a tattoo shop, viewing the various designs offered in the window. I was taken by one design: A big ship with sails, seagulls flying around it. Underneath the blue-inked ship and gulls could be tattooed in red letters: "Homeward Bound."

I figured Hurley girls might be attracted to such a tattoo, which in my mind signified loyalty not only to the U.S. Navy but also the old hometown. Many sailors preferred names of girl-friends at home tattooed on shoulders or arms. If they received Dear John letters, future girlfriends and wives lived with a man tattooed with another woman's name. Being tattooed was a messy business. In a day or two, a tattoo would fester and ooze, become itchy and sore. Sailors couldn't scratch without ruining their tattoos. Getting a tattoo today doesn't appear to be such an ordeal.

Removal of tattoos, before lasers, was a painful and often ineffective process. Most of the tattoos adorning old salts, even strange ones such as with hula girls they made dance by flexing lower arm muscles, had at least a semblance of artistic quality. "Homeward Bound" looked better to me than cobwebbed designs on bodies of young persons today.

I'm told many of these cobwebs are applied while in prison. It is too bad, that if they want to be "inked," pretty colored patterns aren't available in prison.

Now discharged by the Navy, homeward bound without a tattoo on my shoulder, I rode a Greyhound bus. Earlier, I'd written to my grandparents in Victoria, B.C., telling of a plan to visit for a few days upon my discharge. When the time came, however, homesickness prevailed and I couldn't wait to get back to Hurley.

Another mistake, because I never met either of my grandparents on my mother's side of the family. Grandfather Robinson would die April 9, 1952, and Granny on January 3, 1957. As a boy, I retain a hazy memory of seeing Odendahl grandparents for a couple of days during a trip our family made to Colorado. My Grandfather Odendahl died May 13, 1950, with my grandmother passed away in February of 1945.

Greyhound's plan routed me south toward San Diego, then east to Deming and Hurley. In the direction of San Diego, I sat on the aisle next to a well-endowed young woman. "I'm going to San Diego to tryout to sing opera," she said.

As has happened so many times in my life, at the sight of a beautiful woman I immediately found myself near-to-smitten. I wondered, homesick or not, if there were some way I might be able to lengthen my trip home. Footloose and fancy free, I could spend time with her in San Diego. Lots of time! How about in the same apartment!? It soon became clear it would be of no avail to change my bus ticket. First of all, although she talked a lot, her mood toward me never mellowed.

Second, sitting in front of us was an older woman who came aboard at the same time as the chesty one beside me. Having a mother able to listen to our every word also complicated making headway, toward popping any questions about a San Diego stopover. Third, How long did that mother plan to remain in San Diego with her daughter?

The bus pulled into a station for a rest stop. (No toilets on buses then.) The new delight to my eyes took her purse and whatever on the seat, headed for the restroom. I moved into the aisle to let her pass by and she disappeared. The older woman also got up, cleared the rack above her and followed after my heart throb. I perceived they must be in the process of changing buses along with her daughter and I'd never see either again. I looked up and noticed a newspaper-wrapped package in the rack above me. I got up, grabbed it and chased after the older woman, now several feet away from the bus. "Your daughter left this on the bus," I said, thrusting the package into her already filled arms.

"Oh. Thank you very much young man."

Back on the bus after a trip to the men's bathroom, I dejectedly moved next to the window where my well-endowed fantasy once sat. A few moments later, I looked toward the aisle, and there she was! As I struggled to get out of her seat, she looked into the rack above us.

"What happened to my package?"

For one of the few times in my life, I quick-wittedly mumbled a lie. "I don't know."

"It was right there. Someone took it. Did you see anyone take a package wrapped in newspapers?"

"No," this time not as much of a white lie because I *didn't* see anyone take it. I felt overwhelmed enough to be undergoing a sort of out-of-body experience. Whatever she had lost, or simply the fact she had been robbed, put the young woman in a sniffy mood. For many miles she grimly fumed about the "stolen" package and impugned the character of the person robbing her. Silently humiliated, despite a "mother" now out of the picture, I realized no possible progress would be made in my fantasy about moving into some San Diego apartment with her.

When it came time for me to change buses, I wished her the best with an opera career, and crept away. It wasn't the first time I'd ridden a bus from the San Diego area to Hurley. I'd been homesick enough to make the trip twice that year, violating a Navy regulation that one must wander no more than 150 miles from a ship on a 72-hour pass. I did it twice, taking a day on a Greyhound bus to Hurley, spending a fairly sleepless day with family and friends, and another day sleeping on the bus to make it back to the ship on time. I breathed easier each time we were 150 miles from San Diego. If the bus were to break down then, I could call in about why I'd be legally late. Not AWOL.

In her story, *So Many Christmases!* Mom wrote at age 76, "*(Pattie Street, Hurley, Christmas, 1948.) Late Christmas Eve we got word that same son, now 18, that he'd unexpectedly been given leave from the Navy and was on his way home by bus, Wonderful! But under the tree would be no gift for him, (all sent already sent to San Diego!). And The Company store was closed long since. So we switched name cards from a book–about opera–meant for Dorothy. Something he couldn't take with him, unfortunately not too practical! It made our Christmas brighter to have the family complete, even though his hours were numbered. (Could he even spend a night? I think not.)*"

Upon arriving home free from the Navy, I still faced six years of inactive reserve duty. Dad excitedly told me he'd wangled a machinist's apprenticeship at the town's Kennecott mill . "It's not easy," he said, "to get someone an apprenticeship with The Company."

104

An apprenticeship is what I figured on doing, until the next day talking with Freddie Byrd, who that summer lifeguarded at the Hurley swimming pool between semesters at New Mexico State Teachers College in Silver City. "Why'da'ya want to work for The Company for?" he said, looking down from the high perch he sat on.

"Dad says I can't for too long because once I become a journeyman machinist, I'll have to move somewhere else. He said he'd help me go to Detroit to be a tool and die maker in one of the big auto plants there."

"That," Freddie argued, "probably would be a dead end just like working here for Kennecott. Do you have any money?"

"I saved up $500 in the Navy."

"Wow! That's more than enough to pay a year's tuition at Teacher's College. You can work for Kennecott during summers for tuition after that. Get a degree and you can make something out of your life."

"Dad told me, 'You're not college material.' I guess he means compared to Alan."

"Yeah, we all know how smart Alan is, but you could make it through Teacher's College. Look at me; I'm doing it."

"The big problem is: Dad really will get pissed off if I turn down that apprenticeship."

"Well, let me ask you this. Are there any pretty young girls working here in the mill?"

"Nope, not that I can think of right now."

"There are all kinds of them at Teacher's College. You could have a hell of a good time there and learn something, too." That did it. When I told Dad about my decision to go to college, he repeated, "You're not college material. You're making a big mistake not taking that apprenticeship."

That's all Dad ever said, but obviously he *was* disappointed. I realized I was burning a bridge because the apprenticeship probably would never be offered to me again.

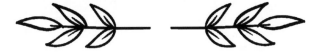

CHAPTER 8 – BEGINNING TO COMMUTE

My Hurley High School friend Jim Robbins had returned from his year's enlistment in the Army, and we rode together to New Mexico State Teachers' College in Silver City for our first day of college classes. Registering a few days before, we'd opted for classes matching our driving schedule, and I'd agreed to help pay for his blue Studebaker coupe's gasoline.

"An un-excused absence will lower your semester grade one point, like from an A to a B– in this class," our first professor, after taking close attendance, warned us. "Three times tardy and your grade drops one point. However, for those of you who commute, see me. If you're tardy, I'll take that into consideration."

After laying out a few more rules, he dismissed us. I moved to the front of his desk. "Sir, I was wondering. Does 'commute' mean those of us who will be driving our cars over to your class from Hurley?"

"Yes, young man," he answered, smiling, "that's what commute means. If you have a flat or your car breaks down, let me know the next class period."

"Thank you sir," I said. The U.S. Navy had taught me usually to know when, to whom and how to say "Sir." But neither in the Navy nor at home had I ever remembered hearing the word "commute." Now I knew what it meant. My college learning experiences had begun!

That first day of attendance began a string at five colleges and universities and 28 years as a professor. New Mexico State Teachers' College opened as a normal school in 1893, changed its name to the teachers' college in the early 1920s, and in 1963 became Western New Mexico University. I moved to the University of New Mexico in Albuquerque the next year, then New Mexico College of Agriculture and Mechanic Arts in Las Cruces (New Mexico State University since 1960), State University of Iowa in Iowa City (University of Iowa since 1964), and finally the University of Missouri at Columbia.

At the University of Missouri

My teaching career would begin in 1964 at the then San Diego State Teachers' College, briefly California State University at San Diego, and its present name of San Diego State University.

Being late for a class in Silver City or anywhere else because of flat tires on New Mexico roads and highways was common. Almost everyone carried a jack, a lug wrench to remove the nuts holding a wheel, and a tool to take the tire off the rim.

It was then a matter of searching for the hole in the inner tube, repairing it either with a "cold" or "hot" patch. Dad preferred hot patches, clamping a metal tray of combustible material over the patch on the tube. You lit the combustible material with a match, and it smoldered several minutes —sealing patch to tube.

For a cold patch, preferred by most in Hurley perhaps because it was cheaper, one applied special glue to a square of rubber over the hole in the tube. You'd wait several minutes for the glue to dry. Either way of patching, you still carefully had to put the inner tube back into the tire, gingerly squeeze the tire onto the rim with the tire tool without scraping another hole in the tube, put the wheel back on the car, and take the jack out from under an axle. The whole process took at least 30 minutes, meaning being quite late for a Teachers' College class.

One often would notice a couple of big rocks alongside a road. Anglos, often prejudicially, referred to those as "Mexican jacks." With occupants perhaps only able to afford glue and tire patches, a stricken car still needed to be lifted to remove a flat tire. A fence post or tree limb was used as a lever and a big rock as a fulcrum. Once in the air, its axel eased down onto a larger rock, the wheel was taken off. It would be a struggle to remove a tube if without a tire tool, to replace it after patching. Working with a lug or other wrench, the wheel was screwed back on the axel. The "Mexican jack" was used to release the rock holding up the car. I, trying to get along with my peer group, certainly held too much prejudice against Hispanics, yet always thought the whole "Mexican jack" operation was very clever. Some Anglos, of course, turned up their noses when seeing those rocks.

In boyhood years, when we rode bicycles, you could buy large toothpaste-sized tubes of Never Leak, and squeeze that sticky liquid into tire tubes to plug tiny holes. When strapped for cash, we'd funnel a small amount of canned milk into bike tubes. Didn't work as well as Never Leak, and when one had a blowout the spoiled milk caused quite the stench.

Because I'd "served" in the Navy, 14 units of physical education automatically had been added to my Teachers' College transcript. I think this benefit, which was proffered under the guise as a reward for our patriotic duty to God and Country, actually came about because WWII vets bristled at carrying out orders, such as doing pushups, from often non-veteran P.E. instructors.

Hispanic vets also literally were changing Hurley. Before the war, many of the Company's older Mexican-American workers, still retaining Mexican citizenship, dreamed of returning home south of the border. Some of them, arriving as early as 1910, were huddled in shacks on "The North Side" across the railway tracks. With almost no upward mobility, Hispanics remained bogged down in manual labor or truck-driving jobs. They were offered neither apprenticeships nor foreman positions. On Dad's mill maintenance "gang," they were called "helpers," even though they understood how to do all the tasks which needed to be done.

"Henry Soltero is as bright as anyone in that mill," Dad said, referring to one of his longtime workers. Dad hoped Soltero would replace him when he retired. That didn't happen. Rather, the position was offered to an Anglo man who never had worked with the "gang." Dad had to train this Anglo man for several months before the transition. Henry Soltero remained unrewarded for his many years of hard work and service to The Company.

It was the closest to slavery I would see in my lifetime. There were no manacles, no whipping of Hispanics. To my knowledge few Anglo Hurleyites, unlike what Thomas Jefferson is reputed to have done with slave Sally Hemings, took advantage of willing or unwilling Hispanic women. Most certainly, what happened to Hispanics working out their years for The Company while living on Hurley's North Side was quite demeaning. They were poor, generally with large families to feed, often with little variance in a diet of cheap although somewhat nourishing pinto beans, tortillas, and hot chilies. Nevertheless, if you look at pictures of us standing in the sun in front of the junior high, Hispanic junior high classmates were not much, if any more, worse-clothed than we Great Depression Anglo boys and girls on The South Side. We all were clothed in the well-worn garb of Hard Times.

It took Hispanic World War II veterans, who had fought as equals for the United States, to force The Company to replace "squatter" shacks with new houses. . A bit of irony was that these houses, with new plumbing fixtures, etc., were more modern than most of those Anglo ones on The South Side. Company houses were maintained by Company carpenters, painters, plumbers, and electricians. This in itself came like a sizeable raise in pay for Hispanics.

Nearly a decade after I'd left Hurley, the Civil Rights movement changed not only the Southern U.S. but also New Mexico. The Company figured a way out of its racial-bias-housing predicament, offered to sell its houses to the occupants. This meant Hurley no longer was a company town. It became incorporated. As houses were made available, either because of original owners dying or moving away, they could be sold to either Company-working Anglos or Hispanics, or anyone else. From anywhere.

My favorite class that year at Teachers" College was geology. Our instructor provided interesting lectures, and even more fun were field trips in a large area surrounding Silver City. On one trip we moved down a canyon and he pointed out the various geologic ages as we passed different layers of rock formations. Walking by scientific evidence of strata of geological periods spanning millions of years certainly did nothing to firm up any belief that God formed the Earth in either six days (or maybe one single day) as written in Genesis. Even six years, or six million years.

On another field trip, we pried trilobites out of a cliff (pretty sure out of limestone).

I still have a couple of those trilobites somewhere, but at the time was more fascinated by a living creature. Her name was Mary White, a tall and very attractive woman who lived in Hurley about a block and a half from our house. She hadn't been there before I joined the Navy. We had a great time talking together on the trilobite-gathering field trip, yet because of still being extremely shy around young women it never occurred to me to ask her for a date.

"Mary White really likes you," Jim Robbins told me. "Why don't you ask her out?"

Jim probably even offered to provide his wheels and to double date with me. Although quite attracted to Mary, I lacked the intestinal fortitude to act upon my feelings. Or, as they used to say, "A faint heart never won a fair lady."

A few months later tall Mary married the even taller center on the college's basketball team. That team was dominated by players from Indiana, where basketball was favored over football. These players weren't the Hoosier state's finest, good enough to play under the likes of the fabled Bobby Knight at Indiana University, but most of them were better than local New Mexico talent.

"Those Eastern bastards," we Hurleyites called them, not only because they prevailed at basketball but also partly because of being newcomers some charmed the local women. Geography was not our forte. We young Hurley men thought anything east of New Mexico was East, didn't realize those players from Indiana should have been referred to as "Midwestern bastards." I still have a different problem with what is Midwest, because many of those states rest more eastern in the U.S. than west. Maybe Midwest was a name picked up as settlers gradually moved west, perhaps not realizing how much further they could go.

When not actually in classes, all of which I attended and took fairly good notes, I studied hardly at all, except an hour or two before exams. This make-believe pattern of "cramming" to be a "student" continued all through my undergraduate days. What resulted was called "a gentleman C."

I spent most of my time with my two best buddies–Sonny Kennedy and George Hailer. Sonny had been graduated from Hurley High with Alan's class. Although not as tall as my just-under-six-feet with shoes on, unlike me he was a natural athlete. Probably his best sport was tennis. While in high school, he dominated all older men in the area. One year in high school Sonny was entered in the state championships in Albuquerque. At the last minute, it was discovered there were insufficient funds to pay his way to the Duke City.

Of course, George Hailer, Jim Robbins and I, along with most of those living in the Hurley area, figured Sonny could and would have been the state high school champion. There is no way to know. I later became aware, while at the University of New Mexico, how many good tennis players were there. At least, I watched them smash the ball as hard as Sonny did.

Sonny could run very fast, was a fine hardball and softball player. He wore thick glasses, perhaps a reason why he wasn't all that great as a batter. On the links, however, Sonny proved himself a good golfer and was a fine bowler. He loved sports and drinking beer. The baby of the family, Sonny had several sisters and an older brother, Nick–named after their father. Most in town figured their tiny, happy-faced mother was a Hispanic, but in his later years Sonny informed George Hailer that she was a Native American. Who knows about that, which doesn't matter, but it might have quite important to Sonny as part of prevailing Anglo prejudice against Mexicans?

George Hailer transferred to Hurley High from a school in Albuquerque. Like Sonny, he was a natural athlete, immediately joining the basketball team composed almost completely of Hispanics. By attending Albuquerque schools, George was non-prejudiced against those of Hispanic origin. Part of this may have come about because many persons living in Northern New Mexico carried genuine Spanish, viewed as aristocratic, blood in their veins. Quite a few held high political offices it the state capital of Santa Fe. At any rate, George got along famously with his browner-skinned teammates. It was something the rest of us Anglos already should have learned to do.

George's mother, a beautiful woman, and mine had become good friends. I also spent some time with George's brother, Jack, in his own right a good athlete. Jack didn't go out for Hurley High teams, but excelled in the classroom. Elected president of the Honor Society, Jack refused to go on stage to receive a certificate acknowledging it. I don't know whether it was shyness, or a sort of mini-revolution against the school system. Before being graduated, George joined the Army. Jack already had graduated and served time in the Navy. While George was in the Army, his mother died.

After that first year at Teachers' College, I decided to transfer to the University of New Mexico in Albuquerque. Soon after, Sonny Kennedy received a "Greetings:" letter and off he went to the Army. When George Hailer finished his Army tour, he began working toward becoming a journeyman carpenter as an apprentice at The Company. He married Darlene Ford, a high school girl who lived to the west of us on Pattie Street. Darlene was the best thing that ever happened to George.

Later, Mary and I were privileged to be a few times with George and Darlene Hailers' kids, Dee and Bud. Not as much as we'd have liked to. A fond memory is the day we fished with Bud at an Apache lake in the White Mountains of Arizona. I expect Darlene and Mary caught more trout than Bud, George and I. We all pulled out enough that day for a great fried fish supper Darlene fixed for us.

Another highlight was when George and Darlene came to La Mesa to help celebrate my surprise 50th birthday party. I couldn't figure out why George said we ought to go to a place I thought didn't have the best Mexican food in our area, or why he insisted we wear sport coats.

After the Hailers bought their Lazy Daze RV, there was the Fantasy Caravan group of motor homes which we joined to go to Mazatlan in Mexico. Also fun was traveling together in our motor homes to New Orleans for my niece Laura's (Alan's daughter) wedding.

The motorhome group

Before that, Sonny and I were single and seemed happy as larks, with nothing much to do in the summer except work for Chino Copper Company during the day and head out together after dark. We usually went to really sophisticated places, like The Bloody Bucket for a couple of beers. The bucket was *The Chino Buffet*—a small bar about a mile north of town which didn't offer any sort of buffet that I ever recall. Heck, we probably didn't know what a buffet was, except we might have eaten at a cafeteria one time or another.

The Chino Buffet was owned by Mildred Clark, who ran the three whorehouses in Silver City, others in New Mexico, and some as far away as Alaska. For a good read, check out

Madame Mille, by Max Evans, 2002, University of New Mexico Press. An example, by Evans about Millie in Silver City:

"I learned from others that during the vicious copper strike in the late 1950s, Hispanic strikers had very little money saved, and they ran out of food. Millie fed their children for months. It was only white bread bologna and cheese, but it was food. The strike was immortalized in the film "Salt of the Earth' which was a film so radical in its time that the director and actors were blacklisted in Hollywood as dreaded Communist sympathizers. Nevertheless, they made the movie. Despite possible boycotts from her wealthy patrons, Millie had her own convictions. She fed the poor. She fed the families of the strikers."

After beers at Mildred's Chino Buffet, we'd drive over to Vi's Drive-in at Bayard for cheeseburgers, fries and often milk shakes. You got'ta be young to wan'na drink a milk shake after several beers. Vi's attached trays to the door of your car when you rolled down the driver's side window. We didn't belong to organizations like the Sierra Club, but had real appreciation for the wildlife at Vi's. They wore mighty tight blouses and very short shorts. Those "wild waitresses" would slink toward us, lean over displaying cleavage while taking our orders. A few minutes later they placed food and drinks on trays, and wiggled back to the kitchen window. The whole process was great exercise for the eyes of multi-processing, multi-hungry, young men.

Then we might go back to The Bloody Bucket for another beer. Or maybe chase another car. The idea was to find some other young man we knew driving along the highway, preferably with his girlfriend squeezed next to him in the front seat. We'd slip up behind and bump his car three or four times. It was really fun if his girlfriend got a bit scared and moved over to her side of the seat. We, in those days, of course, were very interested in protecting the virtue of girls. Don't try that with the plastic bumpers on today's cars, which aren't made out of steel which flexes.

Before moving to Albuquerque (The BIG CITY!!) for a second year of college, I phoned Bob Neel at the University of New Mexico. He lived at the Sigma Chi fraternity house, along with fellow Hurleyites Amos Stone and recently Derrick (Bud) Green. Bud, the son of the superintendent for The Company, had just been graduated by UMN. He had served in one of the armed forces during World War II, later became an engineer for The Company, at someplace besides Hurley.

I asked Bob Neel for advice about which dorm at UNM was the best. He said something like, "They're all the pits. Why don't you live with Amos and me here at the Sig house? We have some empty rooms." Sounded good to me. I also was able to find a job at a UNM cafeteria setting up tables, clearing dishes, and having to take my turn at a real chore–scrubbing pots and pans. The ones with baked-on food were the most difficult and time-consuming. Scrubbing in deep, hot, and soapy water, caused one to sweat. Not good if you attend a class before you could shower.

Nevertheless, can you believe it? There I was at the BIG UNIVERSITY in the BIG CITY, living in a comfortable place with some friendly guys who had been out in the BIG WORLD. Earning a little extra money at the cafeteria to help pay rent at the Sig House, for personal expenses, and by working summers for the Company able to save toward tuition.

In a couple of weeks things changed dramatically. The president of the fraternity came by and told me, "We're sorry, Max, but you won't be able to stay in this room because we're going to be pledging other guys to fill up the house. Of course, if you went through Pledge Week and asked to pledge Sigma Chi and we took you in, you could stay here."

He assured me that it looked favorable for my being accepted as a Sigma Chi pledge. This proved a dilemma, because I'd viewed fraternities and sororities by their very nature to be undemocratic, open only to the select few. Snobbish, for rich kids. Yet, I had made friends with most of those in the Sig house and wanted to stay. The process of Pledge Week consisted of my talking with "actives" at all the fraternities on campus, each touting the advantages of living in their houses. After that, I selected three as my preference in rank order–with, of course, Sigma Chi first. I was accepted as a pledge by the Sig actives.

Being a Sig pledge didn't prove all that difficult. There were one or two bully-like actives who enjoyed attempting to make it a sort of boot camp, even though pre-war paddling and other forms of physical punishment had been outlawed at UNM. Like bringing to an end inadequate housing for Hispanics working for The Company in Hurley, World War II vets at UNM weren't about to be paddled or physically mistreated by younger actives whom Dad would describe as "still wet behind the ears.".

Pledge work was somewhat analogous to my time aboard ship in the Navy. Not as rigorous as boot camp, yet we pledges played the role of enlisted men and the actives that of officers. We performed such tasks as the weekly cleaning and scrubbing of the Sig house.

Although I kept my cafeteria job, as a pledge living at the Sig house I was obligated to take my meals there. This proved to be one example of many benefits I received from fraternity living. I learned, when called upon, to recite a simple, ecumenical grace– something my family never did. My table manners also improved, although it was not due to any deficiency of Mom's. Only that I hadn't paid more attention to her teaching of table etiquette.

What benefitted me most was being able to talk and exchange ideas with Sigma Chi "brothers" from all parts of the United States. A few came from well-to-do families. As a parochial New Mexican, I found myself eager to acquire knowledge and lifestyle customs from cosmopolitan young men from Albuquerque and even larger cities. Probably the most far-reaching benefit was a new-found expectation for at least limited upward mobility.

As noted before, too many young Hurley males envisioned no future for themselves other than working for The Company or joining the armed forces as enlisted men. Among Sigs, I discovered persons looking forward to professional careers, such as the two who lived in one of the rooms and studied together in preparation for dental school. Another, in pre-law, became a Rhodes Scholar before ending up as a partner at a prestigious Chicago law firm.

I attempted to hold on to what I saw as the best of both worlds–a professional career and living in Hurley–working summers for The Company. I began taking courses toward becoming a mechanical engineer, a top-of-the-line Company career for a Hurleyite and something which I figured would make Dad proud of me. Alas, it was not to be. A disaster!

An example of why that happened: The wartime chemistry class at Hurley High, where I'd had the crush on Sara von Tress. While we rubbed hands, our assignments consisted of mixing up strange stuff in test tubes and beakers as prescribed in a workbook.

"If you don't know your valence table, or don't learn it within a week," the UNM chemistry professor told a small auditorium packed with students, "you'll flunk this class."

The multi-colored periodic table of the elements hung ominously on the blackboard, filled with what one dictionary calls "the quality which determines the number of atoms or groups with which any single atom or group will unite chemically." You know, like H_2O —two parts H for hydrogen and one part O for oxygen equals water.

Those graduated from big schools such as Albuquerque High already knew the periodic table. I felt it pointless to attempt to continue and dropped that class. Even mechanical drawing proved a challenge for me. We didn't use modern "drafting machines" at UNM, drew everything by hand with T-squares, clear celluloid triangles, and rulers. After completing a drawing in pencil, you inked the lines with special little tools (such as compasses) filled from ink bottles. Drat! Too often, on the last line of inking a drawing, I'd get nervous and helplessly watch the ink flow under a celluloid triangle–meaning the drawing had to be done all over again.

My grade average fell so low by the end of the semester that it required struggling to make A's and B's in most other courses for the remainder of my undergraduate days. That is, even in order to sneak away from UNM with the minimum requirement of a "gentleman's C" average. I dropped out of engineering, much to Dad's disappointment. Maybe that's what he could have meant in his viewing of me as not being "college material"?

My days with slide rules ended, I decided to become a high school English teacher, still holding onto the idea of returning to Hurley. Just before the next semester, I headed over early one morning to the UNM Education building to check about enrollment. Too early; nobody able to advise me was there. On a whim, I entered the Journalism Building, climbing the stairs to the second floor above the UNM printing presses.

"We can sign you up for classes right now," a professor whose name I've forgotten told me. "Being a journalist is a lot more fun than teaching English in some high school." So that's what I did. I've sometimes wondered, "What if I'd hung in, memorized that 'valence table,' put in enough effort to pass those engineering classes? Could I really have done it? What if someone had been there early that morning to sign me up for education courses? Would I have found success or happiness as a high school English teacher, probably facing disciple problems from unruly boymen with perpetual hard-ons more fantasizing about young women than about learning *anything*?"

While all this was going on (with me also still fantasizing, but enjoying no sex with young UNM women), I faced another obstacle in my college career. The Korean War had broken out. Remember, I owed Uncle Sam six years in the Naval reserve? Yep, I read a headline in the morning *Albuquerque Journal* which shouted, "60,000 Naval Reservists to Be Called Up." I became panicky, not so much out of fear of seeing military "action" or being killed but of being forced to leave college. Returning to some dreary ship for who knew how long as an enlisted man.? Again, Bob Neel came to my rescue.

"Why don't you join the Air Force ROTC like me?" he asked. Bob told me he'd avoided the draft since high school by being in the ROTC, although was obligated to serve years of active duty as an Air Force officer after being graduated by UNM. He yearned to be a pilot.

I joined the ROTC, was told that —because of my previous Navy service–would be commissioned in two years rather than the four required of students like Bob Neel. We were learning how to set up GCA (Ground Controlled Approach), a system of towers which guided Air Force planes onto runways during inclement weather.

That first semester in ROTC went fine; I even was selected to march other cadets because of my vast boot-camp experience. Bob Neel helped guide me though the more technical parts of classes. At the end of the semester, I was called into the ROTC colonel's office, "I've got some bad news for you, Odendahl," the colonel said. "With this war getting hotter, standards are tougher. We can't keep anyone in the GCA program who isn't an engineering student."

"Sir," I exclaimed, "I was in the Naval reserve. Now, that I've resigned that to join the ROTC they'll draft me into the Army."

"Well, son, here's what you might do. (I don't think the Air Force colonel ever relished the idea of marching in the Army with a full pack, either.) New Mexico A&M at Las Cruces is a land-grant college. Part of being land-grant is that it must have an ROTC program available to all students. You could transfer there."

He smiled and joked, "They have to take anyone, even journalism majors." So the second semester of my sophomore year, New Mexico A&M became my third undergraduate college–where I continued with Air Force ROTC. The Aggies were known as The Cowboy School. Many of its students came from homes on ranches–so big hats, Levis, tight shirts with snap buttons, and western boots were common wear.

What I perceived as one advantage of becoming an Aggie was that I could come home to Hurley each weekend. This meant I headed out go to the Chino Buffet with Sonny Kennedy. Sometimes George Hailer joined us briefly at the Chino, but he was a more domesticated married man now. We invariably ordered bottles of Schlitz —which, for no particular reason that I know of, we considered the best-tasting beer. It wasn't the best atmosphere because I wasn't studying at all on those weekends. I did find Aggie classes easier than at UNM, but that probably was because I no longer struggled with engineering.

For some reason I once was offered a two-hour ride back to A&M at Las Cruces by Alan Borenstein in his new Plymouth. Borenstein's Department Store, sitting on a corner of the main street in Silver City, was the largest clothing outlet in Grant County. The Borensteins might have been the only Jewish family in the county. (That is, unless some were among those Jews who came to New Mexico to flee the Spanish Inquisition in Mexico, had secretly switching to Catholicism to remain alive.)

That ride with Alan Borenstein proved a strange trip, for no reason except because I thought it the first I'd ever spent any amount of time alone with a Jewish person. (Actually, one or more of my Sigma Chi brothers could have been Jewish?) I don't know why, but I expected Alan to do something or say something weird or at least act differently from other folks. Of course, he didn't. He even let me drive his new car part of

117

the way, cautioning me not to go more than 50 mph because it still was being broken in. I don't recall ever seeing him after that.

As my semester at New Mexico A&M ended, I found out (probably from Bob Neel again) that UNM's Air Force ROTC now was accepting non-engineers. I returned to the Albuquerque campus. At the end of my junior year I was commissioned a second lieutenant in the Air Force Reserve. We cadets at UNM still were supposed to have learned to be expert overseeing the installation and maintenance of GCA (Group Controlled Approach) towers for landing planes. Just before my commissioning, a master sergeant called me into his office.

"Odendahl," he smiled, "I see from your records that you are a veteran of World War II. So, you have the choice of taking active or inactive reserve duty after you graduate."

The Korean War still was going on and I had no idea when it would end. I also knew it unlikely I was a veteran of World War II for service in the Navy in 1948-49, although one little card I received upon my discharge said something like that.

"I didn't see any action," I blurted out.

"Doesn't matter —if you were in the service when hostilities were going on," he said. By this time I had regained my senses as a military person and remembered never to volunteer further information until asked for or about it. "I'll take inactive, sergeant. I need to make sure I get through college without being called up."

"Okay, sounds good. Then, that's how I'll put you down."

"Say, Sergeant, I've been worried about one other thing."

"What's that?"

"Well, I'm not an engineering student and maybe could run into some problems putting up one of those GCA towers."

"Oh hell, Odendahl, you've nothing to worry about. A master sergeant like me would take care of all of that for you."

"I'm sure he could, but what if he got drunk or something and screwed up. Wouldn't I still be the one responsible?"

"You've got a point there, Odendahl. What's your major?"

"Journalism."

He took a manual off a shelf and shuffled through it. "What about being a Public Information Officer?"

"Yeah, I'm pretty sure I could handle that."

"Okay, Odendahl. Here's what we're going to do. I'll just change a number here and there and you won't have to worry about GCA. You'll be officially down as being commissioned as a Public Information Officer."

"Thanks a lot, Sergeant," I said, as I waved at him and left the room. Probably it simply was a nice favor for a fellow, although former, enlisted man.

When I returned to UNM from A&M, I no longer worked in the cafeteria. I became a "houseboy" at a sorority–Alpha Delta Pi. In return for "dinner and supper," houseboys served those meals to sorority "girls" and washed their dishes. No pay, but here is the how the drill went:

There were four of us houseboys. Two donned white jackets and bow ties to serve the young women. The house mother, seated at the head of the table in the dining room, rang a little bell. One of us in a white jacket would go from the kitchen and stand facing her.

"Yes, Mother Williams?"

"You may serve now."

"Yes ma'am."

Serving was "family style," meaning we carried large bowls and platters to the table. They were filled with food prepared by a jolly and gracious female cook. The young sorority women passed to one another. Meanwhile, two other houseboys were in the kitchen gobbling down their own meal. Young men can eat a lot of food and we crammed our stomachs full twice a day, saving money by, usually foregoing any sort of breakfast.

When the uniformed houseboys removed bowls and platters, plates, knives and forks– preparing for dessert, the others began washing. They were dressed in heavy, waterproof bibs and wore long, rubber gloves which extended almost to their elbows.

One deep basin was filled with very hot, sudsy water and the other with hot, clear, rinse water doctored with Clorox.

One of my cherished experiences while removing a dinner plate from the table was unintentionally dropping a fork down one of the young women's blouses. She lifted it from where it rested in her cleavage, handed it over her shoulder to me, and said with a grin, "I think this is yours."

If Mother Williams was aware of this little episode, she didn't let on. My final year at UNM I moved up to be head houseboy at Alpha Delta Pi. I even recruited another younger Sig pledge, named Grinslade from Santa Rita, to work with us that semester.

While the women enjoyed dessert, the two servers sat in the kitchen gorging themselves. They then cleared the dessert plates and silverware, helped the dishwashers put away everything. Serving lunch usually took less than an hour, dinner a bit longer than that.

We did learn once the hard way about "silverware." What we normally placed on the ADPi table was stainless steel. On one special occasion, Mother Williams told us to use the sorority's silverware, including serving ware. Our mistake was that we forgot that regularly Clorox was added to the rinse water to sanitize everything. The Clorox turned the silverware black and we had to spend a long time polishing it!

Probably the prettiest, and certainly one of the most lively, yet unassuming, of those young ADPi women was Gloria Castillo from Belen. She later moved to Hollywood, where she had a bit part in one movie–perhaps more of a film career. After a popular song of the time, I called her "Little Glow Worm" each time we met

Mother Williams frowned on romances between houseboys and ADPi women, the morality of whom she felt she closely guarded. The women weren't even allowed to come into the kitchen while we were there. A fellow Sig and houseboy dated one of the women and returned her home only about five minutes after the 11 p.m. deadline. She was put on restriction for a couple of weeks. Mother Williams admonished them at the door, "Both of you, of all people, should have known better."

Mother Williams had good reason to guard against lustful Sigs, would have been astounded by a prank regularly carried out. It went this way: During a party at the Sig House, where liquor wasn't supposed to be present, some would have become tipsy anyway. Those not onto the prank would be told, "Maria should be ready for us."

One of several randy young men, often pledges, with ears perked up would ask,

"Who's Maria?"

"Maria lives down by the railroad tracks," came the answer from the ringleader. "Her husband is a conductor for the railroad, but he's a lot older than her —can't 'cut the mustard' any more. She's real horny and he's real jealous."

The story continued that Maria made herself available to multiple men when her husband worked on the train to and from El Paso. What she would do was set a lantern in her window, letting young men know her husband was gone.

"I know he's not there now," the ringleader would say. "Let's go down and see what Maria can do for you guys." Meanwhile, other Sigs had traveled in the direction of an abandoned shack in an open field near the railroad tracks, and placed a light in the window. As the small party approached the house, the ringleader would call out just above a whisper, "Maria. Maria."

Suddenly the door to the shack would fly open and a figure would stand silhouetted in the door frame with a shotgun in his hand. "You wife-stealing sons of bitches," he bellowed and fired the shotgun into the air.

The now not-so-randy young men scattered all directions into the darkness and heard the sound of the shotgun being fired a couple of more times. The ringleader, the shotgun blaster, and other Sigs in on the plot drove off. Those frightened men left scattered behind had to find their own way back to the Sig House. Often they arrived bruised from tripping and falling in the dark. One once even cut himself slightly while running full speed into a barbed wire fence.

Moving into my senior year at UNM, I became at least somewhat more serious about my grades. I still needed desperately to raise to the "Gentleman C" level required not only for graduation, but also toward preparing for a job as a newspaperman.

Keen Rafferty, the chairman who had established the UNM Journalism Department, served as my mentor and favorite professor. He had come to New Mexico as "a lunger," one of many "Easterners" fighting tuberculosis–an extremely virulent disease. No medicine existed to cure TB, and even recently the disease still infected nearly one-third of the world's population, killing almost three million people per year, more deaths than from any other infectious agent. The sickness had become resistant to drugs and AIDS patients easily contracted it.

In Rafferty's case, one of his lungs already had collapsed before he arrived in New Mexico. Many others, often in much worse condition, came to the Southwest, hoping the dry air would stop or slow the disease. As a boy in Hurley, when one of us coughed more than once, another would joke, "You've come Out West too late."

Keen Rafferty came Out West after a distinguished career with *The Baltimore Sun*, where he had risen to become the "slot man." Those editing newspaper stories (referred to as "copy") sat around a U-shaped desk. The person in charge had his (rarely her) chair in the middle of the U–in the slot. So "a "slot man" and "rim men" worked at the "copy desk."

121

Few women edited hard news copy, generally were assigned to soft news such as "society pages." Women often edited, wrote headlines, and positioned soft news in such pages.

Slot men carried heavy responsibility. They decided which stories ran in the newspaper, on what news pages. They assigned typefaces for and sizes of headlines written by "rim men" copy editors, who meticulously checked stories for spelling, punctuation, other errors, and wrote headlines. The slot man penciled onto "dummy" pages the exact length and position of each story to be put together in "the back shop" — the composing room.

A "breaking" story, a news event just happening, especially if underway "on deadline" (just before a newspaper must be printed), found the slot man stretched to his best. A rewrite man sitting nearby often typed breaking stories in "takes" dictated by reporters on telephones at the scene. Takes were handed to a copy editor, checked, and sent to the Linotype machines to be set ponderously into melted lead —"hot type." While another copy editor might be writing a headline, the slot man decided which other stories and/or pictures, often on a front page already filled with significant news, must be removed to make room for the breaking one.

One of Rafferty's colleagues on *The Baltimore Sun* was H.L. (Henry Louis) Mencken. The iconoclastic columnist known as the "Sage of Baltimore" wrote before his death in 1956, *"If, after I depart this vale, you ever remember me and have some thought to please my ghost, forgive some sinner and wink your eye at some homely girl."* Mencken's creed:

I believe that no discovery of fact, however trivial, can be wholly useless to the race, and that no trumpeting of falsehood, however virtuous in intent, can be anything but vicious.

I believe that all government is evil, in that all government must necessarily make war upon liberty...

I believe that the evidence for immortality is no better than the evidence of witches, and deserves no more respect.

I believe in the complete freedom of thought and speech...

I believe in the capacity of man to conquer his world, and to find out what it is made of, and how it is run.

I believe in the reality of progress.

But the whole thing, after all, may be put very simply. I believe that it is better to tell the truth than to lie. I believe that it is better to be free than to be a slave. And I believe that it is better to know than be ignorant.

The Sage of Baltimore also once wrote: *"No one in this world, so far as I know ... has ever lost money by underestimating the intelligence of the great masses of the plain people."*

Mencken's legacy sadly included later being viewed as racist and anti-Jewish. Once during a classroom discussion Rafferty indicated to us he didn't respect the man personally but considered him an excellent writer. He didn't elaborate.

Among several journalism classes I took from Rafferty was one in copy editing, where he perched in the slot with elbows on the copy desk handing out to those of us sitting around the rim stories to edit and headlines to write. I imagined myself working for him on the rim at *The Baltimore Sun.* It later turned out that editing copy, writing headlines, and making up newspaper pages probably were my greatest strengths as a journalist. That was to come about after a long learning process.

Those of us who worked for no pay on *The Lobo*, the UNM student newspaper, took turns making a final "proof" before the presses began to run. Once when it was my turn, I was handed a first copy off the flatbed press. I checked it for errors.

It was common for some Linotype operators working in the noisy "back shops" of newspapers to be deaf . Deafness turned to their advantage. They set type unbothered by clanking linotypes or the nearby roar of rotary presses. A deaf Linotype operator smiled and nodded at me if I'd found any mistakes in that particular issue of *The Lobo.* "Okay?" he asked.

"Yep," I mouthed back, giving him a proud thumbs-up sign to start the press. It felt great to be in charge. He began to laugh, took a leaded line of type out of a page sitting on the press, and handed it to me. It was part of a front-page "cutline," the caption below a picture of several sorority women vying for some honor such as Homecoming Queen. I had quickly and incorrectly read that line of the cutline on the printed page as, "Missing is Sylvia Jones of Such and Such Sorority."

Examining the leaded line, I found it actually read, "Pissing is Sylvia Jones of Such and Such Sorority." That she *could have been*, but it didn't need to be pointed out by *The Lobo.* Laughing even harder, the deaf Linotype operator reached into his apron, took out the correct lead line about the *missing* woman and inserted it into the page. "Okay?"

"Yep," but now with a sheepish look on my face, I gave him a less-than-enthusiastic, more unsure thumbs up.

When Keen Rafferty graded one of our papers and made comments, he signed it K.R. To his face we called him Mr. Rafferty, behind it K.R. For an Editorial Writing class, I turned in a very immature critical piece bemoaning the grade-point system. (Under therapy,

Sigmund Freud might have linked that particular "editorial" to my feeble struggle to become graduated, or later ADHD—which Freud probably wasn't aware of.) It was the result of a last-minute effort, as given most assignments I completed. Okay for breaking news stories, not for editorials —which require serious thought before and during writing. Rafferty returned my paper with a "D" grade and attached the following:

Max:

If what you said were true and sensible, and would improve American college education, and be good for students–including you–and if it were still written as well and with such vigor as the attached, this would be worth a good B.

What shall I do: grade according to the way it's written, or according to my judgment as to, one, whether or not it's publishable in a newspaper as an editorial, and two, whether what it says is sound sense, likely to make readers believe so, and likely to improve the lot of mankind (that is, in this case, of students) ultimately?

I have been wondering how it happens that you are so upset by the university system and how it is you are so sure that you are right. This dogmatic quality, a kind of intransigence which indicates an inability to adjust yourself to other people and to people particularly of more experience and at least more demonstrated brains, lets you into a position in which, if you keep it up, you'll always be up in arms about something in your writing.

Sometimes people in their writing find an outlet for the things they can't do or say under the circumstances surrounding the rest of their immediate lives. But in editorial writing a fellow has no such privilege. The disciplines of writing newspaper editorials are even more stringent upon us that the disciplines of, say, social contact or a military caste system or marriage as a conventional institution, or whether one may urinate in public.

Editorial writing is not a way of finding expression for one's personality, or for one's frustrations. It is, on the other hand, a highly impersonalized thing (or should be), under which the writer attempts to get at an ultimate truth of some kind in the interests of people as a whole. It seems to me that the editorials you have been writing have been for no one's good except to make you feel better psychically for having said them.

K.R.

Of course, K.R. was correct on all counts. About that time I also found myself in hot water with the university's football coach. Someone had recruited me as sports editor for *The Lobo*. Un-athletic, I'd personally done nothing more in sports than running and losing mile races on Hurley High's and New Mexico Teachers' College track teams. I knew little about how to cover or write about sports, only what I'd picked up as a reader of the *El*

Paso Times. In the beginning, I used stories supplied by the university's sports information writer.

UNM had recruited a fairly famous coach, named Dudley DeGroot, and the football team's first game took place out of town. I listened on the radio as the Lobos played a decent first half. The second half turned into a disaster. I wrote in the next issue of the *Lobo* that the team appeared out of shape. A day later the coach left word for me to come to his office. I expected to get some good quotes from him about the game and what was in store for the next one. Perhaps he would praise me saying, "Good story. It's made my boys work a little harder for the next game."

"So," he asked angrily, "you think my team is out of shape?"

"It sounded like that to me on the radio."

"Well," he said as his voice grew louder. "You don't know a damn thing about this team and I doubt much about football either." He had me there and I didn't know what to answer.

"So, here's what you can do. The team will be practicing in about 15 minutes. You can just come down on the field and get in the middle of the players, find out how out of shape they are."

I neither went down to the field nor recall interviewing DeGroot ever again. It was one of a multitude of lessons all journalists continually happen upon. No matter what you experience, good or bad, or what odd bits of data and information you acquire, they often will be useful in some way for you later on. Writing sports stories would later consume three years of my life, during which I interviewed several football coaches–with no ill feeling that I'm aware of like from DeGroot. Baseball is another matter, with worse altercations with a Class C pitcher and a manager. Read about it later as we move along in this epic. For sure, I'm a slow learner.

Another person getting himself into hot water in 1952 was Edward Abbey, the editor of the student literary publication and my brother Alan's close friend at UNM. On the cover of *The Thunderbird*, was written: *"Man will not be free until the last king is strangled by the entrails of the last priest!"* —signed, Louisa May Alcott.

The UNM administration did not think the ludicrous quotation, obviously not what Louisa May Alcott would ever be likely to write, was at all funny. A dean actually rushed over and, like in some low-rated movie, stopped the presses. A day or so later the Publications Board met, with UNM bigwigs determined to receive Abbey's head on a platter. Ed explained how it all came about.

He had contacted the priest in charge of the Newman Center, the campus gathering place for Roman Catholics, and outlined his plan. *The Thunderbird* would devote that fateful issue to anti-Catholicism, to be followed by another—this time an all-pro-Catholic issue, exclusively written and edited by students at the Newman Center. Abbey testified that the priest there agreed to his plan.

The problem was that the majority of New Mexico's residents were Hispanic, many devout or at the least baptized Roman Catholics. The UNM administration saw itself facing a wildfire of grievances, not only from ordinary citizens but also from powerful Hispanics elected to and holding high state offices in Santa Fe. They held the university's purse strings.

Keen Rafferty argued before the Publications Board that Abbey was within his rights, a simple matter of freedom of the press guaranteed under the First Amendment of the U.S. Constitution. A professor from the English Department testified that Abbey was a very talented writer, probably would find his mark as a novelist. Nevertheless, the Publications Board fired Abbey as editor and as far as I know *The Thunderbird* never rose from the ashes to be published under that name again

Edward Abbey later became a well-known environmental novelist and article writer. His funniest book probably was *The Monkey Wrench Gang. A* more serious one was *Desert Solitaire.* His novel, *The Brave Cowboy,* published in *1956,* evolved into a movie with a changed name, *Lonely Are the Brave,* starring Kirk Douglas and Walter Matthau. After Abbey's death, Douglas was quoted as saying his role in *Lonely Are the Brave* was the most honest he ever had portrayed.

In a book called *Slickrock,* Abbey (writing to accompany Philip Hyde's photographs of the Southwest) mentioned a trip in Alan's Chevvie, (I think it was a Ford, can't recall Alan ever owning a Chev) "They said there was no road," Abbey wrote. "They were right. But we did it anyhow, me and a kid named Alan Odendahl (a brilliant economist since devoured by the insurance industry), freezing at night in our kapok sleeping bags and eating tinned tuna for breakfast, lunch, and supper."

For some forgotten reason, I spent a night at the place where Abbey once lived in Tijeras Canyon, east of Albuquerque. I recall trying to rest either in a sleeping bag or on a couch in the middle of the night while he and Alan loudly argued about who should be considered the most important and commendable (leaving out the likes of Hitler and Stalin) person of the first 50 years of the 20ᵗʰ Century. Ghandi, Churchill, FDR and others were dissected until early morning.

After they finally gave up their animated discussion to sleep a few hours, we loaded into Alan's (1946, 1947, 1948?) Ford convertible—maybe the "Chevvie" Ed mentioned? —and drove down through Belen to Bernardo and east to Ladron Peak (Mountain of Thieves) in the Sierra Ladrones, Still in my memory is an excited Abbey racing around the lower parts of the rock-strewn peak in his hiking shoes. (The mountain is 9,147 feet high. Yet, remember, most of New Mexico already stands a mile high, so the peak stretched about 4,000 feet more into the air.)

I don't believe we climbed all the way to the top. We did have fun speculating about tales of at least one secret cave in those mountains. Where Apaches and related Native Americans could have stored gold and other loot stolen from settlers and off civilian and military wagon trains. According to an article in the December, 2003, issue of *New Mexico Magazine,* "Some stories have a basis in fact. An old wooden trunk found on the mountain held a leather-bound Bible belonging to the Spanish missionary Fray Diego Jimenez, who traveled the countryside from 1632 to 1678."

Another time at UNM I took some of my writing over for Abbey to read. He had moved into an apartment off-campus, was now married to his first wife, Jean Schmekel. She was a well-rounded "dish" and I certainly envied his regularly having sex available–which those of us living in dorms and fraternity house generally lacked. Ed quickly but seriously read my stuff and shook his head. He was right; It *was* pretty bad.

When he died at 61 of complications from surgery in March of 1989 at Oracle, Arizona, Ed's friends secretly buried him as he had requested–in a sleeping bag, perhaps behind some big rock —his last act of defiance against authority which demands your veins be filled with chemicals, Alan was not able to be there, or at a later ceremony where other friends drank beer while extolling Abbey's eccentric virtues. I earlier had read about Abbey's death in the San Diego newspaper and, when I phoned Alan, it was the first he was aware of it. We sadly agreed that Ed had been a special person.

Receiving my Bachelor's at UNM

As the first semester of my senior year came to an end, I was well past the flirting stage in my love affair with journalism, seriously enjoying some of the virtues beginning to rub off on me, and looking forward to working under the lofty umbrella of First Amendment privileges. I also found myself drawn to the stirring of another romance.

Her name was Mary Ethel Johnson, a physical education major working as secretary for Keen Rafferty in the UNM Journalism Department office. As she customarily did to others, she smiled brightly at me each time I breezed by on the way to class

"You were always late for classes, Max," she reminded me later. That didn't impress her very much. Part of Mary's job was posting grades and other important information in students' permanent records. "You were the guy who had that awful name to spell." That probably didn't help my cause much at first, either.

While at home in Hurley for my senior year Holiday Break, I sent out only a few Christmas cards. One of them was mailed to an Alpha Delta Pi woman I had my houseboy's eye on. The other was sent to Mary Ethel Johnson. Returning to Albuquerque in January, I mustered up enough courage to ask Mary out. Our first date was to a movie (Huh?–about an opera). The next was to one of Billy Graham's "revivals." Taking a girl on a date to an evangelical meeting had never entered my mind. I held little interest in evangelists, big name or not, and Billy Graham held about the biggest name of all of those traveling preachers.

Mary remarked about what she saw as a spectacular revival being staged in a huge tent nestled next to the Sandia Mountains several miles east of the University of New Mexico, on what at that time was open land. So, I said something like, "Let's go."

Several local church choirs had been enlisted to sing together. I was more interested in finding out what all those people did in that tent. I recall being dressed for the date in brown slacks, a shirt without a tie, and brown leather shoes–all a notch above my standard of a white T-shirt, faded Levis, and tennis sneakers.

For me the highlight of the revival was hearing noted religious baritone George Beverly Shea sing "How Great Thou Art." I failed to fully sense that, although Mary also was captivated by the baritone's rendition of the hymn, the revival held deeper meaning for her.

Slouching in my seat, I attempted to shut out much of what I identified as the droning and shouting of a "holy roller" preacher. Nobody rolled in the aisles or even, as in modern post-denominational churches, leaped up now and again to wildly wave arms in the air. I'm still convinced ADD contributed to my disinterest in Graham's sermon, as it has to those of most other preachers over the years.

At the conclusion of his sermon, the evangelist prayed for something like "tormented souls" to come forward to an adjoining tent and "give yourself to Jesus Christ." I figured the tent was where the souls were hit up for pledges of money. Most, including Mary, had bowed heads. I craned my neck to see if anyone actually was coming forward.

I didn't see any movement at first. Graham kept saying things like, "I can see them coming from the back. There's people on the sides, others moving down the main aisle. Join them if your heart is heavy. Jesus is calling."

The joint choirs sang, "Jesus is calling, is tenderly calling today." A few persons began to ease toward the front of the tent. I figured they were shills (like those paid to attract suckers to carnival games and sideshows). My uninformed speculation was that the evangelist's organization planted them in the audience to induce others to move forward.

I did concede there *might* be folks from Albuquerque-area churches, those from fundamentalist congregations customarily beseeched forward, to fall on their knees at the altar as sinners seeking calls for redemption. Hundreds soon were on their way to the smaller, adjoining tent.

"I didn't care for what that evangelist did while he was preaching," Mary whispered to me on the way out of the main tent. Believing I'd found in Mary Ethel Johnson a kindred

129

spirit concerning religion, I said, "Neither did I. All those shills were the height of hypocrisy, weren't they?"

I don't think Mary knew what I meant by 'shills', "It wasn't so much the shills," she explained, "but Billy Graham kept hitting his Bible with his fist and pounding it on the lectern while he preached. I'd have thought he'd have more respect for the Bible. That really disappointed me."

"They call those guys Bible thumpers," I confidently advised her. I became convinced Mary, with my seeing her as a reasonable and intelligent person, would concur in due time with my cynical view of religion. She in turn had observed me at my best behavior, probably anticipated that I could be converted into a dedicated Christian. Like so many young couples with significant conflicts, each believes the other person will change and arrive at the other's way of thinking. That's rarely the case.

One of our dates was to the Air Force ROTC ball, with a full orchestra. I borrowed a car from a Sigma Chi brother and set out for Mary's house on Lafayette Street. Many of the streets leading off of Central Avenue, Albuquerque's main thoroughfare and part of Highway 66 going directly through the city were named after former U.S. Presidents. So, all I had to do was cruise down Central until I found Lafayette. Right?

Wrong, of course. Lafayette wasn't a President. I found myself lost and almost an hour late to pick Mary up. Along with her mother, older sister Jean and husband Alvin, also waited there to meet me. Not a very good first impression.

That was the date when I wore my topcoat, given to me by Mom and Dad when I moved to Albuquerque. "A boy going off to college needs a good overcoat," Dad said.

Mom agreed, though, always the more frugal one, didn't see as much need for it.

"Where did you borrow that?" Mary asked about the coat which extended beyond my knees.

"Oh, it's mine. Mom and Dad gave it to me when I came to Albuquerque."

"You mean you had it all this time when you've been taking me out wearing that dirty old jacket?" She referred to an olive-colored foul weather jacket I'd acquired while in the Navy.

"That foul weather jacket isn't dirty, just looks like it is because of its color. I've had it cleaned several times. Actually, that jacket is a lot warmer than this topcoat." Mary, perhaps for the first time, gave me what our daughters later referred to as "The Look."

Our romance went forward. In February I had given her my Sigma Chi pin. Mary was disappointed that fellow Sigs did not recognize the pinning by coming to her house and singing the usual *Sweetheart of Sigma Chi* serenade. She was, and still is, convinced it was because she was looked down upon as a GDI (God-damned independent–not a member of a sorority). I felt she wasn't serenaded only because of the logistics of getting to her home compared to walking on campus to a sorority house.

By the time of Spring Break I asked Mary if she would go with me to Hurley to meet my parents. She accepted. As I look back on it, her parents certainly showed exceptional faith and trust in their 19-year-old daughter to allow her to travel unescorted about 250 miles away to spend several days with a young man and his family they didn't know all that well. I realize now what an act of faith and trust they also put in me.

"I knew it was pretty serious," Mom privately told me after we arrived in Hurley. "That was the first time you wrote not asking for money." Although I'd like to think my virtues while attending college included a fair amount of frugality, the fact of the matter was that several times I had to write home asking for money – usually $50 (which I suppose would amount to about $500 these days). I thought great cleverness went into writing those letters, chatting about happenings in my life before mentioning money.

After Mary was settled in (I think she stayed with sister Dorothy in her room) and after supper, I decided to take her to the Chino Buffet. When we arrived, Sonny Kennedy and Bud Green were sitting at the bar. After introductions, Bud asked, "What would you like to drink?"

"A Coke," she told him and the bartender.

"Listen, Mary," Sonny said in a lecturing tone of voice. "If you're going to run around with us, you've got to learn how to drink beer."

"Oh, let her order what she wants," Bud said, and Mary drank her Coke while the three of us quaffed our usual Schlitz–probably a couple of bottles of beer during her single soft drink.

Sonny's first impression wasn't a good one for Mary, although she later would find him a sensitive fellow and also her good friend. Not a smart-ass. I also think Sonny saw Mary posing a threat to the threesome. Already married was George Hailer and it appeared I also was ready to go "down the tubes."

Curiously, that was the feeling I would have for the next few months–not a unique perception at all during that period. In my view, a majority of men in our generation viewed marriage as leading to regular sex and more stability (like not hanging around the Chino Buffet guzzling beer). Most women of that era entered marriage after searching for a man they felt at the time met their standard of a dependable breadwinner, and as the father of their children. I don't recall any man who sought marriage mainly to produce children or any woman primarily for regular sex. Obviously, there must have been a few.

Dad had taken me aside and said something like, "Mary seems like an awfully nice girl. If you're ready to settle down, I think you should think about it now."

After-dark, Mary and I necked in our family car at the bottom of the slag dump. (Slag was the left-over material in the process of pouring copper bars at the smelter. Still red-hot, slag glowed in the dark as it was poured from special railway cars at the top of the dump). Mary said, "Well, I guess all this means we're going to get married?"

Not very romantic, huh? No begging on bended knees by me, with a ring in my hand. My answer: "I guess so." That has proved to be the best decision I ever made in my life.

Mary, back in Albuquerque, told me her family couldn't afford a big wedding, that she would do it mostly on her own. She decided on a date —July 17, her parents' 25th wedding anniversary and brother Greg's 10th birthday.

Miss Mary Ethel Johnson

Miss Johnson, Max Odendahl Wed in June

Mr. and Mrs. Charles W. Johnson, 813 Lafayette Dr. NE, have announced the engagement of their daughter, Miss Mary Ethel Johnson, to Max Odendahl, radio wire editor of the Associated Press in Albuquerque.

Mr. Odendahl is the son of Mr. and Mrs. H. C. Odendahl of Hurley, and will be graduated in June from the University of New Mexico with a bachelor of arts degree in journalism. He is a member of Sigma Delta Chi, journalism honorary fraternity, and Sigma Chi, social fraternity.

Miss Johnson attended the University of New Mexico where she majored in education, and is secretary of the journalism department at the university. She is a past honored queen of Job's Daughters, Bethel No. 2, Albuquerque.

July 17 has been chosen at the wedding date, which also will be the silver wedding anniversary the bride's parents. The cer will take place at Trin odist Church.

I could feel myself swimming on the outer edge of a whirlpool–everything out of my control as the current slowly moved me around. Did "down the tubes" mean the middle of the whirlpool to which Mary and I were being drawn? Everything that happened to us until our wedding date certainly were new experiences for me.

One of her two best friends, Barbara Ostrower, offered to loan Mary her white wedding dress. Somewhere along about that time Mary's father, Charles W. "Chick" Johnson, told me, "Max, there's one thing we've got to stand together on."

"What's that?"

"Well, I don't want to wear one of those monkey suits at your wedding. A plain business suit is good enough for a man to be married in, don't you think?"

"I sure do, Chick." (He was a great guy and by this time was good to be on a first-name basis with.)

"Okay, we'll stand together on that."

Not only did Chick hold a high position as a civil engineer with the New Mexico Highway Department, but also I felt he definitely was head of the household. His wife, Lula Mae, seemed to defer to most of his wishes. So, wearing our regular business suits was a done deal. Or was it? About two weeks before the wedding, Chick said to me, "Have you rented your white dinner jacket yet?"

"What do you mean? I thought we were wearing our regular suits?"

"There's been a change in plans," he said with a grin on his face. "All the men in the wedding party now are going to wear white dinner jackets."

"Oh." As he told me where to rent my white jacket and black pants, I could swear I heard the rushing of water drawing me closer to the tube in the middle of that whirlpool.

The wedding was to be held at Albuquerque's Trinity Methodist Church, with the reception afterwards in the basement. That is, unless it rained. In that event, the church basement was reserved for the Boy Scouts.

When rain was forecast we needed another place for the reception. After receiving an okay from fraternity officers still living there for the summer, we re-scheduled the reception at the Sigma Chi house. Mary, who recently had attended a wedding reception where drinking had gotten out of hand, decided we would serve only soft-drink punch.

"We've got a problem," Chick told me as the women of the family including Mary's mother, older sister Jean, younger sister Phyllis, and others were setting up and decorating the main room of the Sig house for the reception.

"What's that?"

"Lots of my highway department and contractor friends have been invited to this reception," he said, "and they like their booze. I know Mary's against it, but couldn't we set up two punch bowls and spike one?"

"I guess so, but she won't like it."

"This is your chance to make your first decision as a married man."

"Okay, let's do it."

Meanwhile, my parents arrived in Albuquerque and were to stay in a motel while Mary and I used their car for our short honeymoon. Whether or not she had a whirlpool feeling, Mary also felt some reservations about becoming married, was especially jittery on our wedding day. It didn't help that very day I went to a barber shop for a haircut and the only shave in my life with a straight razor. I had been letting my hair grow out, but decided in my nervousness to revert to my usual short flattop. It did rain and Al Cynova, her sister Jean's husband, had to carry Mary across streams of water and into the church. With my new flattop, I appeared like a different person to Mary, beautiful and radiant in her white wedding dress as she walked down the aisle toward me on the arm of her father.

During the ceremony, I nervously said, "With this wing I wed." After being pronounced husband and wife, we arrived at the Sig house, and Mary spotted the two punch bowls. As I explained the situation she frowned, asked which bowl her father had spiked.

"Oh, my goodness," she said following where my finger pointed. In the spiked punch line were the minister (Methodist ministers back then were required to take "the pledge" never to consume alcohol) and Mary's two teetotaler grandmothers. We could do nothing as we stood in another line accepting folks' congratulations, including from those who never before had met me and said things like, "I *just know* you are going to be the *perfect* husband for our dear Mary."

Our wedding day, July 17, 1953

Besides the punch, there only was a wedding cake. No sit-down dinner. No band. No dancing. After cutting the cake and sharing a piece of it, Mary and I headed for the front door of the Sig house where the crowd waited with rice in their hands. Showered with rice, we got into my parents' car and headed out.

I thought Mary planned and pulled off a great wedding. Still do, and see no reason why so much needs to be spent now. (According to *Bride's* magazine, $19,000 per couple is spent on weddings. Lately read a figure of $35,000. Don't know whether those are average, median, or what.) If it costs as much as the down payment on a home, that money for modern lavish weddings could be better put to use helping the young couple get set up. Just an opinion, which I know is going nowhere.

After driving to Santa Fe, we spotted what looked like a decent motel. I carried our marriage license into the motel, thinking it might be needed as proof when registering. Wasn't asked for it, and never have been since. The only time we needed that license was when, after the death of one of her grandmothers, a government bond was left in Mary's maiden name. She had to produce the license for the bank in order to cash the bond.

After changing clothes, we had a steak dinner and a giddy conversation in what we figured one of Santa Fe's swanky restaurants. We went back to the motel to spend our first night in bed together. I'm happy to say we've continued doing so for some sixty-odd years and counting.

With the girls on our 50th anniversary

CHAPTER 9 — WORKING FOR THE AP AND THE WSJ

When we returned from Hurley, word spread around the UNM Journalism Department that Mary and I were engaged. Keen Rafferty called me into his office and shut the door. "I understand you plan to marry my secretary?"

"Yes-sir, that's right."

"Don't you think a young man who plans to get married needs to have a job lined up?"

"I guess so," suddenly sheepish upon realizing about not reflecting enough upon job opportunities after college. Somehow, I'd figured things ought'a work out for the best.

"Well, I certainly think so, Max, and I've lined up a part-time, weekend job for you with AP (Associated Press) until the end of the semester. It may become full-time this summer, but there's no guarantee–and it's very unlikely that you'll be able to stay on after that."

"Thank you."

"I think you can handle the job at AP okay, Max. It's fast-paced. You *will* have to show up on time. You can't be late like you are to most of my classes."

"I won't be."

As what I hoped would be my final year at UNM began, Rafferty earlier had called me into his office to discuss another matter. "Max, I see you don't have a minor. You won't be able to graduate without a minor."

This came as a shock, because I'd taken some amount of pride in perusing of catalogs for New Mexico State Teacher's College, New Mexico A&M, and UNM. All the while juggling credits from the three institutions in order to be graduated in four years, this despite the disastrous semester attempting to become a mechanical engineer.

"I didn't think I needed a minor, according to the catalog."

"Well you do."

"Oh," sort of a sigh, chagrined at missing that information in the UNM catalog.

"Here's what you might do, Max. I see you have quite a few credits in Air Science."

"Yeah, I took those classes to stay out of the draft."

"Anyway, Max. Well, if you took two more classes of Air Science, you would have a minor and could be graduated on time."

"Okay, if you think so, that's what I'll do."

One rule is that very little is easy or simple in a bureaucracy. As was to be my experience for many years after that, colleges and universities are big-time bureaucracies. So, when asking the Air Force Colonel about taking an additional two Air Science classes, he retorted, "You can't do that, Odendahl! You're an Air Force officer now! You would outrank the sergeants teaching the classes!"

"I can't graduate this semester unless I take those classes."

He shifted a bit in the chair behind his desk, "Well.....maybe if you talked it over with the sergeants....that still might be possible. You'd have to let them know specifically that you'd be taking those classes as a civilian."

"Yes sir. I can do that."

When this skinny young man in civilian clothes explained the situation to one of the burly sergeants, he laughed heartily and replied, "Sign up for any classes you need, Odendahl. Just between us, we won't pay any attention to the colonel. What he doesn't know don't hurt him."

That's what I did; minored in Air Science at UNM, and still to this day am without much of a clue about how to set up those Ground Controlled Approach units for landing Air Force aircraft.

Beginning a stint at the Associated Press proved even more an eye-opener due to my lack of experience. The most surprising jolt came right off, simply observing the speedy atmosphere in which AP staffers worked and wrote. For example, Bureau Chief Sanky Trimble typed at close to 100 words a minute from his notes and "copy" flowed from his typewriter at that speed. If I recall, his specialty was cattle trading and his speediest stories came on deadline after covering cattle conventions.

My meager typing skill proved a problem, to the point of irritating newsmen and newswomen phoning in stories from other parts of New Mexico to the AP bureau. Not only could I not transcribe phoned-in stories quickly enough, but also showed ineptitude in putting together my own copy, It became embarrassing.

The main task assigned me was each hour compiling a 10-minute "split" in the national AP radio wire. This 10-minute-break provided news from around the state for New Mexico radio stations. What had been sent on the wire an hour before was re-written to make it sound fresh, with newer items interspersed. These came from phoned-in stories, others teletyped by New Mexico AP-member newspapers, or from pieces copied/rewritten from editions of Albuquerque's newspapers–the morning, independent *Journal* or the afternoon Scripps-Howard *Tribune*.

It took _only_ about 500 words–somewhere around two to three pages double-spaced with added space between items–to fill the 10-minute New Mexico radio wire break. That meant I had 50 minutes, often interrupted by having to laboriously type phoned-in stories, to do the radio work. In the beginning, another staffer helped me get the radio break written in time. During all of those months I worked for AP, rarely were a few minutes remaining before the next break came in the national wire. It *had* to be filled. Veteran AP staffers working the radio wire took only about half an hour, spent the rest of their 50 minutes on other stories. As I did no reporting, you couldn't have called me a "cub reporter" for AP. (Actually, I never heard that term used during the years I worked for newspapers.)

In New Mexico, as elsewhere, AP constantly battled against United Press to be first in print and on the air. United Press began in 1907 with newspaper publisher E. W. Scripps. It would be five years after I worked for AP, in 1958, that our rival became United Press International —brought about by a merger with William Randolph Hearst's International News Service which began in 1909.

A vivid example of AP and United Press rivalry was Operation Little Switch, the exchange of sick and disabled prisoners in April of 1953, during final truce negotiations ending the Korean War.

As the names of United States prisoners (intensified by tension of their families not knowing whether they were dead or alive) appeared on the teletype machine in the Albuquerque AP office, bits of paper ("takes") were ripped off to be retyped and sent out on New Mexico print and (especially) the radio wire. TV news didn't amount to as much in those days, although the names were provided in time for 10 o'clock newscasts.

New Mexico's AP held its lead over UPI only in minutes, sometimes ahead just a few seconds. It was a proud moment that early night in the AP office when we all watched the final New Mexico prisoner's name sent out *before* UPI.

When I arrived at the AP bureau office one morning during the summer, the experienced staffer for whom I usually worked told me, excitement in his voice,

"There's been a riot at the state prison in Santa Fe,"

"What's happened?"

"The prisoners somehow got out of their cells, but they're still inside the walls. United Press is beating the hell out of us on this one." I'm pretty certain it was young Mel Mencher, later a Neiman Fellow and faculty member at Columbia University's Graduate School of Journalism, who was "beating the hell out of us." Mencher was the United Press man stationed in Santa Fe, 60 miles from Albuquerque. He didn't usually covering the penitentiary, but political news at the state's capitol.

"I've got to go to Santa Fe to help AP," my boss told me. "The rest of our guys are already there or headed that way. So, anyway, you're in charge of the bureau."

"In charge?"

"Yeah, just do the best you can to keep things going. You probably can figure it out. I'm off." And out the door he went. Stories about the riot soon moved over the wire, filed from the AP office near the *Santa Fe New Mexican*–where now famous novelist Tony Hillerman then was, or soon to be, editor. Besides furiously typing to keep up in Albuquerque with the usual 10-minute state radio wire splits, I answered numerous phone calls–the gist of many of which I didn't understand.

With no time to honor such requests of AP-member newspapers or radio stations, all I could say was, "Sorry, but everyone else is at the prison in Santa Fe covering the riot."

This seemed to do the trick. It was among my first lessons about a common bond between newspersons sharing breaking stories. Or perhaps those on the other end of the line thought back sympathetically to their days when they were like the greenhorn they were speaking to.

Journalists also had some bad habits. The AP bureau was located on the first floor, just below a shared newsroom. The *Journal* occupied the news, composing, and press rooms in the late afternoon and at night to produce its morning newspaper. The *Tribune* used those same facilities from early morning to late afternoon to turn out its afternoon edition.

On Saturdays, when I began working part-time on weekends for AP, the managing editor of the *Journal* would came downstairs to find out how the horses had fared in quarter-horse and other races at Ruidoso Downs in Ruidoso. Wood shavings covered the floor of the AP bureau and around my desk. Invariably, the managing editor on his way to check the wire would spit into the wood chips next to my desk.

I also learned - because AP received immediate results of horse racing and other sporting events - to pass on to newspapers or radio and TV stations, that staffers were never to reveal those outcomes to anyone on the phone. Get a result from AP on the phone and one could make a sure bet at a local bar, perhaps even with a bookie. Whether the managing editor of the *Journal* simply was curious about how the nags fared or used AP information for betting, I'll never know. I do know I resented his spitting habit.

For my several weekends at AP, before Sanky Trimble became bureau chief, another boss sat at that desk. He would arrive, sit down, place two packs of Camels on the desk, and begin making phone calls. He shouted into the telephone's mouthpiece resting on a pedestal about a foot above his desktop. A headpiece covered one ear, while one of those lighted Camels dangled from the side of his mouth.

Wow! That's the way a *real* newsman looks! So I bought a pack of Camels the next weekend and began puffing away, trying to let a smoking cigarette dangle from the side of my mouth. Camels were quite strong, and it became difficult not to cough, even though

I'd experimented smoking a pipe for a few months before that. The long and short of it was that I developed a bad habit which lasted about 10 years.

Only about a pack a day, but nevertheless a *very* bad habit. The medical jury remained out those days about the ill effects of smoking. One popular magazine article concluded there was evidence that the worst consequence might come from nicotine, which caused a slight jolt to the heart from each of the 20 cigarettes in a pack. There weren't warnings about the danger of second-hand smoke, which filled our AP and newspaper offices around the nation. Both men and women smoked, spurred on by print and radio advertising, free trial packs of cigarettes given out at colleges and universities, and observing movie stars continually lighting up on screen. It would be 10 years later, when lung cancer became generally linked to smoking, before I stopped.

Mary and I lived within walking distance of the AP office, in an apartment on Coal Avenue owned by her Uncle Marvin, her father's brother. We made at least a couple of mistakes as first-time renters. We bought a new refrigerator when the old one "died" and made a real mess attempting to sand the wood floor.

"Why didn't you let me know?" Marvin later asked. "I'd have taken care of those things for you." Live and learn.

Two significant letters arrived at our apartment. One was from the Sigma Chi employment service, in which established "brothers" helped in job searches for those just out of college. The first letter was from -and I certainly should but just can't recall his name -an advertising executive at the *Wall Street Journal* in New York who had recommended me for employment. It certainly was an act of favoritism, because the ad guy didn't know me at all. Yet perhaps not much more than what placement centers at Harvard, Yale and other Ivy League colleges provide by interaction with former and new graduates?

The second letter came from Clayton Sutton, the managing editor of the southwest edition of the *WSJ*, printed in Dallas. It offered to fly me there for a job interview. At least three motives spurred me aboard the airplane to Dallas. The first was that, after an inquiry with Bureau Chief Trimble, it still was "iffy" whether after the summer the AP budget would permit me to stay on full-time with the wire service.

The second was that Mary and I saw an opportunity to strike out on our own. I'm certain Mary wasn't as eager to leave as I was. She felt comfortable interacting with a large and extended family, including visits of relatives from such places as Aztec, New Mexico, her birthplace in 1934. By contrast, the five Hurley Odendahls had lived very much to themselves. I had spent a year in the Navy, and four more at colleges and universities, while Mary never had left the security of her home.

The third reason was that I dreamed of becoming a columnist for *The New York Times*. If really old, you might remember James "Scotty" Reston, that paper's Washington bureau chief and columnist. Well, I figured he'd have to retire pretty soon from the *Times*. When you're in your early 20s, anyone even a few years older appears ready for their dotage–so senile they must be on the verge of retiring or even dying.

Reston was born in Scotland, had moved to the United States with his family at the age of 10. In Dayton, he caddied for James Cox, an Ohio newspaper publisher and 1920 Democratic presidential candidate. Cox loaned Reston money to attend the University of Illinois, where he was graduated in the Hard Times year of 1933.

He began his journalistic career at the Cox newspaper in Springfield, Ohio, By 1939, Reston was working in the London bureau of *The New York Times*. In 1945, he won a Pulitzer Prize for National Telegraphic Reporting and another in 1957 for National Reporting. Reston continued covering stories and writing columns many years for *The New York Times*, not dying until 1995.

Here was my plan: The *Wall Street Journal* always made the various lists as one of the top-ten newspapers in the United States. If I took the Dallas WSJ job, I could move from there to that paper's main office in New York City. Once there, my brilliance as a journalist would shine so brightly that I'd be hired by *The New York Times*. And, once Scotty Reston retired, I'd take over his job as a columnist.

That brilliance certainly didn't shine through in my negotiations with Clay Sutton in Dallas. He offered me a job as a reporter, then asked, "How much is the Associated Press paying you?"

"Fifty-five dollars a week."

"That's what we could pay you."

"Okay." Not smart. A lateral move. I should have answered with something like,

"I don't think I could move here for less than 75 dollars a week."

I'm almost certain Sutton would have offered more than $55 (maybe $65 or $70). After my arrival for work in Dallas, I found out the other reporters were receiving more. Of course, some of them were much more experienced than I. For the first few months in Dallas, money wasn't our main problem because Mary found a job with Magnolia Oil Company. We were even able to eat out often on our two salaries.

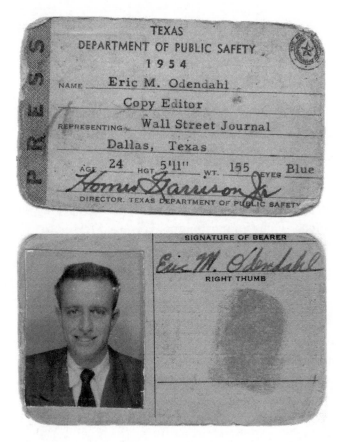

I went to Dallas two or three weeks before Mary completed her obligation as secretary to in the UNM Journalism Department. It became my task to find a furnished place for us to live in. Looking at only a few places, I rented the top floor of an old house next to a seafood restaurant. The place had three beds, would have served a good-sized family. I received lots of kidding about those beds, where undoubtedly our firstborn–Teresa Jean– was conceived.

Working for the *Journal* proved more difficult, and usually wasn't always that much fun or anything funny about it. That partly was because UNM journalism students studied toward a career with regular weekly and daily newspapers. Like how to write an obituary and take notes at a police or fire station. *The Wall Street Journal* was a different kind of animal.

Dow Jones & Company was founded in 1882 by reporters Charles Dow, Edward Jones and Charles Bergstresser. Jones converted the small *Customers' Afternoon Letter* into *The Wall Street Journal*, first published in 1889, and began delivery of the Dow Jones News Service via telegraph. The *Journal* featured the Jones 'Average', the first of several indexes of stock and bond prices on the New York Stock Exchange. In 1941, at the age of 32,

Barney Kilgore was appointed managing editor. Beginning with a circulation of 33,000, he built it to 1.1 million before his early death in 1969.

There were four editions of the *Journal* during my 18-month Dallas tour in 1953-54. The main edition was in New York City, with regional editions —not only in Dallas but also in Chicago and San Francisco. Principal emphasis remained to provide daily listing of total sales and up or down values posted by major stock and bond markets–plus various other tabular financial information such as farm futures.

Listings arrived by telephone from New York City to be printed in regional editions. They spun off all four presses in late afternoons Monday through Friday, in an era of dirty and noisy linotype machines, when composing rooms were referred to as "the back shop."

Producing a solid "line of type," the linotype was developed in 1886 by German-born American inventor Ottmar Mergenthaler. Before computers took over, linotypes were the mainstay in newspaper and other printing plants for almost a century. Operators sat in front of the huge machine's keyboard. From copy (typewritten stories or editorials) they manipulated the machines to set type from hot-lead. They could set up to about 16 lines of hottype per minute. Often less, especially with the smaller "agate" type used for stock market tables and sports — such as baseball and basketball box scores.

Most daily newspapers, especially smaller ones, found slow linotype capacity overfilled by setting local and national news stories, feature stories, editorials, plus sports, society, and other pages. Papers might run a few selected stocks, those considered of most interest to readers in their areas. Eastern afternoon papers, meeting deadlines just past the closing of the New York Stock Exchange, didn't have the time or linotype-machine capacity to publish more.

The goal of *The Wall Street Journal* was to publish almost *all* stock and bond market results and have them in readers' hands early the next morning. Linotypes were operated by a *WSJ*-invented, Rube Goldberg-like, apparatus. As stock and bond market reports arrived by wire in the New York and regional printing plants, the apparatus had boxes which automatically punched down linotype keys. This significantly speeded up the process.

Three main *WSJ* front page stories usually were set into type early each weekday, having been written days earlier by New York or regional reporters and carefully checked and edited in New York. Those edited front- page stories then were sent back by telephone wire to regional printing plants. The *WSJ* at that time rarely printed long, breaking news stories. The two main stories appearing on each side of the front page were called "leaders" and another in the middle the "A-head." Other news on the front pages appeared as snippets like "What's News" or "Washington Wire." A few fairly long stories were placed on inside pages if space was left over from the mainstay tabular material.

Reporters were judged by how many "leaders" (a term probably originated and perhaps still used by British newspapers) they were able to have published. Clayt Sutton, my boss as managing editor of the Dallas edition, held a record at the time. Earlier as a reporter he'd been able to have 25 "leaders" published in the *WSJ* in one year. That factors out to about one leader every two weeks, quite an accomplishment considering more than 100 reporters at the four editions competed for the limited leader- space of 10 per week.

Significant, but counting less toward reporters' advancement, were those A-head stories. To highlight my struggle as a *WSJ* reporter, consider this: In 18 months with the newspaper, I published no leader stories and just one A-head. It was a story about the copper mill and mining operations after a *WSJ*-paid trip back to Hurley and Santa Rita. And that A-head was put together by an experienced reporter and fine writer, Charlie Stabler, after Sutton suggested, "Would you help him out?"

WALL STREET JOURNA

Copyright 1954, by Dow Jones & Company, Inc.

SOUTHWEST EDITION   DALLAS—TUESDAY, JANUARY 19, 1954   Entered as Second Class at the Post Office, Dal

Labor Force Trends

Civilian Labor Force

Unemployed

Employed

1930   1940   1950 1953
Source: Bureau of Census

EMPLOYMENT averaged 61.9 million during 1953, about 600,000 above the 1952 average. Unemployment last year averaged 1.5 million, a dip of 200,000 from 1952. The civilian labor force during 1953 averaged 63.4 million.

New Mexican Town Atop Copper Deposit Gets Shoved Aside

* * *

Modern Methods of Mining Low-Grade Ore Makes for $1.5 Million Migration

By Eric M. Odendahl
Staff Reporter of The Wall Street Journal

SANTA RITA, N.M.—This sunbaked town, perched atop a rock "island" in the middle of an open pit copper mine, is being shoved aside to make way for progress.

New methods of recovering copper from low-grade ore which was once considered worthless have made the Santa Rita site a valuable source of the shiny red metal. So 37 families and their homes are being shifted a mile and a half to the northwest, opening the island to blasting powder and shovels.

Cost of the migration, an estimated $1.5 million, is being borne by Kennecott Copper Corp., owner of the mine and the town itself. Within relatively recent years this company and others in the industry have improved their techniques of extracting copper from ore to the point where it's sometimes now possible to use deposits which once were scorned. Present copper prices of around 30 cents a pound also have encouraged

My one and only WSJ A-head

148

Charlie's father had been financial editor of *The New York Herald-Tribune,* and my young colleague had worked for other papers before coming to Dallas. Contrast that to the *WSJ* being my first real newspaper job. At the *WSJ*, we reporters weren't feverishly pounding out on typewriters short radio "splits" like I did at the Associated Press in Albuquerque. In Dallas we attempted to report and write long, significant stories. It was a whole new ballgame for me.

Also consider that my parents never owned a share of stock or a speculative bond. They put most of their life's saving in very safe U.S. Government Bonds, which we called "war bonds," a habit they developed during World War II. I didn't even know the differences between stocks and bonds.

Charlie and his wife were good to Mary and me outside the office. Several times they invited us to join them at the Dallas Press Club, on the second story above the Pulley Bone Café. (Some of you non-Texan readers may refer to a chicken's pulley bone as a wishbone).

Another reporter invited us to a New Year's Eve party at a local nightclub.

"We'll each put in 10 bucks for the booze. I'll buy it and carry it over there. There's no service charge, so we'll just have to pay for the setups." Cokes sold in stores for 5 to 10 cents, so I figured the few dollars left in my wallet easily would carry us through the night. Surprise!!! I think the dance hall charged one dollar for each setup. There were Charlie and his wife, the other reporter and his wife, and Mary and I—a total of six bucks a setup!

I think we got there about 10 p.m., to dance and wait for midnight. It was embarrassing when I paid for one round, could only put in $4 when my turn came around again. I expect Mary and I deferred on drinks after that. Guess it serves me right for not prying more than $55 bucks a week out of Clayt Sutton when I took the job in the first place. Life was different in those days of few credit cards, and those only good at specific gasoline stations and some other places like for Sears Roebuck – but usable only at Sears.

As I wasn't yet capable of regularly whipping out leader stories, Clayt often had me rewriting quarterly earnings tables sent in by companies–usually small, Southwest region ones. Besides the usually correct table, they would claim something like, "Our earnings have gone up 25% percent."

When I first put that in an earnings-table story, Clayt read it before it was printed and rushed over, "That doesn't mean anything, Max, Maybe this company lost 90 percent of its earnings at this time last year. So, it moved up 25% percent in the last quarter. It's still

65% percent behind. Always look back a year or so, or better yet just present the figures and leave out any of their claims."

Another time a man came in and cornered me at my desk, showing me a paint-like roofing material he manufactured, contending it would make buildings much cooler in the summer. I thought that sounded pretty good and typed up a story. Again Clayt responded, "Plain white paint applied to a roof will make the building cooler, won't it?"

"I guess so."

"Well then, this isn't a story unless we have some sort of proof this guy's stuff would make the building even cooler than white paint. So, we won't run your story until you can confirm his stuff is superior." However, Clayt always was supportive. "Keep looking," he'd say, "and you'll come across a leader."

The *Journal* required reporters to be "self-starters," able to search out and write their own leader stories. It wasn't like at general circulation newspapers, where an editor assigned stories, might have barked, "Odendahl, get over to the DA's office and see how they're coming along with charges against that Jones guy, the one it sure looks like killed his wife with a hatchet."

One Friday, Clayt told me that on Monday I had an appointment with the president of the Katy (Missouri-Kansas-Texas) Railroad. What did I do about it that weekend? Nothing. On Monday morning, before heading over to meet the president of Katy, I remarked to Clayt, "What do you want me to ask him about?"

"Oh, I don't know, but piggy-backing is getting to be a pretty big thing with railroads now. Ask him about that." He went on to explain that piggy-backing was putting the trailers of semi-trucks onto railroad cars. Trailers could be taken off flatcars at other destinations, hooked up to another semi for local delivery of goods .

"Saves on paying drivers for long distance hauls," Clayt continued. "With so many of those long-haul drivers members of the Teamsters Union, that can become expensive." Thinking back, I believe Clayt was putting me on to a possible leader story, hoping the Katy president to be the first of many interviews with railway and union officials. When I arrived at the Katy office, a beaming public relations man was there to greet me, said the president was ready for the interview.

Ushered into the president's office, I found a bald-headed, rather plump man sitting behind a huge desk. He, of course, wore an expensive business suit. I had on a white shirt and tie and at least a sports coat, as did all *Journal* reporters, although ours were much less expensive. This was general practice among journalists, as one never knew when an assignment might come to cover a mayor, a senator, or even the President. In this case, it was the president of a railroad.

I shook his hand and he motioned me to sit down in a leather-covered chair in front of his desk. "It's always good to see a *Wall Street Journal* reporter," he commented. He went on to say that he had enjoyed sessions with another *WSJ* reporter. I had heard of the guy, knew he'd been a shining star (meaning he'd turned out several leaders and A-heads), who now was working in a better-paying public relations position with Shell Oil.

"Yep, he used to fire plenty of questions at me," the Katy president continued, and joked, "Some of them I had a difficult time answering." He paused, smiled, then added: "So, go ahead. Fire away."

I let go with my single question. "What about piggy-backing railroading?"

"What about it?" he answered. He'd turned the table on me. I had nothing more to ask, just stared at him. Finally the public relations man broke in and told the Katy president, "I'll take him to my office, sir, and see what we can do for him."

I could tell the Katy president was mildly disgusted. It was an embarrassing lesson I later passed on to students when teaching reporting. Before going for an interview, especially with an important person, one should research for story ideas and formulate a solid list of questions either on paper on in one's mind. In this case I had the whole weekend to do library research on the Missouri-Kansas-Texas Railroad and its president. I also should have looked over previous *Journal* Katy articles for follow-up questions and other story ideas. However, one lives and learns best by experience.

Another somewhat-famous reporting event, which over the years I've heard retold, occurred while I was at the Dallas *WSJ*. An attractive single woman with the first name of Beth had been hired as a reporter and graced a desk close to mine. One day Clayt called her into his office. She was assigned to have lunch with H. L. Hunt and do a feature story.

Haroldson Lafayette Hunt, born the same year as Dad, 1889, was an oil tycoon, known as the richest man in Dallas. During his life, he had three wives and 15 children. The character J.R. Ewing in the TV series, *Dallas,* was partially based on Hunt.

As Mary and I drove past Hunt's many acres of property around his mansion, an enlarged replica of George Washington's Mount Vernon, one of us remarked we'd never have enough money even to pay for the surrounding white, wood fence.

H.L was very-politically conservative and carried out a colorful public feud with oilman/philanthropist Sid Richardson in Fort Worth. Dallas and Fort Worth moved closer together as remaining open land filled with homes and businesses. The two constantly exchanged friendly barbs about which city provided the best Texas food and showcased premier museums and sporting attractions. When Beth planned to meet H.L at his Dallas office, she held high expectations of his escorting her for lunch someplace such as the swanky Petroleum Club.

As she sat down across from his desk, H.L. Hunt reached into a drawer and pulled out two brown bags. They were their lunches. When Beth arrived back at the Dallas *WSJ* she was irate about the lunch fiasco, and whether or not she'd been duped in a PR ploy for newspaper coverage. Could it have been routine daily behavior of tightwad H.L. Hunt?

Another time, Clayt sent me to visit the factory of an emerging Dallas firm.

"They're going on the Big Board (New York Stock Exchange). We already have all we need from them for a story, but the president wants to talk personally with a *Journal* reporter. We're doing this as a courtesy. You don't need to bring back a story, but take some notes anyway."

Again, a PR person ushered me into the president's office. I don't recall anyone then ever called a chief executive officer or CEO. I had a nice conversation with him, after which he told the PR person to guide me on a tour of the new plant. The PR person walked me by several offices, saying, "There are folks with master's degrees in there" or "folks with PhDs."

At one office he introduced me to a Dr. Ford, who held up a tiny glass object and explained, "This is a transistor. It was developed by Bell Laboratories and we are using it for our products here. Transistors are smaller, last much longer, and will soon replace all the vacuum tubes in electronic equipment."

I was familiar with vacuum tubes, those pesky little glass things which regularly had to be replaced in radios and early TV sets. You could buy vacuum tubes many places, even in drugstores. What you did when a radio or TV set went on the fritz was take any suspicious (usually blackened) vacuum tubes to a hardware or drugstore and re-plug them one-at-a-time into a waist-high testing machine.

The needle on a meter showed if tubes were defective, and you bought new ones, careful to make certain the plugs on the bottom matched the old ones. You went home, where you plugged new vacuum tubes into an ailing radio or TV. If you were lucky, you'd replaced the defective tubes and the radio or TV sprang to life. If not, you might go through the process of removing more tubes and again carrying them down to be checked out–or throw your hands in the air and carry the set to a shop for more-expensive repairs.

When I came home, I told Mary about my experiences at the Dallas plant. "How much is the stock selling for?" she asked, knowing we couldn't afford to buy any. "Five dollars a share," I replied.

The name of the company? Texas Instruments. The president of that company later became the mayor of Dallas. And, those with the means to purchase the company's stock at $5 per share increased their money many times over. Question: Would my advance knowledge constitute "inside trading." I doubt it, with the few stocks we might have afforded — even with borrowed money.

In the meantime, Mary had her own problem with Magnolia Oil. She was holding down a secretarial position in that company's tall Dallas building with a huge "Flying Red Horse" on top of it. I joked to folks that Mary's job was to clean up the manure from that red horse each day. She didn't appreciate my attempt at humor, especially as I repeated the gag over and over again, a habit I've never cured myself of.

Mary did have a good deal as far as benefits provided by Magnolia. A certain amount of her pay could be put into Magnolia stock and, after a year, the firm would begin to match each share. If I'd opted to stay with the *Journal,* and Mary could have with Magnolia, we probably would be living in retirement in a comfortable, air-conditioned home along one of the better streets in Dallas.

That was not to happen, because Mary could no longer work after she "showed" — when it became evident she was pregnant. The fact that she was married didn't seem to matter to those drawing up or instituting their plan. It wasn't any questionable policy of morality. I can't tell you the reasoning behind Magnolia's conduct, because countless women who "showed" worked physically harder at home than Mary at work, perhaps taking care of several children, or also adding a job to make ends meet. Some performed fairly heavy labor in outside-the-home jobs.

Mary to this day doesn't know the exact reason Magnolia let her go after she "showed" at five months pregnant. I figure it was because she worked in a male-dominated company, one in which males didn't want to have females around they saw as becoming less beautiful, or contend with what they considered a situation which might result in their idea of profound mood changes. Jobs for married women who became pregnant at many other firms suddenly became temporary ones.

Not only did Mary find herself jobless but, because she was laid off four months before our baby was born, she also received no paid maternity leave. Such leaves generally were to come many years later. What was questioned was Mary's station in life as a woman. The common view was that she and other new mothers should stay at home and take care of their babies, a calamity faced by unmarried mothers earning their living with no outside resources. I don't recall ever hearing the term "single mother" at that time. As Mary earned more than my $55 a week, this turn of events cut our income by more than half. I needed to tighten my belt. Mary literally couldn't do that because her waist was getting larger. We became more frugal.

It was a good time for Mary's mother to visit. The plan was for the three of us to go east by bus to Shreveport, Louisiana, to visit with Lula Mae's aunts. We were packed and ready to go one morning when Lula Mae went into the kitchen to get a cup of coffee. She let out a small scream as a large rat ran out of a cupboard door and across her slippered feet. This didn't do much to make her believe her son-in-law had chosen an acceptable place for her daughter to live.

Mary and I knew the rats were there, but this was the first one we'd seen. We'd heard them at night running up and down inside the walls and above the ceiling. As the house was next to a popular seafood restaurant, we figured the rats originally arrived from there, maybe before that from some ship by way of a box or container of fish. Maybe even part of a sort of romantic seafaring story? Rats out of sight, out of mind. Now out of sight no longer?

Lula Mae shocked us by mentioning that rats would eat, or certainly were capable of seriously biting, babies in their cribs. It was an easy decision to look for a new place to live before our baby was born.

The trip to Shreveport was a fun one. Almost all of Lula Mae's aunts, sisters of her mother, for whom my Mary was a namesake, had big butts. Viewing big butts was nothing new for me, but the behavior of the cousins and "kissing cousins" was. They gave you a peck on the cheek and a tight hug, their breasts packed tightly against your chest. College girls in New Mexico never hugged me like that. Southern hospitality took on a new meaning.

Their wonderful home-cooked food reminded me of Grandma Mary's and Lula Mae's. Before we left Albuquerque and on several visits after that, Lula Mae's mother would lay out a spread of vittles which filled the dinner table. Like daughter Lula Mae, Grandma Mary would proclaim, "It's just potluck. You'll have to get by with it." Potluck might mean ham, a platter of fried chicken, and roast beef (all on the table at once). Surrounding that would be bowls of mashed potatoes, vegetables, and chicken gravy. I suppose usually there was a salad, but certainly a dessert–maybe a couple of kinds of pie or a cake with butter frosting. Often both.

I just kept saying, "Thank you ma'am" as the food kept passed around dinner tables in Albuquerque or Shreveport. Calories were no problem for me. I ate until I could eat no more. Concern about "low-fat" diets would come years later.

One night, one of Lula Mae's male relatives —either nephew, cousin — took us to a nightclub in Bossier City, just east of Shreveport. Our host paid for our drinks. While very jovial, he sternly warned us not to go into the basement below the nightclub. Apparently illegal gambling went on down there, despite the fact that during the evening our host introduced us to a couple of Bossier City's plainclothes police officers.

A pregnant Mary tired a bit after midnight. She and several others were driven home, while Lula Mae and I remained with our host, and two or three of those pretty kissing cousins/nephews, and their husbands. The finale before the nightclub closed was a dance by a voluptuous woman holding two lighted candles, dripping wax on herself. Her body appeared heavily oiled but, even so, I wondered if the hot wax might be painful.

Her grand finale came naked when she placed one of the burning candles upright on the dance floor, gyrating around it. Finally, she slowly sat her nude body down on the burning candle–quite a novel way to snuff one out. When at the breakfast table the next morning, I tried in the least graphic terms possible to describe the candle snuffing to Mary. "Law zee," Lula Mae kept saying over and over again, not adding anything to my story. "I'm glad I wasn't there to see that," Mary stiffly retorted.

I don't recall Lula Mae adding anything to her "law zees." I suspect she was nearly as fascinated by the culmination of that dance as I. It's difficult for me to use good-enough judgment about when to stop, once I begin telling stories, so I probably added, "I saw a woman smoke a cigarette like that."

I think Sonny Kennedy, George Hailer, Dutch Robertson and I were among those at the Chino Buffet north of Hurley the night a fellow brought a not-especially attractive woman into the bar. He collected $5 from each of us for the strip show, which began in a room adjoining the bar. He promised a special ending.

In dimmed light the woman went through the usual slow routine of a stripper removing all her clothes. Then she lit a cigarette and, as the lights dimmed more until her nude body became a silhouette, spread her legs wide apart. The cigarette glowed as she inserted the mouth end into herself. The lights were turned almost completely out, and for several minutes the cigarette intermittently glowed bright and softer.

I don't know whether she actually puffed in such a manner, or if she added some gimmick to the cigarette after it became quite dark. At any rate, about 20 guys had forked over $5 apiece to provide the woman with $100 for a few minutes' light work in the dark. We

Three Musketeers and maybe Dutch Robertson left the Chino Buffet and headed over to Vi's Drive-In three miles away at Bayard for our usual cheeseburgers and fries. I wouldn't be surprised if, meanwhile in Chino Buffet's parking lot, that woman wasn't gathering considerably more money by providing expensive trysts for a few guys in the back seat of her car.

Soon after Mary's mother had returned to Albuquerque, we told our Dallas landlords, an older woman and her daughter, that we were moving because of what rats might do to a tiny baby. The women didn't own up to the presence of rats. Maybe it was the prospect of a baby bawling in the apartment above them, but they didn't argue about us leaving. Later, they probably also were relieved that we didn't report the rats to health authorities–as we should have.

Mary had found a much nicer place to live at a brick apartment house on a street corner. No rats, but its drawback was a street-car line with tracks which creaked as the heavy vehicles moved slowly around the corner every 10 minutes or so. Nevertheless, after a few days and nights, we became used to the loud creaking.

A couple lived in the apartment upstairs. The woman became quite friendly with the jobless Mary. Her husband's given name was T.C., or some other initials. He was a male chauvinist. As an example, one night the three of us were watching a situation comedy on the upstairs TV. T.C. came home, wanted to see a boxing match. He switched the TV to the match and sat down in his favorite chair. He did offer us a beer. I think he was oblivious to his rude behavior.

One day the upstairs couple drove us to a small airport. T.C. rented an ancient bi-plane (two wings–one under the other) and convinced me to climb into the rear cockpit. Once in the air he began making loops with the plane, stalling it, stuff like that.

He earlier had said, "I haven't been up in a plane for a while. I need to keep up with my flying."

It *was* fun riding along for flying stunts with the Red Baron at the controls, not so when T.C. attempted to land. On his first try, T.C. bounced the plane hard on the runway, pulled back on the joystick, lifted us off and we flew around in a circle for his next landing attempt. This one was successful. While I was wobbly legged getting out of the plane, a very pregnant Mary was quite agitated. "I thought both of you were going to be killed when that plane bounced on the runway. I don't want to be a widow"

T.C. just laughed at her. I thought to myself, "She's right. What a stupid thing for a guy who's going to be a father any day now to do." We met another couple that day and the guy gave Mary a ride in his little, MG roadster. I don't think the MG made much more than

60 miles an hour, but sitting so close to the ground with the wind blowing through her hair, Mary had a speedy feeling.

One afternoon soon after that she and I walked (more likely rode the streetcar which stopped at our place) to one of our favorite cheapo eating spots. For $1.50, you received a plastic basket filled with a quarter of a delicious fried chicken, French fries, and salad. We were at a children's playground, either eating or finishing our chicken baskets, when Mary held her large belly in both hands and quietly said, "Uh, oh!"

So we went home, gathered what was necessary, and T.C. drove us to Baylor Hospital. It was confirmed that our baby was ready to make his or her appearance. (As far as I know, you couldn't determine a baby's gender ahead of time then. At least we didn't.) It would be a long haul for Mary, lying in a bed in a hall outside the hospital's delivery room.

Every few minutes a man or woman in a white frock came by, pulled the sheet off Mary's legs. She raised her knees; they spread apart her legs, and took a look. "Not quite yet," they'd say, checking her against a chart on the wall next to her bed which looked like a target, laid out in centimeters. When a woman's centimeters were large enough to match the proper size on the chart, she'd be transferred to a gurney and rolled into the delivery room.

"Any weirdo could wander around this hall," I remarked, "raising the sheets on women to take a looksee." Mary gave me a glance of derision, almost as disdainful as that which our children later came to call, "The Look."

It was early the next morning, June 6, 1954 before Mary matched the centimeter chart, and by that time she felt an urgent need to go to the bathroom. The delivery-room attendants paid no heed as they rolled her away–perhaps figuring her need was only the pressure of the baby. I was sent to a waiting room. In about two hours, a doctor appeared and said, "Mr. Odendahl, you have a baby daughter." I nervously asked if all the fingers, "stuff like that" were okay, and he grinned and said, "Yes. She's fine."

The doctor was the gynecologist who had been leading Mary through her pregnancy. The thing is, I never saw him before she was wheeled into the delivery room and Mary, before she was put partly under, found only an intern and nurses in that room. We think the intern probably delivered the baby, and perhaps our doctor showed up during the final minutes. "I guess interns have to learn how to do it on their own," I later told Mary. We both agreed it was fortunate there were no complications.

We had decided to name the baby, if it was a girl, Teresa Jean. The name honored Mary's sweet Aunt Teresa, then living in Denver, and also kept up the tradition of having a Teresa for generations in my Grandmother Robinson's family. Middle-name Jean was for

Mary's older sister Jean, and also mine —the Jeanie who died in Alberta shortly after her birth. And, of course, for my Mom, Jean.

I had taken a look at our daughter before being allowed to visit Mary in her hospital room. "What does she look like?"

"Beautiful," I replied, "except for her chin. She doesn't seem to have much of a chin."

"Oh no!!!"

A dumb remark, especially to a new mother weak from hours of ordeal delivering her baby. Our healthy daughter, whom we called Terry, had nothing wrong with her chin. After Terry's early-morning birth, I'd gone home to get some sleep. Before sleeping, I phoned the *WSJ* office about the good news. The next day, after I arrived at the office, "Red," the fellow in charge of "making up" (putting together) the Dallas edition of the newspaper chided me, "Guys here don't usually take off a day just because their wives have a baby."

Sure surprised me, because if measured by the quantity of my work, the Southwest Edition of the *Wall Street Journal* didn't require my presence in order to be published. Bringing a baby home from the hospital constitutes an extreme change in the lifestyle of a couple – especially those as young and naive as we were, and undoubtedly for those older and wiser, too. Mary, who stayed alone at home for many months, found her life revitalized with the responsibilities of caring for Terry.

I began to feel no longer "numero uno" in Mary's life, now that I must share her love with Terry. Most men, I believe with no firm data to back me up, have difficulty facing up to this turn of events, even though their love also pours out to that little guy or gal each time those tiny fingers wrap around one of theirs.

Meanwhile at work, the job I really began to aspire for was Red's. Because of my lack of performance as a "self-starter" reporter, Clayt Sutton had assigned me to the copy desk. Others at another copy desk far away in New York wrote the headlines and edited front-page and most inside *WSJ* stories, automatically set into type at regional editions. We on the Dallas copy desk occasionally wrote headlines for stories only published in the Southwest Edition. It amazed me how proficient those on the New York copy desk were in conjuring up heads for leader and A-head stories–pieces often pretty dull once past the first three or four paragraphs.

Those first "grafs," according to the *Journal* writing formula at that time, might have read:

"MULESHOE, TEXAS–A farmer stands forlornly looking over a barbed wire fence at the parched acres of his small spread.

"Joe Zilch is among thousands of Texas farmers experiencing the worst drought since...."

As I recall, in this particular case, the dateline–place of origin–for the drought leader or A-head had been sent to New York as originating from another small Texas town. A copy editor in the Big City became captivated by "Muleshoe" mentioned somewhere in the story, hence the dateline change.

"I guess it doesn't matter all that much," Clayt said, laughing about the dateline change for "our" story. "There must be some farmer 'forlornly looking over a barbed-wire fence' somewhere near Muleshoe, too." At any rate, we on the *WSJ* Dallas copy desk might write for a regional story a jazzy headline like,

"Cotton Prices Rise During Fall Quarter"

We didn't conjure up non-business-newspaper heads such as,

"Wife Shoots Husband to Death After Finding Lipstick on Collar

Our job mainly involved checking grammar, spelling, and facts of stories before they were sent to "the backshop" to be set into type for the Southwest Edition, and to proofread the completed paper before it ran off the presses. These were very important tasks, as I found out to my chagrin.

One Friday an advertising salesman came by and showed me the front page of the day-before *Journal.* In a summary of world news events were a couple of paragraphs explaining how President Dwight D. Eisenhower had been forced to cancel a trip to Japan, because of anti-American rioting there. The President has gotten as far as, I think, Guam when advised it would be too dangerous to continue on to Japan.

Part of one sentence in print in the Dallas edition read something like: "*President Eisenhower was forced to delay his trip to the Fart East because....."*

The ad guy thought that fart part really funny. No way. I immediately knew it was not funny and not good, especially because I'd proofread the front page the day before. Apparently, Clayt didn't find out about the error until after we'd all gone home. The next morning, I received a call from him about an emergency Saturday meeting of the whole editorial staff at the *Journal* office.

"This is the worst mistake I've seen since working on the *Journal* for 19 years," Clayt began as we all stood in his office that Saturday. It could have been another figure than

19, but I felt that Fart would blow me out of a job. Clayt had retrieved the proof sheets and there it was on the sheet containing the Fart: A big "OK" with my initials after it.

Clayt didn't fire me, but did sternly admonish the staff to be more careful. I think that, despite their inconvenience of coming in on a Saturday, most of the gang felt sorry for me and my honest mistake, but I had the idea Red was unsympathetic. Somehow, I also felt my days at the *Journal* might be numbered.

Once or twice Red asked me to join him for some small task in the backshop. He was quite proficient at putting the paper together under deadline pressure. A light bulb went on in my head. Working under such creative pressure seemed like fun. Makeup deadlines at the *WSJ* were only moderately stressful. For example, we didn't cover breaking Dallas news stories requiring quickly redoing the whole front page's layout, moving and/or eliminating other stories and pictures. At that time, there were no front-page pictures as part of the stodgy, everyday-the-same vertical makeup recognized each morning by readers of the *Journal*.

My thought: with a little training, I could do what Red did. Fat chance! There was no indication of Red's promotion to New York or any plans of his to move to another newspaper. Meanwhile, Mary's mother and younger sister Phyllis arrived in Dallas for a short visit to help with Terry. Boy, was I glad to see them! My sister Dorothy also spent some time aiding Mary and the baby. After that, Mary had the tough job of any mother caring for a new baby while her husband is at work.

Our financial situation was in the pits, so low that we moved to a very small wood-frame apartment in an alley behind a large house on one of the better streets of Dallas. African-American servants lived in other such apartments along the alley, frequently passing back and forth by our place. It was the closest I'd ever lived to these folks, their skin darker than Mexican-Americans I'd gone to school with. We exchanged friendly smiles and "Hello" or "Nice day, isn't it" but never had long talks or became friends with any of them. Different times, yes, but prejudice, ignorance and fear made for a sad state of affairs. We probably missed an opportunity to learn more about another culture and the plight of the poor.

After I went to work the day we moved in, Mary, looking at our scattered belongings in that tiny apartment while holding a tiny baby in her arms, was moved to tears. No air conditioning, the only moving air on hot and humid Dallas nights coming from a 6-inch fan directed into Terry's crib. Mary became determined to move "back home"–somewhere (anywhere) in New Mexico.

We took a vacation trip to Albuquerque in our first car, a white, four-door, 1941 Chevrolet, advertised in the *Dallas Morning News* for $120. The "older guy" selling the car, after I'd looked it over at his house one evening and agreed to buy it, made me do this:

We met in a Dallas bank the next day. He coaxed a bank clerk to be a witness while I counted out $120. He signed the "pink slip". He took the cash, handed the keys over to me, pointed to the car at the curb, wished me the best, and left the bank.

Mary had a cousin in Weatherford whom we'd gotten to know. Dorsey Johnson suffered from birth defects, had some difficulty talking while moving his mouth in a strange way, and walked with a limp. He also was one of the finest human beings I've ever met in my life.

For a week, not too long before Terry arrived on the scene, Mary had gone to Weatherford to care for Dorsey's father – Uncle John, a retired Methodist preacher and brother of her Methodist minister grandfather on the Johnson side of the family. I arrived to spend the next weekend when Aunt Emma and Dorsey returned. Aunt Emma rewarded us with wonderful home-cooked meals, including her to-die-for breakfast biscuits.

Another time at Dorsey's, Uncle Jessie —also a former Methodist preacher and another brother of Mary's grandfather, himself a Methodist preacher–and Alf Utton of Aztec, New Mexico, were all seated with us at the breakfast table.

Now, Aunt Emma's biscuits had convinced me hers were the best I'd ever eaten. They came hot out of her oven and she pressed them on you. I wouldn't be surprised if I didn't eat five or six at a breakfast sitting, along with eggs, and either ham, sausage, bacon– probably also some grits. Aunt Emma, like my Mary's Grandma Mary, beamed wider the more you ate. A young buck like me had no problem putting away a scandalous amount of food.

Before we ate at that particular breakfast, Uncle John began a long blessing of the food. After he finished, Uncle Jess picked up on his own extended blessing. This was followed by a few of Alf's words thanking the Good Lord for our well-being as well as for the food piled on the table. Trouble was – that food was getting cold. With bowed head, my eyes watched a platter of those exquisite-tasting biscuits losing their prime.

Not only did he make us a part of his family, but also Dorsey did things like take us to a large arena in either Dallas or Fort Worth for a fabulous ice show. Just before Terry was born, he found a puppy for Mary–which we called Suzie. The puppy, from a litter of cocker spaniels, turned out to be a white fox terrier with black spots. Its tail had been cut off because that was the fate of cocker spaniel puppies.

When we proudly brought our '41 Chevy to Weatherford for Dorsey to see, he learned we planned to drive it to Albuquerque. Quite concerned, he had me "motor" to a local "shade tree" mechanic's place. The mechanic tuned the engine, also took down the oil pan, tightening the connecting rods.

Noticing lots of sludge at the bottom of the oil pan, the mechanic poured some gasoline in it and set the whole works afire. Burning the sludge out of the pan, the fire also exposed and cleaned a pretty-well-clogged wire oil strainer. Somehow, I don't think we would have made it to Albuquerque and back with all that sludge moving through that engine.

I didn't have enough money in my pocket to pay the mechanic after he'd put the screws and a new gasket on the oil pan, reattached it to the block, and filled the engine with clean oil. "Don't worry about it," Dorsey laughed, waving me away with his hand. "I planned to pay for this work for you kids. I just worried this car with you, Mary and the baby would break down along the road. Even now, I'm not so sure about it."

At any rate, we headed for Albuquerque on a Friday after I got off work at the *Journal*. Gasoline sold in Dallas for 25 cents a gallon, and I figured we could make the round trip on the scant amount of money we'd saved. Poor figuring. When we crossed over the border into New Mexico, we noticed the price of gasoline higher – maybe 35 cents a gallon. It also seemed café food became higher-priced along the way. After spending several days sponging off Mary's folks, eating for nothing at their table, my worried wife declared, "I'm going to have to borrow $10 from Daddy for gasoline to get us back to Dallas."

"Don't do that," I almost shouted.

"Why not?"

"Well, when I married you I said I'd take care of you and that's what I plan to do. I can't be a part of borrowing money from your dad."

"What are you going to do? We don't have enough money to make it home."

"I saw a sign on Central Avenue, there along Route 66, offering white gasoline for 25 cents a gallon. We have enough money to fill up a tank on that to get us to Hatch. Then, I'll borrow $10 from my dad and we can make it home on that."

Mary laughed. "What's the difference from borrowing money from my daddy and yours?"

"Lots. Borrowing from my own family isn't the same as having to take a handout from yours."

Mary just shook her head. As we left for Hatch, her mother, fortunately not privy to our conversation, handed us what she called a "Care Package" of sandwiches and potato salad to eat along the way. I stopped to fill the Chevy with white gasoline at that "Get Your Kicks on Route 66" station. Problem was, white gas didn't have much of a kick, was sold mainly for use in camp stoves and lanterns.

As a boy in Hurley, we'd used a fancy cook-stove which burned white gas. Although white gas burns a fine, hot blue flame, it provides less octane than required for an automobile engine. The two-lane road between Albuquerque and Hatch (now four-lane I-25) snaked through several canyons. The Chevy clicked right along on the white gasoline on the flat stretches and going down into the canyons. Pulling itself and the three of us out of the canyons was another matter.

There developed a heavy ping, almost a knock as the car burning white gas labored out of the first canyon. I pushed the pedal to the floor going down into the next canyon (we're talking here of a top speed of about 70 with old tires and a baby in the car). Even making runs for it, several times the car barely pinged its way out of a canyon. We made it to Hatch without obvious damage to the car.

Mom and Dad had moved to Hatch from Hurley in 1954 after he retired October 1 at age 65 from the Chino Mines Division of Kennecott Copper Corporation. Moving from Hayden. Arizona, after Alan was born May 1 of that year, Dad first began work in Hurley for the Nevada Consolidated Copper in November of 1928,. As previously written, our family lived in Jerome, Arizona for 17 months during "Hard Times" of 1935-36, where Dad worked as a machinist for Phelps Dodge Corporation. We moved back to Hurley in 1936.

"On behalf of the company," Chino Mines Division general manager W.H. Goodrich wrote Dad, "I wish to take this opportunity to express our appreciation for your long and faithful service. This enterprise could not have continued to prosper without the services of men like yourself, whose abilities, devotion to duty and integrity were of the highest. My sincere wish is that you will continue to enjoy many years of happiness."

Mr. Goodrich had given me a ride several times while in high school when I occasionally hitchhiked to Silver City. He always seemed like an amiable man.

"I know there is always some emotion," wrote assistant general manager F.C. (Cooper) Green of the Utah Copper Division from Salt Lake City, "with leaving a job in which you have been happy a good may years...I notice also that you are building a home in Hatch and wondering if you have some farming ground with which to keep busy....In addition to my sincere congratulations over many years of work well done, I personally add my own thanks for the help you gave me while we worked together...Good luck and best regards to Mrs. Odendahl"

Green was a longtime superintendent of the mill and smelter at Hurley before moving to a better position with Kennecott in Utah. I don't think Dad ever was all that happy about his job, for years looked forward to retiring. Mom and Dad also did not build a house at Hatch, but bought one which they turned into a nice home.

Cooper Green was the father of Derrick (Bud) Green, who when on vacation from the University of New Mexico, occasionally drank beer with Sonny Kennedy, George Hailer, and me at the Chino Buffett. Bud also was one of the "Hurley boys" who attracted me to Sigma Chi at UNM.

Mary and I and the baby stayed in Hatch for a few days. I "borrowed" enough money from either Dad or Mom for us to drive home to Dallas on regular gasoline.

CHAPTER 10 – SPORTS EDITOR? SPORTS WRITER?

The editor at the independent *Albuquerque Journal* returned to our tiny Dallas apartment my letter applying for a reporter's position. He scribbled on the bottom a brief, "Thanks, But No Thanks," note. Later, while on that trip to the Duke City visiting Mary's parents, I made a visit to the office of the editor of the Scripps-Howard *Albuquerque Tribune.*

"Have you ever covered city hall, the police station, the sheriff's office? An election?"

"No."

"I have a lot of respect for the *Wall Street Journal,* and you probably learned something about being a writer, but your experience there wouldn't help us at all. Besides, I don't have any openings for a beginning reporter."

I wondered if he mistakenly thought I was making more money at the *WSJ* than he could match at the *Tribune.* He certainly was correct about my being a greenhorn about the workings of and - reporting for - a regular newspaper.

Our ticket out of that small, hot Dallas apartment arrived as a Christmas present in the form of a letter from Don Wright, editor of the *Daily Record* in Roswell. He offered me a job as "sports writer". "I don't know all that much about sports, but it's basketball season," I told Mary, "and I covered a few games for the *Daily Lobo* at UNM. I'll get to know the sports editor and he'll help get me straightened out by the time baseball season rolls around in the spring."

Ah, the confidence of youth. It didn't take long after Mary and I talked it over for me to telephone Wright, and accept the job. When I told Clayt Sutton I was leaving the *Journal,* he seemed surprised. "It takes quite a while to get the hang of how we work here. But, I can see you've made up your mind. Was it money? Guess I should have given you a raise. I just was too busy to think about it." I told him that didn't matter; couldn't tell whether he actually would have preferred for me to stay with the *Journal* or felt somewhat relieved to see me leave.

Mary and baby Terry went home to Albuquerque for a few days, must have been by bus. Our white, 1941 Chevy four-door rolled into Roswell with me alone at the wheel on a Friday afternoon just after New Year's 1955. After having spent about a year and a half with the *Wall Street Journal,* I immediately went to the *Daily Record* office to check in with Mr. Wright. (It would be a week or two before I would call him Don.) A thin, hawk-nosed man with kind eyes, Wright probably was in his late 60s.

"Good to meet you. First off, what can we do to get you settled?"

"My wife and I have a little baby. We'll need to rent a house."

"We can help you with that. But first, take the weekend and see if you can find one on your own. I'd have liked to have gotten you started at work tomorrow, but we'll get by until Monday."

"Where is the sports editor? I'd like to meet him."

"Sports editor? Sports writer?" Wright smiled as he answered with a shrug. "All the same thing here. You're it now."

"Oh," I silently muttered, thinking about a wife soon on her way to Roswell with six-month-old Terry. I'd severed ties with the *WSJ*. Wright was correct. This was *it* now. "What time do you want me to come in on Monday?"

"Six in the morning. Let me give you a sort of outline of what you'll be doing on your job here."

Wright pointed to the Associated Press teletype machine which delivered national and state sports stories. He explained about the two sports pages I would make up early each morning for Monday through Friday afternoon editions of the *Record*. How I'd work late Saturday on the Sunday morning edition's sports pages.[2]

With only two hours to complete all the makeup work of the sports pages on weekdays, by an 8 a.m. deadline, Wright said the rest of my time would be spent covering local sports at two high schools: the public Roswell High and the Roman Catholic St. Peter's. In addition, I'd attend some games at New Mexico Military Institute, a junior college, and cover the Class C Roswell Rockets during the baseball season. Saying nothing, I simply felt overwhelmed.

"Have you had much experience with making up pages?" he asked.

---

[2] Producing newspaper pages in the 1950s meant the backshop working by hand with solid lead columns of type and clamping them together into heavy "chases." I would soon learn that my part of "making up" the Record involved selecting which national and state sports stories to be run along with my local ones, writing headlines for all of these, plus composing captions for selected photographs and illustrations–referred to as "art." All this was penciled on "dummies," layout sheets to guide union workers in the composing room placing columns and pictures/illustrations around advertisements. Those layout pages already had ads dummied in before we in the newsroom received them.

"A little," quite a bit of a fib because casually fooling around with sports pages on the *Daily Lobo* in college and occasionally helping and watching "Red" put together the Dallas *WSJ* hardly qualified as very much makeup experience.

Wright must have seen through me, as he said, "Al Stubbs can help you with that." He motioned for Stubbs to come over and shake my hand, the beginning of a lifelong friendship.

Al also was a thin man. (My, how thin and flat-bellied most of us young men were in those days.) He stood taller, probably about 6'2", had a broad grin on his face as he looked down at me through horn-rimmed eyeglasses. His title was news editor, and/or city editor. Whatever, as I was to find working for a small newspaper meant having to pitch in to do any job in the event of vacations or illnesses.

Stubbs helped Wright assign stories to the paper's two reporters. Al also made up all the newspaper's pages besides sports and "society," or those carrying Don Wright's editorials and local letters-to-the-editor and nationally syndicated columns and others. Wright edited those pages himself and they usually were set into type a day ahead of publication.

"Oh yeah, Max," Wright said as the three of us stood together, "you'll also be writing a sports column three times a week. It's called 'Riding Herd on Sports'." I thought to myself, "Riding Herd about what? Good Lord." To say that I was overwhelmed was becoming an understatement.

"See you Monday."

"Yes sir, Mr. Wright." When I arrived on the job just before 6 a.m. that first Monday, Al Stubbs saved my bacon (as he did many times during my tenure at the *Record*). Noticing how bewildered I was, he began ripping apart copy piled up behind the Associated Press teletype and placed national and state sports stories on my desk.[3]

You wrote a headline for an Associated Press wire story, then took a corresponding teletypesetter tape off a hook, and on that tape wrote the first word of the head and its size. Then you carried those tapes to the backshop (composing room).

Operators in the backshop fed the tapes into teletypesetters, black boxes attached to linotype machines.

---

[3] Each story had a number on it, and a Teletypesetter tape machine attached to the Teletype spewed out tape to go with each story. You read numbers on the tape which coincided with numbers on stories being typed out of the Teletype machine. Tape was torn apart and hung in numerical order on a row of sharp nails.

This system, somewhat similar to the mechanism which actually punched linotype keys at the *Wall Street Journal*, allowed one *Roswell Record* operator to feed tapes to two or more linotypes at the same time. Besides faster typesetting, it also cut down the payroll from the days when each linotype required an operator.

Local, typewritten stories were handed over a counter through a cubby hole to the back shop, where two women spent their shift converting them into tapes for feeding into the teletypesetters. Stubbs pointed to the two layout (dummy) sheets for the sports pages, "If you'll start writing some heads," he said, "I'll begin making up your pages."

Well, now, I'd written no headlines for Associated Press, only a few for *Daily Lobo* sports stories during my college days at UNM, and a very few for the *Wall Street Journal*. We did learn at UNM that a capital W or M, for example, required more space in a headline than a capital I. You counted it out–with the larger the head size the fewer counts you had to work with.

Using a pencil, I began to write and carefully count them. I did this for a couple of days or more while Stubbs put together the sports pages. Finally, he gently said,

"You can do it faster, Max, if you'd write those heads on the typewriter."[4]

(I have only an inkling about how one writes headlines and edits stories on a modern newspaper's computer. Or, how to make-up put-together newspaper pages on the new 'contraptions'. Those ink-wretched days have passed me by. Newsmen and newswomen no longer are rubbing their hands over leaded pages covered with ink as they help guide the composing room where to place stories.)

Al Stubbs was a patient, gentle man and a good teacher. With his ability to get along with people, he'd have been very successful teaching print journalism at a college or university. I think he might have been unhappy not chasing down stories and feeling the thrill of working under pressure, especially handling fast-breaking news.

How did the makeup of sports pages go in those first few days after Stubbs hesitantly left me to my own devices? Fairly well, at least in my view–probably not his or Don Wright's. It took several days before I could put those two sports pages together in two hours. I copied dummies of pages previous sports editors had laid out back in issues of the *Record.* If there were a three-column and a two-column picture with, say, three big sports

---

[4] He explained how, if you'd leave a bit of room, most heads will average out about right if the number of letters one types equals the count one is allowed for a certain size headline. It wasn't writing headlines for perfection to fill the columns, but it was necessarily faster. Head counts vary according to the "fonts" (type style) used by each newspaper. You simply have to memorize counts after a while.

stories, I'd find an old issue with two pics and three stories and lay my page out almost exactly the same.

That three-time weekly "Riding Herd on Sports" local column proved to be the highest hurdle. Although a fairly regular, yet hardly fanatical, reader of sports pages, I'd never looked at athletics in much of an analytical way. So, what did I do? I became a copycat again until I felt my feet on the ground. The *Record* received "exchanges," trading complimentary copies of our paper for freebies of other newspapers from around New Mexico. If the sports editor of the *Albuquerque Journal*, say, was asking the Albuquerque High School basketball coach some questions for his columns , I'd copy those down.

Then I'd go by Roswell High or St. Peter's High and ask their basketball coaches the same questions. Sometimes the answers would be identical to those in Albuquerque; often they would be quite different. Didn't matter. Fodder for "Riding Herd on Sports." Of course, after a while, I devised my own questions and came up with original ideas for the column.

Undoubtedly from the beginning, and as time flew by, I didn't fool many readers. A man named John Rush of Dexter, a town just south of Roswell on the highway leading to Artesia and on to Carlsbad with its famous caverns, wrote:

"Your small bulletin on the Bronco game indicates what a really small person you are. [The Broncos Rush referred to was the football team of New Mexico Military Institute.]

"Putting the blame on the coaches for not doing your job for you. If you were worth a nickel you could have gotten the information – if in no other way you could have listened to the radio.

"Did you know that the Michigan-Michigan State game was the leading game in the nation. Where is the coverage?

"We understand your entire sport background is the Wall Street Journal and we believe it."

Among other shortcomings, I'd somehow failed to put in that all-Michigan game, must have neglected or screwed up in some manner reporting on that NMMI game, and according to the sports fan wrote unfairly about its coaches. Attempting to be fair, I led off one of my "Riding Herd on Sports" columns with Mr. Rush's complete letter.

The *Record*, despite limited space compared to large daily newspapers, attempted to squeeze in stories every Sunday about Saturday games involving the nation's top 10 Associated Press college teams, along with those in New Mexico. With Roswell in the southeast corner of the state adjoining Texas, of more interest for many transplanted Texans and/or Lone Star State college alumni were games involving teams in the

Southwest Conference such as the University of Texas, Southern Methodist, Baylor, Rice, and Texas A&M.

A phenomenon of the mid-1950s was the rapid growth of television viewing, as more and more homes acquired their first black-and-white sets with small screens. This meant that while I was working Saturday nights putting together the *Record's* sports pages, TV viewers actually were watching many of those games. It took me awhile to fathom and appreciate why readers, now avid TV watchers, were becoming so much more knowledgeable about sports. Why they took me to task, became more critical of my perceived ignoring of their favorite TV teams.

I also received a letter from the Rev. Mathias Heile, priest at St. Peter's Church:

Dear Friend,

May I thank you sincerely for the fine article relative to athletics at St. Peter's High that appeared in your column "Riding Herd on Sports" in the Roswell Daily Record of March 5, 1956.

This is certainly a fine tribute to the boys and a special incentive for them and I do appreciate your most favorable publicity.

So thanks again for this and all past favors of the recent basketball season.

With every best wish,

Upon arriving in Roswell, I had learned from reporter Brownie Emerson, a Catholic convert and a member of St. Peter's, that there was widespread negative judgment at the church about our newspaper. It concerned the way the Crusaders were being covered by the *Record* compared to the Coyotes of the public Roswell High School.

St. Peter's did not compete in football. I'd begun to make every effort to cover and write stories about all basketball games of both teams. Usually I sat next to Father Mathias, who kept score for St. Peter's team home games. It took me awhile to discover what the major problem was. When the Crusaders lost an out-of-town game, nothing was phoned into the *Record*. No Crusaders story, but we had published one about the Coyotes

At first, I thought perhaps some of these St. Peter's road games simply were completed too late for our Saturday night deadline. Finally, it dawned on me that only when the Crusaders won were the results phoned in. So I asked the coach about it.

"I don't have any personal problem with you or the *Record*," he answered. "It's just that when we lose I get so down-hearted that I can't call in."

"Okay, maybe we could try this. I can see how you don't want to talk after losing a game, but what about asking the kid *(I was not much more than a kid myself)* who keeps score for you to phone in just the box score? Wouldn't take him very long. I can write a story for you from that."

"I'll try to do that from now on." And he did. "The kid" called in the losers and the coach the winners. Writing a story from a box score wasn't as complete as covering a game and/or talking to a coach about it afterwards, but it can be done. The idea remained to put the hometown team in the best available light.

Like, when losing: "Although the Crusaders led 36-32 at halfway." Or: "Despite Big (I *already knew he's a tall guy*) Jack Smith's pouring in 16 points...." I was surprised when St. Peter's invited Mary and me to its year-end banquet. Somewhere during the festivities, the coach got up, smiled, and said, "We have a Protestant sports editor and his wife here with us tonight." Then he began to tell two or three mild and inoffensive Protestant jokes. I'd heard lots of jokes much more offensive, most of them off-color, about Catholic priests and nuns. It never occurred to me that there was ongoing ribbing of Protestants by Catholics.

After the coach had finished his jokes and thanked me for the newspaper's coverage of the team, Father Mathias strode to the microphone. He also fired off a Protestant joke or two and made Mary and me laugh and feel even more welcome.

I'd never come across the word "ecumenical," nor did anyone else use it during that wonderful evening. But that's what was happening for Mary and me as we sat with new-found friends.

I certainly didn't know much about covering baseball either, despite those boyhood fantasies of following in the flashing footsteps of New York Yankees Joe DiMaggio and Mickey Mantle, hitting all those home runs and making jumping-into-the-air, sterling catches at the center-field fence.

I'd memorized a few baseball records, such as those held by the likes of Ty Cobb and Babe Ruth. Growing up without TV, the best baseball I'd seen in Hurley was its semi-pro team. The Company, Kennecott Copper Corporation as you'll remember, provided jobs in the mill for past-their-prime baseball players, most of whom had played out their youth in the West Texas-New Mexico League. I think they were once a Class A league. The idea was for these men, lacking much education or job skills, to be able to provide for their families while still playing the game they loved.

They carried such names as shortstop "Happy" Spangler, who told me he wore a metal cup under his jock strap to protect the "family jewels," keeping his wife happy in the event a baseball he fielded took a "bad bounce" between his legs. There was "Chief," first baseman Dave Byington. Obviously having some Native American blood coursing through his veins, the big fellow could hit the ball a mile. After his baseball and softball playing days ended, when The Company sold the town to its workers, Byington became Hurley's first mayor.

Our Hurley team once even traveled to the Semi-Pro either National or World Series, didn't advance very far, perhaps winning its first game. We young Hurley lads were gravely disappointed because we felt those guys, especially when rangy "Cowboy" Thornton pitched, were just about invincible on the baseball field. Incidentally, the manager's name my first year covering the Roswell Rockets was "Stubby" Greer. His real first name was Hayden, and I don't know whether they nicknamed him Stubby because he was short, because he might have had stubby fingers, or for some other unknown reason left to your imagination.

Covering the Rockets further exposed my lack of sports writing skill and knowledge about athletics possessed by those who held the job before me. An earlier sports editor was the son of Harold Green, one of the *Record's* linotype operators. Bob Green moved on to become national golfing writer for the Associated Press. Harold shook his head when pointing out my difficulty in making up statistical tables such as batting averages, team won-loss records, and pitchers' earned-run averages. He never said it, but in the back of my mind I always heard, "My Bob never had *those* problems."

The *Record* sports editor just before me had been "Buck" Lanier. It was Buck's good fortune to be around during the 1954 baseball season of our Class C Longhorn League when Roswell Rocket Joe Bauman hit his 72nd home run at Artesia, another small city about 40 miles south of town.

That came on September 5, the last day of the 1954 season - -a doubleheader. In the first game the left-handed Bauman hit his 70th homer over the 365-foot-way right field fence. In the second game he hit number 71 and 72. It would be 47 years later before Bauman's record for organized baseball would be broken, when Barry Bonds of the San Francisco Giants hit 73 homers in 2001. Joe used no performance-enhancing drugs as Bonds did. Maybe a beer now and again. Nevertheless, Bonds faced major league, not Class C, pitching.

Times change. Joe Bauman received about $600 a month, with some extra money Roswell fans pushed through the fence when he hit a home run–*only* during those months of the year he played for the Rockets. In contrast, Barry Bonds received **$18 million** in 2004. In Bauman's playing days, only a few major leaguers were paid $100,000 a year.

I found 6-foot-5-inch "Big Joe" to be a great guy. Once during difficulties writing about Roswell Rocket players and serving as official scorer — making decisions whether batted balls were hits or errors, Joe advised me, "Don't worry about it, Max. What I think is that sometimes you're right and sometimes you're wrong. But, I'll get my hits. It all averages out."

My fledgling efforts as official score keeper provided an extra $5 for each Rocket home game covered. During a 72-home-game season that amounted to an extra $360, which in 1955 provided a lot of food on the Odendahl family table. Being paid about $60 a week by the *Record*, it totaled to an extra month-and-a-half's wages.

My scoring troubles perhaps were coupled with what could have been my Attention Deficit Disorder. Being official score keeper forced intense on-the job learning, because I'd never come in contact with a baseball score book.[5] It may have been ADD or simply a lack of sleep which caused lapses in judgment while scoring the baseball Rockets. Covering that team was a young man's (or young woman's) job. Then, women journalists were usually society editors.

After arriving sleepy at the *Record* office at 6 a.m. to make up those two sports pages, I spent the day during seasons talking with basketball or football coaches - perhaps writing a *Riding Herd on Sports* column. In baseball season it would be after dark and the field lights would be on when I climbed the ladder into the press box overlooking the fans behind home plate. The game often lasted past 10 p.m. I drove directly to the *Record* office, where I compiled a complete box score and wrote a story on the Longhorn League teletype wire.

After typing the story and box score on the teletype, they moved by wire to, say, the sports editor of Midland or the Odessa, Texas, newspapers. When the Rockets played in Midland or Odessa, that sports editor would teletype a box score and story to me. Worked pretty well except for tiring out sports editors.

During baseball season I'd really be pooped, arriving home before midnight, getting up to be at the office at 6 the next morning. So, let's say the next night I looked down trying to keep the score book accurate when a player–either side, didn't matter–cracked a ball off

---

[5] I'd worked with basketball score books in college and Coach Dewey Johnson of the Roswell High Coyotes provided me with statistics after each football game. Someone also showed me how to crudely chart a football game on paper imprinted with squares. I employed this method for New Mexico Military Institute games. You laid out 100 squares for the length of a football field, using different-colored pencils for each team. Copying from the official program numbers for players–like say, the quarterback was number 8– one plotted in by player number each pass, ground gain, loss, etc. Then you counted the squares for total number of yards gained, lost, length of passes, and so forth. A tedious process, especially when writing a story fighting a Saturday-night deadline.

his bat at the opposing shortstop. By the time I glanced up, the ball already was in the outfield.

Now, if the ball went between the shortstop's legs, that would be an error. If "the old horsehide" shot past him with no reasonable chance of his fielding it and throwing out the batter, that would be a base hit – perhaps even resulting in a double. There were two buttons to push – one for an error and another for a hit. Which light should go up on the scoreboard, for that hit or error I hadn't even seen?

Sometimes Charlie Wells, covering the game for the local radio station, saw what had happened. Charlie also worked a tough schedule early each morning covering city hall, police, fire department and such. Many times neither of us knew, after a bat cracked, exactly what had occurred.

In that case, I'd just pushed a button. No yell from the crowd probably meant all was okay. If not, they'd scream, especially if they thought my error about an error hurt the Rockets. Often they simply screamed or loudly moaned for the hell of it, even if Charlie and I saw exactly what had happened and agreed on the call. That's what fans – call them short for fanatics if you wish -pay for to do at ball games. That's also what Big Joe Bauman meant when he kindly said, "It all averages out."

Another dilemma was when Rocket players and managers told me that score keepers always gave the benefit of the doubt to home team players. "We get our hits and fewer errors at home. It costs us on the road. Score keepers do that, even in the major leagues."

I wasn't convinced that big city score keepers, although naturally writing favorable stories about hometown players, went so far as to be dishonest in favor of their own teams. My guess would be that there are several sets of eyes in major league boxes keeping up with what's going on. Many times it's simply a matter of judgment between scoring a hit or an error. Since watching TV, there are some major league calls which I disagree with—especially whether the first baseman has put his foot on the bag after catching a ball to make an out. Then again, what the TV camera sees isn't always the same as what's before the referees' eyes.

Major league ballparks also are better groomed. Roswell players often contended they shouldn't be charged with an error when a baseball "took a bad hop," perhaps caused by striking a piece of gravel in the infield. On the other hand, that meant an undeserved hit for a player on the opposing team. A score-keeper's dilemma.

An unfortunate incident occurred one night when my, at-that-time young, brother-in-law (Mary's brother Greg) came to sit in the press box with me. It was the score keeper's job to go to the dugouts and receive the starting batting lineups and record them in the

174

official score book. Coming out of the Roswell dugout, I was accosted by an unhappy pitcher named Ralph Buckingham.

"You're giving me too many wild pitches when they should be pass balls," he growled. The "aging" (maybe 30 or 35) Buckingham, whom I saw as already unhappy on his way down as a Class C Roswell Rocket after having been a Class AAA pitcher, was referring to another score keeping dilemma. It is a wild pitch if the ball hits the ground before the catcher misses it. My interpretation from reading the rule book (no one taught me these rules, I had to figure them out myself as I went along – sort of like setting up your own computer from an instruction book) was generally if the pitch went past the catcher, without hitting the ground beforehand, should it be scored a pass ball. The primary problem arrived with a rookie Rocket catcher who had as much difficulty blocking errant pitches as I did unraveling scoring rules.

"I don't hear any of the other pitchers griping about wild pitches," I, in too much of a wise-ass way, replied to Buckingham, A mistake. He swung at me, yet his fist missed and I was able to grab around him. Other Roswell players pulled us apart as we sort of wrestled on the ground.

Taking a swing at an official scorer is like doing so to an umpire. So, Harry James, president of the Longhorn League and operator of the Nickson Hotel in Roswell, decided to take official action against Buckingham. He was fined $50 and his contract returned to a Sacramento, California, team.

"That lefthander missed me like he usually does home plate," I ungraciously later joked to someone about the incident. Actually, I felt bad about what had happened. Buckingham probably had a wife and children who were cut off from support in the middle of a baseball season. I should have kept my mouth shut and let him tell me off. At the age of 25 to 35 males tend to be too cocky and competitive to do that. I've learned and now try, no matter how bizarre a comment or opinion might be, not to use some acid rejoinder — but to say something like, "That's an interesting way to look at it." Or "I've never heard that idea before." Sometimes, that is — not as many times as I should.

There were frequent altercations on the field between the Class C players over such insults as one calling another a "busher," a term treated as offensive as if referring to someone's mother as a female dog.

Buck Lanier had made a good bit of extra money in 1954 phoning around stories after Joe Bauman's exploit.[6] Moving on to one of the larger El Paso, Texas, newspapers, Buck re-

---

[6] In 1954 Bauman also set a Longhorn League record with 224 runs batted in while posting a .400 batting average. He also had a .916 slugging average, plus 199 hits, and 188 runs.

visited the *Record* a couple of times. He noted how much cheaper it was for him and several other El Paso newsmen to live in Ciudad Juarez, across the bridge over the Rio Grande in Mexico. "You can buy a bottle of beer for a dime if you know the right place to go."

Despite being hampered with illness, Big Joe Bauman had a good season in 1955 with 45 home runs and a batting average of .336. The next year Bauman retired, with the press release claiming it was because of a chipped bone in his left ankle. However, Joe told me it also was because, *"They're throwing past my power."*

That was one of the best quotes I ever heard from a baseball player. Joe quietly went back to work at his Texaco gas station. He and his wife, Dorothy, attended the First Methodist church in Roswell where Mary and I did. Don't know if they were there the day the plaster fell from the ceiling. I wrote the story about it for Monday's *Record*,

"The solo "Bless This House" was next on the order of worship but the blessing came early for the congregation at First Methodist Church, Second and Penn, at the late service yesterday morning.

"People sitting in the back rows of the packed church narrowly averted serious injury or death when plaster plummeted from the ceiling of the overhanging balcony....

"Apparently the only injury was to Paul McEvoy, advertising manager for KSWS radio and television. KSWS was broadcasting from the church all during the near-calamity.

"A piece of the falling plaster caught McEvoy's coat and pinned him to the floor. He was struck on the right foot and crawled from the sanctuary – apparently the last one from under the damaged area. He said his ankle was sprained."

All of us in the balcony slowly made our way down the stairs and out of the church. McEvoy estimated there were at least 25 to 30 people under the balcony when Dillon made his announcement.

"There was a crack in the ceiling," McEvoy said. "All the people moved out and the plaster fell. There was a full minute's notice. If there hadn't been, it would have killed 12 or 15 people. It was providence or something."

Mary and I were sitting in the balcony when the minister, Dr. Austin H. Dillon, told everyone, *"Please get out from under the balcony and come to the front."* If that was divine direction, I ignored it almost too long in paying little attention to Roswell Little League teams. Never covered their games. Depended on managers to bring results to the newspaper office.

176

It was my surprise when I found the Roswell Lions Hondo All-Stars (then, as now some of those boys playing weren't that little) were on their way to Williamsport, Pennsylvania, for the Little League World Series. The *Record* had no individual pictures of the players, only a couple of team shots the manager brought in before they left.

The Roswell team continued its winning ways at Williamsport, first a 3-1 victory over Upper Darby, Pennsylvania, and next 6-3 over Winchester, Massachusetts. The paper began to be deluged with telephone calls demanding much more coverage of the Little Leaguers than provided by the Associated Press Bureau in Albuquerque.

I asked Al Stubbs, who had become managing editor after Don Wright retired after suffering a heart attack, if I could fly to Williamsport. Stubbs relayed the request to publisher Bob Beck. It was denied for two reasons: A purported lack of funds and there would be nobody to cover the Rockets and make up the sports pages. The situation became more serious as the irate phone calls continued.

The day before the championship game, AP in Albuquerque wouldn't verify if a complete story could be provided. A running, inning-by-inning story would clog the New Mexico teletype wire connected to all member newspapers in the state. Those teletype machines relayed stories at about the speed of a fairly fast typist, very slow compared to today's instant links between computers. Other New Mexico newspapers, likewise on deadline – hoping to receive latest stock market quotations or "fast breaking hard news" on that sole teletype wire – had much less interest in the outcome of Roswell's Little League game.

There also was the problem, that once it arrived by teletype, of getting the story into hot type with linotype machines which produced only a few lines of type each minute. In addition, the *Record* would have to hold up publication of its final afternoon edition until after the regular deadline. While pondering all this, a Little League light bulb went on in my head. An announcer for a local radio station had gathered enough advertising revenue to pay his way to Williamsport. He would be announcing the championship game the next day.

So, here's the way it went on Friday, August 24, 1956. As the announcer radioed his play-by-play report, I put it all down on one of my official score sheets provided by the Class C Longhorn League. During advertisements, I wrote my story in "takes" – short paragraphs which were set into type by two or more waiting linotype operators in the "back shop."

The complete front-page story and box score were set in boldface type, leading off with a Williamsport, PA., dateline and *(Special to the Record). Well, producing a newspaper story from a radio announcer's gab was pretty special.* Anyway a headline in red ink Roswell Wraps Up World Series adorned the top of the page, with a repeat of the previously published team picture beneath it.

The lead to the story read, "Tommy Jordan clouted a three-run homer in the fourth inning for the Roswell Hondo All-Stars here this afternoon as he struck out 14 Delaware Township, N.J., batters to win the Little League World Series 3-l." Within minutes after the end of the game, papers began to roll off the press.

On Monday, the champion Little Leaguers arrived home by train to Roswell. They were greeted by a crowd estimated between 3,000 and 5,000. Part of my story said, *"The afternoon belonged mostly to the boys. Some appeared shy and some cocky throughout the proceedings, but it was written across the faces how proud they were. And the faces of the crowd mirrored the pride of the boys."*

About a month before Roswell won the Little League world championship, a very much more important event in my life had occurred. On July 22, 1956, Pamela Maxine Odendahl arrived at the local hospital. Mary's parents were living in Roswell at the time, and Lula Mae expected to be called immediately when the time arrived to make the dash to the hospital. We, however, prided ourselves in wanting to take care of the big event on our own. Our primary physician scheduled to deliver Pam (Dr. Brown, the kind of friend you would see and talk to around Roswell) was out of town when Mary went into labor, with an ob-gyn specialist on call for Brown's patients. As the delivery moved along slowly, the ob-gyn guy, a stranger to us, said to me, "I think we need to induce labor to get this over with. What do you think?"

"Sounds good to me," I replied.

I don't know whether Mary was asked her opinion about inducing labor. A husband, one hopes, wouldn't be the exclusive decision maker in this day and age. After Pam was born early in the morning, I went by to present Mary's mother with the good news. Lula Mae showed herself more than a bit distressed about not being in on the big event. Over a cup of coffee, I tried to describe how Mary and I wanted to do this on our own. Finally, she looked at me, smiled, and said, "Okay. I'll fix you some bacon and eggs for breakfast."

That was typical of Lula Mae. A wonderful mother-in-law. In all the years, we never had an angry argument. Pam's birth came about a month after that of Caryl Lynne Stubbs. Al and Florence (Flossie) Stubbs were ecstatic after already having produced two boys, Bruce and Chuck. I guess whatever causes babies to be conceived must have been in Roswell air nine months or so before Caryl (who doesn't especially like the Lynne added to her name now) and Pam were born. Incidentally, Mary planned to call our baby Max if he were a boy–hence the Maxine middle name.

"Two girls are boy enough for me," I told Mary. As it worked out, that was the end of our production of children. Whew!!

Me with my girls, 1958

Terry, Mary and Pam

179

The usual routine at the *Record* was that Al Stubbs would remain in the office each morning while some of us gathered for coffee at "The Greek's" cafe down the block. We'd bitch about this and that concerning Al's decisions. When Stubbs took his vacations I would fill in as pseudo editor for two weeks. So, down to the cafe we went and everyone remained silent. Suddenly it occurred to me that I was in charge and they now needed to bitch about me. So, I decided to stay behind with ears burning. It would have been "fun" to have been a fly on the wall at The Greek's.

I usually assumed the added duty of filling Al's editorial pages. For some reason, perhaps because the *Wall Street Journal* at the time was winning Pulitzer prizes for its editorials, many small newspapers plugged some of them in during editors' vacations. While I worked at the *WSJ*, that newspaper routinely gave permission for stories and editorials to be duplicated by other publications. There was one condition: That the complete story or editorial must be re-published, in order that facts, figures or opinions wouldn't be taken out of context.

I began to try my hand at typing out editorials and editorial columns. Probably my best column got me the most heat but is remindful of the old saying," If you can't stand the heat, stay out of the kitchen" The column was a satire about the John Birch Society, an ultra-right-wing organization established in Indiana in 1958 to combat what it perceived to be widespread infiltration of Communism into American life.

The founder was Robert H. Welch, producer of Welch grape juice and other products. The society, named after a Baptist missionary who had been killed by Chinese Communists in 1945, had gone so far as to accuse World War II hero and ex-four star-general, and at the time Republican President Dwight D. Eisenhower, along with CIA Director Allen Dulles, and Chief Justice Earl Warren, of being "dedicated, conscious, agents of the Communist conspiracy."

My satire, *The Jack Spruce Society*, made Roswell John Birch Society members furious. One of those in a dither requested a private meeting with me. Over coffee at the Greek's cafe, he chastised me about my ignorance of the dangers of Communism. He held two paperback books in his hand and passed one over to me. This meeting was quite serious business to him.

"Here is *Masters of Deceit* by J. Edgar Hoover, which I bet you haven't read," he said sarcastically. "I'm giving this to you." Hoover, the longtime director of the Federal Bureau of investigation, made a practice of stirring up Americans against Russia and

Communism. Many of us figured this simply was Hoover's way of continuing to hold onto his job for so long.[7]

"This other book in my hand is *The Blue Book of the John Birch Society*," sputtered the man whom I had made an enemy of with my *Jack Spruce Society* column. "If you want to read it, you'll have to pay for it."

"That's fine," I said. "Be glad to. How much is it?" Probably less than $5 for the paperback. I paid him for it, he handed it to me, and I could tell he still was very angry with me as he strode away.

The man was a contractor who installed insulation into walls and ceilings of houses, something not routinely done during construction in Roswell and many other places not having severe winters. Mary had been to his own house several times to play bridge with his wife as part of a female foursome. After the *Jack Spruce* column, Mary never was invited there again.

The Greek-American running the restaurant often treated coffee to those of us working on the newspaper. Perhaps like free meals for cops. Feeding cops with the intention that the bad guys around town would notice cars of the law frequenting certain restaurants and decide those are not smart places to holdup. Perhaps The Greek thought he might require good press sometime, but I doubt it. I think he simply was a generous fellow and realized we "ink-stained wretches" weren't paid all that much.

"You need a good wife to be successful in running a restaurant," he once told two or three of us newspersons sitting in one of his booths. "You also need to know how to cook." The Greek explained that cooks he hired often got drunk, especially on Friday and Saturday nights, wouldn't show up for work the next morning.

"So, you have to be able to roll up your sleeves, go back into the kitchen, and cook. That also means your wife needs to come in and watch over the cash register. Waitresses aren't naturally dishonest, but a cash register full of money is a real temptation. They often are between husbands, or live with mean boyfriends, and are strapped for money."

He explained that a waitress usually wouldn't steal directly from the register, but simply wouldn't log in all "tickets," and pocket that money. Times change. I notice waitresses

---

[7] John Edgar Hoover became director of the Bureau of Investigation in 1924, which in 1935 was established by Congress as the Federal Bureau of investigation. Hoover held the director's job for almost half a century, until his death at age 77 on May 2, 1972. When President Richard Nixon heard the news, he was shocked but reportedly said about the director who was known as a closet gay and cross dresser: "Jesus Christ! That old cocksucker!" Publicly, he called Hoover a "truly remarkable man" and "one of his closest friends and advisers."

routinely operate cash registers now, perhaps because of computerization it appears most customers pay with credit cards. Also, in many restaurants – especially chains such as "Denny's" – waitresses and waiters punch in orders to the kitchen by computer. Thus, there is an electronic record of orders and revenue must match that record. It appears more complicated now to get away with theft.

It's also now considered socially unacceptable to call someone "The Greek," even when he or she can hear you say it and might not appear especially offended. Sixty years ago it was still fairly common to refer to a person – at times even in his presence, as say to remark, "you big Swede." In my Dad's youth, when there was widespread immigration from Europe, poverty-stricken national and ethnic groups would gather together by necessity in their own parts of a city. This made them identifiable even more such as Irish, Italian, German, Polish, or Catholic, Jewish among many. Most immigrants, especially Jews, who suffered prejudice, often found it necessary to live together in "ghettos" and help one another in order to survive.

The backshop foreman for the *Roswell Daily Record* was a fellow named Bob Bear. For my first few months at the newspaper, his sister was society editor. The Bear family once had owned all or much of the *Record,* now part of a small chain of newspapers headquartered in Lake Charles, Louisiana. I don't know exactly what had happened financially to Bob Bear, but now he was stuck running the backshop and obviously he resented it.

Bear sometimes could be very irascible. When in a bad mood, he'd put together pages of the paper the way he thought they should be rather than following our "dummies" sent to him from the newsroom. This could lead to heated arguments. Yet, Bob Bear had what still seems to me a strange or perhaps special personality. For example, let's say the two of us were in the middle of a mild argument about placement of a story or picture on one of "my" sports pages. "Dammit, I'm not changing it for you," he'd shout, then might follow softly with, "Let's go down to The Greek's and get a cup of coffee."

Bob would remove his ink-stained apron, lay it across a "chase" partially filled with metal type, and we'd walk – usually silently – out of the office. Once on the street, Bear's personality was transformed. He might ask after Mary and our kids. Or he'd discuss sports. Over coffee, he'd often talk about his favorite trips with his wife to Las Vegas, Nevada. Going by car from southeastern New Mexico, mostly on two-lane, bumpy roads, took many arduous hours – including driving at night facing the piercing lights of oncoming traffic.

What Bob and his wife enjoyed most were the little shows performed next to bars in many Sin City casinos. Not big-name singers such as Frank Sinatra or Sammy Davis, Jr., but he raved about those like Louis Prima and Keeley Smith — others maybe getting their starts as Las Vegas entertainers. Bear said there were no tickets or cover charges. You just sat at a table or stood next to the bar and enjoyed drinks and the performance. One could tell as he talked that these trips briefly alleviated the pain of having to work at the *Record.*

You'd return to the newspaper with Bob Bear, and he'd put his apron back on. The Bear of the Backshop, back in his gloomy element, would stare with a bit of anger and declare, "I'm still not moving that damn story for you." When Bob Bear's sister finally retired as society editor, a beautiful younger woman replaced her. Beverly Ragland was the sister of a famous professional football player, Tom Brookshier.[8] She had been Miss New Mexico twice, competing in Atlantic City for Miss America. After that, she had done some modeling.

Beverly was thin with beautiful legs, but not busty. "This helped me when I was a model because I could wear all kinds of clothes," she once told me. "I posed as myself when a thin girl was needed. They also could wrap a large, filled bra around me, or put pads on my butt before I dressed and walked down the ramp."

When Beverly was on vacation, either Al Stubbs or I put together her society pages. Usually she had left behind pictures and stories and we only had to make up her pages and write headlines.

"I can tell a four-column wedding when she walks through the door," Beverly once said. What she meant was that wedding coverage was determined by the bride's (often the groom's) standing in Roswell's social circles and/or the size of the wedding. The *Record* prided itself in providing space for every wedding, but this meant occasional four-column photos with long stories for a major social event. Three-column, two-column pictures/stories were decided by Beverly, with one column and no photo - only a short story for what she considered brides having little or no social status.

Beverly was divorced, and as a Catholic apparently didn't plan to be married again. She could have had boyfriends, but as far as I knew showed no interest in anyone working at the *Record.* Probably in her mind none of us, except for married publisher Bob Beck, was a four-column person.

---

[8] Born in 1931, so only a year younger than I am, Brookshier was graduated from the University of Colorado in 1953. For nine years after that he was a defensive back for the Philadelphia Eagles, named a Pro Bowler in 1959 and 1960 and had his number retired. The Eagles won the National Football League Championship in 1960. Brookshier became an NFL, Super Bowls and other bowls sports broadcaster and in 1975 teamed up with Pat Summerall.

Nevertheless, Beverly was cheerful and personable to us slaving in the newsroom. Man, her face sure was pretty as she worked at her desk about six feet away. And, when she got up to walk around the room those legs were really something worth pausing to glance at. Besides religiously keeping a close eye on pretty faces and well-turned ankles which wandered in and out of the newsroom during my first three years at the *Roswell Daily Record*, I became more aware not only about sports but also local news.

Editor Don Wright had suffered a serious heart attack, tried to come back to work, but had to retire after more than 50 years as a journalist. This was before heart bypasses or angioplasty. A person then weakened by one attack might only live a quieter life, waiting and worrying about another, often-fatal episode.

Al Stubbs was named editor of the *Record.* This meant someone had to be hired to take over as news and city editor. There were several persons who filled this position, three of whom I remember. As my desk was butted up next to that of Al and the persons who followed him, I was able to observe how they put together the main part of the newspaper.

Because of all of the time it took for linotype machines to tediously produce hot type, most of the newspaper had to be made ready the day before publication. Not only advertising pages but also pages filled with editorials, political columns, and letters to the editor. Society pages, feature stories, and any special sections also were prepared early. As soon as one day's edition rolled off the press, type in the heavy metal pages was melted down, replaced for the next day. Ads and type were arranged in what were called *chases.*

Around a few ads, space always was left open the day of publication for "my" two sports pages. On the news side, there was the full front page and one or two "jump pages." "*Jumps*" were continuations of front-page stories. Like sports, the jump pages were only partially open for news, with the remaining space filled with ads.

The way it worked was that the number of pages to be printed for a certain day was determined by the amount of advertising which had been sold. That department would *dummy* in ads and the news department filled in the remaining space. "News doesn't pay for this newspaper or your paychecks," those in the advertising department sometimes would, it seemed to me a bit too gleefully or haughtily, remind us, "Advertising does."

A rough rule of thumb was that what one paid either subscribing to or purchasing a newspaper off the newsstand about equaled the price of the paper it was printed on. The remainder of the revenue came from advertising. At any rate, putting together the front and jump pages was a bit different than sports pages. A sports editor usually had a pretty good idea of what those pages were going to look like.

For example, if I covered a winning home game of the professional baseball Roswell Rockets, I might have decided the night before to make that the lead sports story – perhaps with an action picture taken by our photographer. Then I'd simply add the few other local stories which I might have written the day before, fill in the rest of the space with state and national sports stories taken off the Associated Press wire. As mentioned before, this procedure began at 6 a.m. and my deadline for finishing filling sports pages was 8 a.m.

"Making up" the front page was another matter. The news editor usually had no idea how his pages would look until coming into the office each morning, checking the Associated Press wire and perusing stories by the two local reporters, already written or soon to arrive that morning at his desk.

While watching all this, it wasn't that I was completely unsatisfied with being a sports editor. Looking back, I'd say that my first year was a learning experience, the second one which I was pretty much satisfied with my work, and by the third it began to become somewhat boring. Often, sports writing is viewed by budding journalists simply as a starting point, a first job. For others, it becomes a whole career. After covering 72 home games of the Roswell Rockets for each of three seasons, there was and still is little appeal left for me about watching slow-moving baseball games. It still stays with me, however, that winning isn't what's most important to look for and enjoy at a sporting event. It's athleticism.

Like the Rockets once acquired, maybe from Cuba or elsewhere in the Caribbean, a gifted shortstop. He could dart over behind second base, make a sterling stop, and throw out a runner before he reached first base. But he couldn't bat very well, not even against a Class C team. As far as I know, the fellow never became a star. Yet his shortstopping was a wonder to behold. I didn't see a shortstop make plays like that until one night watching Ozzie Smith. Nicknamed "the Wizard," Smith won his first Golden Glove award playing for the San Diego Padres before being traded in 1982 to the St. Louis Cardinals. A great-hitting shortstop, he was elected to the Baseball of Fame in 2002.

Career-minded sports writers usually arrive at each event as if something new or exciting is about to happen. Sports can become the most important aspect of a journalist's life. . Many sports writers are former athletes who can't stay away from games. The rest of us have been referred to jokingly as "jock sniffers." That may be, because we longed to excel as athletes and lacked the physical ability. We collected some of that glory by writing or broadcasting about it. Some former athletes believe it truly impossible to understand or write about sports unless having physically participated in them.

During my first sports writing days, Al Stubbs wrote in his "West of the Pecos" column:

Max Odendahl, Record sports editor, was the busiest man in Roswell over the weekend, and the work is not all accomplished. Roswell Invitational Basketball Tournament started Thursday and Max has seen more basketball since then than he cares to admit. Games day and night. Check the Record's sports pages today and you'll see what's meant. And Golden Gloves starts here Monday.

Max, a University of New Mexico graduate, came to the Record Jan. 3 from a job in Dallas, Texas, with the Dallas branch of the Wall Street Journal. He admits there's a little more variety to his sports job than there was with the Journal, which deals mainly with figures and interpretive news on the financial and stock market world.

Keen Rafferty University of New Mexico School of Journalism head, was fortunate in having Odendahl's wife, Mary, living in Roswell during the press convention which ended last night with the presentation of Shafer awards. Mrs. Odendahl served as secretary to Rafferty at UNM and has helped with registration at other New Mexico Press Conventions. She was a "natural" for the job here at the Nickson Hotel Thursday afternoon and Friday morning.

One of the *Record* news editors I observed closely was named Rick Raphael. One day I asked him, "Rick, how do you keep track of, decide which stories you're going to put on the front page?"

"Oh, that's easy," he replied. "I just put them in three piles."

"How's that?"

"The first pile is *Page One Stories*; the second pile is Page One *Maybe*; the third is *For The Jump Page*. As better wire stories come in or important local ones from our reporters, I move them around in the piles."

"Like how?"

"Like early in the morning I've pulled apart the AP wire and put those stories, along with local ones I already have, into the three piles. Maybe at that time I pick out the lead page-one story. As the morning progresses there may be breaking wire or local stories which have to go on the front page, maybe one of them the lead story. In that case the former lead story goes lower on the front page."

"That would mean you'd need to move a story or two on top of the Page One *Maybe* Pile?"

"Right, and take some of the Page One *Maybe* stories and put them on top of the *For the Jump Page* pile. Some days, I don't have to move much around. On others, there are so many breaking stories coming in that I fill the jump page without using any from the *For the Jump Page* pile."

"What do you do with those?"

"Either throw them away, or if they are real lively —-such that the news isn't likely to change or more maybe it's a feature story - I might have time to put headlines on them to fill up inside pages for the next day."

"Looks like a good system."

"It works for me."

And it worked for me when I moved up to that job. Later, when teaching Copy Editing classes at San Diego State University, I still thought this a great system – one worth passing along to students. Some would look at me with glassy eyes. Guess those who didn't put my advice into their notes thought it would be something unlikely to be on a test. Their philosophy: "If it ain't gonna' be on the test, it ain't worth much."

Rick Raphael, as many journalists with itchy feet are prone to do, moved on. Early one night I got a call from him. He still was in New Mexico, now working for the *Alamogordo Daily News.*

"I've got a tip for you," he said, and went on to give me the location of the dead body of a child. What had happened was that the young girl had been kidnapped from her home by either a Hispanic-American or Mexican man. Apparently he had some sort of reputation or record as a sex offender and authorities feared the worst had happened to the girl.

The man fled into Mexico, considered a safe haven for wrong-doers who commit crimes in the United States. But Mexicans, outraged by sex offenders, captured the man, held him for extradition. Roswell Police Chief Tommy Thompson went into Mexico to bring the suspect back to the U.S.

We at the *Record* knew this much of the story, but not where the girl was – although we presumed her to be left somewhere dead after the man had committed unspeakable acts. We suspected either Tommy Thompson or Mexican law officers had elicited from the suspect (probably in a manner it best we didn't learn about or we would have had to publish it) the location of the dead girl's body.

"Tommy doesn't know I heard him talking with the FBI on the police network," Rick told me. "There's a State Police relay station near Alamogordo which we listen to, although they don't know it. Mum's the word."

"Right."

I was agreeing not to divulge the source of information for a news story. To keep it confidential. Journalists have gone to jail or prison rather than name a source they have pledged confidentiality to. In this case, there were two sources of news which couldn't be revealed – Rick and our knowledge about the police radio relay station.

As soon as Rick told me the location of the child's body, I called the *Record's* photographer, raced by in my car to pick him up, and we speeded to the location. Huddled around the dead girl's body were sheriff's deputies, an ambulance crew, and an FBI agent. She lay on the ground with a large screwdriver protruding from her chest. The FBI agent looked up, became enraged, and asked us, "What the hell are you guys doing out here? How did you get here?"

"We just came here to get a picture," I told him.

"Yeah, Freedom of the Press!!" he growled. "That's the way you bastards work. You come out here to get a picture of a poor little dead girl with a screwdriver sticking out of her chest."

"Nope," I said. "We don't publish pictures of dead people unless they're covered up." By this time the child was being loaded on a gurney, and one of the ambulance crew – whom we had worked with before — did his usual, covered the little body with a blanket.

"Okay," the photographer said, "any of you guys who want to can stand behind the gurney."

The FBI man walked away in a huff. The published picture showed a small form with something sticking up–all under a blanket–on a gurney with the ambulance crew and two dean-pan deputies wearing their cowboy hats.

That wasn't the end of it. Chief Thompson and the FBI man sought to find out where the leak had come from. To plug it. Finally, they centered on one of the deputies–a guy named Pinky. He was married to a teletypesetter operator working for the *Record*. They became convinced Pinky somehow had notified his wife about the location of the body, and she had phoned us.

It was a dilemma, as Pinky said his job was in jeopardy. I went to the office of his boss, the sheriff, told him that Pinky was not our source. Of course, the sheriff wanted to know who was, and I wouldn't tell him. The sheriff went away angry. I don't know whether because he thought I was lying to him or that I wouldn't cop on the real source. In any case, Pinky kept his job and both he and his wife thanked me for it.

There still is controversy over journalists refusing to reveal confidential sources. The furor at this writing reaches into the offices of the President and Vice President of the United States, who often parcel out information "on background" without a source. But the principle remains the same. It is much more difficult for the media to publish or broadcast controversial stories when their confidential sources are at jeopardy of being revealed because of subpoenas.

After Rick Raphael had gone his merry way from the *Record*, Al Stubbs hired a man almost literally off the street to take Rick's job. (I think Al met him in the Greek's café.) I can't recall the guy's name, but he was a big-time talker about his newspaper experiences in Texas. Neither Al nor I believed many of his stories. It seemed to me his main problem was not arriving for work on time.

Perhaps that was because he had a small trailer parked on the edge of town into which, so we heard, he constantly was attempting to lure women. I don't think such off-the-job behavior would amount to a hill of beans now, but making it public was frowned on in those days. In many ways they were days of hypocrisy. In this case, it was acceptable to be macho but one should be discreet about such behavior – especially if the marital status of any woman lured was uncertain and information about what was going on was "getting around town."

At any rate, because of late on-the job, off-the job behavior, or both, he "didn't work out" and he was "let go.'" Nowadays, folks talk about being "fired" when they mean "let go" or "laid off." A firing used to mean something like an angry order from a boss that "here's your 'pink slip', clear out your desk, pick up your paycheck, and never come back," rather than gentle notification of a certain number of days' remaining on one's job.

The next news editor came from Trinidad, Colorado, one of the newspapers in our little chain headquartered in Lake Charles, Louisiana. His name was Bill Bloom and he was a perfect gentleman. He was punctual, a hard worker, and a pleasure to be around. His problem was that everything was new to him. He found it difficult to keep up with the very-fast pace of the one-person tasks of sorting out the news, dummying pages, and writing headlines – all while facing the *Record's* tight deadlines.

The first edition had to be off the press around noon in order to be loaded on buses to outlying areas and up into the mountains to places like the resort town of Ruidoso. The second edition usually wasn't changed all that much. If I recall, the deadline was 2 p.m.

189

There was more time to put together the Sunday morning paper, with the news editor coming in early in the afternoon and the deadline about 11 p.m. No paper was published on Saturday.

As it became obvious Bloom was continuing to have difficulty keeping pace, Al confided to me that he regretfully also would have to be "let go" – but perhaps would be able to have his old job back in Trinidad. As I had been watching the process for a long time, I told Stubbs I'd like to take a crack at being news editor.

He complimented me on my work as sports editor, said he'd hate to lose me from that job, but agreed to let me give it a try. He and I worked together putting out both sports and news pages for a few weeks until another sports writer/editor could be hired.

TUES., OCT. 20, 1959   ROSWELL DAILY RECORD—PAGE 7

DEPARTMENTALIZED—The Roswell Daily Record is departmentalized like any other newspaper. Three departments are represented in these pictured across the top of the page. In the upper left picture, the Editorial Department is represented as Max Odendahl, city and news editor, talks with Woman's Page Editor Beverly Ragland. In the center picture is Bob Ruede at work. He's classified advertising manager, with two women working under him. On the right is Business Manager H. M. Higginbotham, with some of the front office or circulation and business office staff. Women, left to right, Emma and R

All smiles at the Roswell Daily Record

Right off, I found out what Bloom had been up against as news editor. (Later I had the title of city editor also attached to it, although Stubbs usually still made assignments of stories for the two reporters. My, how hard we both worked, especially when one of us was on vacation.) The news editor first had to figure which of that particular day's stories was most important. Rick Raphael's three-pile system saved me there.

Another demanding trick always was to keep the slow linotype machines clanging away. The sports editor arrived at about 6 a.m., and the machines were his to keep busy until an 8 a.m. deadline. As news editor, one had to be on the job – about 6:30 to 7 – and keep teletype tapes of stories ready for the linotypes, along with headlines, dummies filled out, and conferences with printers. The news editor kept the backshop buzzing to meet the noon deadline of the first edition.

I stayed with that job until leaving the *Record* to go to graduate school in journalism at what was then called The State University of Iowa in Iowa City. A couple of years later, still studying journalism at the University of Missouri, I was appalled at myself for some of their "rules" I had broken in headline writing and page makeup tasks. Yet the *Record* was produced six days a week by a short-handed editorial staff. That in itself was a miracle of sorts, one constantly repeated by small daily newspapers around the nation.

While learning the ropes as an editor tying together the news, on occasion I also left the office to cover stories as a reporter. Looking back over my shoulder, I've come to the conclusion that—had I continued newspaper work as a lifetime occupation—my future *wouldn't* have been very successful as a reporter. Maybe ADD had something to do with it. Never quick-witted enough to pin down sources with hard questions. Never an ace reporter for sure, only a small-numbered card. But, *perhaps.*

(1) I'd have moved to the "rim" on a larger newspaper and continued editing stories and writing headlines, eventually becoming its "slot man" who made up front and other news pages. I also realized that age - almost the same as with athletes - eventually would take its toll. As Al Stubbs, although he stayed in the business for a working lifetime, once said, "Newspapering is a young man's job."

(2) I might have been fortunate enough to move into a job as editorial writer at another newspaper - or, better yet, have written some sort of column. When young, I imagined humorous-ridiculous pieces about ordinary life. Who knows, I might have become another Erma Bombeck. She was born three years earlier than me, didn't begin writing her columns until 1964. Besides talent, much of newspaper success is being in the right place at the right time.

"Anybody who watches three games of football in a row," Erma once wrote, "should be declared brain dead."

Boy, did I so often feel the same while covering sports. Wonder what would have been the reaction from fans if I'd written about that boredom in one of my "Riding Herd on Sports" columns. Not good, and with the advent of TV many more men and women became avid watchers. Super fans. Like watching a football game, you never knew what was going to happen when putting together the news side of a paper.

One day as news editor I'd made up what I thought was an especially neat and balanced front page. An original one, for me anyway. Maybe about 10:30 a.m., Al comes by and says grimly, "There's been a big crash on the runway at Walker Air Force Base. It's looks as if several guys have been killed."

"Oh, no!" I say, not only in sympathy for the surviving families of those killed but also because my great "original" makeup of the front page is going down the drain.

Memory tells me what happened was a green student pilot was taxiing either a KC-97 or KC-135 (both fuel tanker planes for B-47 and B-52 bombers) down a runway at Walker Air Force Base about six miles south of Roswell. A heavy gust of wind hit and the plane's wing crashed into three or four other parked planes. I think there was an explosion or explosions which killed several men. It was the worst, or one of the worst, stateside military airfield accidents in Air Force history.

We held-up the first edition until one of our reporters received sufficient information to write a story about the tragedy. A base photographer had supplied us with a large front-page "cut," a picture. That meant, of course, that the front page had to be completely remade. The presses then rolled with the new page for two combined editions. Sad business but still exciting for ink-stained wretches.

Roswell was a good place to raise a family. One saying was, "I wouldn't take a million dollars for one of my kids but I wouldn't give two bits for another one." It seemed as if almost every young couple had two or more children and none of us would have had enough money to pay much ransom, so there was little worry about any of them being kidnapped.

After renting for a while, Mary and I had lucked upon a fairly-new, three-bedroom, cinder-block house priced around $9,000. With a GI mortgage, it cost us about $60 per month. The neighborhood around 1111 Rancho Road was filled with kids. They would gather in one backyard and the mother there would keep an eye on them. The next day they might wander over to another yard under another mother's watchful eyes.

Those mothers' eyes and ears would mainly be tuned to the possibility that one of the children had become injured or to intervene in squabbling which had gone on too long. There was little worry about children being abducted, although the kids were warned, "Don't talk to strangers and never get in anyone's car unless you know them."

There had to have been sexual deviants around, but I don't recall much talk or real concern about them. We at the *Record*, for example, didn't run periodic stories about "perverts" and their locations – which appears to be common in journalism now.

Anyway, mothers randomly took turns watching small children, which gave them time to perform their other myriad household chores. It was a different world, with fewer mothers working outside the home, with husbands' paychecks usually sufficient to raise a family. I recall head-shaking conversations about kibbutzes in Israel–where parents left their children from morning until almost night because both of them had to work outside homes helping the new state take form.

"I just don't see how those mothers could do that," was a common comment, "leaving their children alone with somebody else all day. What kind of a family is that?"

Of course now, with the necessity of two parents working in so many U.S. families, kibbutzes here are called day-care centers.

On the lighter side, Terry had a small record player. She sat in front of it while "Peter Pan" played over and over until she had memorized the lines of all the characters. She loved to organize kids in the neighborhood to play the different roles, teaching them their lines – with her as Peter Pan, of course. Pam would be given some minor role.

When the kids were ready to present *Peter Pan*, or some other performance, parents would gather around. We knew all our neighbors – at least superficially. The man next door worked for the telephone company. Two doors up the street was perhaps Roswell's most skilled surgeon. Down the street on the catty corner lived Ferron Cummins, who owned and operated a clothes washateria.

Ferron had grown up in Lake Arthur, a few miles south of Roswell. He enlisted in the Army Air Corps in 1940, was sent to Manila in November of 1941. When the Japanese bombed Pearl Harbor on December 7, on December 8 they attacked the Philippines, and by April Ferron was a prisoner of war.

He endured the notorious Bataan Death March. In his "This Is My Life" (a copy was given to Mary and me by his wife Lora after his premature death – which happened to so many others who survived the Death March) Ferron describes how 13,000 Americans began the march and only about 8,000 survived. In 1944, he was shipped to Japan, performed slave labor with little food until the atomic bomb was dropped on Hiroshima in August of 1945.

Arriving back in the United States, Ferron spent time in hospitals before being allowed to head home to New Mexico. He tells this poignant, yet wonderful, story:

"They sent a B-17 to take me to Roswell Army Field (a place I didn't know existed) and the other Air Force airman to his place near Lubbock. The second lieutenant pilot requested a staff car to take me from Roswell to my home in Lake Arthur, a distance of about 30 miles. The pilot was only carrying out orders and I didn't realize what he had done.

"Shortly after we landed I found myself, along with the pilot, standing in front of the Wing Commander's desk. The Wing Commander was Colonel (Later General) Blanchard. He wanted to know who I thought I was demanding a staff car (I was only a Staff Sergeant). I told him I really didn't want a staff car and if he would allow me to use the phone I would call my parents and they would come for me.

"He then asked where I had been and when I told him I had been in the Philippines and a prisoner of the Japanese for three and a half years he pointed to his staff car and the driver on the curb and said, 'Take my car and driver and keep them as long as you want them.'

"I, of, the course, sent them back as soon as I got home. On the way home, at about 3:30 in the afternoon, near the Mossman loading pens, we were about to pass my Dad and his Santa Fe section hands going home on the railroad motor car.

"I asked the driver to stop and when Dad saw me he jumped out of the motor car and came running. Dad would never let anyone else drive his motor car but, that afternoon he told the crew to take it on in and he rode the rest of the way home in the staff car with me. IT WAS GOOD TO BE HOME!"

Across the street from us lived Major Milton Poole, a navigator on a B-47. That plane was the dominant Air Force (note that Ferron Cummins' Army Air Corps was no longer part of the Army but a separate military force) bomber before the B-52.

Milton, who lived with his beautiful wife, Thelma, and two young daughters a year or two older than Terry, was a jolly fellow around the neighborhood. He would run his gasoline-power mower across the lawn with a mug of beer in one hand. This maneuver infuriated Novella Lynch's mother to no end.

Novella was a single school teacher who lived next door to the Pooles with her strict Baptist mother who didn't believe in drinking alcohol, much less making such a public display of it. Yet, she liked Milton, who did many favors for daughter and mother – such as minor repairs to their home.

The mother appeared to be constantly criticizing her daughter. One evening just before dark, Novella came across the street and sat on the lawn next to Mary and me. My good wife had to go into our house for a few minutes and Novella's mother across the street spotted the two of us sitting together. The mother had a conniption fit, began yelling at the top of her lungs for Novella to come home. She obeyed – scurrying back across the street!

Wonder what "the Old Lady" thought Novella and I were up to in front of God and everybody else on the lawn? Several years after leaving Roswell we learned that Novella died in a nursing home at an early age. It's a good bet her mother was much of the cause of driving her there.

Two doors to the south of us on Rancho Road lived Tech Sergeant John Goolsbee and his wife, Patricia. Pat was John's British bride, and at the time they had just one son, about Terry's age. John's job was flight engineer on a KC-97, where he sat just behind the pilot and co-pilot. This was in the era of General Curtis LeMay

One biographer says of LeMay that "the men called him 'Iron Ass' because he demanded so much, but he was immensely respected." In 1949, LeMay had taken over leadership of the Strategic Air Command, which included Walker Air Force Base at Roswell.[9]

The crews of SAC planes, both the refueling KC-97s and KC-135s and the bombing B-47s and B-52s, were keenly judged for promotions on the readiness of their aircraft. It was as if General LeMay was standing behind each one of them.

Just after dark one day, a mock emergency order came and John Goolsbee's plane quickly lined up, ready to take off with other KC-97s next to a Walker runway.

On command, two of the planes took off. Looking over a myriad of gauges, John spotted something amiss with his aircraft – something so wrong that he decided the plane was unsafe for takeoff. It was his prerogative, even as a technical sergeant sitting behind two officers, to cancel the takeoff. The conversation went something like this, minutes or seconds before the okay from the tower to take off:

"We have to abort, sir," John said. "We have a serious problem."

"God damn it, Goolsbee," the pilot shouted, perhaps seeing his promotion from captain to major vanishing, "I'm going to have your ass in a sling over this."

"Can't help that, sir. This aircraft isn't ready to take off."

"Damn it," the pilot repeated. "Okay, Goolsbee I'm calling in that we've aborted."

---

[9] The biographer wrote: "He headed SAC until 1957, overseeing the transformation into a modern, efficient, all-jet force. Along the way, he acquired a large fleet of new bombers, established a vast aerial refueling system, started many new units and vases, began missile development, and established a strict command and control system.

Very soon after that came the order from the tower for all the remaining planes to cancel their takeoffs. The first two KC-97s had lifted off the runway, then quickly crashed with many casualties. Whatever was wrong with Goolsbee's plane also affected the others, but they'd taken off anyway.

When John told me this story, I knew it was coming from a very brave and principled man. The last time we saw John and Pat was at a Mexican Café alongside the river and at their home in San Antonio, Texas. John had just beaten back prostate cancer with the injection of radioactive material, but it caught up with him and he died a few years later.

On October 29, 1957, A KC97G tanker took off on a classified survey mission – testing flying at less than 1,000 feet which might allow bombers during those Cold War days to fly under Soviet Union radar. A story from a 64-year-old Navajo sheepherder in the July 1, 2001, *Arizona Republic* recalls what happened at Gray Mountain.

"We could see the fog all around us...I remember (at 20 years old) telling my mom, 'Mom. It sounds like that plane is too low,'" Loretta Mexican Begay said. "All of a sudden we heard the impact of the crash, and we heard rocks rolling down, and I told mom, "Mom, the plane crashed, it sounds like a plane crashed'."

When the KC-97G slammed into Gray Mountain on the western edge of the Navajo Reservation in Arizona, it killed all 16 aboard. One of them was Milton Poole, our neighbor across the street. The Cold War had come home to Rancho Road. The pall of Milton's death hung over the neighborhood, settled there for many days. A grieving Thelma Poole soon decided it best to go back to her home in Michigan.

Mary and I kept track of Thelma and her daughters only with Christmas cards. It would be 35 years later, in 1992 when we were on our post-retirement motorhome trip that we sat down with Thelma in Michigan for coffee. We talked about Roswell and about our daughters. Both of hers were married, one of them a dentist. Thelma was taking care of her 90-something-year-old mother, never having found anyone to replace that happy guy who used to mow his lawn with a stein of beer in his hand.

A few times it was my good fortune to be able to ride high in the sky with members of the Strategic Air Command. Once, I actually flew one of the Air Force's largest planes. Sorta. That is, handled its controls for several minutes under the watchful eye of a real pilot. The plane was a B-36 Peacemaker[10], one of only 385 ever built. Invited along with 40 Air

---

[10] The B-36 was the largest bomber of its day, weighing 200,000 pounds and with a wing span of 230 feet–larger than a Boeing 747. It was powered by <u>six-pusher</u> prop engines, with four jet engines added to later versions. In service with the Air Force for about 10 years, it gradually was phased out and replaced by the B-52 in 1959.

Force Academy cadets as guests on five Walker Air Force Base , we took short turns in the pilot's seat flying the huge aircraft.

Somewhat like when backing up a fifth-wheel trailer once you began to steer the huge B-36 one way, it didn't want to move the other. Turning slowly was the answer, and it took lots of words of encouraging instruction from the pilot to get the plane straightened.

There was even a little bit of excitement for those of us returning in the big plane that day, April 17, 1957, I wrote:

"With minutes left before hitting the runway, trouble developed in number six engine – the outside propeller engine on the right wing. The blades were feathered parallel with the body of the plane but still the propeller turned slowly like a windmill on a fairly calm day. Oil streamed out of the engine, but luckily it didn't catch on fire. The plane began to let down with five engines and the roar became louder. The 'window rattlers' had returned to Roswell. With five engines, the plane still has 90 percent of its power, according to a crew member."

In 1950, a B-36 based in Carswell Air Force Base in Fort Worth, Texas, had experienced icing conditions and multiple fires flying over the Canada and Alaska area. The crew bailed out, and the plane carrying a nuclear device (a "Fat Man," the same as one dropped on Nagasaki, Japan, in 1945) crashed in the ocean. There was worry about the bomb resting on the ocean floor and its resulting release of radiation.

A continuing argument is whether by order of President Harry Truman the United States should have dropped atomic bombs on Hiroshima and Nagasaki[11] Those in favor claim a million Americans might have died invading Japan, where its army was dug-in. Opponents contend Japan soon would have surrendered without an invasion, that perhaps the atomic bombs should have been dropped in the ocean near the two cities to show their power, rather than directly on civilian populations.

In January of 1957, I'd taken a ride in a propeller-driven KC-97 aerial tanker and watched in awe as it refueled a B-47 bomber at about 30,000 feet:

"The sleek, lighted nose of a B-47 bomber pushes slowly out of the darkness, sways slightly to the left, then to the right. Swinging in unison with the nose of the bomber is a cylindrical boom dangling from the tail section of a KC-97, Air Force refueling plane. The pilot of the almost-stalled bomber and boom operator on the slow-moving tanker jockey for position.

---

[11] On August 6, 1945, the B-29 Enola Gay dropped a "Little Boy" atomic bomb on Hiroshima, resulting in the death of about 140,000 persons. Three days later the "Fat Man" from another B-29 Superfortress hit Nagasaki — with an estimated 39,000 to 74,000 more killed.

The end of the boom lines up with the lighted well in the bomber's nose. There is a whir as the boom extends, sinking firmly into the well. An automatic lock clicks. Bomber and tanker are joined 30 to 40 feet apart....Minutes pass, tanks are full, the flow of fuel stops. The operator disconnects the boom, the bomber falls back, then slips quickly past with a silent rush.....Cabin lights flick on, and the boom operator gets out of his prone position while guiding the tricky boom. Smiles creep across faces, packages of cigarettes slip out of zippered pockets of flying suits."

In October of 1959, I rode in a KC-135 jet tanker as part of what Air Force personnel called the "Strategic Air Command World Series." The actual name was the Strategic Air Command, Bombing, Navigation, and Air Refueling Competition. I reported from McCoy Air Force Base in Florida:

"Ten fliers from Walker Air Force Base will be taking off on a mission that could be the most important of their military careers since World War II. Only in the event of an enemy attack and the subsequent mission of retaliation which each man is ready to fly 24 hours a day , yet prays he'll never have to, could the outcome be more important...No bombs will be dropped. Simulated bomb runs will be made and scored by radar accuracy. Accuracy is measured in feet and a direct hit is called a 'Shack'. The bombing mission will be flown at speeds of more than 450 miles an hour. Missions should take seven or eight hours to complete."

Before going up in the World Series, I took "Physiological Training" at McCoy which included going into a decompression chamber. Several of us at the same time in the chamber experienced physically what would happen inside an aircraft if it lost its compression. That is, if the outside pressure flying at high altitude somehow were to suddenly equal that inside.

I also was issued a parachute, with a small tank of oxygen. Both hung on a hook next to the KC-135's door. "You'll be the first out if something happens, that's for sure, even if we need to push," a sergeant told me. "Civilians have to be cleared before we can go." It might not be all that simple. He explained, "Even if we pushed you out, you might hit the tail. Or you'd probably open your chute too soon and run out of oxygen."

We'd been told during our training at McCoy what to do after leaving the plane–say at 25,000 feet. Before opening our parachutes at night we should fall until lights on the ground below became very distinct. In the daytime, before pulling the rip cord, we should be able to make out objects like barns clearly. If we didn't wait, opened our chute too soon, the small oxygen canister wouldn't last long enough for us to survive as we floated down.

"It also would be bad news if we bailed out over water," he continued, pointing out that waves would tangle me in the parachute or its ropes and I'd drown, and that only a few minutes in the cold water of the Atlantic would do me in.

"What we'd try to do is splash down in the water. The plane will stay afloat for a while, long enough to launch the life rafts and for us to get into them." Still, those parachutes became reassuring. During my first commercial flight later, I suddenly felt something missing, said to myself, "My God, I don't have any parachute!!"

Our 6th Bomb Wing from Walker AFB tied for third place in the SAC World Series with the 22nd Bomb Wing from March Air Force Base in California. Bad luck played its part that night for the Roswell team as sextant shots of the stars couldn't be taken because of storm clouds rising as high as 40,000 feet at check-off points. Of course, this was before the GPS (Global Positioning System) common in many of today's automobiles – which connect with satellites straight through clouds to give an exact position.

Two years earlier, the United States and the Soviet Union had become engaged in the Space Race. Al Stubbs and I and one or two other hearty *Roswell Daily Record* staffers were quaffing beer in the bar of the Nickson Hotel, catty-corner across the street, just before midnight on October 4, 1957.[12] The bartender handed Al the phone from Bill Richardson, the young Albuquerque bureau chief for the Associated Press (not the man with the same name who became New Mexico's governor and a U.S. ambassador), on the other end of the line.

"Bill says the Russians have shot something up into space and its circling the world now," Al told us, "and it's pretty important — according to AP."

"Think we need to re-plate?" I asked. Re-plating meant taking the half-round, lead metal front page off the press, perhaps even "stopping the press" if it had begun running. None of us, in either the editorial room or the backshop, liked to do that unless something happened of exceptional news value. Besides extra work, plus expense for the newspaper, it meant all of us would be up long past midnight.

"I guess we need to," Al said, repeating that Richardson said it was "a big deal."

So we local newsmen, ignorant about space matters and not thoroughly convinced of the story's newsworthiness, left the bar and trudged back across the street. The front page was changed, but only reluctantly with a paragraph-or-two, bold-faced insert which told

---

[12] In a procedure not much approved by wives, we gathered in the Nickson bar for at least a half hour every Saturday night while in the composing room the final lead pages of the newspaper were laboriously made ready. At least one of us had to make our way back across the street to double-check the first papers off the press for such errors as transposed pictures.

about the world's first artificial satellite. Sputnik was the size of a basketball, weighed only 183 pounds, and took 98 minutes to orbit the earth.

The enormity of the Soviet Union's achievement quickly became apparent. The Russians not only were ahead in the "Space Race," but also the American public soon began to fear the Soviets could use satellites to launch ballistic missiles from Europe and pinpoint them to targets in the U.S.

On November 3 of 1957, Sputnik II was launched–with a heavier payload and carrying a dog named Laika. On January 31, 1958, the United States launched Explorer I – a satellite carrying a scientific payload which eventually resulted in the discovery of magnetic radiation belts around the earth. They were named after James Van Allen. (More about him when I get to the State University of Iowa.)

News media around the country began to get into the groove about the space age. What was curious was that the Roswell area was the place where a pioneer rocket scientist had carried out many of his experiments.

His name was Robert Hutchings Goddard. I wrote about him in March of 1959:

"There is no formal countdown and only one man in charge as the rocket lifts from its launching tower northwest of Roswell. A smoke trail floats off to the left, giving an erratic appearance to the eye as the flame from the rocket engine pushes it straight and true 7,500 feet into the air. The year is 1935 and another experiment is finished by the 'screwball' who keeps the heads of many Roswell area people shaking."

The next month marked the dedication of the Robert Hutchings Goddard Memorial and Space Museum by dignitaries headed by Dr. Wernher von Braun. The German-born scientist led that nation's U-2 program which rained armed rockets on London. Now, an American citizen as director of the Operations Division of the Army Ballistic Agency at Redstone Arsenal, Alabama, Von Braun figured to be the top missileman in the U.S.

"Authorities such as von Braun, "I wrote, "consider that the United States would be 18 to 20 years ahead in the space race if Americans had listened to Dr. Goddard."

Goddard in 1919 had published a report that a multi-staged rocket weighing 10 tons could land a small payload on the moon. He began firing his rockets at a farm near Auburn, Mass. After residents there protested, Goddard moved to Roswell. Charles A. Lindbergh, first to fly across the Atlantic Ocean from New York to Paris in 1927, came to Roswell and observed Goddard's experiments. "The Lone Eagle" then persuaded the Guggenheim Foundation to grant Goddard $25,000 for his studies.

Mary and I were able to meet von Braun and other dignitaries such as Goddard's widow, during a cookout at a cotton farm south of Roswell. It was hosted by State Senator Morgan Nelson (I'm not certain whether it was because of my stories in the *Record* about Goddard that we were invited, or because I'd gotten to know the state senator at a speaking club–called the Toastmasters. I had found him to be one of the most intelligent and amiable persons I'd known during our Roswell days. At any rate, it was a fun event and Mary's and our first taste of tasty buffalo burgers.)

Another Roswell politician I got to know was Jack Campbell, a Democrat and speaker of the State House of Representatives. Election Night required almost all the editorial staff to take part in the coverage. At least a couple of times, after the votes had been counted, Campbell invited Al, me, and a couple of other *Record* staffers over to the Nickson for a drink. His office also was just down the street from the *Record,* and he was a friendly sort - always ready for a short chat.

Campbell had been a Marine in World War II and an FBI agent. He and his older law partner had gathered some of their money in a novel way. There was a period when Roswell-area cotton farmers and sheep ranchers were contacted by oil companies about mineral leases. The farmers and ranchers doubted there was oil or natural gas under their land, but they came to the Campbell office for the legal work.

Campbell and his partner charged nothing at the time for this legal work. They either drew up, or would oversee, the lease papers - only gambling for a small percentage should any oil or gas revenue come in. Lo and behold! There was a major oil field discovered near Artesia to the south, a refinery was built, and soon the Roswell area was dotted with oil wells. It was a bonanza for lucky farmers and ranchers, but also for Campbell and his partner.

After our family had left New Mexico, Jack M. Campbell was elected governor of the state from 1963 to 1966. He died in 1992 in a retirement home after a long illness at the age of 82. According to his obituary in the *Milwaukee Journal* Campbell was credited with, "Enforcing a non-partisan civil service system for state employees and modernizing services for the mentally ill. He was the first New Mexico governor to appoint a science advisor."

Just before the 1960 Presidential election, Al told me, "Lyndon Johnson's in town. I can't be there, but someone from the paper should be to meet him." Off to the Holiday Inn I went to find the Democratic Vice-Presidential candidate running with John F. Kennedy.

Texan Johnson was moving like a whirlwind through Southern and Southwest states. His efforts on the ticket could have made the difference in that very close election when

201

Kennedy defeated Vice President Richard Nixon. When I arrived at the Holiday Inn east of town, Lady Bird Johnson was greeting everyone coming into the lobby. I told her who I was. "Oh, Lyndon always likes to meet with you folks from the press," she purred with a gracious show of excitement, a true politician's wife. "You just go right on in. Lyndon's waiting for you in the next room."

The Senator sorta was. I got in a line, shook the hand of and mumbled a few un-notable words with the man who would become President of the United States that awful day. November 22, 1963, when John F. Kennedy was assassinated while we were at the University of Missouri.

Which reminds me of trivial tricks-of-the-trade while editor or headline writer. Like to spell assassination, just write "ass" twice and go from there. And to spell Soviet Premier Nikita Khrushchev correctly, you need to put in three h's.

A sort of final note about my series on Robert Goddard. I sent it in as competition for the annual contest of the New Mexico Press Association. Thought I had a good chance there. Didn't make it with those stories, but *sorta* did with editorials/columns. Al Stubbs won first place, Bill Stoddard of the *Artesia Daily Press* second and Tony Hillerman of Santa Fe's *New Mexican* third.

The chairman of judges wrote in February of 1960:

"You said only three places, but if I ever want to hire a good editorial writer, I will settle for Bob White, (Farmington); Jeter Bryan (Carlsbad); Jess Price (Tucumcari); Norm Newcomer (Artesia), or Max Odendahl (Roswell). Generally speaking, the group is outstanding."

Licking my unofficial, honorable-mention wounds, I rationalized about only occasionally writing editorials or columns (like when Al was on vacation). Because the rest of the group did theirs year-round, they had more material to choose entries from. Yeah, right.

Al later beamed with pride that he beat out Tony Hillerman, the yet-to-be famous mystery novelist, in that editorial division two or three times. While never a close friend of Hillerman, I consider him more than a nodding acquaintance. A couple of times a year New Mexico Associated Press-member editors and wire editors would meet in Albuquerque. Over drinks provided by AP, we'd sit (usually in the bar) and talk about how to make our wire service work better by mutual sharing of stories. I don't recall any meeting when amiable and dedicated-newsman Tony wasn't there. During that time, AP put out the following little blurb:

"ALBUQUERQUE (AP)–Max Odendahl, wire editor of the Roswell Daily Record has been named state chairman of the Associated Press Managing Editors Association. Odendahl was

elected at a Sunday night meeting and succeeds Tony Hillerman of the Santa Fe New Mexican."

In the 1960s, Tony left the editorship of *The New Mexican* to pursue graduate studies at the University of New Mexico in Albuquerque, while at the same time doing public relations work for the university. He later became chairman of the university's Journalism Department.

It was during this time that he began writing his best-selling novels featuring Navajo law enforcement officers Joe Leaphorn and Jim Chee. His first novel was *The Blessing Way*, followed by *The Fly on the Wall*, about newspaper persons. The story is that when Tony submitted his first Navajo-oriented novel to an agent, the reply was something like, "We probably could get it published if you got that Indian stuff out of it." Tony found another agent, and, as they say, "the rest is history."

Tony, his wife Marie, Mary, and I spent time together during meals at a national conference of the Association for Education in Journalism and Mass Communication when I taught at San Diego State University. Hillerman certainly became a bit more successful with his writing career than I. (That's a joke, son.) Several years ago there was an article in a New Mexico publication noting the richest persons in the state. Tony was listed as being worth an estimated $25 million. That was a few novels ago. He also wrote many non-fiction pieces.

In the spring of 1960, the *Record* sent me to Columbia University in New York City for a two-week seminar at the American Press Institute for publishers, editors, and chief news executives. There were 26 newspapers with a circulation under 50,000 represented, including six from Canada. It was a great learning experience as we heard lectures by experts and critiqued each other's papers.

But my country bumpkinship was evident. I knew virtually nothing about the life of homosexuals, except that ignorantly we straight men still referred to "queers" or "fairies." Most of us thought two women living together generally were nothing but "old maids," although we had heard a little about short-haired "dykes."

One method to identify a gay man (nobody I was aware of used that term then – to be "young and gay" meant something quite different) somehow had crept into my mind. Guys in generally desert-like New Mexico had convinced me that carrying an umbrella identified a man as a homosexual.

One gray New York day, two or three of the participants at the American Press Institute showed up with umbrellas. "Aha!!" I thought. After the lunch break, almost all the men around the large table packed umbrellas. Was I surrounded by newspaper "fairies?"

Nope, it began to rain in the middle of the afternoon and only two or three of us ignorant dry-landers went out into it without an umbrella. We got wet.

I went to the Great White Way near Times Square to take in a couple of plays, including "The Music Man," with Eddie Albert in the starring role. I recall one of those subway trips as an example how racist and frightened of "negroes" many of us were. If you got on the subway at Columbia University going one way (I think it was Downtown) you'd be able to get off near Times Square and close to the theaters. But if you boarded the Uptown subway, it would take you past Harlem. Most of us white New Mexicans thought Harlem represented untold dangers, perhaps even to our very lives.

On one of my trips–all dressed up in suit and tie, I mistakenly got on the Uptown subway. (Uptown. Downtown. Sounded the same to me.) In only a few minutes I could tell we were in an African-American area of New York - the dreaded Harlem. Dredging up some courage, I actually asked a black woman what I ought to do. Told her I was headed for a play. "Oh, you're okay," she reassured me with a smile. "Just get off at the next stop. Go up the stairs, across the tracks in the building, down the stairs and catch a Downtown train going the other way."

Thanked her, got off at the next stop, and can tell you that was a mighty quick bit of walking up and down those darkened stairs. Nervous, quite a bit scared, waiting for the next subway, for the first time in my life I was surrounded by black folks. Guess what? I survived and enjoyed the play.

Randomly choosing those plays, getting in with walk-on tickets, I sure wasn't as organized as some other American Press Institute participants. On Monday, one asked if I'd gone to a Sunday service at the Marble Collegiate Church in Manhattan to listen to Norman Vincent Peale. Born in 1898 and ordained as a Methodist minister, Peale in 1932 changed to the Reformed Church in America. He was pastor at the Manhattan church for 52 years as it grew in membership from 600 to over 5,000. He was most noted for "Positive Thinking." His best-selling book, *The Power of Positive Thinking* stayed on the New York Times best-selling list for 186 consecutive weeks.

If Mary had been with me, she probably would have convinced me to go with her to Peale's church, but I wasn't much impressed by the minister's techniques, agreed with critics who referred to them as "self-hypnosis." Harvard scholar Donald Meyer wrote that Peale's view actually was a grim and depressing one of those afraid to take on the challenges of life - resigned to the status quo, to anger, and even impotence.

I think somehow, maybe because of growing up in a small town, getting next to "personalities" never impressed me quite as much as it has so many others. Although, I would have liked on my New York trip to have met either of the two Joes, DiMaggio or Louis.

Serving the Navy in San Diego in the late 1940s, I was a homesick kid who came home by Greyhound bus all the way to New Mexico on 72-hour passes. Recall a couple of other sailors who also took a bus trip during their leave, but went to Los Angeles to listen to Frankie Laine. He had a distinctive voice and belted out such songs as "The Cry of the Wild Goose" and "That's My Desire." Laine also recorded duets with some of the most popular female singers of that time – such as Patti Page, Doris Day, and Jo Stafford.

If anything, the accolade-of-stars situation has gotten worse – or better, according to most of the younger set. For example, at this writing some hard news on the second page of the *San Diego Union-Tribune* has been partially replaced with such soft trivia as who Paris Hilton might be sleeping with or whether Madonna should have adopted a baby in Africa. This 21ˢᵗ Century "sign of the times" showed that the *U-T* felt pressured to compete for circulation with *People* magazine and popular television shows such as "Entertainment Tonight" – which glamorize movie/TV stars and other entertainers.

Leaving Gotham in 1960, I flew to Washington, D.C., where a few hours was spent taking a first look at the nation's capitol building and the memorials to really important people like George Washington, and Thomas Jefferson.

I looked out from the steps of the Abraham Lincoln Memorial at the reflecting ponds, where thousands later would gather to hear the Rev. Martin Luther King make his "I Have A Dream" speech. And from there took a long walk to make a somber visit to Arlington National Cemetery and silently observe a changing of the guard at The Tomb of the Unknown Soldier.

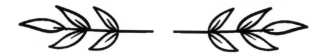

Chapter 11 – Leaving Roswell's Little Space Creatures Behind

Along about this time, Al Stubbs promoted me from News Editor to City Editor. It simply was a change in title. The *Record's* two reporters, Hank Smith and Brownie Emerson - experienced, independent–self-starters knew how and what to cover on their beats.

It never became like scenes in the movies. Where I'd sit around with a cigar hanging out of my mouth, barking out orders, "Get off your fat asses and over to City Hall and find out what the hell's goin' on over there." Besides, neither Hank nor Brownie had a fat ass.

My job continued to be to put together, still often frantically on deadline, the news pages of the paper before deadline each day. Could I have worked for the *Roswell Daily Record* for maybe 30 years before retiring. Who knows about that, but it eventually came down to the amount of salary for a fellow raising a family.

Without any sort of written agreement, I'd begun in 1955 at the *Record* at $55 for a six-day-week. The deal which became apparent was that each six months I'd receive a $5 weekly raise. By 1961 I'd reached an annual salary of over $5,000 a year. By comparison, Tony Hillerman told me he never received less than $10,000 yearly as editor of the *Santa Fe New Mexican*. And, although Al didn't say so, Stubbs's salary must have been somewhere near Hillerman's.

What happened at too many small newspapers in the country was that they hired, at meager salaries, bright-eyed and bushy-tailed journalism school graduates chomping at the bit to change the world. Or those hoping quickly to be recognized as great writers like Mark Twain or Ernest Hemingway. Low beginning pay didn't deter us. We fantasized about eventually receiving huge royalties from our Great American Novels.

If we eager and over-worked young men and women remained with one newspaper without some sort of major promotion, we would – usually regardless of gender[13] – reach what decades later became known for women as "the glass ceiling." That's what happened to me in 1961 as newcomers in the *Record* newsroom received their raise in wages, but I didn't.

---

[13] And, of course, females – journalism graduates or not — generally were relegated to jobs on newspapers such as writing about society, fashion, or other soft news such as architecture. On TV, they would be the Weather Girls. One such in San Diego, Raquel Welch, moved a long way ahead of that in movies.

"Bob Beck says it's all he can pay you," Al told me when I complained. I talked with the publisher who, although he didn't appear very happy about it, confirmed his decision. Beck, a handsome and nice fellow, in World War II had piloted a C-47 over The Hump – a dangerous 530-mile passage across the Himalayan Mountains. The planes supplied the Chinese, who kept the Burma Road open and hundreds of thousands of Japanese troops preoccupied.

After the war Beck married the daughter of the *Record's* owner, who ran our small chain of newspapers out of Lake Charles, Louisiana. Mrs. Beck's experience sort'a paralleled Katherine Graham's, where her father named her husband publisher of the *Washington Post*. It was only after her husband's suicide that "Katy" Graham assumed her duties as publisher and gained much fame after Watergate.

"The Old Man," as Bob Beck's father-in-law was referred to at the *Record,* probably operated all of his papers with a salary limit for "non-key" personnel. That's the way the cow ate the cabbage. Neither Mary nor I can remember whether the *Record* paid for our Blue Cross health insurance (which covered Pam's birth), but we don't think it did. There was no specified retirement plan of any kind, although a couple of longtime, retiring employees testified that, "The Old Man will take care of you. He did me." Trouble was, The Old Man would be dead long before I would retire from the *Record.* What then?

Not only was I miffed by this troubling financial turn of events, but also a decision had to be made what to do about it. In early 1961, I was 30 years old and not likely to replace Al Stubbs as editor. Also in his 30s, Al had grown up in Roswell, showed no interest in moving up to a larger newspaper anywhere else.

An offer from the *Albuquerque Journal* several years earlier to work in the Duke City as a sports writer brought little interest from me in returning to sports coverage. With scant experience as a reporter, editorial writer, or columnist, I'd probably need to look for a job putting another newspaper together somewhere.

Mary at least once had told me, "If you ever decide to go back to school, I'll work as a secretary to get you through." Sounded good. My only teaching experience had been leading a very short course about newspapering for the Roswell YMCA. I liked doing it. So, I began looking through catalogs of various universities offering graduate courses in journalism. What enticed me most was what *seemed to be* the curriculum at the State University of Iowa, now simply the University of Iowa.

Times certainly have changed. I'm almost dead-certain that, with my barely-passing, undergraduate grade-point-average at the University of New Mexico, I'd not make it into any respectable graduate program now. Lady Luck led me by the hand because of my experience in the journalism field, and two excellent recommendations. One came from Al Stubbs, who graciously didn't try to do anything like "get even" for my deciding to leave the *Record* shortly after I'd taken that all-expense-paid trip to the American Press Institute at Columbia University in New York City.

The director of the Roswell YMCA, with a name I sheepishly can't even remember, wrote the other recommendation. Maybe he'd heard good things about my short YMCA short course in journalism. Several times I'd had coffee with him at The Greek's café down the street. "Hope you made a generous pledge to The United Way," he once remarked. "We sure need the money."

"I did," and, kidding him, added, "but what I wrote on the pledge card was: 'None of This Goes to the YMCA ','"

He chuckled and said, "It would take lots of you miserable malcontents to take away any YMCA United Fund money. We still get our certain percentage." It was a fickle finger of fate at another coffee meeting, that I mentioned leaving Roswell. Out of the blue, the YMCA director volunteered, "If you need a recommendation, Max, I'll be happy to write one for you."

He did, and along with Al's they somehow must have impressed Leslie Moeller, the director of the School of Journalism at the State University of Iowa. I received a letter saying I was accepted into the master's program. To this day I have no idea what my Graduate Record Exam score might have been.

Bob Neel, who you recall sat next to me at Hurley High School because his name began with N and mine with O, and a Sigma Chi fraternity brother, said to me one afternoon walking across campus at the University of New Mexico, "They're giving a test this afternoon for those who want to go on to graduate school. I think I'll go by and take it."

"Is that very important?" I asked.

"Maybe? Who knows what we might decide to do after this Korean War gets over with?" So, Bob and I took the test. As far as I know, Bob Neel never completed any graduate work – although he might have taken additional courses at UNM. After being an Air Force pilot in the Korean War, Bob married and worked until retirement as an engineer at Sandia Base. He and Mary's brother-in-law, Tom Hill, knew one another there. Bob's and my nonchalantly taking of the GRE probably would boggle the minds of those now cramming, fretting days before the essential exam, struggling so hard for high scores hoping to lead to a graduate degree and BIG BUCKS.

Before having readers leave Roswell, guess this is as good any place in this long-winded narrative to make known my meager knowledge about the city's now-famous Outer Space creatures. "The Roswell Incident" was before our family arrived in 1955. The *Roswell Daily Record* on July 8, 1947, printed a story originating from Roswell Army Air Field. It told about the capture of a crashed flying disc. Over the years, the story has been magnified into a "Believe-It-or-Not" tale that aliens, some possibly still alive at least for a while, were recovered.

The Air Force has faced charges of massively covering-up of knowledge about the incident. Even that a nurse - pledged to silence about working on the alleged little bodies -disappeared, perhaps even could have been murdered. The other side of the tale is that, during the 1940s and 1950s, the Air Force had a highly classified program going known as the Mogul Project. For the "cover-up" the military claimed the crashed disk amounted only to a "weather balloon." In fact, the Mogul Project may have been a method of monitoring secret Soviet nuclear denotations and radiation by placing sensitive special equipment in balloons at high altitudes.

Some of these experiments originating at Alamogordo Army Air Field could also have involved launching balloons carrying and then ejecting dummies or chimpanzees. Equipped with parachutes the dummies or chimps would show how best to return pilots or astronauts to earth if they had to eject at high altitudes.

One even-less-mentioned scenario is that chimps could have landed near Roswell with their fur singed off. Was it chimps secretly whisked away, perhaps to Ohio, by the U.S. military so that the public wouldn't panic, or be offended about the way the chimps were treated? Or was the panic because of a threat of *something* from Outer Space our military didn't understand? Or couldn't protect us against? You be the judge.

To put what little I know in context, Al Stubbs might have casually mentioned about the Roswell mysterious flying disc and/or an Air Force cover-up once or twice. It certainly didn't hold much significance for us at the *Record* while I was there. It was many years after Mary and I with two young daughters had left New Mexico that we learned about the possible gravity of the "Roswell Incident."

However, if the purported UFO landing/little-creatures chronicle had "stayed alive" it would have been a major focal point in all of my stories about the Robert Goddard Space Museum. Either Al Stubbs, I, or someone else I surely would have asked Wernher von Braun what he knew or speculated about it. And so forth.

Nevertheless, stories about Unidentified Flying Objects being sighted weren't unusual. A number of folks in New Mexico during the 1950s saw what convinced them were Flying

Saucers, or other-shaped UFOs. Common stories were about observing a horizontal, cigar-shaped light hovering somewhere, which zipped away at a tremendous speed. In a 1997 *Time* magazine cover story about "the Roswell Files," Jimmy Carter was mentioned, "While running for the presidency, (Carter) admitted he had seen a UFO, but then, once in office, reneged on promises to open the government's flying saucer files." Why did Carter renege? What, if anything more, or sinister had he learned?

Mary and I saw one or two large "falling stars" while necking on the mesa outside Albuquerque in 1953. A professor at the University of New Mexico was keeping track of this rather unusual number of nightly meteorites and requested those seeing them to call him. Mary told me after phoning the prof, "He asked me whether they looked as big as a silver dollar, a half dollar, a quarter, or a nickel. I wasn't sure, because that's not the way we looked at them."

"Yeah," I agreed, "they just were larger and had longer tails than ordinary falling stars." Could these have been the tails of fiery entries of space vehicles into our atmosphere? Tom Hill, Mary's younger sister Phyllis's husband, had been graduated in the same 1953 UNM class as I. A mechanical engineer, Tom then was working in deep Sandia Mountains tunnels at the Sandia Corporation next to the Albuquerque airport. Sandia engineers produced nuclear weapons which came from designs of scientists operating just above Santa Fe at Los Alamos, the birthplace of the atom bomb.

"One night Tom and I saw a flying saucer," a convinced Phyllis told Mary. "And it wasn't anything we Americans have because he knows just about everything top secret we are doing in that area."

On the other hand, the *Record* staff usually looked at such stories as something WE knew about and the United States was doing it . For example, one day those at the *Record* were privy to a tale about a line of cars leaving White Sands Proving Ground between Alamogordo and Las Cruces. Suddenly, the rumor went, a flying saucer hovered over the cars and all stopped dead in their tracks. After a several minutes, according to the story, drivers were able to restart their cars and continue toward homes. "Aha!" someone at the *Record* commented, "We got those Ruskies by the balls now."

The Soviet Union reportedly had a much larger row of tanks facing those of NATO (the North Atlantic Treaty Organization), not only toward Europeans but also United States forces there. "So," the staffer continued, "if we go to war, one of those flying saucers of ours could fly over that whole line of Ruskie tanks. Bingo! They all shut down, can't get 'em started. Like sitting ducks. Meanwhile, our tanks move in on them and soon it's all over."

Maybe? Just one battle. However, the real threat to humanity remained. Both the Soviet Union and the United States were stockpiling enough nuclear weapons to be delivered by rockets which could wipe out the cities of both nations several times.

The *Record*, and other newspapers, didn't publish unsubstantiated stories like about any flying saucer shutting down automobiles. During the Cold War, we of "the liberal press" did attempt to keep the defense secrets of our country.

Another example: While I was working part-time for the Albuquerque Bureau of the Associated Press early in 1953, a couple of AP staffers were doing a story at Los Alamos. Apparently, they went to a bar with some engineers and/or other scientists such as physicists and asked a few questions.

When they finished writing their story in Albuquerque, they submitted it to the nuclear experts at Sandia Base to check for factual errors. That's when you-know-what hit the fan. It seems the story contained several "top secrets" deemed helpful to the Soviets. So that story was killed and never ran in any AP newspaper, or was aired by a member radio or TV station.

"Secrets" were determined by the government, especially military branches of it. Yet, what remained a secret or whether it should be kept "classified" wasn't easy to determine. When I flew as a guest on that Strategic Air Command World Series trip, we journalists were cautioned never to use the word "cell'. While the KC-135s refueled the B-47s, we were in a "cell." Because all U.S. planes flew at a lower speed to connect and disconnect, in a real war they'd be vulnerable to fast Soviet fighter planes and ground-to-air rocket attacks.

After returning home from Florida, I picked up a *Life* magazine reporting the SAC World Series. It used the word "cell" to explain what was happening during hookup. When I asked the Public Information Officer at Walker Air Force Base about it, he chuckled, "Oh well, *Life* publishes back East closer to Washington and some high-ranking military person probably gave the OK to declassify 'cell'. We just have to live with those kinds of things."

I knew it wasn't going to be easy to leave such fun of newspapering behind. Or news sources who had become friends. And, especially, pals at the *Record*. It was even more difficult for Mary, who once she gets to really know you acquires a friend for life.

One of both our pals was reporter Brownie Emerson, who had converted to Catholicism. He had been married, but the gist of the story I got was that his wife left him. "You know, we were married as Catholics," he would mutter nearly in tears after a couple of beers. "She also should know that as a Catholic, she's still married to me."

A lonely guy, a good reporter later who suffered a heart attack and never actually was able to return to work. My listening to him repeat his sad marital tale over beers made me late for dinner more than once, a procedure not viewed too kindly by my good wife. What I often did to avoid facing any heavy music was to bring Brownie along for warmed-up dinners.

It was in a bar after work late one May afternoon of 1961 while Brownie was crying into his beer that he and I witnessed what probably was not only a local Roswell, but also a national, change in attitude about civil rights for "Negroes."

During civil rights protests in Birmingham, Alabama, the Birmingham Commissioner of Public Safety Eugene "Bull" Connor had used fire hoses and police dogs on black demonstrators. A thousand children had stayed out of school. Connor brought firefighters out and ordered them to turn streams of water on the children. Most demonstrators ran away, but one group refused to budge. The firefighters turned even more powerful hoses on them, the force of the water so hard it rolled protesters down the street. Connor also called out police dogs, which attacked those trying to enter a church.

"Jesus," a guy drinking at the Roswell bar and watching the brutality on TV shouted, "take a look what they done to those niggers."

"I never liked niggers much," the man sitting on the stool next to him added, "but that's goin' too far. It just ain't right to treat nobody that way." Brownie and I nodded heads to each other knowingly. When guys in bars who freely let the "N" word roll off their tongues were fed up with the way those with dark skin were being treated in one Southern city–change was in the air.

Earlier, on March 11, 1960, Brownie–on his trusty typewriter with triple-sized letters — had written a letter.

"Dear Mary:

"Thanks for your note in connection with the birthday present, my small and inadequate return for all the kindness shown to me by you and Max.

"I've said it so many times it sounds like a broken record but just the same I'll say it again: you and Max are two of the finest–and this is no buildup for me asking favors now or hereafter.

"Not only is Max a top-flight newspaperman but he is the grandest guy I've ever known to work with. He has plenty of humor and common sense, a sense of fair play – and these qualities are rare.

"Believe me this comes from the heart. The reason for putting it in writing is that this old broken-down wreck has about had it – and I wanted to put this in writing before the time comes when I won't be able to write.

"Please forgive the long letter. Those as ancient as I am talk too much and bore folks.

"Once more thanks for all your kindness and may God pour forth his blessing on you both and the children.

"Sincerely,

(Signed)–'Brownie'

"Brownwood Emerson"

March 11, 1960

Dear Mary:

Thanks for your note in connection
with the birthday present, a small and
inadequate return for all the kindness
shown to me by you and Max.

I've said it so many times it
sounds like a broken record but just the
same I'll say it again: you and Max are
two of the finest--and this is no buildup
for me asking favors either now or hereafter

Not only is Max a topflight
newspaperman but he is the grandest guy
I've ever known to work with. He has plenty
of humor and common sense, a sense of fair
play--and these qualities are rare.

Believe me all this comes from the
heart. The reason for putting it in writing
is that this old broken-down wreck has
about had it--and I wanted to put this in
writing before the time comes when I won't
able to write.

214

Please forgive the long letter. Those
as ancient as I am talk too much and bore folks.
Once more thanks for all your kk
kindness and may God pour forth his blessings
on you both and the children.

Sincerely,
Brownwood Emerson

Before he left the *Record*, Brownie offered me his large-print typewriter, which I declined because of younger eyes. But he did give me a long pair of scissors and a magnifying glass–which I still treasure. Brownie's letter to Mary was as close to any journalism prize I ever received.

There wasn't yet any hope for medical miracles like heart bypasses, or even angioplasty. Heart-attack victims like Brownie only waited in fear of their next attack. For example, Brownie was too frightened to climb courthouse stairs to cover stories. Kind-hearted Al Stubbs tried to lighten his load as much as possible, but a terrified Brownie soon quit his job. He was befriended by a priest and lived on Social Security (disability) next to the Catholic church. He died only a few years later.

In 1959 and the early 1960s, we watched "Rawhide" on television, starring Clint Eastwood. He was born three days after me, May 31, 1930, in San Francisco. Eastwood played wrangler Rowdy Yates, with trail boss Gil Favor portrayed by Eric Fleming. The trail boss would yell at the wranglers after each night's rest on the long cattle drive to "head 'em up, move 'em out!" It was time for our little Odendahl herd of four Roswellites to head ourselves up, to prepare ourselves to move out toward Iowa.

We'd bought and filled a 1947 Ford pickup to pull a U-Haul trailer. Problem was the tough little pickup had a faulty oil pump with little pressure when exceeding 45 miles per hour. Mary was forced to drive the same tedious speed behind me in our Nash Rambler station wagon. The girls, however, reveled in taking turns riding in the crowded cab of the slow pickup.

'Twas an odd and difficult year for me at the State University of Iowa, unlike any ever experienced before as an undergraduate at those three separate Land of Enchantment colleges (New Mexico State Teachers College at Silver City, New Mexico A&M at Las Cruces, and the University of New Mexico at Albuquerque). First and foremost, it became gravely serious on the home front when Terry developed pneumonia and was in an Iowa City hospital several days, including Christmas Eve. We drove those 20-mile round trips across the icy two-lane highway every night to visit with her.

After Terry came home from the hospital, she continued to suffer from allergies. She had to take a series of shots for that. What doctors did was determine from skin tests what she was allergic to (like household dust) and inject small amounts of those offending substances. After a few weeks, her allergies appeared almost to go away.

Mary was working full-time on campus as a secretary at Hillcrest men's dorms- and-dining. I had landed a part-time job in the news and information (university PR) office. My hours had to be juggled between classes, the job, and being there for Pam when she arrived home from the country grade school.

Pam and I spent lots of time playing games on afternoons before Mary and Terry came home, which included making weird faces at one another, One day, Pam's teacher called Mary in for a counseling session. She told Mary that Pam had been "acting out," was a difficult child to control. So, I stopped goofing around with Pam.

We worried Pam's problem was more serious than that, and were relieved when we moved on campus the second semester and her new teacher reported things were working out well.

Besides added time driving on icy roads, our heating bills were very high at the place out in the country. Luckily, Mary's boss was able to pull a string here and there and found married student housing for us on campus -- half of a World War II Quonset hut. Tow-headed Pam found a great new friend in a girl her age living in the other half of the Quonset hut, a "Negro" who had skin as dark as hers was fair. It was our family's first experience, and a good one, living close to African-Americans.

Ah, and how COLD it was! Something we never had experienced in New Mexico where snow only occasionally fell in some years, but rarely more than six or eight inches deep.

Normally, most of it melted to patches by the next afternoon. Not in Iowa. When a cold front moved in, with snow or not, the thermometer continued to register well below freezing – sometimes still near zero in late afternoon even as the sun shone brightly.

Once, coming home from work at dusk, Mary was caught in an ice storm which made the highway so slippery that, when proceeding up a slight hill, the Rambler spun completely around. She didn't know what to do, so trudged through the snow to the nearest farmhouse. A young man accompanied her back to the car, easily was able to turn it around, drive her on up the hill, and left with a friendly wave of his hand.

Another time, after visiting Terry in the hospital, the Rambler station wagon simply stopped on the road home. Finding the nearest telephone somewhere (decades before cell phones), I called our neighbor living in the red-brick house next to us.

"Don't you have any Heet with you?" he asked.

"No, it's colder than hell out here," I replied, thinking he was referring to heat–the temperature.

"It's H-E-E-T. Comes in a can. I'll bring one out and see if we can't get you started."

He did, and it worked. He also probably squirted a couple of shots of ether from an aerosol can into the carburetor. What had happened was that the gasoline line, which he tapped on with the nearest available tool, was frozen. After that, on his advice, the routine for cold weather driving included:

First, always keep the gas tank as full as possible, so moisture does not get into and freeze gasoline lines. Second, pour in a can of Heet with each fill-up. Third, carry an extra can of Heet with you in the glove compartment for possible gas line freeze-ups. Along with a pressurized can of ether for extremely cold startups with a low battery. And, fourth, keep a piece of a large cardboard box ready in the back of the station wagon. That allowed the car's heater to do its work. The Nash Rambler's heater wouldn't put out much hot air unless you attached cardboard in front of the bottom half of the radiator to block cold air coming through .

One needed to remember to apply brakes long before a stop sign to avoid skidding right through the intersection on the packed snow. Dangerous. Bought snow tires for the rear wheels. Put up storm windows on our little house. And so forth. Mary and I and two children lived in a new world.

Iowans were used to dressing for the cold. No New Mexico hatless mode, grabbing a jacket, going outside and - only after you became cold - quickly putting it on. Rather, one went through a ritual – perhaps while already wearing a wool sweater and even long-John underwear – of wrapping a long scarf around the neck, pulling on a heavy coat, donning a cap which also covered the ears (or a hat with earmuffs), and finally placing hands in gloves. All this done before opening any door and going outside. Of course, if snowing or much snow on the ground, one wore warm boots.

One time Mary's dad came to see us for a short visit during a freezing spell. We stopped at the airport to schedule his flight home. Going back outside, the Rambler wouldn't start and I had forgotten to have Heet. Spotting a gas station a little over a quarter of a mile away, I asked Chick and the others to wait inside while I walked to the gas station. By the time I returned with the Heet and got the Rambler running, my frozen ears were smarting. For several years after that skin on the tips of my ears peeled off. Should have had earmuffs or been wise enough to let someone drive me even that short distance!

Cold or snowy weather didn't deter many Hawkeye football fans. One of Mary's bosses had wangled tickets for good seats next to them in the stadium, which was close to our little Quonset hut. Parallel to the stadium ran railway tracks and trainloads of Iowans unloaded there for the games. While the men huddled in warm coats during the games talking football, many of the women appeared to be toughing out the cold or snow in their faces simply to observe or be observed in fashionable clothes. This occurred before newer TV generations of women became as knowledgeable about sports as their male counterparts. How many of those Iowa women were expert about football, I know not.

To get to the mass communication building, I had to walk each day on a bridge across the river. The wind seemed to blow colder along the river – my first real experience with what is meant by the "wind chill factor." No matter how bundled up, I felt chilled to the bone by the time I arrived for classes.

Juggling time around in this "new world" didn't work well for me academically that first semester. The main factor was insufficient time studying. With no medical proof, I use one excuse for part of it as ADD. It still is quite difficult for me to remain focused very long on one task. Because we lived out in the country that first semester I was unable to take part in much of the camaraderie among the mass comm grad students. They gathered at a small bar on campus in the afternoons. I recall being there only once. Grad students also met regularly during evenings in the basement of the mass comm building, where the foibles of profs and classes were discussed.

Working part-time at the university PR office, rather than as a graduate assistant for a mass comm prof, might have added to not being as privy as other students to what was expected. Lame excuses. The truth of the matter simply came down to that I didn't cut it academically as a graduate student that first semester in Iowa.

I was "awarded" a C in a radio production class taught by a prof named Andrews, who had as his grad assistant a fellow named Joseph Benti. One class project was to put together a half-hour segment for a weekly program aired by the campus radio station. Professor Andrews had heard me talk, so wouldn't permit me to go on the air with my New Mexico-Texas twang. He agreed another student and I should do the project together.

It was near the end of the semester, so I came up with the bright idea our half hour could feature short segments of the best programs others in our class already had produced. My classmate had that good, clear voice noted for Iowans - with no accent, just right for radio. After we chose portions of the best programs of the semester I wrote segments of introduction and he read them in his deep voice.

We turned our tape into Joe Benti and felt pretty proud of ourselves. We would hear our program on the air the next week. Big problem. We unknowingly hadn't adjusted the "levels." that is, some of the other programs that semester were taped at a different volume level than our introductions. This meant listening to the short segments was sorta like to classical music on a car radio, when you barely can hear a single violin and suddenly the whole orchestra comes on to overpower your ears.

Benti was furious because he had to go through our whole taped program and adjust the levels. He might have passed his vehemence against us on Professor Andrews. Even though neither he nor Benti[14] earlier had ever told us anything about adjusting tapes for "levels," I figured that episode mainly was the cause of my C in the radio production class.

The other Waterloo "C" grade came in a research methods course, taught by Art Barnes – the head of the mass comm graduate division (*not a good course to receive a C in*). Each student was supposed to design a mass comm research project. At a loss about how to proceed, a fellow student working part-time in the news and information center appeared to have an answer.

"I'll bring in the paper I turned in last semester," she said. "You can look it over and it will give ideas for your own project. I got a B on it." Now, this shows you where I was at that time as a grad student. I thought, "Well, if she made a B, I can come up with something about like hers and also get a B."

That's what I tried to do. If really a Gung Ho grad, I would have thought, "I'll look hers over. Maybe it will give me an idea about how to improve my paper, turn it into an A."

---

[14] Handsome Joe Benti later moved to Los Angeles, where he anchored news programs for the CBS station there. The word was that he was heir to replacing the aging Walter Cronkite. But Benti married an LA anchorwoman, retired, and far as I know, neither returned to TV.

In other words, I still was thinking in terms of doing just enough work to get by, like I'd always done as an undergrad. And, I paid the Piper. Barnes marked a C on my paper after finding a couple of errors one of which I recall being that the size of my sample wasn't correct. (It was about the same size as hers, but I guess he missed it on her paper.) It would have been helpful if I'd carefully studied the textbook about sample sizes and other aspects of the project, rather than partly so much on what my working partner had done.

"Wow!' she said, when I told her about my grade. "I'm sure glad Old Barnes didn't find any of those mistakes when he graded my paper."

I had logged in As and Bs for my other courses, but worried about those two Cs, had a conference with Les Moeller, the director of the mass comm school. "No," he said in a serious voice when I asked about continuing toward a PhD after completing a master's. "Doctoral students here have almost an A average."

I knew that was it for me at Iowa – a masters, even though Mary already had agreed to continue working on her PhT, Pushing Hubby Through. She had become friends with a woman who was the head dietitian for the men's dorms. Her husband was working toward a PhD in mass comm, a fellow who constantly bragged about his 4.0 (straight A) average.

"Well, you know what they say," he told me, "working toward a PhD is a struggle between the student and the university. And, the university frequently wins." It would have been helpful if I'd asked that 4.0 student to look over my research paper before I turned it into Professor Barnes.

As you can imagine, I was in the doldrums between semesters. Things grew brighter the second semester. One of those "things" was that I didn't receive any C grades, was beginning to fathom the life of a grad student.

The second was Mary's and my friendship with Ron and Gayla Farrar. Ron also had real newspaper experience, with much of his working for the *Arkansas Gazette*. Moeller had promised Ron that if he came to Iowa he would be the publisher of *The Daily Iowan*, the student newspaper produced in the mass comm building. But Ron said Moeller had reneged on his promise, made him a regular graduate assistant. "Moeller just has me doing things like carrying around Coke bottles from one place to the other."

Ron let us in on a secret. Despite making high grades, he was planning to jump ship, to transfer to the University of Missouri. He and Gayla had visited Columbia, Missouri, and talked with the graduate advisor of the journalism school there. It was a done deal. Ron and Gayla were leaving Iowa.

Mary and I talked it over. She agreed to continue working full-time if I earned a PhD. It didn't seem to make much sense to enter a college teaching career without the PhD, and both Terry and Pam – although I now realize how difficult it must have been for them - were somewhat used to moving from one school to another.

After receiving advice from Ron and Gayla, I drove the Rambler station wagon to Columbia to meet with William Howard Taft (undoubtedly an ancestor of the U.S. President of the same name). As graduate advisor at the School of Journalism at the University of Missouri, Bill Taft was very congenial. I already had sent along my transcripts. Either he hadn't seen those two C grades, or it didn't matter all that much to him, and as an "old Navy vet" I wasn't about to volunteer anything about them unless he asked. It was the beginning of a life-long friendship with another mentor, as close as that about a decade earlier with Keen Rafferty, Mary's former boss and head of the Journalism Department at the University of New Mexico.

One day, while the Farrars and Odendahls were in the midst of plotting their escapes as Iowa fugitives heading across the state line to Missouri, I got word that Moeller wanted to see me in his office. Ron and I had become enough paranoid as grad students that we worried that somehow Iowa profs might be striking back, maybe lowering our grades that semester if they had found out about our treasonous intentions. Perhaps Moeller had gotten wind of our transgressions.

"Max," Moeller began. "I know you're disappointed not to be continuing here toward a doctorate. But I've found you a good journalism teaching job." It was, as I recall, in San Antonio – perhaps Trinity University which might have been Trinity College at that time. In retrospect, as a lifelong Southwesterner, I think I might'a learned to be fairly comfortable as a Texan and believe it probably would have been a pleasant place for me to teach. Yet, in my mind, I already was committed to move to the Show Me State and continue my education.

So, I thanked Moeller and spilled the beans, without naming Ron as a co-conspirator. Looking back, I figure Moeller might already had gotten wind of what was going on. Even so, he probably considered that at the time little research was required by faculty at the Texas college and I probably could hack it there as a journalism teacher with a master's degree. After that meeting, despite Ron's bad experience with him, I classified Les Moeller as a Class Act.

Still hanging over my head was completion of a thesis. So figure this one – that is, who would be best to choose as thesis chairman? I selected Art Barnes, the prof who had graded me as C in his research methods class. My reasoning: Barnes would make sure my project was feasible and be certain to guide me to its successful completion. Barnes didn't blink an eye and agreed to be my thesis chairman. It may have been at that meeting, probably another, that I said something to him about his being a Roman Catholic.

"Where did you get that idea?" he asked.

"Because you have so many kids." (As I recall he had nearly 10.)

"No," he laughed, "my wife and I just are careless Methodists."

By now acutely aware of my limitations as a mass comm pedantic, such as not understanding how to put together a rigid scientific study involving statistics, Barnes agreed I should do a content analysis. Reported in April of 1961 by the *Overseas Weekly* – a privately-owned newspaper with wide distribution among soldiers in West Germany - was that Major General Edwin A. Walker was using John Birch Society literature in educating troops including the U.S. Army's 24ᵗʰ Infantry Division.

Of course, I immediately was intrigued by the story because of writing the "Jack Spruce Society" spoof column for the *Roswell Daily Record* and provoking the wrath of John Birch Society members in that New Mexico city. You'll recall that its founder Robert Welch in a 1953 letter to friends had accused President Dwight David Eisenhower and his brother, Milton Eisenhower, of being Communists.

Overseas Weekly said that in 1960 General Walker had addressed 200 men of his division and their dependents at a Parent-Teacher Association meeting. The newspaper reported that the general described former President Harry S. Truman, former Secretary of State Dean Acheson and Eleanor Roosevelt as "definitely pink" and Columbia Broadcasting System commentators Eric Sevareid and Edward R. Murrow (who then was director of the United States Information Agency) and newspaper columnist Walter Lippman as "confirmed Communists."

General Walker denied making the statements, saying the purpose of the "Pro-Blue" program he had initiated was to teach his troops about Communism. He further stated it had nothing to do with the John Birch Society. Suspicious coloring – because the "Blue Book of the John Birch Society" was a sort of Bible of Robert Welch's group.

Anyway, the general was relieved of his command and assigned to the Army's European Headquarters at Heidelberg while his case was investigated. The result of the investigation was an "official oral admonishment" of General Walker for his Pro-Blue program and also for trying to influence the votes of his troops, a violation of the Hatch Act.

Another general reported that although Walker *was* a member of the John Birch Society, he was sincere in saying the Pro-Blue program *was not* derived from the John Birch Society. A few months later, Walker announced he was resigning from the Army. He forfeited about $1,000 a month pay that he would have received if he had not resigned his commission.[15]

It was decided that my thesis would concern the number of favorable and unfavorable comments about General Walker. Publications selected to be studied were:

1. Four "prestige" newspapers: the *New York Times, Christian Science Monitor, Wall Street Journal,* and *New York Herald-Tribune.*

2. Four Iowa newspapers: *The Des Moines Register, The Cedar Rapids Gazette, The Keokuk Daily Gate City,* and *The Oskaloosa Daily Herald.*

3. Three news magazines: *Time, Newsweek,* and *U.S. News & World Report.*

4. Eight right-wing publications: *The Manion Forum, Independent American , Closer-up, Don Bell Reports, Counterattack, Dan Smoot Reports, Common Sense,* and *The Cross and the Flag.*

It was fortunate that the State University of Iowa had made a point of collecting right-wing publications in what became known as the Tension File. No doubt the most fun in the study, and relief from peering at so much material in the library and at the State Historical Association in Iowa City, was driving several times in the Rambler station wagon through the green Iowa countryside to Oskaloosa and studying the Walker case in the *Daily Herald's* bound volumes.

When presented with the first draft of the study, Barnes suggested much of the material also needed to be presented in tabular form. So, that's what I did—provided tables he indicated to go along with the writing. At the next meeting, he told me there were too many tables. So, I took some out. The third time around, he pointed out where more tables were needed (almost all the same ones taken out). So, I put them back in.

By now, I knew the routine: Certainly never grumble to any profs, especially on your thesis committee. Trudge ahead to do whatever necessary to compile a body of work which meets faculty approval.

There was little unexpected found in the results of the study. The ratio of favorable to unfavorable assertions about Genera Walker varied with the type of publications. There was a range of favorable assertions in the prestige newspapers, Iowa newspapers, and

---

[15] $12,000 a year was a hefty one to give up in 1961.

the national news magazines. On the other hand, nearly all the assertions in the right-wing publications were favorable to the general. He was their guy.

I left what I hoped would be the final draft of the study with Barnes as we prepared to leave for Missouri. He promised to give me a call there after he had read it.

A U-Haul trailer was rented ahead of time, but on moving day wasn't at the rental yard as promised. Several friends, including Mary's boss, had gathered early that morning to help load the trailer and pickup. It was frustrating, and we didn't obtain the U-Haul trailer and load it until noon.

The Odendahl family pulled out of Iowa City early that afternoon, headed for another new adventure. As Mary and I had become a bit wiser about life in the "cold country, we moved into a comfortable, brick, two-bedroom, married-housing unit at the University of Missouri. We lived on the south end of the campus, within walking distance to classes and work. No more driving on snowy or icy roads unless we had to.

Directly to the northwest of married housing was the university hospital. Not long after moving in, we received word to be on the lookout for a "flasher" - referred to as a "pervert" — who apparently was exposing himself after opening his car door in one of the hospital parking lots. When we warned the girls about him, Terry said nonchalantly, "Oh yeah, some of us saw that man do that the other day."

If "that man" were to show up again, Mary and I warned Terry and Pam, "Run away, don't talk to him." They just looked at us. It registered that children had a sounder perception about that flasher's behavior than we adults. *Of course*, we wanted the kids to stay away from deviates. Yet they were experiencing an inevitable part of living near a hospital with its psychiatric unit. Probably - flashers were generally harmless?

What might have turned into a dire consequence of the children obeying us, however, happened soon after to Pam. One well-below-freezing and a bit windy morning Mary and I already were at work/classes as Pam stood on the corner near us waiting for her school bus. For some reason the school bus didn't come by that morning. But brave little Pam, perhaps even because of the flasher incidents and warnings to her never to wander until the bus arrived, stood waiting who knows how long.

Luckily, a neighbor across the street observed our cold and forlorn daughter's plight. He later told us it took some real persuasion to convince Pam to cross the street and into his warm college apartment. The neighbor was Jerry Bailey, who was working toward a doctorate in Industrial Studies. He and his wife Norma had two children, Roseann and David. It would be part of the beginning of a friendship between the two families which has lasted to this day, with them celebrating 65 years of marriage. (More about the Baileys later.)

Besides flashers, "ordinary" sex also became more open near us. Adjacent to the same hospital parking lots frequented by the flasher stood a grove of trees. Usually at dusk, especially on weekends, we'd observe students as couples heading into the trees. One of them invariably carried a blanket, noticeably doing nothing to hide it. We knew what they were up to: much the same as what often went on furtively in the seats of cars parked on or off campuses in New Mexico years before.

"This is the Show Me state," I commented to Mary. "That's what those students are doing: getting to see more of each other than they could in some cramped car." As so often the case, Mary didn't think my attempt at humor especially funny.

We found ourselves in the middle of what was being called the Sexual Revolution. Helping to get it started was the publication of two books, the Kinsey Reports: *Sexual Behavior in the Human Male (1948)* and *Sexual Behavior in the Human Female* (1953) by Dr. Alfred Kinsey, Wardell Pomerey, and others. Kinsey, a zoologist at Indiana University, also founded the Institute for Sex Research.

After Kinsey's volume about males and sex hit the bookstores, a graduate student in sociology at Northwestern University, Hugh Hefner, wrote a term paper about sex laws. In 1953 – the year Mary and I married - Hefner published his first edition of *Playboy* magazine, featuring a color centerfold of Marilyn Monroe in the nude.

Unheard of. A general-circulation magazine with pics of *naked* women! Sometimes displayed openly in newsstands, although in the beginning more likely under the counter widely available by subscription for horny *or whatever* men. Even perused by women, because of stunning nude photos of beautiful women they might long to be. Hefner wrote many of the articles himself which advocated openness about adult sex. He also paid top prices for models – the more famous the woman the better for posing in the nude for talented photographers. Articles on various subjects were by some of the nation's best writers. The magazine sold like hotcakes.

In 1960 the Food and Drug Administration licensed a birth control pill for women which had been developed in 1957. The Civil Rights Movement also was heating up. One if the first breakthroughs came in 1954 when the Supreme Court ruled in *Brown v. Board of Education of Topeka, Kansas*–unanimously agreeing that segregation in public schools is unconstitutional. A victory for the National Association of Colored People and its attorney, Thurgood Marshall, who later became the nation's first black Supreme Court justice.

In 1955, Rosa Parks, an NCAAP member in Montgomery, Alabama, had refused to give up her seat at the front of a bus to a white person. That same year Martin Luther King, Jr., established the Southern Christian Leadership Conference. In 1962, President Kennedy had to send 5,000 federal troops to the University of Mississippi when James Meredith became the first black student to enroll there.

In our married student complex at the University of Missouri lived a negro family. The father was studying medicine and, luckily while we were there, was graduated by the university as its first negro physician. A large group of his family and friends gathered at the small apartment after his graduation. Oh, how they did celebrate loud and late into the night. They kept us awake, but it was worth it.

While walking across campus to classes, I also became acquainted with another negro student. He was working toward an EdD, was destined to hold the first doctorate in education granted to a negro by the university. Like most of us grad students, he was a bit paranoid that somehow, or because of something, or someone would keep him from his goal.

He always carried a tightly-gripped briefcase with him, and when I commented about that he told me, "There's a copy of my dissertation I'm working on in it. There's another copy at home, but I'm scared something might happen, like maybe my apartment might burn down." Another time when I asked the nervous, briefcase-carrying fellow how it was going, he replied, "Pretty well overall, I guess. But, you know, I went to a movie just to relax the other afternoon. About halfway through it, I said, 'Oh my God, what am I doing wasting time here when I should be working on my dissertation?' So I ran out of that movie, came home and got back to work."

I was honest when I told him I knew how he felt, because my own dissertation hovered somewhere past the horizon. At the time, there generally were two kinds of PhD journalism dissertations completed at MU. I already had decided to do some sort of historical study and to ask Bill Taft if he'd agree to serve as chairman. Several other PhD journalism students were working with what I'd now call "the guru." Professor William (Will) Stephenson's domain was a lower floor of a journalism building which became known as "The Basement."

A British psychologist, Stephenson had done research studies which included naming the Studebaker "*Lark*" and the Ford "*Thunderbird.*" For most of his research, Stephenson had developed what was called Q Methodology. Q factor analysis examines how people think about a topic by reducing many individual viewpoints down to a few "factors." Simply put, this factor analysis comes from a series of "Q Sorts" – a ranking of variables typically presented as statements printed on small cards. But the problem for me was that

226

statistics were required as part of reaching Q-Sort conclusions. Aware of weakness in math, I wasn't about to tackle classes in statistics which almost surely would lower my grades.

I did take a non-statistical class from Stephenson, in which we processed a small Q Sort about hospitals. We prepared for this by practicing another Q Sort about personal grooming. As part of the practice run I interviewed Mary about grooming and she repeated the "test" for me. After reviewing the results, Stephenson joked to the class, "I don't how this couple can be living together.

Obviously, Mary and I had different views about what it meant for a person to be well-groomed.

I really applied myself studying that semester, all A's except for one C. It came in Earl English's semantics class. *Not good!! He was dean of the School of Journalism.* But I didn't study enough to do better than average in that class. Without the added effort I simply couldn't decipher enough of his tricky multiple choice questions, like: The correct answer could be "a., b., c. or d." Or it might be "a. and b." or, perhaps, "a. and d."

Once, as the dean was lecturing, he appeared to be looking out the window and droned in a serious voice, "Yes, The Map is Not the Territory." Jogging myself out of my usual ADD doldrums during what to me were his dull lectures, I raised out of my seat and looked toward the window, wondering what map he saw out there. Dean English gave me a strange look. Of course, what he endeavored to explain to us was the principle that words or phrases are a map, but they don't ever contain the whole meaning – the territory. That's the kind of semantic theories we were tested on.

A young woman who sat next to me in this undergraduate class aced every one of the dean's tests – often administered by his secretary as he was frequently out of town. My classmate liked, "really dug," the class, couldn't understand why it was so difficult for me, especially because I was a graduate student. It still seems to me that semantics – like music – has a beat to it better picked up by some than others.

My friend Ron Farrar went to the head of graduate instruction, Bill Taft's office, and pointed out that I'd made 10 units of "A" grades, with the one "C' in the dean's class only two units out of a total of 12. I don't think Taft had been privy to my grades. On learning this, Taft made a personal appeal to either the dean and/or a faculty committee, and he/it agreed I could be a PhD candidate at the University of Missouri. I still feel indebted to Ron Farrar and Bill Taft. When Taft told me of the decision, I also felt something else: That, finally, despite being a non-serious undergraduate and self-diagnosed victim of ADD, I probably almost had *Paid the Piper.* That is not to say that I'd given up my paranoia, only that if I continued to work hard there might be "light at the end of the academic tunnel."

Ronald T. Farrar was born in Fordyce, Arkansas, July 3, 1935, and graduated with a journalism degree from the University of Arkansas. As mentioned before, one of the places he worked for was the *Arkansas Gazette,* a very well-respected paper at the time. Ron's PhD dissertation was about Charles Ross, a newspaper man who helped begin the School of Journalism at the University of Missouri with founder Walter Williams in 1908 – the first in the nation. Ross later became press secretary for President Harry Truman.

After his graduation, Ron Farrar headed up a couple of journalism schools, wrote several journalism textbooks and in 1998 a biography, *A Creed for My Profession: Walter Williams, Journalist to the World.* Farrar retired as Associate Dean for Graduate Studies and Research at the University of South Carolina.

Earl English was dean of the School of Journalism and remained popular with Missouri editors, partly because he could sit down in their back shops and still produce lead-like-metal stories on their linotype machines. Yet , it seemed to me, former dean Frank Luther Mott still carried the most prestige for the school.

Mott was born near a place called What Cheer, Iowa, in 1886. From 1927 to 1942 he was director of the School of Journalism at the State University of Iowa. From 1930 to 1935, he was editor of *Journalism Quarterly.* Sorta Like Ron Farrar and me, Frank Luther Mott (always *respectfully* referred to by including his middle name) moved from Iowa to Missouri – where Mott was dean of the School of Journalism at the University of Missouri from 1942 to 1951.

He probably was best known for his editions of *American Journalism,* at the time the best history of U.S. newspapers. In 1939 Mott had been awarded the Pulitzer Prize for *A History of American Magazines* – which became a four-volume work by 1952. Mott for many years taught the required-of-all-undergraduate-journalism-students History and Principles class in a packed hall. It was a class long remembered in the lives of most J grads, not only because of the pithy content of Mott's lectures but also because of the esteem in which they held the man. After Mott's retirement at Missouri, my mentor there, William Howard Taft proudly had taken over the coveted History and Principles class and taught it for many more years.

It was a privilege to be able to take a seminar with the retired Frank Luther Mott. We met once a week in his study, surrounded by shelves of books, and were served ice tea and cookies by Mrs. Mott – who graciously flitted in and out of the room. During this time

Mott's autobiography, *Time Enough,* was published. I should have bought a copy of the book and asked Mott to sign it. It would be worth a lot, at least to me, now.

Besides an old, wise, and learned man, Mott was kind and gentle. Just before the master's comprehensive exams each semester, Mott would leak information about them. Not the exact questions, of course, but he'd go around half-whispering something like, "It might be a good idea to look over *Blank* and also *Blank's* books before your exam." Later, just before taking my PhD comps, one highly respected prof–Eugene Sharp, also suggested a reporting book I ought to be familiar with. Part of a tradition? Historian Frank Luther Mott died in 1964, the same year our family had moved to San Diego.

While pursuing work at Missouri in the Western American History area, I came across in library study another historian with a similar affinity for graduate students. His name was Walter Prescott Webb, a native Texan who taught at the University of Texas. He'd written his master's thesis on the Texas Rangers, did a year's more study at the University of Chicago. In 1931 he published *The Great Plains*, which led to his being awarded his PhD the next year for his work on the book. In 1939 The Social Science Research Council declared *The Great Plains* the outstanding contribution to American history since World War I.

Webb was my kind of guy, searching for simple answers. *The Great Plains* contended the revolver, barbed wire, and the windmill had significant influence in settlement of that arid, treeless region. Some other Western historians viewed Webb's theories as too simplistic. In a quote I'm not taking the time to look up, but do vividly recall Walter Prescott Webb writing, went something like this, "I like to sit on those committees when the hapless grad students are defending their work so I can vote for them. Fact is, I don't know the answers to most of the questions the other professors are asking." Walter Prescott Webb died in 1963, at about the same time I was reveling about his kinship with grad students.

The first semester at Missouri found me working at the School of Agriculture, putting out a newsletter. One day my boss there invited Mary and me to a cocktail party at his home. We found a home - lighted, with guests inside - and greeting me at the door was Ed Lambert, head of radio-TV at the J School.

"Please, come on in," he told us. "Have a drink."

I believe I was holding a drink in my hand by the time I asked where my boss was. "Oh," he lives next door," Lambert said. We apologized and sheepishly prepared to leave. But Lambert laughed about it, assured us all was well. I guess he had recognized me as a J grad student, so spontaneously invited us in to *his* party. My boss also got a kick out of it when we arrived next door and told him what had happened.

One day a native Missouri student living in our apartment complex brought us some carp – enough for several meals. "Carp will eat about anything, like what comes out of sewers," he told us," but these were caught by me this weekend in a fresh-water lake. They are good eating." And they were, although after cooking the carp Mary and I were hesitant about putting the first bites into our mouths. That neighbor also had a custom, when it appeared a night might be especially frigid, of taking the battery out of his car and keeping it inside his warm apartment. The next morning he'd carry the battery back outside to his vehicle, reattach the cables on it, and his car would start right up. Alas, one cold morning he attached the wrong cables to the battery and it literally split apart.

There appeared another novelty at a house just around the corner from the married student apartments. While visiting a student and his family renting the house, Mary and I observed him doing a strange thing with something in his hand. He was changing the channels on his TV with a *remote control*! Before that, everyone we knew always got up and down from their chairs, and walked to and from their TV, pushing buttons in order to change channels or adjust the volume.

By the next semester I'd moved job-wise across campus from the School of Agriculture to become graduate assistant to Dale Spencer, who taught newspaper law, copy editing, and also oversaw students helping to put together *The Columbia Missourian*. Its uniqueness was that it *wasn't* a student newspaper, rather a professional daily which circulated in Columbia. Complete with Associated Press statewide, national, and international wire stories, undergrad J students covered and wrote local stories under the guidance of faculty. Students also, under Spencer's steady hand, edited, wrote headlines, and helped him make up *The Columbia Missourian* each day.

My job was to assist Spencer with his copy editing classes – grading papers and administering his tests. Meanwhile, Mary worked as a secretary in the Social Psychology Department for an egotistical fellow named Bruce Biddle, who actually fancied himself as one of the few academics in the United States who produced anything worthwhile.

One of the male profs in Mary's department, not Biddle, oversaw a graduate student doing a unique psychological project. The female student took a baby or very young chimpanzee home with her and raised it for a period of time as if the chimp were her child. The aim was to find out if that chimp would flourish to a greater extent intellectually and/or socially in such a setting. The chimp proved too much trouble for the female student and her companion to raise so the project was abandoned.

It was between classes on noontime of November 22, 1963, when I learned President John F. Kennedy had been shot in Dallas. About a half hour later we students found out the President had died in the hospital of a bullet wound in the head.[16] Camelot had ended. I went numbly to my next class – one in political science. The prof dismissed us, but first explained the succession to the presidency. "If we should find out that Vice President Lyndon Johnson[17] also has been killed," he told us, "the next President will be the Speaker of the House of Representatives. I assume he was not in Dallas."

I went home, where Mary and the girls soon joined me. Over and over on our small – maybe 14-inch-screen, white-cabinet, black-and-white TV – we watched the pandemonium in Dallas. It included LBJ being sworn in as President while new widow Jackie Kennedy stood near him in a blood-smeared dress. All classes were canceled at the university the next day. By this time Lee Harvey Oswald had been captured and appeared to be the killer, not only of Kennedy but also of a Dallas policeman. It would become *stranger*, a part of TV for several days without any ads or regular programming as we watched Oswald being led through a hall in the basement of the Dallas courthouse. A nondescript fellow named Jack Ruby suddenly darted out with a pistol in his hand. Ruby shot Oswald in his stomach. It was announced that Oswald quickly (it seemed to many of us *strangely* too quickly) had died.

It was first speculated that Ruby was so fond of Jackie Kennedy, was so deeply moved that he had to avenge her husband's death. Few TV watchers believed that or ever became convinced either Ruby or Oswald had acted alone, rather that it all was part of some monstrous plot. All of it *very strange.*

After thousands filed by to pay their respects at JFK's casket in Washington, there came the unique funeral for a President, including a procession with a riderless horse carrying his boots reversed in the stirrups of the saddle. All these TV images will never be forgotten by those who saw them, nor will most of us believe that the whole truth of that *strange* and tragic event will be told during our lifetimes – if ever.

Sometime, when not watching these weird events, I walked over to *The Columbia Missourian* and talked with Dale Spencer, who had put together the November 22 special issue of that newspaper. "I just tried to remember," he said, "front pages like Pearl Harbor or the end of World War II, and made up ours the same." Noticing the waste basket next to his desk overflowing, I dug around and found news copy which Associated Press had provided on its teletypewriter at the time of the assassination. Spencer said I could keep it.

---

[16] I can't recall whether it was on campus, or later a rerun at home, that I saw Walter Cronkite, taking off his glasses and with tears running down his face, announce Kennedy's death.

[17] Johnson was riding two cars behind the Kennedys and Texas Governor and Mrs. John Connally.

"Number 179:

"LEAD KENNEDY SHOT

"DALLAS (AP) President Kennedy and Gov. John Connally of Texas were shot from ambush today.

"It was not known whether either was killed."

Number 183:

"BULLETIN

"DALLAS (AP) President Kennedy was given blood transfusions today at Parkland Hospital in an effort to save his life after he and Gov. John Connally of Texas were shot in an assassination attempt."

Number 184

"URGENT

"DALLAS–add Kennedy lead

"AP reporter Jack Bell said Kennedy lay on a seat of a car. Blood stained his clothing.

"Mrs. Kennedy was weeping and trying to hold up her husband's head when reporters reached the car."

Number 192

'BULLETIN

'DALLAS (AP) Two priests stepped out of Parkland Hospital's emergency ward today and said President Kennedy had died of his bullet wounds.

"The priests came out of the ward at approximately 1:37 p.m. CTS

"The announcement by the priests brought audible sobs from a crowd of scores of newsmen and other citizens crowded around the emergency entrance."

On CBS-TV, Mary and I had watched reruns of Walter Cronkite weeping as he delivered this same news.

On the brighter side, I'd revived my interest in "cowboys and Indians" – specifically by taking classes in Western United States History. This was motivated by the requirement that PhD journalism students pass comprehensive exams not only in two J areas but also some other academic discipline.

My mentor in the History Department was Lewis Atherton, with whom I took undergrad and graduate courses. He was born in Missouri, received all three of his degrees – A.B., M.A., and PhD at the University of Missouri. He published four books: *Frontier Merchant in Mid-America, The Southern Store, 1800-1860, Main Street on the Middle Border,* and *Cattle Kings.* When looking up Atherton's background on the Internet to include with this memoir, I found he taught at New Mexico Military Institute in Roswell in 1928 and 1929. He married Mary Louise Webb June 5, 1929, in Roswell and had three children.

Atherton had moved to St Joseph Junior College in Missouri by 1930 (the year of my birth), so maybe none of his children were born in Roswell, as Pam was. Yet it could well have been that there still were others of the Webb family in Roswell at the same time as the Odendahls. If I'd known it, that might have been good to chat with Atherton about.

It became interesting how this area of history was presented and contemplated. As a native New Mexican, my idea of the "West" was looking up and down the U.S. map to find Texas/ Oklahoma, New Mexico /Colorado, Montana/Wyoming and states westwards from there. The present American Automobile Association map of the Western States/Provinces doesn't even include Texas or Oklahoma.

Not so with Western American History classes, which began with the movement west from the East Coast. The guru at the time I studied, although he had died 30 years or so earlier in 1932, was Frederick Jackson Turner, who was best known for *The Significance of the Frontier in American History.* His "Frontier Thesis" first was published in 1893 in a paper read to the American Historical Association during the Chicago World's Fair. Part of Turner's thesis was that there was a series of frontiers in the push westward across America. One source claimed, "The forging of the unique and rugged American identity occurred at the juncture between the civilization of settlement and the savagery of wilderness."

As subsequent Eastern areas of the U.S. became more heavily populated, frontiers also became referred to by other scholars as "safety valves." "The West" – beginning with non-Native Americans moving over the Allegheny Mountains - provided places of relief, somewhere to go for the poor, the discontented, or those a step ahead of the law. As Horace Greeley, editor of the *New York Tribune* had advised, "Go West, young man, go West."[18]

---

[18] *Go West, young man* was said to be about Manifest Destiny. Although popularized by Greeley, it actually probably was first written by John Soule.

By my time of study fewer scholars still generally agreed with Turner's thesis. Those in disagreement argued there were several other factors bringing continued expansion, even after land frontiers ended at the Pacific Ocean. For example, it was argued one of these factors could be continued economic growth through "free enterprise" as a "safety valve."

Atherton advised us grad students during one of his undergraduate classes that we would have to decide that semester whether we were "Turnerians" or "anti-Turnerians." Each of his tests contained an added question for the grad students and he'd not yet asked us about Turner. I figured the question would come along with others in the final exam, and I prepared myself as a loyal Turnerian. Sure enough, there came the question. But Atherton asked, "Discuss Frederick Jackson Turner, one half as a Turnerian and the other half as an anti-Turnerian."

I quickly wrote in my bluebook arguments for much of the Turnerian half, but then quickly racked my brain to unscramble the remainder of my pro-Turnerian ammunition into an anti-Turnerian second-half-answer. By now I'd become more fascinated and caught up with Western American History than in my journalism classes and favored history as the area which I'd like to teach. That was out of the question because earning a PhD in history would have required two or three more years of solid overall study for a person without a bachelor's degree in any area of history.

Not only would that have been too much of an added burden for my loyal family to bear, but also there would have been the ordeal of an ADD person's continued struggle to pay attention enough to maintain A and B grades. I already had found younger history students not only to be bright —along with possessing great memories - but also very competitive, such as staying up all night studying for tests the following day. I could feel my being over 30 years old.

And who knows whether I'd have even survived teaching history with academia moving rapidly into the "publish or perish" era? Maybe some hidden box or boxes – a treasure trove of Old West material - would have come into my possession? Could I have milked those musty manuscripts or letters for a few articles leading to a book or two? Intriguing for me are these kinds of accounts:

(1) Lewis Atherton told our graduate seminar that, despite the constant barrage in movies and on TV, there weren't all that many "High Noon" gunfights in the Real West. The beginning of the myth may have been with The Virginian, a Western novel by Owen Wister published in 1902,

Therefore Trampas spoke. "Your bet, you son-of-a —."

The Virginian's pistol came out, and his hand lay on the table, holding it unaimed. And with a voice as gentle as ever, the voice that sounded almost like a caress, but drawling a very little more than usual, so that there was almost a space between each word, he issued his orders to the man Trampas: "When you call me that, SMILE." And he looked at Trampas across the table.

Yes, the voice was gentle. But in my ears it seemed as if somewhere the bell of death was ringing; and silence...

In the 1952 movie High Noon, Gary Cooper plays the marshal of Hadleyville, Kansas, and his wife is Grace Kelly. As a matter of honor, he faces four gunmen in a middle-of-the-street shootout and defeats them - only with his wife's help. Cooper won an Oscar for his portrayal.

"Why would you go out in the middle of the street to commit suicide," Atherton asked about this sort of ubiquitous fiction and film scenario, "and challenge some fellow who was a better shot and could draw his pistol faster than you could? More likely you'd hide behind a tree and shoot him in the back after he rode by on his horse."

(2) In 1970 Dee Brown, who had written 15 books on Western American History, published *Bury My Heart at Wounded Knee*, which was listed on the dust cover as "a documented account of the systematic plunder of the American Indians during the second half of the 19th Century, battle by battle, massacre by massacre, broken treaty by broken treaty." Part of the beginning toward ending another myth, that of portraying Native Americans almost always as the bad guys.

At high noon one day in the late spring or early Summer of 1964, our home telephone rang. I was warming up canned chicken noodle soap to share with Terry and Pam. Mary was at work. "My name is Jim Julian," the voice on the phone said, "and I'm chairman of the Journalism Department at San Diego State College. We have an opening on our faculty and I'd like to talk to you about it."

I immediately assumed he was calling from San Diego. Other graduate students seeking jobs had warned me to be sure to get the complete lay of the land - such as salary and health insurance - before making any sort of commitment to any college or university. So, I began to pepper Julian with such questions.

"We could talk about all of that," he replied. "I'm here in Missouri at the Journalism Library. Could you make it over to meet with me?"

"Of course. I'll be right over."

I rushed across to the next married student housing unit and arranged with the woman there to finish feeding the kids and watch over them while I was gone. Her husband was a medical student, and they were a Jewish couple named Rose, with their own children.[19]

I arrived at the library and Julian and I shook hands. He opened the San Diego State College catalog to the Journalism Department and handed it to me. "Which of these courses can you teach?"

Quickly looking them over, I said (probably with too much bravado), "I really don't know much of anything about advertising or public relations. I might be able to teach photography, but sure would have to brush up on working in the darkroom before I could help students with that. I think I could handle the rest of those classes."

"Okay," Julian said. "I'll have a talk with our vice president and see what happens. I'm on my way to Europe for several weeks."

That was about the extent of my first meeting with Jim Julian. Didn't continue peppering him with my questions, also can't recall his offering any specific salary, or if I were likely to be offered the position.

When Mary arrived home, we agreed San Diego would be a good place for me to begin a teaching career because Mom and Dad now were living in an apartment in La Jolla, only a few miles up on the Pacific Coast.[20] We also agreed that with such a brief and informal meeting with Julian my chances of being hired by San Diego State College were pretty slim. So we were pleasantly surprised when a letter arrived from Donald Watson, vice president of San Diego State, offering me a job as assistant professor in the Journalism Department beginning with the fall semester. The pay would be $7,300 for the 1964-65 academic year – meaning there would be three months of 1965 summer vacation.

We decided I should take the beginning teaching job, even though I'd not even selected, much less begun, working on a dissertation. I would not recommend such a procedure to others, but our funds were running very low. Also, Watson's letter did not specifically state that completing a doctorate was a requirement of my being hired. Somehow, however, we knew that might be the hidden case.

Mary and I thought it worth the gamble, because if we remained in Missouri it would only be to finish a dissertation. The worst case scenario might be that if I didn't hack the

---

[19] Her father owned a department store (perhaps in New York State). She once advised Mary never to buy anything in a department store unless it's on sale, that regular prices are jacked up.
[20] Actually, La Jolla was and is a part of San Diego. Rich La Jolla residents, though, like to think of themselves as living in "The Village."

dissertation another - perhaps even smaller than San Diego - state college probably would hire me with a master's degree and some teaching experience under my belt.

In that late summer of 1964, I had to give up something very close to me. I sold the sturdy 1947 Ford pickup which had carried all our possessions from New Mexico to Iowa, and to Missouri. I'd paid $150 for it in Roswell. Two young Missouri fellows closely looked it over, and even after I'd told them about the engine's low oil pressure, agreed to give me $150.

Good deal? Maybe, but when they drove away, I had the feeling as if watching an old girlfriend walk off – after declaring she'd never wanted to talk to or see me again. I still wish I had that old truck, with a newer, more powerful engine and snazzy paint job. Somehow, I guess, American males hold a lifelong herding instinct when it comes to females and/or vehicles which have been close to them.

Mary and I decided it would be foolish to pay shipping expenses to bring along to California the old and very heavy, solid oak, roll-top desk I'd bought for $25 in Roswell. It also had become close to me. A neighbor had coveted the desk and when I offered it to her for $75 she rushed over with a check. After arriving in San Diego, we discovered a desk of that size and that good condition was worth close to $1,000. No telling what the price would be now. You can't measure lost love in dollars and cents.

Were we headed to California as still a part of historian Frederick Jackson Turner's search for a "new frontier" he'd alluded to more than 70 years earlier? Or was it a "safety valve" because we almost were out of money? Nevertheless, excitement filled the air. Editor Horace Greeley was shouting, "Go West , young man." With adventure beckoning us ever onward, the four of us readied ourselves to drive toward California in the again-heavily-loaded Nash Rambler station wagon.

CHAPTER 12 — CALIFORNIA, HERE WE COME

Our station wagon rolled away from Columbia, Missouri, slowly increasing its pace to 60 miles per hour (which in 1964 felt like a pretty fast speed to most of us – the fastest lots of people ever drove). As the outside temperature grew hotter, the car's air conditioner began to fail.

Even though we couldn't afford it, our sweating family stopped in Oklahoma to have an expensive air-conditioner repair. Didn't do much good. The half-fixed air conditioner barely kept up. Not that it made much difference. Catch-22. Most of those old cars were built with smaller radiators than present ones. When the outside temperature hovered above 100, with the air conditioner on, the Rambler's engine overheated. When the temperature gauge moved into the red zone, the air conditioner had to be turned off.

As we perspired, I kept extolling to Mary and the kids about what a lush place San Diego was during my Navy time in 1948-49, about how we soon would be swimming in the cool Pacific Ocean, lolling on sandy beaches. It wasn't easy to convince them as we pushed through the heat - seeing mirages off the highway in New Mexico. Past even hotter Yuma, Arizona, bridging the Colorado River, entering California, and driving across blowing sand dunes. Most of the road still was two-lane, undivided U.S. Highway 80 as we climbed up out of the desert into the mountains east of San Diego.

"Look at all of those huge boulders!" Mary exclaimed as we left the heat, winding through what appeared to be an unearthly landscape. As the kids said, "Yeah, Dad," I began to wonder about my memory of San Diego. Was it only green a few blocks from the ocean? It wasn't until we passed larger trees on the sides of the road through Alpine, about 30 miles from San Diego, that we felt out of the desert.

When approaching the outskirts of San Diego in 1964, we might have been listening to an eight-track recording which included Patsy Cline singing my favorite, *I Fall to Pieces*. Patsy had died in March just a year earlier when on her way home to Nashville. The Piper Comanche in which she was riding flew into severe weather and crashed. Ten years after her death she would become the first female solo artist voted into the Country Music Hall of Fame. For me, there has never been another female voice like hers singing what I call "cowboy" songs.

Just about the time Mary and I began dating, on January 1 of 1953, Hank Williams died in a chauffeured Cadillac after injecting himself with B12 and morphine. I remember him singing on the radio such songs as *Jambalaya (on the Bayou)* and *Your Cheatin' Heart*. His final single was titled *I'll Never Get Out of This World Alive*. Still ranked in 2003 number two among the *40 Greatest Men of Country Music*. Williams never was my favorite as much as Eddy Arnold, or Jim Reeves.

Eddy died at 89 on May 9, 2008, 19 days before my birthday. Eddy and I went back a long ways. To Hurley, where every weekday morning as a teenager I listened to a clear-channel radio program from Dallas sponsored by Pearl Beer. It began and ended with Eddy singing and yodeling *The Cattle Call*:

The cattle are prowlin', the coyotes are howlin'
Way out where the doggies roam
Where spurs are a jinglin', and the cowboy is singing
His lonesome cattle call
(yodeling)
He rides in the sun, 'til his days work is done
And he rounds up the cattle each fall
(yodeling)
Singing his cattle call
For hours he would ride, on the range far and wide
When the night wind blows up a squall, his heart is a feather
In all kinds of weather
He sings his cattle call
(yodeling)
He's browned as a fairy, from ridin' the prairie
And he sings with a western drawl
Singing his cattle call

From 1945 to 1954, Eddy had 57 consecutive singles in the country Top 10.

In July of the 1964 summer we arrived in San Diego, Jim Reeves was killed. The small aircraft he was piloting crashed during a thunderstorm near Nashville. He and Patsy Cline both killed in airplane crashes in the same vicinity barely more than a year apart.

Eddy was my favorite, but Jim's velvety voice crooned many of the same songs.

Country, jazz, and classical are all I've needed to listen to. Perhaps because of failing hearing, I've never moved on to appreciate rock or rock 'n roll. To my bad ears it sounds like constant shouting into microphones. On TV, I see singers pacing back and forth on the stage, among lots of dry-ice smoke, with some fireworks and other stuff going on.

Arriving in San Diego, we stayed with Mom and Dad in their La Jolla apartment.[21] Dad's hearing at age 75, as mine now, required aids in both ears. Pam's younger and more shrill

---

[21] They were paying about $300 per month for the apartment, with a partial view of the Pacific. The rent now is 10 times that–at the least $3,000.

voice bothered him and they never became as close as he and Terry did. She would listen for hours as Dad told family history and other stories. I'd heard them so many times as a youngster that they usually bored me, even though I should have remembered more.

Dad, Terry, Alan, Pam, Me, Mary, Mom

It took us three weeks to find our own place to live, a rented house on Broadmoor Street in La Mesa while a high school teacher was on sabbatical. Next door were the Roeslers–Elmer (Ike) and Phyllis and their two sons, Doug and David. They welcomed us warmly to La Mesa and took us to the Methodist church there, where we became members. Ike managed a large photography supply store close to downtown San Diego. He was a World War II hero, a paratrooper who had been wounded in the hip on one jump in Europe, voluntarily went back to his unit to make two more jumps. He later died in their home and Phyllis, who suffered from fairly severe Alzheimer's, received the necessary care a few more years in a nice facility.

When I reported to the Division[22] leader, David Milne at San Diego State College, he told me, "I've worked out a Fall Semester schedule for you because Jim Julian hasn't returned from Europe yet." He told me that I'd be teaching two sections of a Beginning Public Relations course. "That will make it easier for you because there will be only one preparation while you are getting on your feet here." I realized at that moment Julian hadn't informed the Division leader about our conversation in the University of Missouri

---

[22] Other departments in the Social Science Building at the time included Political Science, Geography, and Health Education.

journalism library. That an area which I felt I *wasn't* adequately prepared to teach was public relations, along with advertising and photography.

The scene was reminiscent of when I arrived in Roswell nine years earlier, thinking I'd been hired as a sports writer and found that not only was I a one-person staff as sports editor but also expected to write an unfamiliar column on local sports three times a week. The situation was the same. Beginning a new job with a wife and family to support, I was in no position to argue. I'd just have to make the best of it.

"Oh, well," Journalism Department Chairman Jim Julian told me when he returned, "PR shouldn't be too hard for you to teach. You can get the pros to come in and do lots of guest lectures for you." By "pros" he meant men and women holding public relations positions in the San Diego area, loosely defined as "professionals." So that's what I did. Called up the list Julian supplied and most seemed happy to oblige.

The textbook, the leading one in PR, was written by Scott Cutlip and Allen Center. It became the beginning source for most of my lectures. By and large, journalists looked down on PR persons as "flacks', meaning they only presented their employers in the best light while "flacking" for them.

The "pros," many of them former news persons, invariably viewed it the opposite way. "I have much more freedom to write or say what I want to now than when I worked on newspapers (radio, TV, etc.)," they would tell students. Obviously, they also knew much more than I about the real business of public relations and were able to provide good information to the classes, along with workplace anecdotes.

One of the best guest lecturers was a young sergeant named Bill Kolender, doing PR work for the San Diego Police Department. "My mother asked me," Kolender said, "what's a good Jewish boy like you doing being a cop?" Kolender rose to become Police Chief, worked in a high position for the State of California, and returned to San Diego County to become its Sheriff – a position he held into his 70s.

The beginning PR course was taught in the Business Building, all the way east across campus from our Social Sciences Building. If I had impromptu conferences with students just before those classes, or if an only-occasional rain hit San Diego, it could be a struggle either to get to class on time or stay dry.

During my first semester or two at San Diego State College, The Public Relations Society of America decided to accredit members who were willing to take and pass a test. As the only one teaching in the public relations area at State at the time, I was asked to help prepare some of the "pros" for this test - as an extension course. Our family needed the extra money so, despite no experience as a pro, I agreed to lead the course.

Figuring most of the questions would come out of the Cutlip and Center textbook, that's what we "centered" on. (A joke, son. A joke!) It *was* a fun course. Also briefly reviewed were other texts about PR, figuring some sort of bibliography might be asked on the test. One of them was an older title called *The Making of a Public Relations Man.*

On announcing this book's name, a female pro raised her hand and commented,

"I haven't found that making a public relations man is any more difficult than any other man. Maybe even easier." Laughter ensued. I'm happy and proud to report that, as far as I know, all the pros in that class who took the test passed and were among the first ones able to place after their names on office doors, stationary, business cards and the like, "Public Relations Society of America, Accredited."

Not as proud that earlier, at one of our new faculty meetings, I'd recognized Clinton Jencks from my days at Hurley. He would be teaching courses in the Economics Department. It probably was unfair to mention that to more-conservative-than-me Jim Julian, who was faculty advisor for *The Daily Aztec*–the student newspaper.

The Aztec published a story about Jencks being on campus and his history. Julian, whom I discovered had developed all sorts of campus sources and also many at the Copley newspapers, told me after publication of the *Aztec* story that SDS President Malcolm Love had called Jencks to his office and warned him:

"You cause any trouble and you're fired."

"Don't worry," Jencks is rumored to have replied, "I won't be causing you any trouble." The kind of "trouble" Love referred to happened during the McCarthy era. Marjorie Cohn, a professor at San Diego's Thomas Jefferson School of Law[23] recalled[24] how Jencks had been the leader of the Bayard District of Mine, Mill and Smelter workers. Bayard was about four miles north of Hurley on the now-blocked-off old highway to Silver City.

She said that Jencks, while working in Bayard, had been "convicted of falsely swearing in a non-Communist affidavit required of officials under the Taft-Hartley Act." It became a landmark case in 1957 – Jencks v. United States.

The Supreme Court of the U.S. reversed Jencks's five-year prison sentence because the government refused to turn over to the defense statements made by prosecution witnesses. Cohn relived the story of how witnesses included Harvey Matusow, a former Communist who had gone to work for Senator McCarthy.

---

[23] Also president-elect of the National Lawyers Guild and U.S. representative to the American Association of Jurists.
[24] After Jencks's death December 15, 2005, of natural causes at 87.

Later, in the book, *False Witness,* Matusow recanted his testimony against Jencks. The Supreme Court ordered the government to give Jencks full access to its records. The FBI refused and the government dismissed its case against Jencks. Three months later, Congress passed the Jencks Act. Cohn said the act provides that no statement of a government witness shall be turned over to the defense until after the witness has first testified in direct examination.

She wrote that Jencks, even though "a highly decorated war veteran," also was blacklisted – unable to find work for many years. "The FBI is very powerful and far-reaching," she quoted Jencks as saying, and that a California State employment counselor told him, "I think you may be politically unemployable."

His luck changed in 1959 when awarded a Woodrow Wilson Fellowship for training university professors. In spite of being ordered to appear before the House Un-American Activities Committee (HUAC) and FBI pressure, the foundation stood tall and bravely refused to rescind his fellowship. Jencks was graduated by the University of California at Berkeley with a PhD in economics and taught at San Diego State for 22 years.

"Why was I singled out?" Cohn said Jencks asked and answered his own question, "I was a good organizer. I was dangerous in that sense" Jencks said his work involved at least three struggles, "The proliferation of union organizations after the Great Depression and World War II, the new struggles of Mexican-American workers, and women."

As for women, the movie *Salt of the Earth* portrayed their role in a 15-month strike which began in 1950 against Empire Zinc Company about 10 miles away from Hurley, with union workers demanding equal pay with Anglos, plus better safety conditions, and healthcare. The strikers, including Jencks, portrayed themselves in the film. When Hispanic men were stopped from picketing, their wives and other women walked the picket line. The men became house-fraus - pretty radical in the 1950s. Cohn said the strike was successful.

Salt of the Earth was a low-budget movie, made by blacklisted film-makers with few professional actors. Cohn recalls how many theaters refused to show the film after pressure from HUAC, the Screen Actors Guild, and the International Alliance of Theater and Stage Employees. Cohn said *Salt of the Earth* is one of the most widely viewed films in the world, one of only 100 elected by the Library of Congress for the National Film Registry.

Dolores Huerta, co-founder with Cesar Chavez of the United Farm Workers said of Jencks, "His life was one of extraordinary bravery. He was a pioneer, such a leader in an organization of mostly Spanish-speaking people. He earned everyone's respect."

I lived in Hurley when Jencks led the Empire strike, just those few miles away close to Santa Rita where I was born. During that time, Jencks and a caravan of cars filled with Mexican-American members of the International Union of Mine, Mill, and Smelter Workers occasionally would drive up and down the streets of Hurley honking their horns. For example, when a strike appeared to be going their way.

It's almost certain that the majority of Anglos in Hurley viewed Jencks as a treasonable Communist and a trouble maker. Most of them were against strikes, living fearfully month-to-month on paychecks from Kennecott Copper Corporation. Some were "journeymen" carpenters, electricians, painters and pipe-fitters who might find work elsewhere. Yet for others, many of them middle-aged and approaching retirement and dependent on Social Security and small Kennecott pensions, the only steady jobs they'd ever held were as "operators" – special shift-work. Alternating on three shifts – watching over and keeping the Hurley copper mill and smelter operating 24 hours a day.

Modern unskilled Wal-Mart employees, so difficult to unionize, appear by their attitude and fearful demeanor to be like those of the Kennecott workers. Young Hurleyites lucky enough to attend, and those graduated by colleges and universities, frequently left the area to seek their fortunes away from the smelter and mill.

It was a dilemma for me. In my gut I knew Jencks was doing the right thing, while many in my young Hurley peer group dismissed him as "that Commie." I never was a close acquaintance of Jencks, either at Hurley or San Diego State, only waved at him a couple of times on campus and he responded with a smile.

Clinton Jencks was a lion.

He faced a dilemma, and also one for me when we arrived at San Diego State. New faculty were to sign an oath of allegiance required of every employee working for the State of California. Referred to as the "non-Communist Affidavit," it began, "I do solemnly swear (or affirm) that I will support and defend the Constitution of the United States and the Constitution of California against all enemies, foreign and domestic...."

I'd already affirmed the U.S. part when joining the Navy in 1948. I'd wondered that in the event of any sort of disturbance or revolution by U.S. citizens, wouldn't it be quite difficult to determine who was "the enemy"? After all, that's the way the United States was founded, by revolution. The domestic enemies worried about during our "Founding" days usually were the Tories, those who supported the British during that revolution. Not too many of those around in the U.S. now. Who were we so worried about now? "Communists" was the pat answer.

What made it seem even more ludicrous was my status still as a First Lieutenant in the United States Air Force Reserve. I'd raised my right hand the second time to defend the U.S. Constitution 12 years earlier, when commissioned after ROTC at the University of New Mexico. So, we're just adding California, now, I guess?

Were I a Russian spy or engaged in espionage for another country, I'd readily have been the first to sign. I suppose I must have shrugged my shoulders when penning my name to the California thing, without even carefully reading through (still haven't – wonder how many did?) the state's Constitution I was promising to defend. Meaning with my life, merely pledging to argue for it as an academic, or what?

An analogy is placing one's hand or hat over one's heart and repeating the Allegiance to the Flag, which I did so many times in Hurley's grade school. How does one have allegiance to an object - a flag? Swearing so once in a lifetime ought to be sufficient, if you believe that somehow makes you a true patriot. There's also the problem of constant parroting "with freedom and justice for all" when, unfortunately, the United States hasn't yet quite reached that lofty goal. I always place my hand on my heart, not only with pride about living in this country but also with the hope justice for everyone might arrive in the near future. At any rate, you'd imagine any real spy, to avert suspicion and a possible death penalty would press a right hand tightly against his or her chest.

A classic loyalty case already had transpired at San Diego State 10 years earlier, in 1954. Harry C. Steinmetz, a longtime professor of psychology, was dismissed from his position on grounds on insubordination stemming from "allegations of subversion and communist affiliation."[25] The House Un-American Activities Committee in 1953 called Steinmetz before it and he invoked the Fifth Amendment to the U.S. Constitution (certainly within his Constitutional rights) and refused to answer whether he was a member of the Communist Party.

"Whatever I have been," he was quoted as telling a newspaper reporter during a recess, "I am ashamed of nothing." At the time, his refusal to answer HUAC's questions didn't constitute "unprofessional conduct" as defined by California law. That later was changed by the Luckel Act. Authored by Assemblyman Frank Luckel of San Diego, a retired Navy commander, it became known as the "answer or be fired law."[26]

Ominous to my not remaining on the faculty at State wasn't because of being suspected as a spy or communist. It was that I was teaching with an ABD (All But Dissertation), had

[25] Information about the Steinmetz case comes from *The Journal of San Diego History*, Fall, 1989, Volume 35, Number 4.
[26] Steinmetz eventually received the non-paying title as professor emeritus at State. He died February 15, 1981, at the age of 82.

245

neither passed the necessary pre-PhD comprehensive exam nor had anything in mind to research as a dissertation.

There were many professors teaching journalism in 1964, not only up and down California as part of the State College System but also across the nation, combining their media experience with master's degrees. Yet, Mary was to find a definite pecking order among the wives of faculty members which reflected that San Diego State, along with San Joe State, perceived themselves superior to others in the State College System.

'Where did your husband receive his degree?" she would be asked.

"Oh, he has two degrees from two universities and is working on another." To raised eyebrows, she soon discovered the "degree" the other wives were asking about was the doctorate. Wives of husbands who had been graduated with doctorates felt they carried a bigger feather in their hats.

Studying for the PhD comprehensive exam at the University of Missouri, my primary worry wasn't so much about journalism questions but what Lewis Atherton would come up with to test my knowledge of Western United States History. As you recall, that was the third (outside) area for my PhD program, with the other two others in journalism.

I really hit hard my notes from Atherton and other Western History profs' classes, as well as reviewing bibliography – looking through several of the "classic" books – such as *Mining Camps* by Charles Howard Shinn, originally published in 1884.[27] There was quite a bit of apprehension when I traveled to Missouri for the comprehensives. When I passed them, only the dissertation stood in the way of receiving a doctorate.

Because Missouri was such a distance from San Diego, I figured it too inconvenient to tackle some project in the pipeline there as a dissertation. I'd also become wise enough to avoid any quantitative (numbers crunching or statistical) study, and opted for an historical (qualitative) project.

The Copley News Service celebrated its 10th anniversary in 1965. It was founded by James Strohn Copley, owner and publisher not only of the morning *San Diego Union* and *San Diego Evening Tribune* but other smaller newspapers in California and Illinois.

There was the story - which I never was able fully to verify - that, at a meeting somewhere, President Dwight David Eisenhower had alerted Jim Copley about what the President saw as an imbalance of news coverage, especially concerning the dangers of communist threats there.

---

[27] I suspect historians don't consider many of these old books all that important now.

Hence, so the story went, the first emphasis of the Copley News Service was on Latin America. By 1965, CNS had expanded coverage to other areas of the world, and established a Washington, D.C., bureau. After I'd received preliminary approval to proceed from Copley officials, Bill Taft agreed to be dissertation advisor for my researching the history of CNS. Other University of Missouri journalism faculty members serving on the committee were Eugene Sharp and Ed Lambert. My former boss Dale Spencer, for whom I'd worked as a J grad student, also gave his OK to join the committee, as did Western U.S. History professor Lewis Atherton.

At this point I found myself more than a bit concerned about being able to gather sufficient information for a dissertation. Not only was I a Yellow Dog Democrat and the Copley organization decidedly Republican, but also there appeared to be a Copley aura of secretiveness. For example, many "Letters to the Editor" of San Diego Copley newspapers often were published unsigned – or with initials, something like "J.S., Coronado." As if someone evil was lurking around the county, seeking out newspaper letter writers, planning to do them some kind of bodily or other harm?

Another example: When I'd worked for Associated Press in Albuquerque, *The Wall Street Journal* in Dallas and *The Roswell Daily Record*, our doors were wide open. This open-door policy partly was intended to encourage anyone to inform us about something newsworthy (or what even they might mistakenly consider newsworthy). This led to minor stories and, occasionally, even the beginning of more important ones.

Public officials, politicians, PR folks (say, like the spokesman for a Red Cross funding drive), sauntered in to talk with advertising managers, news editors, and reporters. Mortuary workers came in with information for obituaries, women arrived with wedding pictures, and so forth. Not at the Copley building.

One did not traipse into the building at Third Avenue and Broadway where the *Union* and *Evening Tribune* were published – and where headquarters of the Copley News Service was located. A guard at the door intercepted everyone. If he didn't recognize you as an employee, or you weren't listed in his appointment book, he'd phone upstairs and someone there had to vouch for you before admittance to the building.

Actually, I found myself treated cordially by everyone in the building, especially John Pinkerman, executive news editor of Copley News Service. Nevertheless, there appeared tension I'd not experienced in other newsrooms. The aura seemed to me as if there was worry that Jim Copley himself suddenly might appear and shout, "What the hell is this guy doing nosing around here."

Perhaps the concern about my legitimate nosing around simply to write a history was explained in the late 1970s, long after I'd completed the dissertation. It was reported that the Copley News Service was used by the Central Intelligence Agency as a front in Latin America. Reporters Joe Trento and Dave Roman also added that the whole Copley Press organization had been used as a front for the CIA, that Jim Copley had been cooperating with the CIA since 1947. They reported that at one time two dozen Copley employees were working for the CIA, and that the CIA had funded the Inter-American Press Association.

Carl Bernstein, who in 1972 had teamed with Bob Woodward at the *Washington Post* to report on President Nixon's Watergate scandal, in 1977, wrote a 27,000-word story for *Rolling Stone* about the CIA and the media. "The Agency's involvement with the Copley organization is so extensive that it's almost impossible to sort out," Bernstein quoted a CIA official as saying. Other Agency officials, according to Bernstein, "said then that James S. Copley, the chain's owner until 1973, personally made most of the cover arrangements with the CIA."

It also has been reported that the *San Diego Union and Evening* News spied on antiwar protesters for the FBI. When Mary and I marched a couple of times in downtown San Diego against the Vietnam War, we noticed men standing on street corners taking pictures of those passing by and thought it rather odd.

It's not all bad news about the shady history of the Copley News Service. In 2006 CNS and the *San Diego Union-Tribune* won the Pulitzer National Reporting Prize for their disclosure that former Congressman Randy Cunningham received bribes. It led to his criminal conviction and imprisonment. Noted for their work were reporters Marcus Stern and Jerry Krammer.

I treaded lightly those years earlier, unaware of any of the above CIA-FBI accusations. Somehow I sensed to avoid asking standard questions such as whether or not the venture had proved profitable, or even the range of salaries being paid. Talk about my own paranoia –not about the CIA but that someone at CNS might not allow me to finish my study! In addition, I worried all through the writing of the dissertation that some member of the University of Missouri faculty committee might demand I probe much deeper into the working of CNS. If I couldn't produce, would I have to abandon the project and pursue another?

I'd heard enough horror stories about dissertations, especially in the sciences, when a graduate student would almost complete his or her study – only to discover someone else had just published similar findings. Back to the drawing boards. Luckily, I discovered there were biographical sketches of those at CNS since the beginning until that present time, and duplicates of stories which had been gathered during all those 10 years. Thus the title of the dissertation became *The Story and Stories of Copley News Service.*

For several months, when I could spare time to break away from teaching and family obligations, I'd gather material in downtown San Diego and take it home to process into the project. I also interviewed Executive News Editor Pinkerman and several others working at the CNS headquarters.

The 268 final pages and all the drafts of the dissertation were composed on the typewriter. If you pecked out 15 pages of a chapter, were for some reason to decide in the middle of the night to slip a couple of paragraphs into page 3, that meant the next morning or later retyping the remaining 12 pages. No computerized automatic spacing of inserts, cut and paste or copy. For perspective, think about this: office computers – with personal computers (PCs) in their infancy in the mid-1960s – often were bulky contraptions with reels of tape hanging on them. They took an engineer's mind to fathom.[28]

Typing of the final dissertation had to be on specified bond paper, precisely meeting standards and rules required by the Graduate School for margins, spacing and footnotes. Mary cheerfully performed this Herculean task and is acknowledged with gratitude.

"It took the confidence and assistance of Mary J. Odendahl, the author's wife and typist, to make this project a reality."

The first draft, also typed precisely by Mary – copied from pages of my messy pecking and scratchy editing – was mailed to Taft. It came back with a few recommendations. Such as that I often became too wordy (if you've read these pages – you believe). Taft pointed out unnecessary portions to delete and that much material would better be handled as footnotes. Back to the typewriter for both Mary and me, another draft mailed to Taft. It came back with only a few more suggestions, which when accomplished would mean an OK for the final typing.

The last day of Mary's final typing on bond paper, she and I argued. I'd become too picky, still wanting to make minor changes – which meant more work for her and not getting the tedious job completed. Nevertheless, she finished her beautiful work. We mailed it off and decided to go out for an early dinner and take in a movie. After dinner we sat in the

---

[28] Bill Gates was 10-12 years old at the time. The name Microsoft wasn't registered until 1976. It was after 1980 before Microsoft (software) and IBM (International Business machines computers–hardware) joined together using DOS (the Direct Operating System) the standard for most PCs other than Macintosh ones called Apples.

theater unaware of what kind of movie it would be – only choosing it because it starred Elizabeth Taylor and Richard Burton.

Guess what? A professor and wife appeared on the screen, began to engage in endless arguing and feuding fueled by too much alcohol. You guessed the name of the movie? *Who's Afraid of Virginia Woolf*, released in June of 1966, with Taylor and Burton, along with George Segal and Sandy Dennis. Taylor played the daughter of a university president married to history professor Burton. One reviewer called it "a literate and profane night in the pathological marriage of two tortured souls, a middle-aged New England professor and his carping wife."

Mary and I recovered from that experience before I again had to return to Missouri to "defend" the dissertation. I survived the moderate questions by the committee, because after they retired to take a vote and returned, Bill Taft told me I'd passed. "Congratulations, Dr. Odendahl," Lewis Atherton added, as he reached out to shake my hand. It's quite an honor in such a situation for a Hurley boy to shake the hand of a distinguished Western History scholar and author.

That wasn't the finale, because the University of Missouri required that students awarded doctorates must be present at the graduation ceremony, Later, again from California to Missouri, Mary and me together this time. A doctorate hood was dropped over my head and draped around my robed shoulders. After the ceremony, Mary and I went by earlier invitation to Bill Taft's home, where he and his wife Myrtle served us lemonade. We assumed liquor never was in the Methodist Tafts' home. Nonetheless, it was a wonderful gesture from professor/graduate and advisor/dissertation supervisor to his student of several years. It also was a bonding of one family to another, marking a special occasion for all four of us.[29]

For sure, plenty of personal light stuff - along with heavier stuff nationally - happened during our first few years in the San Diego area. When ordering checks from a local bank, I decided to print a more complete name on them, changing from Max Odendahl to Eric M. Odendahl. That actually wasn't too radical because I thought my real first name was Eric Maxwell Odendahl. I once contemplated using Maxwell as a first name, because Maxwell Perkins was one of my idols.

Charles Scribner's Sons' Editor William Maxwell Perkins also went by his middle name. Perkins edited the novels of F. Scott Fitzgerald, his first *This Side of Paradise* in 1920 and Ernest Hemingway's, his first, *The Sun Also Rises*, in 1926. The biggest challenge for

---

[29] A few years later Pam and her friend Jan–along with Pam's dog Josh–rode in a VW Squareback across the country and into Canada. They stopped in Columbia, looked up Taft in his office, and had a good visit with him.

Perkins came editing the works of the first Thomas Wolfe – with Perkins talking Wolfe into cutting 90,000 words from *Look Homeward, Angel* in 1929.

And they endured a two-year battle over reducing *Of Time and the River,* published in 1935.

"Wolfe left Scribner's after numerous fights with Perkins," according to Wikipedia, and, "despite this, Perkins served as Wolfe's literary executor after his early death in 1938." Before his own death in 1947, Maxwell Perkins published books by J.P. Marquand and Erskine Caldwell, *The Yearling* by Marjorie Kinnan Rawlins in 1938 (winner of a Pulitzer Prize), and Alan Paton's *Cry the Beloved Country* in 1946. Perkins also is credited with in 1945 talking James Jones into working on *From Here to Eternity,* 1951.

I fantasized in my youth that, if I didn't become the writer of The Great American Novel, perhaps I'd turn into a prominent editor like Perkins.[30] The name change to Eric seemed to go smoothly in San Diego, but our family in New Mexico to this day still calls me "Max" – which is fine with me. I did hear second-hand that one non-San Diego acquaintance in academia said, "He thinks he's hot stuff now that he has a PhD, even changed his name from Max to Eric."

It wasn't trying to place myself on a pedestal, but rather escaping memories harkening all the way back to childhood. A change initiated to pull free from a name in the boxing world. Slapsie Maxie Rosenbloom had been light heavyweight champion of the world from 1932 to 1934. Of course, as I grew up in the 1930s, my teasing playmates thought it great fun calling me Slapsie Maxie.

I didn't like it at all. The real Slapsie Maxie suffered from so many head punches that his motor functions deteriorated. "Slapsie" was a common term for punch-drunk.

Another boxer named Max I didn't like was drafted in 1939 into the German Air Force (Luftwaffe), was unjustly considered a Nazi although apparently he wasn't especially a fan of Adolf Hitler. Earlier, in 1936, Max Schmeling had knocked out African-American Joe Louis in the 14th round of a heavyweight fight in New York. The Germans claimed it a world victory for Nazism.

Americans cheered when, in the 1938 rematch in Yankee Stadium, Louis pounded Schmeling with furious blows and scored a technical knockout in the first round. But lots of Americans found the Brown Bomber unappealing because he was an African-

---

[30] A great deal of change in the less-personal role of editors came with the emergence of the personal computer, when tedious re-typing and editing, checking spelling, etc. ended and novels began flooding publishers' offices.

American. They wanted some Great White Hope to appear to take the heavyweight title away from the Brown Bomber.[31]

A mystery which I've never gotten to the bottom of bobbed to the surface in San Diego while Mary and I applied from San Diego for a passport for our European trip in 1984. The U.S. bureaucracy demanded a copy of my original Santa Rita, New Mexico, birth certificate. When it arrived from Santa Fe, my first name shown is Carl – Carl Maxwell Odendahl – with the printed Carl crossed out and Eric written in above it

Carl in German is the same as Charles in English. Dad's middle name was Charles and my Grandfather Odendahl's first name was Carl. I asked Mom, who was getting along in years, about the reason for the change from Carl to Eric and she said she couldn't remember anything about it (or didn't want to answer for some reason).

I knew she never got along too well with my grandfather when she and Dad were first married and farmed on side-by-side homesteads in Alberta, Canada "He smoked a pipe," she grumbled more than once during my growing years.

At San Diego State College, my first office was shared with Frank Holowach. He had been editor of the newspaper in Titusville, Pennsylvania, where the first producing U.S. oil well was drilled on the Drake Farm in 1859 and then the Funk Farm well in 1861 flowed at 3,000 barrels per day. The Holowach family with three children – two sons and a daughter - had come to San Diego because Frank's wife, Joyce, suffered from multiple sclerosis and doctors hoped she might fare better in a warmer climate.

Frank, along with Jim Julian, had been students of Arthur Wimer at then State University of Iowa (now University of Iowa). Wimer experienced a long newspaper career, especially in the financial area, and had started the Journalism Department at San Diego State.

In 1964 I became the fourth full-time faculty member with the department. Wimer, first with a master's from Iowa. Julian, second with a PhD from Iowa. Holowach, third, with a master's from Iowa. Me, fourth with a master's from Iowa at the time struggling toward a PhD at Missouri. And we soon added other faculty from Iowa, George Sorensen, Jim Buckalew , and Joe Spevak with PhDs. The department occasionally became dubbed "Little Iowa."

---

[31] As I edited this chapter—one of many times — in November of 2008, African-American Barack Obama has just been elected President of the United States. We've come a long way, baby, although we certainly could do much better solving racial and religious differences.

Meanwhile, on the national level, plenty had happened. The Civil Rights Act of 1964 had been signed July 2, outlawing racial segregation in schools, public places and employment. The central figure besides Martin Luther King leading to passage of the act was President Lyndon Johnson, and if LBJ had continued such leadership it might have nominated him in history as one of our greatest Presidents.

His fortune changed just a month later, on August 2, when the destroyer I'd served on in 1948-49, the U.S.S. Maddox (DD-731) *reportedly* engaged three North Vietnamese P-T boats in the Gulf of Tonkin. The U.S. already had become involved in South Vietnam by providing military advisors in 1959, but it was the 1964 Gulf of Tonkin "incident" which LBJ promoted which led to this nation's full-fledged entry into the war.

The war at that time lasted the longest in our history, until 1975, with 58,159 U.S. dead (another 304,000 wounded) plus 3 to 4 *million* Vietnamese killed, along with the deaths of 1.5 to 2 *million* Laotians and Cambodians. By 1969, young American men began being drafted to fight in the war; this changed the whole atmosphere on college and university campuses.

When I arrived at San Diego State College, the faculty member uniform-of-the- day was a business suit with white shirt and tie for men - and dresses with hose for women. I can't exactly recall, but probably only had a single suit when I arrived, quickly purchased another one. Do remember buying a new suit each fall about the time one almost wore out. I eventually kept three suits/sport coats[32] of different colors to appear spic-and-span as the days/classes of the weeks changed. It seemed pretty ordinary because I'd already worn suits, white shirts, and ties working for newspapers. A downside was the fairly-high cleaners' expense, so we wore/aired-out our suits as much as possible between cleanings.

I still kept my hair cut in a short flattop as I generally had since high school.

That would change as the war continued, and students protested it – increasingly after the 1969 draft. Many faculty members like me who in the beginning had expected a short offensive, had turned against the war. We looked for ways to be closer to the concerns of students. One way was to dress more like students, not to appear to be lording over them in business suits.

Somewhere during this ever-changing period the leisure-suit arrived. It featured a coat which looked like an unbuttoned, long-sleeved sports shirt not tucked in. Below were pants minus regular belts or belt loops. An attached, wide portion of pants cloth

---

[32] Bought a name-brand, light-blue-checkered sports coat at a thrift shop for $2 to $4 which I wore for several years.

stretched across your belly as a belt, with buttons showing. You wore a sports shirt (always without a tie) under the coat–usually with the collar of the shirt outside over the collar of the coat. Some faculty members only wore this outfit in the evening for "leisure" events, but others soon arrived on campus in it.

During the Vietnam War period I began going to Hillcrest to have my hair cut by Catherine Foster, a Hillcrest barber and noteworthy artist. "Just let your hair grow out," she ordered me, "and I'll take care of it." What happened in a few weeks was that my hair style looked something like that of popular folk singer John Denver – hanging down the back just above my collar and around my ears, with bangs across my forehead.

Some male faculty members began to wear blue jeans and T-shirts when teaching classes and hanging out on campus. Younger faculty became difficult to distinguish from students. I decided to compromise, wore slacks and long-sleeved shirts without a tie – in the winter sweaters, both pullover and cardigan, over the shirts.

I put on a suit when going to meetings in downtown San Diego. The "rule" for males was that just about anything sartorial went for meetings reaching from San Diego State to Mission Valley directly to the west, but suits and ties still were required to look respectable (and keep up the image of the university) downtown next to the ocean.

Meanwhile, Terry and Pam had been shuffled from one La Mesa grade or middle school to another. The school for each the first year we lived next to the Roeslers on Broodmoor, the second when we rented another year from a faculty member on sabbatical, and the third when we moved into our own little place on Vista Drive. That was very difficult for them with new teachers and friends every year.

There was a period when both girls went through a dress-up stage. They wore short-skirted dresses and panty hose. Active girls quickly put runs in panty hose and parents found it expensive replacing them. As the Vietnam War wore on, even pre-college students became activists against it. Girls began frequenting thrift stores looking for such clothes as baggy shirts, either to cover with overalls, or wear over the overalls with the shirttails hanging behind.

"Well, I'm not sure I'm too happy about what they're wearing," one sort'a baffled mother commented to us, "but it's sure a heck'uv'a lot cheaper than paying for all those panty hose."

When Mary attended her first meeting of faculty wives at San Diego State, she discovered Norma Bailey there. The Baileys[33], unbeknownst to us, also now were part of life at San Diego State College. Mary and Norma decided they would attend together as many meetings and events as they could. One of Jerry's older and tenured colleagues in the Industrial Arts Department[34] had advised me, "There are many ways to get promoted at San Diego State. It really helps if you are a nice guy, if your wife is supporting you, and you have a decent family."[35]

Mary and Norma, both very attractive women with some amount of resemblance to each other, often were mixed up. To some older faculty women, familiar with the children's novels, they laughingly became known as the *Bobbsey Twins*.

Journalism Department Chairman Jim Julian had decided that he no longer wanted the added responsibility of being faculty advisor for the student newspaper, *The Daily Aztec*, turned that job over to me. I found it to be a curious position. The job was to be *advisor* to young people (I wasn't all that much older) who were reveling in their independence from parents and other authority and *didn't particularly wish to be advised* about much of anything. Yet, putting together *The Daily Aztec* provided students with college credit in a class called Newspaper Production. Students receiving grades realized they lived under some authority.

I certainly respected their First Amendment right to freedom of the press in regard to whatever stories they wished to cover, or editorial positions they might take. On the

---

[33] You probably remember the story about her husband, Jerry, rescuing Pam from bitter cold one day at University of Missouri married housing.

[34] The name later was changed to Industrial Studies.

[35] This was to change in subsequent years as more faculty, males and females, had "significant others" and those married had spouses who also worked and were unable to attend daytime campus events. Research and publication also became dominant. "Publish or Perish"!

other hand, whatever was printed in the campus newspaper was a reflection on the university. "The Buck Stops Here" was with me.

It was a rapidly changing, yet still a conservative time in regard to acceptable language in a college newspaper. For example, I recall Sports Editor Tom Gable, who later became a public relations practitioner and wine expert in San Diego, coming to my office and asking, "Is it okay for me to use the word 'transvestite' in my column?"

Not only was I aware Tom was attempting to duplicate the writing style of a noted sports columnist of the *Los Angeles Times* named Jim Murray, who used big words and historical references in his columns, but also this Good Old New Mexico Boy had no idea what a transvestite was – what the word meant.

Overly cautious, I replied, "No, I think you better not use that word, Tom." After he'd gone and I'd quickly looked up the word in the dictionary, I really felt stupid. I imagine Tom and others on the *Aztec* staff were laughing up their sleeves at me for that decision. We mill-and-smelter-town Hurley boys were unaware of transvestites, would have bigotedly called them "queers." We grew up cussing like sailors, but knew we'd be in BIG trouble if we ever did so around girls or women.

It was an attention-getting surprise for me early one morning in the *Aztec* office when a male editor admonished a female reporter, "You really fucked up that story of yours yesterday!" I was preparing to grab the young man by the arm, escort him out into the hall, and give him a piece of my mind when the young woman shouted back in anger, "How did I fuck it up, **you tell me that**. Just **how** did I fuck it up!!!"

I eased myself out of my chair, quietly left the room as they continued their argument. At that moment, I knew California college students were living in a different campus world than that which I was accustomed to.[36]

In January of 1967, the *Aztec* staff buzzed all day about a Friday the 13th bad-luck bombshell story which appeared that afternoon in the San Diego *Evening-Tribune:*

"The coed managing editor of the Daily Aztec, the San Diego State College student newspaper, is in county jail in connection with smuggling marijuana into the country.

"U.S. Customs agents at San Ysidro said they found 44 pounds of marijuana in the girl's car as she was entering the United States at San Ysidro from Tijuana.

"The girl is ....."[37]

---

[36] I also wouldn't have imagined at the time that *almost anyone* would ever use that now more common written word in his or her autobiography.

"Customs agents said . . . , a senior honor student major in English journalism at San Diego State, and two other students were taken into custody in connection with the smuggling....

". . . has a 3.2 point grade average out of a possible 4.0 She is a member of Mortar Board, a senior women's academic honorary society, a senior class officer, and former member of the Student Council."

Almost a year earlier, in February of 1966, *The Daily Aztec* had been named the state's top overall college newspaper by the California Intercollegiate Press Association. The association was comprised of 24 state and private universities. I was very proud to have been the advisor to the *Aztec* that day and sad the next year to learn of her predicament. She was not only a bright student, but also a fun person to be around. I always thought, and continue to, that she was a fine person who may have somehow found herself in with a bad crowd.

I'm still ignorant about how marijuana affects lives. At this writing (2017; California has just made it legal to sell), it appears that marijuana is like alcohol – perhaps not too bad for you if used in moderation. Those of age should be able to refuse using it or use it at their own risk. The vast and murderous underworld of major drug dealers, generally not arrested like their underlings and users, make millions of dollars off the herb.

By 1969, still advisor for the *Daily Aztec*, I'd been promoted from assistant to associate professor, and had received tenure. Receiving tenure seemed much easier than later for faculty members in the department. One morning, Julian came by and told me, "Well, Eric, it looks as if you now have tenure. Wimer and I just took a vote and it probably will go through all the committees and the president will sign off on it."

---

[37] There is no point in listing her name again. She was 21 at the time, would be in her sixties at this writing. Hopefully, she outlived all this and pursued a happy and productive life.

"Just what does tenure mean," I asked.

"It means they aren't going to fire you for what you say - within reason - in your classes. You do still have to be careful about not doing anything like patting the coeds on their butts."

Obit break: During this writing received word that Tony Hillerman, the author known for his Navajo mysteries, died in Albuquerque of pulmonary failure October 26, 2008, at the age of 83. His first book, *The Blessing Way,* was published in 1970 and introduced Lt. Joe Leaphorn. Officer Jim Chee arrived in *"People of Darkness"* in 1978. The second novel he had published in 1971 was "*The Fly on the Wall,*" which revolved around newspapers.

"I feel like I've lost a close friend," Mary sadly said, "but we all have to go sometime." Mary and I and Tony and his wife, Marie, spent some time together at an Association for Education in Journalism (AEJ) national meeting, which she recalls being in Seattle.[38] Tony never was a close friend but certainly a good acquaintance.

You'll recall my University of New Mexico J department mentor, and for whom Mary worked as his secretary, Keen Rafferty.[39] When he retired, Rafferty wrote a letter encouraging me to apply for his job as chairman. I applied from San Diego State College, but the job went to Hillerman - who Rafferty later said was a sort of shoo-in because Tony had done PR work for the university while working toward his master's degree. (Rafferty had a thing against those receiving J degrees and then going into public relations - he called it "selling out.") Certainly, it was good for New Mexico and the writing world that Tony stayed at UNM and began to turn out his Navajo mystery novels.

Tony never lost the common touch. I think the same goes for John Grisham – for example, with his non-novel "*The Innocent Man.*" Exactly a month before Tony Hillerman, September 26, 2008, Paul Newman died – also at age 83. He and Academy Award-winning actress Joanne Woodward had been married for 50 years. I read somewhere that Newman once was asked how he felt about being sexually approached by other women. He is supposed to have replied, "Why go out on the streets looking for hamburger when you have steak at home?" It is difficult to think of a more handsome man or beautiful woman as a movie couple than Newman and Elizabeth Taylor on the screen in *Cat on a Hot Tin Roof* in 1958 – the same year Paul and Joanne married.

---

[38] An earlier chapter detailed how Tony was editor of the *Santa Fe New Mexican* when I was news editor at the *Roswell Daily Record,* how we ink-stained wretches gathered in Albuquerque (with plenty of beer) a couple of times a year for Associated Press editors' meetings.

[39] Rafferty had been "the slot man" —-made up the front page and edited stories for the *Baltimore Sun* when the old curmudgeon, H.L. Mencken, was there. Rafferty came to New Mexico as a "lunger" —had lost one to TB and the dry weather of New Mexico kept him from losing the other. He started the J program at UNM.

Back to a less starry-eyed-level - seven years after that - in June of 1965, *The Quill* which called itself "The Magazine for Journalists," had published my article "What Do Editors Think of Today's Journalism Graduates?" Editors' comments ranged from, "Anyone who questions, or has to comment, on the value of a college education, doesn't deserve one," to: "one of the best all-around professionals I ever met never finished high school. So where are we?"

The idea for all this came after Keen Rafferty wrote (by letter – which took more time to pen or peck out on typewriters - in those days with no e-mail) suggesting I replicate his Fall, 1954, *Journalism Quarterly* article about whether J grads were moving ahead into newspaper work.

I followed his questionnaire and *JQ* published my 10-years-later piece in the summer of 1964.[40] The two articles were enough to help me become promoted to associate professor. A female full professor in the Economics Department on the division promotions committee later told me, "I was so happy to see *someone* in the Journalism Department publishing that I decided to vote for your promotion,"

Actually, Julian had produced what was a good-selling beginning reporting textbook which he regularly updated. Wimer also had written textbooks and continued to sell general-circulation magazine articles to "keep up" with students in his magazine-article writing class. But these weren't considered especially "academic" by many as San Diego State moved closer to the "publish or perish" mode of faculty of colleges and universities around the nation.

In February of 1967, a letter arrived from Donald Brown, chairman of the Journalism Department at Arizona State University in Tempe:

"I came across an old letter of application written by you, and as I was strongly impressed by your fine practical experience, by your academic degree, and by your writing, I wrote around the country to find where you had moved, and Art Barnes told me you were teaching at San Diego State. I suppose Jim Julian would not be happy to lose a good man, but I thought there would be no harm in inquiring (1) if you are happy in your present position or (2) if you know of someone with good practical experience who would be interested in teaching at Arizona State.

It was a flattering letter, sort'a an early job offer (no salary range or figure listed).

---

[40] I felt bad in 1974 after convincing newly-hired full-time colleague Barbara Hartung to again replicate the article as a 20-year checkup. She worked hard on it, but it wasn't a third-time charm when *JQ* turned it down. I think that by this period the journal was into seeking more sophisticated material with highly-developed statistical data.

Mary and I talked it over and decided to remain at San Diego State. For my part, it would be a lateral move – that is, it wasn't as if officials of the University of Missouri were camping at my doorstep, besieging me to come back to teach at Columbia with a much higher salary as a full professor.

For Mary's part, she was making special friends among faculty women, and at the Methodist church in La Mesa. She had begun to settle into the good life of California. For our daughters, a move to Tempe would mean another change in schools, again shuffling them away from friends. We had no idea how Arizona schools compared to those in California.

And there was the old adage, "The grass always looks greener on the other side of the fence." For all of us, the prospect of life in Tempe – which Brown called "located in the thriving Phoenix metropolitan area," one of the hottest spots in the nation – looked even less green and unappealing. I don't think we considered that Arizonians lived in refrigerated air conditioning, only a few days each year necessary in San Diego lives. The closest we'd come to really hot summers was basking in air pushed through evaporating water, a "swamp cooler" on top of our home in Roswell.

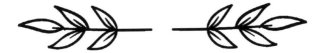

CHAPTER 13 — DEPARTMENT CHAIR (OR WHATEVER?)

An eventful change came two years later, when Jim Julian stepped down as chairman and the Journalism Department faculty voted for me to fill that position.

I've never been certain why Jim Julian, after serving from 1956 to 1969 (more than four times the expected three-year-rotating term), appeared reluctantly to step down from the Department Chairman's[41] position he seemed to enjoy so much.

Years later, I was told it was a decision by Dean Harold Haak[42] (we now had become part of the College of Professional Studies). All I know for sure is that colleagues George Sorensen and Jim Buckalew came by my office one day, said a replacement was needed for Julian, convinced me to take the job, and I was voted in.

The most logical candidate would have been Sorensen himself, who had held administrative positions on other campuses. He was familiar with the ropes of college administration, having for seven years been director of public relations at Monmouth College at Monmouth, Illinois, and another two years as assistant to the president at Moorhead State College at Moorhead, Minnesota.

However, a very bright fellow, Sorensen knew from experience that little was to be gained as department chairman compared to the misery which easily might envelop him. He appeared to enjoy teaching, was receiving high marks from students in both his Sociology and Journalism classes, and was well on his way to promotion without shouldering any such consternation.

Buckalew, who taught classes in radio and television - also very keen and competent - could have stepped into the position. He had previous experience teaching part-time at the University of Hawaii and the University of Iowa. "Moonlighting" for extra money, reporting the news from radio station KCBQ mostly in very early mornings before classes, Buckalew possessed an almost photographic memory. He quickly memorized rosters of all the students in his classes, so could greet them by their first names.

---

[41] It was years later before, because of gender equality issues, that men and women began to be referred to as "Chairs." Those inanimate-object references seemed to me worsen the identity problem. No one ever asked me, but why not just be either a Chairman, a Chairwoman or a Chairperson?

[42] Haak went on to become president of one of the California State Universities. I've lost track of him since then.

The popular prof might be having a conference or a pleasant chat with a student immediately before one of his classes, say journalism history. He'd walk down the hall and deliver an almost seamless hour-and-15-minute lecture about, perhaps, early American journalist Benjamin Franklin and others. A graduate student once told me, "Dr. Buckalew is a walking encyclopedia." Buckalew simply was too busy at that time. Years after I'd retired he did his stint as chairperson.

It became obvious that Julian wasn't a happy camper about leaving. As he moved down the hall to a regular office and I into the larger and swankier department office, he took more than personal files[43] with him. There I was in that bigger office – yet standing alone as if in a batter's stance with three strikes ready to be thrown at me.

Strike one: No files to review which really gave me a clue about what had gone on in the chairman's role in past years. Strike two: As an associate prof, I needed to watch my Ps and Qs with both Julian and Art Wimer. With a wife and two daughters, I fully understood those full profs would make the initial decision about my promotion to their rank as a full professor. Strike Three: The department secretary suddenly had left her job and Julian hadn't time to hire a replacement. I was well aware of the old adage that secretaries make or break the operation of a smooth-running department.

Yet, despite all this, things seemed to go relatively well. No strikeout. Julian offered to help me, sans files, any way he could. Julian never hindered me in my fledgling performance as chairman. Neither he nor Wimer ever threatened something as severe, say as a no-promotion, about any matter. And, I was able to hire a new secretary.

With routine office work piling up, and after waiting several days to be sent someone to interview for the position, I decided to take matters into my own hands. I interviewed and hired Elena Castro, who was just across the hall working as an assistant secretary in the Political Science Department office.

As she began to settle in our office and tackled the stack of secretarial paperwork, Wally Miles of Political Science – perhaps the only African-American professor on campus at the time – stopped me in the hall. "That's a great thing you did, hiring Elena," he said.

I wasn't sure what he meant, but – after he continued – discovered it was because Elena was Hispanic. Certainly I was aware of that, but – honestly – the only way I'd figured in that factor was Elena would be most helpful in fielding the occasional telephone calls received in Spanish from across the Mexican border just a few miles away. Perhaps I'd begun to lose some of that awful prejudice I'd learned in my childhood and youth in

---

[43] I guess he considered files of any department matter he had handled as personal?

Hurley? In any event, Elena Castro remained to be department secretary for several "chairs."

On yet another day, Sorensen and Buckalew came by together again. Both were good friends, but I realized something was up. This time it was to convince me that the department should seek accreditation from the American Council on Education for Journalism. The three of us agreed it was a good idea, and took our oral proposal to a meeting of the whole department faculty. After much discussion, we received a positive vote.

All of us faculty members were well aware that teaching in an accredited department, besides gaining prestige for the department and institution, would be feathers in our own caps. San Diego State would have the distinction of being considered almost in the same league with our graduate *alma mater* Iowa and other Big 10 schools, along with universities with noted journalism departments and schools such as Missouri, Texas, Pennsylvania – and so forth. Besides, even my undergraduate *alma mater*, the University of New Mexico, long had been accredited in journalism.

The down side was that accreditation meant giving up quite a bit of independence. This is the reason competent faculties often decide to opt out of the process. Some of what the AEJ accrediting team looked for *was* pretty Mickey Mouse. For example, I learned from Julian that a local high-ranking official of Copley Newspapers recently had been part of an AEJ accreditation team. The Copley official cordially invited me to what turned out to be a two or three (or more? – can't remember) martini lunch[44] at the noted Top of the Cove Restaurant in La Jolla. "One of the things they're doing is checking out libraries," he told me.

"What do you mean?"

He explained that AEJ team members might visit our library to determine how many books journalism faculty and students had checked out. "I guess they figure," he continued, "that a department which isn't using the library very much isn't all that academic."

This was one of several such nuggets I took back to our faculty. One of my classes required a term paper. I began to demand students not only include standard footnotes but also library call numbers of books which they cited. Students checking out books left behind a record for the accreditation team. Now a question is: Did it make any difference

---

[44] Those martini lunches were the vogue, but the problem was keeping one's self on track as to what the meeting was all about.

academically whether students simply took books off shelves in the library and copied information there, or whether they checked them out?[45]

We still were San Diego State College, and the academic year of the evaluation visit was 1970-71. My job was to prepare an official, pre-visit report which was prefaced saying that it "makes it possible for the visitors to study more thoroughly the characteristics of the journalism program which cannot be understood except through an on-the-campus observation. The team studies the report carefully before making the visit." Man, did that pre-visit report turn out to be lots of time-consuming work, not only for me but also for the rest of the faculty! We now had eight full-time faculty members. Besides Jim Buckalew, Frank Holowach, Jim Julian, George Sorensen, Art Wimer and myself, there were Jack Haberstroh teaching advertising classes, Joe Spevak, news-editorial, and Fred Whitney, public relations, By this time, Spevak had taken over my duties as advisor to *The Daily Aztec.*

Here are a few items from that pre-visit report which might interest the reader: There were 131 undergraduate journalism majors (70 women and 61 men) and one student taking graduate work in a program which only had begun that year. There were 420 students other than journalism majors which had taken journalism courses during the year preceding the accreditation visit. In that academic year, 1969-70, San Diego State had conferred 20 degrees to those completing their journalism and other required courses.

The AEJ actually didn't accredit departments, but what it called "sequences."[46] We sought accreditation for our news-editorial (newspaper) sequence which offered the most classes and had the most faculty with years of experience working on newspapers. They were listed as Holowach, Julian, Odendahl as "sequence head," Spevak and Wimer.

However, even though the AEJ was examining news-editorial, it was obvious that more than outstanding strength was added to the department by all of the other four faculty members.[47] At the time, the maximum nine-month salaries (although spread by checks over 12 months) for full professors was $19,224, for associate profs, $15,036, and $11,904 for assistant profs.

---

[45] Now, of course, students can surf the Internet and never set foot in libraries. This can be a dangerous practice regarding accuracy unless Internet information is manually checked against original sources in the library.

[46] However, departments across the country, whether with only one or several sequences accredited, certainly didn't make this distinction. They touted themselves in catalogs, etc., as "fully accredited."

[47] During the actual visit, it seemed to me the team spent about the same amount of time visiting with and questioning each of us.

Overall, we were what then would be considered middle-aged or close to it (on one side or the other). Wimer was 66, Julian, 56; Holowach and Whitney, 50; Sorensen, 45; Haberstroh, 43; Odendahl, 40; Spevak, 38; and Buckalew, 36.

All of us provided 16-week course outlines. There also was a complete listing of the rooms in which we taught and the cost of equipment utilized there. There was a section on the library in which all U.S. and foreign newspapers were listed, along with specific journalism magazines and periodicals. We also gathered the names of such reference books as dictionaries and almanacs available in our classrooms. Finally, I had to find out and list the name and address of each student who had been graduated in journalism from the news-editorial sequence in the previous year and where he or she was working. Most toiled for publications in the San Diego area.

Dean Haak also signed the report and it was mailed to AEJ. It was a nervous few days as the team arrived and began its examination and questioning of not only the journalism faculty and Haak, but others on campus including the college president. As the team left, we felt fairly confident that we had passed muster and a letter to that effect arrived shortly. That was a happy day for all of us.

(One with a fleeting memory obviously needs to be very cautious about giving impressions when writing a composite about former students. Like that they are "favorites." Even attempting to make such judgments leaves out many others also as worthy. For example, a mass communication class I taught probably averaged about 50 students from across campus each semester. Obviously, I'm unaware as to what happened to most of those students, or of their achievements which are measured not only by job or monetary success, but also by unknowns such as character and numerous other life aspects. It's like economists and weather-persons who cope with too many variables to predict overly accurate results. Often there is at least one student more knowledgeable about a topic being lectured about or discussed.)

My diminishing memory was jogged by one of Nick Canepa's recent sports columns in the slowly being diminished-by —many-pages *San Diego Union-Tribune*.[48] A troubling sign of the times for print journalism.

Canepa wrote sports and hung out at the *Daily Aztec* office while I was advisor in the 1960s. I thought he had the makings of a more purposeful newspaper writer. "Nick," I

---

[48] At this writing the U-T had published fewer pages, laid off or retired more than 200 J staff and other workers, and David Copley just sold it to another corporation for a reported $50 million. It was the end of the 81-year Copley family ownership era for the U-T, which began in 1928 when Ira C. Copley bought the morning *San Diego Union* and afternoon *San Diego Evening Tribune*.

said, "You ought to think about getting past this jock sniffing[49] and begin to write some serious news stories or columns."

He merely smiled, shook his head, gave me a disdainful look. I even coaxed *Aztec* editors to assign him a few non-sports stories. That didn't take, and after his 1969 graduation Canepa in 1974 began a sports writing career for the local Copley newspapers.

In 1977, he was named best writer for San Diego State athletics. Canepa continues to mimic the style of the late Jim Murray, longtime departed sports columnist of the *Los Angeles Times*. Murray continually alluded to historical events and characters. Like referring to an athlete: "He had the speed of Mercury . . ."

Canepa's June 2, 2009, column referred to Ted Giannoulas, known as The San Diego Chicken. I still was department chairman (would have been a "chair" later) when ambitious journalism major Giannoulas dropped by my office with a question, "Don't you think I should get a minority scholarship?"

"I don't think so, Ted. You're neither Black nor Chicano."[50]

"Well, I'm Greek. There aren't many Greeks on this campus. That makes me a minority, so I think I'm qualified."

It *was* something to think about, but there was little evidence Greek-Americans were facing inequity as much as persons of color. Turned down by me (and I assume subsequently by others on campus), he still left with a grin on his face. Enterprising Ted had the last laugh when he became very wealthy – much richer than any SDSU faculty member or staffer I'm aware of.

It wasn't too long after our meeting that the immigrant from New London, Ontario, Canada, became the radio station KGB Chicken, which morphed into the San Diego Chicken. A biography on Google reports how it all began in 1974:

"On the campus of San Diego State, a representative from a rock 'n roll station (KGB) arrived to find anyone who'd agree to wear a rented chicken costume for a promotional

---

[49] A "jock sniffer," which certainly applied to me when I was sports editor of *The Roswell Daily Record,* refers to writers who gather some of their material in team dressing rooms. It is a pejorative, usually meaning that the writer is/was not an athlete himself/herself but enjoys associating with those who are. I have no idea about younger Canepa's athletic career or accomplishments.

[50] Chicano was what appeared to be the preferred and broader reference replacing Mexican at that time, later Latino (male) or Latina (female). Hispanic often is common. Those of us attempting to be socially conscious also dropped the term Negro, then referred to Black, later Afro-American, and now African-American.

gimmick. It was just a one week, temporary job offering to visit the local zoo and giveaway candy Easter eggs. The pay was $2 an hour . . . .

"He has performed at more than 8,500 games and amazingly, has never missed one due to injury or illness. Moreover, he has more than 17,000 total appearances when parades, trade shows, banquets, conventions, TV and radio dates are factored in."

Sporting News editors once included Giannoulas as one of The Top 100 Most Powerful People in Sports in the 20th Century. At this writing he still works as The Chicken at 50 events from June through Labor Day, mainly in minor league ballparks. He told *SD Union-Trib* writer Mark Zeigler, *"The performing is not the problem, but waking up in the morning is a little tougher, there's no doubt. And the flying is not as fun as it used to be."* It was the 35th season for the 55-year-old Giannoulas,

I have no real idea which SDSU J student over the years has pocketed the most change. It well could be Andy Rathbone. Although graduated in 1986 and technically a major in comparative literature, Andy was editor of the *Daily Aztec*. He worked for the *La Jolla Light,* was an editor at *Computer Edge*, and freelanced for *PC World, Computer World and CompuServe*. At the time when most of us were confused by computers (many of us still are), Rathbone wrote *Microsoft Windows for Dummies,* and other Dummy and computer books.

Just a few months ago at this writing friend and member of our family David Goff (more about him in the next chapter) and I had just sat down for lunch at Jimmy's Café in Santee. Former SDSU journalism student Cathy Clark and a female friend noticed us, dropped by to say hello. Cathy had a 36-year career in San Diego as both a broadcast and print journalist. She was one of the first female anchorpersons on any San Diego TV station.

She worked at KFMB (1972-79), KNSD (1979-1989), *The San Diego Tribune* (1990) and KUSI (1990-1999). From 1993 to 1997, she served as president of the San Diego (now Pacific Southwest) chapter of the National Academy of Television Arts and Sciences. She produced the chapter Emmy awards for eight years and in 2006 was honored as a Silver Circle inductee of the Academy.

Cathy and her husband, Roel Robles, formed Robles Production in 1996. The company became Oaktree Productions, Inc., in 2001. Robles is an Emmy-winning photographer. That day she was having lunch at Jimmy's, she was working on a project in the East County area. She's still admired by many in San Diego. Full of fun, smart, and courageous, Cathy seemed to me always destined for success.

San Diego Magazine's longtime editor-in-chief was Tom Blair. He became one of the editors of the *Daily Aztec* while I was advisor. I remember him as a well-behaved, courteous, conservative Republican who had a fine singing voice. He was a friend of a fellow conservative and my colleague, Jim Julian. Back then being conservative and Republican was a plus for San Diego State journalism students hoping for a career in the city. It certainly was a more moderate type of conservatism than advocated by many Republicans today.

The ultra-conservative Copley newspapers reflected the majority San Diego viewpoint. It only has been in the last few years that the voices of Democrats have been a bit more accepted by those newspapers. Some attribute the beginning of the change to the building of the University of California at San Diego,[51] with several Nobel Prize winners and other top researchers and scholars putting San Diego more on the academic map.

Blair began his newspaper career in 1972 as a reporter for Copley's *The Evening Tribune* and was, for some 20 years one of its columnists. He was named editor of San Diego Magazine in 1995. In 2005, he was honored with the Harold Keen Award for Outstanding Contributions in Journalism by the San Diego Press Club.

Another *Daily Aztec* staffer during my time as advisor there was Sue Farrell. She was the daughter of U.S. Navy aviator Ted Farrell and they lived on Coronado Island.[52] After being graduated, Susan (I don't think she liked being called Sue – which is understood by a guy who changed his name from Max to Eric) joined KCST television station as a reporter. She moved up to anchorperson, where she remained for many years.[53] Susan later worked in public relations for the San Diego Opera and as president and chief executive officer of the San Diego Council of the USO.

Rory Devine, a J grad, after my time with the *Aztec* but while I still taught at SDSU, now is an anchorperson on weekend mornings at KNSD. In 2017, she still was reporting for that station.

There also is pathos connected with the lives of some SDSU journalism students of my acquaintance. One involved a most terrible event. After being graduated in 1973, Adrienne Alpert landed her first broadcasting job at KSDO News Radio in San Diego, eventually having a Sunday night talk show. By 1977, Adrienne was working for San Diego's ABC affiliate KGTV, where she remained as an anchor/reporter for 19 years. Alpert joined KABC-7 in Los Angeles as a reporter in 1996.

---

[51] UCSD actually is in La Jolla, a suburb of San Diego. The city's fathers wouldn't hear of naming it the University of California at La Jolla. That has a more exclusive and nice ring to it.
[52] North Island Naval Station adjoins the city of Coronado.
[53] The call letters now are KNSD, and it is an NBC affiliate.

On May 22, 2000, Adrienne was on assignment for KABC-7 in Hollywood. It allegedly was a photographer who raised the 42-foot telescoping mast of their news van into an overhead power line. Alpert stepped out of the van. Reports were that electricity shot through the van and through her body. As the result of the electrocution, Adrienne lost half of her right leg, half of her left arm, part of her left foot, and several fingers of her right hand.

Alpert settled a lawsuit against ABC, Inc. and other companies stemming from the accident. Both Alpert and ABC agreed not to disclose the details of the settlement. She continued to work as a reporter for the Los Angeles station. She and her husband, Barry Paulk, had a son, Michael.

As the years passed by, SDSU journalism students continued to distinguish themselves. One notable is Max Branscomb, a graduate of Bonita Vista High School in Chula Vista. He was graduated with a bachelor's degree in journalism by SDSU in 1980 and a master's degree in mass communication in 1982. I was chairman of the committee for his master's thesis about Simon Casady, longtime publisher of the *El Cajon Valley News.*

Mary and I attended a couple of melodramas which Max wrote. He directed students at his alma mater Bonita Vista High School. It proved fun hissing at the villains and clapping for the heroes and heroines. Bonitafest Melodrama was a full-scale musical, once pegged as San Diego County's longest running theatre production. Max also wrote more than 30 Christmas Pastorelas for Teatro Magica, and theaters in Los Angeles and Tucson.

Branscomb worked as a reporter for newspapers, for magazines, in radio, in educational public relations, and as a drama critic for several newspapers–including *The San Diego Union-Tribune.* In 1996, Max joined the faculty of Southwestern College. While advisor for the community college's student newspaper, the *Sun*, it has won many distinguished awards.

He received SWC's 2005-2006 Teaching Excellence Award. In nominating Branscomb for the award, Shannon Pagano, former editor-in chief of the *Sun,* wrote:

"Max has changed the lives of all of us in profound ways, His dedication to his students and to journalism remains unmatched in our community...as the advisor for the Southwestern College Sun...he has taught his students the invaluable lessons of journalism ethics and has led the way for the Sun staff to become the top-ranked community college newspaper in the nation."

The California Chicano News Media Association of San Diego also honored Branscomb with its La Pluma Lifetime Achievement Award. The group's president, Janine Zuniga, said:

"Max and CCNMA have had a long mutually beneficial relationship over the years...he has touched so many young people's lives during his career. We as journalists are grateful for his dedication and involvement."

Branscomb and his wife Leslie, a *Union-Tribune* reporter, have two daughters – Michaela and Chantal.

Dr. K. Tim Wulfemeyer at this writing is a full professor in what is now the School of Journalism & Media Studies at SDSU. He has degrees from Fullerton College, SDSU, and Iowa State University. He taught at Iowa State, New Mexico State, and the University of Hawaii, has published books and journal articles, and presented research papers at conferences.

"He was one of the brightest students I've ever taught," colleague Jim Buckalew once told me. I replied that Tim's wife, the former Lori McFadden, also was one of the best I'd ever had in my classes. Tim was a place kicker for the Aztec football team during the glory-winning-days of Coach Don Coryell, who later coached the professional San Diego Chargers. The handsome Tim and pretty Lori met as J students at SDSU. Lori, the last that I knew, was an assistant dean at the local Thomas Jefferson School of Law and taught radio news writing classes part-time as SDSU

Several years ago I picked up a Sony color TV for $40 to hang in our bedroom.[54] Mary and I mainly used it to watch the news while getting ready for bed. When there is a major fire, the TV spokesman for fire agencies usually was Maurice Luque.

While Maurice was a J student at SDSU, he once invited Mary and me to go some weekend to a special place he had found for lobster. "It's about halfway between Tijuana and Ensenada," Luque told me. "What happens is that when the lobster boats come in, this lady buys what they can't sell and cooks them in her little café. It's hit and miss – sometimes there is lobster and sometimes there isn't."

The location later became well-known as Puerto Nuevo, where many restaurants feature Pacific Ocean lobster, with beans, and tortillas – and cerveza and margaritas. Puerto Nuevo now is packed, especially on weekends. We never took Maurice up on his offer, but since then Mary and I with others have enjoyed the fare at Puerto Nueva. Most figure it doesn't compare with Maine lobster. Natives of Maine have a definite accent, and most don't speak Spanish. Lobster taste varies, as does language.

---

[54] These bulkier used TVs are selling cheap these days as folks move to thinner, wall-mounted, HD (high definition) models.

270

During our lifetimes we're all joined together in this world. Like: The two Calvano sisters took journalism classes at SDSU at the same time. After being graduated, Rita and Joni both began work with area newspapers. Rita remained with a Copley newspaper until early retirement. Joni reported for a newspaper in the North County, later was graduated from law school.

She became a lawyer for the American Civil Liberties Union, fighting in courtrooms for the Constitutional rights of citizens. Joni married a doctor, Sam Halpern, became independent enough to devote *pro bono* representation and advise the poor and unjustly treated.

Joni Halpern and 12 parents on public assistance founded Supportive Parents Information Network in 1998. The women were struggling to complete their educational training, but were being forced to take low-wage, temporary jobs to satisfy President Bill Clinton's welfare "reform" demands.

Joni said that she and the mothers at S.P.I.N. who have found self-sufficiency are volunteers who feel themselves:

"surrounded by people who have given up and the only thing left is if someone can reach their hand out to them, hold it tight enough so they can get a grip and climb up." S.P.I.N has no paid staff.

"We at S.P.I.N. she added, "are an office of people who have nothing to give but themselves. And every day we come here to make something happen. We create a feeling of hope."

Joni said that after leaving the ACLU, she day-dreamed about how she could be going to a gym several times a week, having more lunches with friends, and spending added time with her children:

"But what would I have said about the gifts that God gave me?" she asked. "What would I have said about how I used them? I don't think those gifts are just for us; they are for something you really care about. For me, it's all about those forgotten parents and children who put their heads on the pillow and think, 'This is how you die.'"

SDSU journalism grads have been on staffs awarded Pulitzer Prizes. Several were working for the *San Diego Evening Tribune*, awarded the 1979 Pulitzer for Breaking News Reporting when the PSA 142 jetliner flying over North Park in San Diego collided with a small plane. In 1993. A J grad on the staff of the *Los Angeles Times* was presented with a 1993 Pulitzer for covering the 1992 Los Angeles Riots after the vicious arrest and beating of African-American Rodney King. Incidentally, Jonathan Freedman, who worked for a period as a part-time J faculty member, won a Pulitzer in 1987 for his editorials in the *Evening Tribune* urging passage of the first immigration reform in 34 years.

In 2015, Lora Cicalo was promoted to managing editor of the *San Diego Union-Tribune*. She joined the *San Diego Tribune* in 1987 as a copy editor. Lora received a bachelor's in journalism and a master's in communication at SDSU. "I have worked closely with Lora for five years," Jeff Light, president and chief operating officer for the newspaper, said. "She is an extraordinary journalist and one of the most admired people in our newsroom. I'm delighted to have her in this role."

Lora's mentor was my colleague — and Mary's and my good friend, Dr. Barbara Hartung. Before her teaching career, Barbara worked several years for local Copley newspapers. She broke through the glass ceiling, was the first full-time SDSU Journalism Department faculty member. She became department chair, later assistant two University presidents. She is a San Diego native who was graduated by Hoover High School (where Ted Williams attended) and who received her bachelor's and master's degrees from San Diego State.

At this writing early in 2017, former student Karen Beth Pearlman covers the East County for the *San Diego Union-Tribune*. She joined the *U-T* in 1996. Her beat is a large one, including La Mesa, El Cajon, Santee, Lakeside, and Lemon Grove. Karen's also writes stories from further east like Alpine, Buckman Springs, Jamul, and Jacumba.

Pearlman was graduated by Patrick Henry High School, Grossmont College, and by SDSU with a degree in Journalism (New Editorial Emphasis with a minor in Health Science). She covered finance and sports four years for the *Daily Aztec*. After graduation Karen worked three years as a sports writer for the *Star News* in Chula Vista and 10 years for the *Daily Californian* in El Cajon.

Mary and I, during these writings, returned from New Orleans, where we had proudly watched our granddaughters, Eleanor and Claire, perform in "Oliver" at Tulane University. Their mother, Terry, joined us along with their father, Michael Bernstein – who is vice president and provost at Tulane. Driving us back that Sunday to Houston, my sister, Dorothy, and her husband, Bill Voss, stopped for lunch at a Cajon café in Lafayette, Louisiana. While enjoying seafood and such delicacies as frog-legs, we watched three generations of people eating and dancing to a Cajun band. I didn't know exactly what Cajuns are supposed to look like, but these folks – who probably had just been to church – appeared a hodge-podge like anywhere else in the United States.

During this period, Provost Michael presided at Tulane while daughter Eleanor was being graduated with a degree in Theater Arts. It was the most joyful graduation ceremony I've ever attended, beginning with a jazz band marching into the auditorium tooting out *The Saints Are Marching In.* Mary and I listened in awe as granddaughter Ele beautifully sang the National Anthem. Another who also sang, receiving an honorary doctorate, was Stevie Wonder.

Ele and Jeremy

Michael later told us a story about the noted blind singer: A Tulane faculty member escorted Stevie down an elevator while taking him back to the New Orleans airport. She remarked, "You know, Stevie, my teen-age daughter just loves all of your songs."

"Is that so," he replied, "What is her favorite?"

The mother told him, and Stevie asked, "Do you have a cell phone? If so, hand it to me." She did and Wonder, after stating the teen-agers' first name, said," This is for you . . . . " sang the girl's favorite into the cell phone. My, can you imagine the delight on the face of the daughter when she listened to that song on her faculty mother's cell phone?

"It's a small, small world," as the Disneyland ditty goes. Upon arriving home by plane, Mary and I began the tasks of catching up with email and snail mail. One of the magazines I subscribe to is *This Week* and the June 26, 2009 issue carried an obit of Norman Brinker, who I noted was just a year younger than I. What further caught my eye as I read along was that he grew up poor – raised as an only child (in the *Washington Post* obit referred to as a "hardscrabble farm") near Roswell, New Mexico. Then he attended San Diego State College, and *This Week* obit reported how Brinker became president of the Jack in the Box franchise (started by San Diegans). By 1966, he was in Dallas creating Steak and Ale which became a national chain growing to 109 units which he sold to Pillsbury. Brinker took part in the rise of chains Bennigan's, and Chili's Grill and Bar. He is credited with the idea of providing a salad bar in restaurants. His eating empire at his death was listed as 1,700 establishments in 27 countries.

Besides my interest being piqued by the Roswell and San Diego State connections, something more about Norman Brinker rang a little bell. So I looked him up on the website of the *San Diego Union-Tribune* – as we'd stopped newspaper delivery while in New Orleans.

Viola!!

"The former athlete and his first wife, the late tennis star Maureen "Little Mo" Connolly, met in San Diego," the U-T's obit reported, *"and lived there until moving to Arizona in the 1960s."*

Ah, who could forget Little Mo, once a darling of the media and one of the most popular personalities in the U.S.? Born in San Diego in 1934, by age 14 she'd won 56 consecutive matches and at 16 won the U.S. tennis championship. She became the first woman to win all four Grand Slam tournaments during the same calendar year and was ranked the number one females' tennis player in the world in 1952, 1953, and 1954.

Her professional career ended by an accident. On July 20, 1954, Maureen was thrown from a horse which became "spooked," was hurled into a cement truck, and her leg was shattered. She announced her engagement to Brinker on the day she retired from competitive tennis and the couple married in San Diego five months later. As a member of the U.S. Olympic equestrian team, he'd become acquainted with Little Mo in San Diego through their mutual love of horses.

Earlier at Roswell, Brinker had begun raising rabbits and by age 14 started trading and selling horses. He earned enough money to attend New Mexico Military Institute in Roswell, and joined the Navy in 1952. He married Maureen Connolly in 1955.

While I was sports editor at the *Daily* Record, she came to Roswell and I wrote a "Riding Herd on Sports" column about her impromptu lesson for a young Roswell High School tennis player, John Bassett. Brinker was at the court with her.

"This is the first time I've had a racquet in my hand for a year and a half," she told me for the April 1, 1956 column.

"She wasn't supposed to have the racquet in her hand at all. It just happened that way. Finally, with urging from Coach Stan Kubiak and Brinker, Maureen grabbed a man's racquet and began to play against Bassett >. . . .

"At first her balls were too far back, too high in the air. But gradually each began to drop into Bassett's side of the court with precision. The power that earned her the nickname 'Little Mo' was evident...

"'She'll never be able to play in a tournament again," Brinker said, watching her drives sizzle across the net . . . .

"The blue scar that kept the muscle on the back of her leg from rippling properly lent a somberness to the scene. Without the scar Little Mo and her youth are almost sure to have made the great records of all-time . . . .

"And, when she couldn't quite reach the ball, she flashed her famous smile – lending a radiance for all those watching."

Brinker began fidgeting, nervous that his wife was overdoing it. He said they had to meet with his mother, and they *"clasped hands, walked gaily to their car, and drove off."* Maureen Connolly died of cancer in 1969. She and Brinkman had two daughters.

One day my niece, Kim Schuelke – daughter of my sister Dorothy and Bill Voss – emailed me asking for a copy of *Balm of Gilead*, one of the unpublished novels her grandmother wrote. While searching in our shed for and finding a carbon copy of Mom's manuscript, which we mailed to Kim, I came across a couple of clippings about Mom's father.

My Canadian grandfather, Alexander Robinson, was born February 24, 1863, in Sussex, New Brunswick, "of Irish immigrant stock." Mom said her father was the seventh of 12 children of James and Jean (Magee) Robinson.

Dr. Alexander Robinson

He was graduated by Fredericton Normal School, where he began his love of Greek and Latin – winning the Lansdowne Silver Medal in language competition. After teaching at Campbellton, New Brunswick, at the age of 26 "Sandy" arrived in Vancouver, British Columbia, as principal of that city's first high school – "one room in the Central school of that day"[55] Reported another famous professor who knew him well, "He was the most dynamic personality ever to head a class in British Columbia."[56]

My Grannie, Emma Hay, also was a teacher. A graduate from Amherst, Nova Scotia, she came to Vancouver, B.C., in the summer of 1888 when the population was estimated at 7,000. She was given the primary classes at the town's "east end school," where she

---

[55] Full tabloid-size page article by Vivienne Chadwick *The Daily Colonist, page 16,* Sunday, November 7, 1971. Some of the information came from my Aunt Pru (Prudence Mulloy).
[56] Ibid.

found she would be teaching at least 100 students. Once, when asked her average attendance, she answered, "It was 108, and the greatest number was 118."[57]

Grandfather met Grannie in Victoria. Mom a couple of times told me the story of what happened after her father and mother had become engaged. Because of an emergency or some other reason, Emma had to go back to be with her family in Nova Scotia for a period of time. During that period "Sandy" fell in love with Emma's sister, Alice.[58] When Emma returned, Sandy announced that he had decided to marry Alice.

"Mother wouldn't stand for it," Mom explained to us kids. "She told Father in no uncertain terms that he must honor his word and marry her. And, that's what Father did."[59]

They were married ("*witness my hand in Victoria*" the minister signs off) March 14, 1892. In part of the pledges printed on the marriage license, Grandfather promises "to love her, comfort her, honour and keep her in sickness and health." Grannie says she'll do more, "*obey him*, serve him love, honour, and keep him in sickness and in health."

The couple produced 16 children, eight of whom died at childbirth or very soon thereafter. Mom, born in Vancouver, B.C., at 5 p.m. December 24, 1892, was the oldest of the eight who survived. The others were Harry, August 29, 1894; Teresa, November 29, 1895; Helen, July 30, 1899; Cecil, March 31, 1903; Emma Patricia (known by her middle name), May 16, 1905; Prudence, April 26, 1907; and Edward (Ted)[60], November 12, 1909.

Uncle Ted was killed by Germans during World War II while flying over the English Channel. His death was taken very hard by Mom but, sadly, never having met my uncle at the time, I didn't fully appreciate her grief. On a happier note, Mom related another neat story about Grandfather and Grannie. "Once, while Mother was having all those children, her doctor told her that for her health it would be wise to get away from Father. So she moved back to Nova Scotia for a period of time. But, as soon as she returned, she became pregnant again."

In 1899, The Robinson family moved to Victoria, B.C., where Grandfather became superintendent of schools for all of British Columbia. He held this position for 20 years.

---

[57] *Vancouver Sun,* magazine supplement, February 21, 1948, when my grandmother was 78.
[58] I have no idea whether the relationship was Platonic, or what.
[59] Another story Mom reluctantly told is that on his deathbed, Grandfather kept calling for my great-aunt: "Alice! Alice!!"
[60] My Uncle Ted was killed during World War II when the military airplane in which he was riding disappeared into the English Channel, presumably shot down by Germans. It was the only war death I know of in our immediate family, except that one of my Canadian nephews also may have been killed.

"He was a grand, old gentleman, 'Sandy' Robinson," wrote D.A. McGregor[61] after Grandfather's death at the age of 90 on April 9, 1952, "with his thatch of white hair, his proud carriage, his flashing eye, and his friendly smile. He felt he knew what was best for British Columbia in the matter of education and had no hesitation fighting for what he wanted. He was a hard man, his opponents said, stubborn, intractable, exasperating. No doubt he was all that. But if he was with you he was a tower of strength."

I also ran across a manuscript about Grandfather Robinson written by one of my aunts (probably Aunt Prue) – because Mom's notations and suggestions to her were in the margins. "But he had a hot temper. And we children suffered when he gave vent to it. For instance, should any of us say 'It is me" instead of It is I, we heard about it in no uncertain terms. On these occasions Father, always quick to detect the slightest inaccuracy in grammar or pronunciation, would thump his clenched fist on whatever object was nearest at hand and thunder, 'How many times must I tell you that the verb, to be, takes the same case after it as before? When will you remember to say, It is I?'"

Mary tells me, "You're much like your Grandfather Robinson." I'm sure she couldn't mean being randy, having a roving eye, or ill-tempered at times? She must be referring to both of us having "thatches" of white hair? Then, of course, on Grannie's side of the family there is the story of the randy Duke of Kent and his presumably passionate mistress. My sister Dorothy doesn't put much faith in that story as part of our family's history. "Half the people in Canada," she huffed, "think they're related to royalty,"

Nevertheless, the Duke of Kent story is my cup of tea. Born as Edward Augustus, the Duke of Kent was the fourth son and fifth child of the 15 offspring of King George III. It was during the reign of George III that the British lost 13 colonies in North America which became the United States.

The duke was destined to become the father of Queen Victoria -- maybe my "Cousin Vickie"? How and why? Because as his older brothers died, the duke was the only one eligible for the throne and had to return to England to carry out his royal duties.

Did nobility slip into the Robinson family through my Grannie? Did that royal blood surge from Mom into Odendahl veins (or drat, perhaps it didn't.) One source minced no words saying the Duke of Kent "lived with a middle-aged French mistress for 27 years."[62]

I've always figured the "mistress" was the real love of the randy duke's life, rather than _that_ Victoire Maria Louisa of Leiningen, Princess of Saxe-Coburg-Saalfeld, and a widow

---

[61] _The Vancouver Province_, page 3, Monday, April 21, 1952.
[62] A pretty good version of the story can be found in the November, 1965 issue of the Canadian magazine, _Chatelaine._

with two children –- who became the mother of Queen Victoria. The Duke's mysterious mistress was Alphonsine Therese Bernadine Julie de Montgenet de St Laurent, Baronne de Fortisson. A refugee from the French Revolution, she had a husband and small daughter when she met the Duke of Kent in Geneva, Switzerland, in 1789.

"There have been Teresas in our family in every generation since[63]," Mom told us, but she didn't like the idea behind the Duke of Kent story. Mom admired British royalty, yet - like most women seemed to in the period while I was growing up - had a strong aversion to any hint of illegitimacy in her family. "If the Duke of Kent had a mistress," Mom figured, "then they weren't married and any offspring would be illegitimate."

Julie St Laurent probably moved to Canada with the Duke of Kent in mid-1791. She was "small, dark and slender, with big dark eyes (*like Mom's?*) and a pretty tilt to her upper lip." The Duke of Kent was described as "tall, red-headed, bluff, modest and affable." Edward had a dark side. He mistreated British soldiers serving under his command. One such punishment resulted in a sergeant being flogged to death. It was under this "cloud of cruelty" that the Duke of Kent was moved to Canada with Julia St Laurent.

I've always thought it didn't matter at all what the duke and his mistress were up to, and now times *have* changed.[64] "So there's real blood," I kidded Mom, "and illegitimate blood?" Mom responded that, even if the Duke of Kent and his mistress had married, the Royal Marriage Act of 1722 would have annulled it. The act denied nobility to the offspring of illegitimate or morganatic alliances. Julie St Laurent, a Catholic rather than a member of the Church of England, may also have been considered a commoner.

"On top of that," Mom explained, "Julie St Laurent was a divorced woman, which heirs to the throne like the Duke of Kent simply aren't allowed to marry."[65]

"Who cares about divorces, all that stuff?" I argued. "Isn't there the proof right there in our family Bible?" Birth dates of Mom's family members listed in the Bible (now owned by my sister Dorothy's daughter Kim[66]) reach back to Mary Elizabeth Rees, who was born

---

[63] Our daughter was named Teresa Jean Odendahl. The tradition continues.

[64] Perhaps partly because of so many often single mothers raising offspring of various men–and women in varied relationships —the terms "bastard" or "illegitimate" seem almost lost from our common vocabulary? It's certainly better for children not to have to live under such stigma.

[65] You'll recall the sad tale of Princess Margaret, born in 1930, the same year as I. (And perhaps with about the same amount of the Duke of Kent's blood in her veins?) She as a teenager fell in love with young World War II hero, Group Captain Peter Townsend. He was divorced–at that time forbidden by the Church of England. Her older sister, then and since was Queen Elizabeth. The passionate princess was ordered by her sister to break off the relationship at the age of 25. She died at age 71.

[66] It has been a tradition in the Robinson family that the big Bible passes to the oldest daughter– hence: Grannie to Mom, Mom to Dorothy, and Dorothy to Kim.

in 1798. Some in Mom's family contended Mary Elizabeth was a daughter of the Duke of Kent and Julie St Laurent.

Plenty of other families in Canada have laid claim to that royal lineage, with reports of six other possible children - including Mary Elizabeth's brother, John Edward Rees. "It's probably just a lot of nonsense," Mom once said, " but I must admit sometimes it is a bit of fun just thinking about it, isn't it? It would be much more charming, though, if the Duke of Kent had married Julie St Laurent."

By the time the *"Chatelaine"* article was published in 1965, our family of four drove almost every late Sunday morning to La Jolla for one of Dad's meals. The main course of the sumptuous dinners (who would dare call them a "lunch") usually consisted of a large pork loin roasted along with potatoes, carrots, onions, and celery.

Dad always preferred a very hot oven and I've never been able to quite duplicate those grand potatoes. "Potatoes always seems dirty to me no matter how much I wash them," he claimed, "so I prefer to peel them." The whole, peeled potatoes would be boiled for a few minutes[67] and then placed in the hot grease around the almost cooked pork roast. They would brown on one side in the grease, and then Dad would turn them over. The result would be potatoes with a brown crust on both sides and soft in the middle.

Meanwhile, Dad would have prepared a small salad, already topped with dressing, in a bowl for each of us – usually consisting of head lettuce, tomatoes, and cucumbers. For dessert we invariably each had a large, cored, green-variety apple–baked next to the roast with brown sugar in the core-holes. The baked apples then were served with half & half cream poured over them.

There always was more food prepared than all of us needed to eat, yet Dad would become upset if we brought an unexpected guest with us. He wanted to know ahead of time so any guest or guests, besides having a generous portion of pork roast, would each be presented with a whole potato, salad, and baked apple.

At this particular writing it's now August of 2009 and Mary and I have just hosted a fun-time, mini family reunion – with daughters Terry and Pam, and grand-kids Eleanor, Jeremy and Claire.[68] I asked for recollections of our family's life just after we came to California.

Pam recalled her dog, Sandy, a collie/sheltie, and remembers going out into the country to choose him from several litters of "pure-bred" puppies. I recall the wiry woman selling

---

[67] The potato water was saved to add to the pork drippings for the gravy.
[68] More about them when we arrive at the times of their births.

the dogs was unshaven under her arms and gave us two pieces of advice which I overruled. She said a spayed female dog usually was more gentle than a neutered male – would be better-suited for the girls, and that her smallest shelties were better choices than the larger ones. I helped choose one of the larger males, which we named Sandy. Guess I just wanted another male in the family.

Although Sandy certainly became mainly Pam's dog and a good pet for all in the family, he could be aggressive and territorial – such as occasionally snapping at the mailman. I should have listened to that tough lady selling dogs. Pam also recalls those big dinners cooked by Dad. And other family food treats and trends: "Mom (Mary) made special birthday dinners," she said. "I always wanted beef stroganoff."

Her Grannie (my Mom) gave the girls tea and shortbread cookies. "Grannie had beautiful geraniums on her porch; we went to the Children's Cove in La Jolla to play with the shells and in the sand; you could see a glimpse of the ocean from their apartment."

Pam remembers that we always had dinner as a family every night. "Dad ate chicken down to the bone–ha!" I give as an excuse that this habit of mine came out of the Great Depression – Hard Times, when food on the Odendahl table may have been scarcer for a family of five than I care to remember. His past of being hungry as a youngster might explain why Dad always cooked so much food.

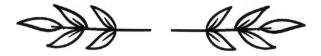

CHAPTER 14 — BEST NOT TO ORDER A MARGARITA IN RUSSIA

This chapter mainly focuses on the Odendahl family's love of traveling, even though certainly I'm still not a seasoned expert. Like, one evening in 2005 while in St. Petersburg, Russia, with Mary and friends Sue Berry and Barbara Sorensen, I ordered a margarita. Dumb. Nyet. Terrible margarita. When in Russia, better to order vodka. In Mexico, tequila or cerveza. ¿Comprende?

I've already mentioned how long ago in this weighty tome that against Mary's sound advice after we arrived in San Diego, we bought on time a four-door 1964 Dodge Dart, with a small V-8 engine. Yep, kind'a dumb. Broke after graduate school, should have kept our old Nash Rambler station wagon a bit longer until we found ourselves firmly on financial feet.

However, that Dart *was* a great car — on my list as a classic. It had a button shift on the left side of the dashboard to control its automatic transmission. And that little V-8 would really make the car move out. Dad had warned me before we arrived about needing power for "hills" in San Diego, but a dependable Dart 6-cylinder would have done the trick, plus saved on gasoline. Only about 14 miles per gallon from the V-8.

The joy of the Dart came several times when the four of us would load up "at first light" in La Mesa, headed for Santa Fe. Our first stop usually was for breakfast, where Terry invariably ordered a hamburger with fries. No problem hardly anywhere now, but in those days most restaurants served only breakfast items until about 11 a. m.

Waitresses often checked with the kitchen to see if Terry's "strange" request could be honored. Usually, it wasn't. Yet, one time a cook came out to our table, looked at Terry and told her, "OK, little lady, I'll fix you a burger with fries."

With the speed limit in Arizona generally 55, and the V-8 purring softly, we'd "barrel" along at about 60, searching for highway cops hiding behind giant saguaro cacti. A quick stop for lunch (where the rest of us usually dined on hamburgers while Terry ordered something else - if she'd gotten her burger for breakfast). Mary would spell my driving an hour or so in the morning and also in the afternoon. It too often was her luck when she took over behind the wheel that we'd come across a highway construction zone and she'd have to weave between markers and machinery for several miles. Or it would begin to rain.

We'd arrive in Santa Fe well after dark. Mary's mother always had something ready for us to eat. "You'll just have to do with potluck," she'd say, before laying out what appeared to be a feast fit for kings and queens. For the trip home, Lula Mae would provide her "care package" filled with sandwiches and other goodies. Our plan in those 1960s and 1970s always was to make the long, one-day-trip as cheaply as possible. Our money problem was aggravated because we were riding in a new car overriding our budget with payments.

A car or two later, we'd stop for one night along the 800-plus-mile journey to Santa Fe or Albuquerque. In our motor home, it usually took two-and-a-half days, maybe "camping" at Flagstaff, Arizona, the first night. At Gallup, New Mexico's neat little Red Rock campground, the second. And roll into our destination around the middle of the third day. I still have a trucker's heart beating inside me.

Me and my motorhome

Those 1960s days were before major bank credit cards, when each oil company competed with its own card. While buying gasoline, you signed on a card for it and the gas stations/oil companies often did not bill you for your purchases for two or three months. Thus, the fuel expense of our trips would be spread out over that time — not like at present when each purchase is computerized and one immediately owes for all of it on that month's bill.[69]

Mary's father and another New Mexico highway engineer had figured their shortest/quickest route between San Diego to Albuquerque or Santa Fe. Chick showed me on maps how to go toward Phoenix, weave around that city on two-lane roads through Arizona towns like Casa Grande and Coolidge. On to Globe, through beautiful Salt River Canyon to Show Low, where after a few miles you veer off Highway 60. Driving northeast through a couple of other small Arizona towns, we'd head east across the Zuni Indian Reservation on an even narrower, but well-paved road. Finally, we'd zip onto Interstate 40 in New Mexico just east of Grants, headed directly to Albuquerque. If to Santa Fe, on up I-25,

During one trip just before dark, it began to snow as we wound through Salt River Canyon. Heavy flakes fell by the time we reached the pitch-black turnoff to drive across the Zuni Indian Reservation. Our headlights showed no tracks at all in a few inches deep snow on that eastward road. "If the Indians aren't driving this road in their four-wheel-drive pickups," I told Mary, "we better not chance it."

Not with a dear wife and two precious daughters riding with me. If I'd been by myself, would "adventure beckons ever onward" have enticed me down that "shorter," dark road leading into the below-freezing night? At my age I certainly would proclaim, "No way, Jose." For sure, it would have been dumber than dumb driving a snowy road with no friendly, and smarter, Native Americans around in case help were needed. I could have run off the road and frozen to death.

Nevertheless, after backing off the road to Zuni and turning north, snow fell even heavier, piling deeper on the road. Our lone car's headlights beamed toward Sanders and Interstate 40. As we began moving east on the Interstate, we felt less lonely, certainly safer. We pulled in behind a semi-truck pushing snow in front of it.

"Well," I commented, "as long as this semi plows the snow and stays on the road, we're okay." By this time the girls weren't asking, "When are we going to get there" but were as apprehensively watching and involved in this new adventure as Mary and I.

We discovered another semi headed north on Interstate 25 but, as I recall, the snow wasn't falling as heavily there. Porch lights were on when we arrived late at the Johnson home in Santa Fe. Inside a real fireplace blazed with wood and coals, and Mary's mother

---

[69] There wasn't available (or at least we didn't have) any credit card which would be accepted by a café or restaurant. We needed to carry along enough "cold cash" for meals, go hungry, or survive on Mary's mother's "care packages."

quickly took some "potluck" out of the oven. Through the windows, we could see the snow still falling. It was the beginning of one of best Christmases I've ever had.

Another great Christmas was spent in Soda Springs, Idaho, with Mary's sister Jean's family. One of the highlights was riding on nephew Tommy's snowmobile. We attended Christmas Eve Mass with the Roman Catholic Cynova family. After the service I moved forward to shake the priest's hand, took my sweet time looking over candles near the altar. Coming out of the church, I found the others had gone.[70] Soon the town's police officer came up to me on the sidewalk. "Looks like Cynova has left you behind?"

"Yep."

"Well," he laughed, "I'll take you to their place." On the way, he related how he'd been a Mormon, but had converted to Catholicism after marrying for the second time. I got the feeling he simply loved his new wife, and finding the "correct ship" to sail on his spiritual voyage was not that much of a big deal for him.

As we reached the block where the Cynovas lived, the officer turned on his flashing red lights and activated his siren a couple of short times. Al Cynova (who until about that time had always been called Alvin by all in the family) came out to the street, laughing. The officer rolled down the window. "So, this is how you treat your brother-in-law?" he kidded Al.

During one stay in Santa Fe, I came down with what I believe is the worst case of influenza I've ever experienced.[71] Confined to bed, I'd perspire until the sheets were soaked, then begin to shiver under a heavy pile of blankets or quilts. Even more embarrassing was being a stinking guest. Each day after work, Mary's father would pop into the bedroom, "Here's a little tonic for you," Chick said, handing me a glass of about six or eight ounces of whiskey.

"Neat," as they say on TV. Yep, those drinks were really neat. Although far from a connoisseur of whiskey due to avoiding it after my awful high school experience, this stuff seemed to be a real help in the battle against the flu. Especially, if in a shivering mode, the whiskey warmed me to the core and I soon fell back asleep.

It was a sad trip to Santa Fe in March of 1970, after we received word that Mary's father had suffered a massive heart attack.[72] Mary flew to Santa Fe and it appeared that by

---

[70] We arrived in two cars, so each driver figured I was in the other one.
[71] At this writing there is a nationwide epidemic of H1n1, or Swine Flu, Some claim any of us over the age of 64 already may have had a similar flu? Mine in Santa Fe?
[72] There were no "miracle" super-blood-thinners or angioplasties. Heart attack victims either survived, or didn't.

sheer willpower Chick lived until his three daughters, his son, and Aunt Ethel were at his bedside.

It was determined his funeral service would not be for several days, time enough for Terry, Pam, and me to drive to Santa Fe. However, "Big Bill" Johnson — a Navy Chief Petty Officer and Mary's double-first cousin by way of Mary's mother's sister, Lodee[73] — offered to drive us in his car. "I have air conditioning," he explained, "and we'll all be more comfortable going across Arizona."

That afternoon we moved along at a good pace past Yuma, Arizona, almost to a wide place along the north side of the freeway called Aztec.[74] Suddenly we heard a very loud noise and Bill pulled over to the side. The cooling fan had come loose from the water pump and driven its way into the radiator. There was a tiny garage in Aztec, but the mechanic there said repairs were too much for him. So we waited for a wrecker to come about 60 miles from Yuma. When it arrived, Bill's car was hooked to it and the three of us rode back to Yuma in the big wrecker's cab with its driver.

The dealership there wasn't able to work on the car until the next morning, so we spent the night in a Yuma motel. It wasn't until the next afternoon, after Bill shook his head and paid a hefty repair bill, that the four of us were on our way again. We breathed a sigh of relief and laughed as we whizzed by Aztec.

Arriving in Santa Fe, Mary's sister Jean asked if we'd like to go to the funeral home to take a look at Chick. Not me. I'd rather remember what a person looks like when living. Nevertheless, Mary's mother opted for an open-casket funeral—so the next day at the end of the service we traipsed past for our last look at Chick. As I got out of the car at the sunlit cemetery that afternoon, Mary's Aunt Ethel could tell I was in pretty bad shape. She took hold of my hand, and as she walked me to the graveside, said, "Isn't this a beautiful day?"

She reminded me that death is a part of life. Ethel Utton was "The Angel of Aztec," New Mexico, the person who comforted the needy. Good deeds ruled her agenda, like showing up with soup when someone was sick. Mary and her sister Phyllis have been inspired by their Aunt Ethel, followed in her footsteps — helping and reassuring those in distress.

The Uttons operated a dairy just outside of Aztec. Several years after Chick's funeral, on a very cold day Aunt Ethel walked out to the highway next to the dairy to pick up mail from the box. A hit-and-run driver left her beside the mailbox to freeze to death.

---

[73] Aunt Lodee had married Mary's father's brother, Uncle Brady Johnson, so that made Mary and Bill double first cousins.
[74] An ironic situation, as both Mary and Bill had partly grown up together in Aztec, New Mexico.

It wasn't until 1984 that Mary and I began our international traveling. We'd been briefly to Canada and Mexico, but I'd never considered that "international." Terry had completed work on her Ph.D. in Cultural Anthropology at the University of Colorado in Boulder. We shared ownership of a house up "Four-Mile Hill" west of Boulder.

We decided to sell the house because, with renters so far away, it would be too much effort to maintain. With a now-seemingly-paltry amount from the equity, Mary announced, "Let's take the girls on a trip to Europe." We signed on for a trip with Cosmos, at the time probably the cheapest tour provider - with American Express perhaps the most luxurious. Arriving in London in a misty rain, the four of us waited in a dark square outside the airport for one of those unique little English black cabs to take us to our hotel. It was a long wait.

Admittedly, most of the group weren't Ugly Americans, yet the longer they waited the more unhappy campers some became. For no good reason, the four of us thought the rainy situation was hilarious and began laughing. "You people," one of the unhappy campers told us, "must be crazy."

Cosmos offered one of those hurried European trips recalling the phrase, "It must be Tuesday, we're in Belgium." Actually, when we left London for Belgium, one of the ferry's twin engines conked out and the trip took twice as long. We arrived very late and were so tired we missed breakfast before touring Brussels. The remainder of the trip was great with "the girls" urging Mary and me on to do things like climb (by elevator) the Eiffel Tower in Paris, listen to music in Vienna and tour Rome's ancient edifices and the Vatican.

Although we often carried our own baggage — sometimes because of no elevators, struggling up stairs into "second-class" quarters - a plus in Venice one night was all the wine we needed gratis. It seemed Terry and Pam had a pint of beer ready for us at least once a day, often tucked away at a shady table in a town's plaza. And quaffing that beer didn't bother my stomach like the American stuff can do — despite some U.S. breweries claiming not to include additives.

We viewed the art treasures of Florence. Terry had spent a school year in Florence during college at San Diego State. She loves the place (we could see why) and stayed there a couple of extra days – catching us later on the tour. Mary wasn't very impressed when Terry showed us the Florence apartment she shared with other students. It would have worried Mary if she'd known how ordinary American students, in order to make ends meet, live closely together in foreign countries.

After the Cosmos tour, we took a few extra days to explore London, including a day out in the country to visit my Aunt Patsy (Mom's sister) — who took us on a jaunt to an old, castle-like mansion, then to a pub for a pint of ale and lunch. It was something to ride around with Aunt Patsy driving on the "wrong" side of the road.

In the summer of 1989, Mary and I joined our friends Lorna Ross and Linda Mason for a trip in a 13-passenger van. It began in Vancouver, Washington, and we ferried over to Victoria. We drove through part of the rest of British Columbia, and included a dip into Alaska. One of the highlights of that trip was celebrating Lorna's 60th birthday at a garage dump. The way it happened was that a white (albino?) bear was said to show up at the garage dump on random evenings. Luck was with us and he/she arrived to paw through the garbage. "That's the first time," our delighted driver and tour guide told us, "that I've ever seen that white bear." After the bear took its leave, we tourists and guide shared a frosted cake to celebrate Lorna's 60th.

Mary was antsy about that time, not from the evening at the garbage dump, but because Terry and her significant other, Michael Bernstein, were expecting our first grandchild. Mary was hoping we'd be able to return to San Diego in time for the big event. That didn't happen and we arrived home in San Diego after the birth of Eleanor Odendahl Bernstein, named after Eleanor Roosevelt, on August 19, 1989. But Mary was able to stand just outside the room with son-in-law Sheldon Quant in Oakland on September 24 - just over a month later that same year - when Pam gave C-section birth to Jeremy Nicolas Quant.

Mary and me with Ele and Jeremy

I loitered in the hallway at Kaiser Hospital in San Diego as Terry was in labor with her and Michael's second child. A close friend helping Terry through the ordeal, artist Doris

288

Bittar, came out in the hallway and said, "You might as well come in and see your grandchild born." I did. No more waiting to ask some doctor whether all the fingers and toes were there. I was right in the room with Michael, Mary, Doris, a midwife, and an obstetrician. Eleanor's (Ele's) mouth grew wide as her sister's head crowned. Terry was so courageous about bearing up under her birthing pains with all of us there. Claire Odendahl Bernstein arrived safely into the world August 16, 1995. It sure made me glad I'd never given birth.

Eleanor, Terry, Claire and Michael

Eleanor and Claire

The March 23, 1992 edition of *The Daily Aztec* carried a story that I would be retiring from San Diego State University in June, or as a student reporter quoted me as saying I'd be *"riding off into the sunset"* and it would be an end to stories about…*"the infamously obscure starting point at which Odendahl tells all his students they will end their careers — there, or Barstow, but not the* Los Angeles Times . . . *with his ever-present smile he creates stories in his New Mexico drawl . . . he just seems like a born story-teller."*

"He sometimes rambled on," one student added, *"but he always had a point. His stories made class more interesting, and I learned a lot."* Journalism Department Secretary Muriel Kulikowski opined, *"He's easygoing, very supportive, not demanding. Staff, secretaries, media technicians and colleagues all think the world of him. He's not a prima donna; what you see is what you get."*

Terry and Mary joined me at my final J department banquet in 1992, held each year to honor the meritorious work of SDSU students. The back of the program listed "A Career of Achievements: 1964-1992." That program now hangs above my desk at home with a Sharpie pen notation. FOR OBITUARY, it reads, for help whenever someone might need to write it up:

Professor Eric M. Odendahl retires after 28 years of service at SDSU. He joined the faculty in 1964 while completing his University of Missouri Ph.D. in journalism. He was awarded a master's degree in journalism from the University of Iowa. He earned the Bachelor of Arts degree in journalism from the University of New Mexico.

Before his academic career, Professor Odendahl worked in newspaper journalism. After completing his undergraduate degree in 1953, he joined the Associated Press staff in Albuquerque. That same year he moved to Dallas, Texas, where he joined the Wall Street Journal as reporter and copy editor. In 1955 he returned to his home state of New Mexico for six years as news editor, city editor, and sports editor of the Roswell Daily Record.

Professor Odendahl was faculty adviser to the Daily Aztec when the California Intercollegiate Press Association named it the best college newspaper in 1967. He was department chair when the Department of Journalism first achieved national accreditation in 1971. He was Mass Communication graduate program coordinator, 1979-82, and journalism undergraduate adviser, 1981-83,

He and his wife Mary have two daughters and two (Claire wasn't born until 1995) *grandchildren. Mary will retire next month from her position as executive administrator of the Presbytery of San Diego.*

We pulled away in July of 1992 in our small Itasca Class A motor-home towing our little blue, four-wheel-drive Suzuki Samurai, with a fairly-firm promise from San Diego State that I'd receive early retirement at age 62. With a "Golden Handshake" of four extra years added to my 28 years of SDSU teaching.

Mary and I found ourselves quite relieved several weeks later during our joint "Retirement Tour." Son-in-love Michael Bernstein, teaching history at the University of California at San Diego, watched out for us. He understood the slow process as it unfolded at SDSU, sent word while we were on the road when my retirement finally was in the bag. Mary already had retired after 17 years of service for the Presbytery of San Diego.

Her first job in "America's Finest City" had been working at SDSU in Career Planning and Placement. It was there that she developed a lifelong friendship with Mary Pat Gannon, a Roman Catholic nun. At a social gathering, we somehow asked each other what we'd like to be in the possibility of reincarnation. When my turn came around, maybe after a beer or two and in a good humor, I answered, "I'd like to be a prize bull. I could eat almost all the time and farmers constantly would bring in cows to be serviced."

"Oh no," Mary Pat quickly admonished me. "When you die, Eric, you'll end up as a monk alone living on top of a mountain. You'll be copying the Bible by hand, and you won't be allowed to change a word of it."

A Presbyterian friend interviewed Mary and recommend she be hired as secretary for the presbytery of the San Diego district. A presbytery is the ruling body in Presbyterian-church districts. It consists of ministers and elders representing congregations within the district. Not that it even really matters all that much, but did more in those days - Mary's first presbyter boss was an African-American, Casper Glenn. She also worked for a Latino presbyter, Raphael Sanchez, and interim presbyter Barbara Worthington. "Mary," Barbara Worthington once declared, "is the heart of the Presbytery."

At the time, the Presbytery fostered a Crisis Center, which provided food, clothing and counseling for the poor, and others in need. At first when Mary worked there, two Military Parish Visitors aided military families in their own times of crisis. Doing that good work alone for several years became the responsibility of Janet Williams, who has been a special friend ever since. The three of us camped many years with the Mission Bells RV Club, and took a cruise together to Alaska.

The March, 1992, issue of *Good News of the Presbytery of San Diego* announced Mary's retirement as Administrator and said she has been recognized as the *"heart and soul of the presbytery office."* Executive Neil Brown added:

"It will not be difficult to replace Mary; it will be impossible. She lives her faith every day in her work and in the relationship with all the many people whose lives she touches. I will miss her terribly. My sadness at her departure is overcome only by my happiness for her and Eric, knowing that she richly deserves all the rewards retirement will bring."

During our joint-retirement trip in 1992, Mary and I lived three months and drove 13,000 miles in the motor-home. Our first treat was to camp with Pam, Sheldon, Grandson Jeremy and Shel's mother Marge at Pinecrest, California. Next stopping at Lake Tahoe, we moved on to Soda Springs, Idaho, to see Jean and Al Cynova. On to Afton, Wyoming, to visit nephew Tommy Cynova and his wife Brenda.

With one of them taking turns driving behind in their car, Jean and Al rode along in our motor-home until we visited the Black Hills Passion Play. (It wasn't the kind of passion I expected to view in a play.) Next came Mount Rushmore and the Devil's Tower. When the four of us arrived at Sturgis, South Dakota, we were in for a surprise. Some 50,000 motorcyclists, most of them riding Harley Davidsons, were there for a rally. It first was a bit scary, with our visions of being trapped — surrounded in the RV park by "dangerous" Hell's Angels and the like.

It didn't turn out that way at all. A middle-aged motorcycle rider camped in a tent next to us in the park came up and explained, "We like to have fun and drink some beer, but we'll try to shut down all the noise by 11 o'clock. If you have any trouble, just let me know." We had no trouble from anyone. We were drinking beer ourselves now and again on that trip, and the noise stopped around 11. The next day we excitedly toured Sturgis, taking in sights of leather-clad riders, their bikes, and various swap meets—mainly where Harley Davidson parts and regalia were exchanged.

After the Cynovas turned back toward home in their car, Mary and I continued on our leisurely journey all the way to New Brunswick. Then down the East Coast to Key West, Florida, west to New Orleans. We drove up through Jackson to Memphis, on to Branson, Missouri, and westward home. All along the way we stopped to see friends and relatives. As my memory fades about various trips we took and when, luckily it's jogged by Mary's annual Christmas letters and photo albums.

In 1993, 20 church and camping friends went to Lake Powell for a week on two houseboats. We were guided by Steve Thomas, son of Esther and Tommy, who earlier had worked on Lake Powell. That same year Mary and I took an Interhostel trip to Ireland with retired SDSU J colleague George Sorensen, and his wife Barbara. "It was," Mary wrote, "a marvelous experience in which we learned about Ireland's history, culture and folklore. We saw beautiful countryside, medieval ruins of castles and churches, and really enjoyed meeting the wonderful Irish people."

I had a mild heart attack in March of 1994, requiring angioplasty to remove an obstruction from a 90-percent-clogged artery. My brother Alan was not so fortunate, suffering a massive heart attack in July. He had phoned after my angioplasty and I warned him to be careful about what and the amount he ate. We both had figured, with parents never suffering from any heart problems (except Mom's pretty natural congestive heart failure just before her death after 90), that we would be long-lived.

Mary and I were travelling in Alaska in her sister, Jean, and brother-in-law, Al's, motor-home. Along with us in another motor-home were Martha and Gerald Kogle and Esther and Tommy Thomas. We were camped at Haines, Alaska, when word came of Alan's attack. His proved a major one, with his heart stopped quite a few minutes before adequate help arrived.

293

Friends, retried San Diego Deputy Sheriff John Bauer and his wife, were custodians at the Haines RV park. Barbara had cooked many years at the First United Methodist Church of La Mesa. For two or three days, Barbara drove me by pickup into the town of Haines so that I could phone Alan's daughters to keep track of his condition. "I also have a really bad heart," Barbara sympathetically told me the first day we drove into town. She said she hoped to be on the list for a heart transplant, but, "I'm just barely below the requirement." Sadly, later on their way home to San Diego, Barbara had a fatal heart attack.

After our Alaska trip, I flew to be at his hospital bed as Alan remained in a three-month coma. I came back again to Silver Spring, Maryland, for his memorial service that October. His obituary in the *Washington Post* read:

Alan Odendahl, 66, an economist who retired last year from the Small Business Association, died Oct. 20 (1994) at Langhorne, Pa., of complications related to a heart attack.

Mr. Odendahl, of Hyattsville, was born in Hayden, Ariz. He graduated from the University of New Mexico and received a master's degree in economics from Yale University. During the Korean War, he served in the Army.

In 1961, he came to the Washington area to work in the Department of Commerce. He joined the SBA in 1966 and worked in the office of industry analysis, the office of policy analysis, and the office of size standards, from which he retired.

Mr. Odendahl collected antique and classic automobiles, and he was active in Parents Without Partners.

His marriages to Alice Stehle and Anne Hitch ended in divorce.

Survivors include two children from his first marriage, Nora Odendahl of Lawrenceville, N.J., and Steven Odendahl of Madison, Wis,; two children from his second marriage, Laura Odendahl of Williamsport and Cynthia Odendahl of Silver Spring; one brother, Eric Odendahl of La Mesa, Calif.; and one sister, Dorothy Voss of Portage, Mich.

Alan's daughters and son arranged for the funeral, which Dorothy and I attended. His friends recalled many good memories about and being with him. Alan's offspring buried him with a grand view in beautiful Parkland Memorial Park in Rockville, Maryland..

That year Terry and Michael found 63 acres of undeveloped land near Cerrillos, between Albuquerque and Santa Fe. At the time, the four of us planned to build two retirement houses on the land. Concurrently, Mary and I were into our six-year-long, once-a-week period of delivering meals, mainly to HIV victims. Mama's Kitchen honored us in 1998 as Volunteers of the Year for the East County.

Our 1998 Volunteer of the Year Award

We had begun delivering meals to David Goff, who has become a beloved part of our family.

Pam, David and Terry

David was living in an El Cajon apartment with his little dog, Allie. Mary immediately took a liking to both of them. Soon after Mary and I met David, he moved to a pretty-run-down trailer park in Lakeside.

Mary and I became acquainted with David's mother, Vi, an accomplished artist living in her Lakeside home. We visited Vi often during her hospice period, and arrived with David a very short time after his mother died. With his inheritance, David was able to move into a nice manufactured home, in the Meadowbrook Park in Santee just a mile or so from us.

At this writing, although at that time only minutes away from observing Vi Goff's death, I actually never have been with a person when he or she died. The closest to that probably was with Robert Wilton. In October of 1999 Mary and I had flown to Oaxaca, Mexico, with Kimberly and Robert Wilton for Day of the Dead festivities. It was there that we met a woman coming out of the cemetery who told us she had spent several hours beside the grave of her deceased husband. "It was a good visit," she told us.

Sometime after arriving home, it was discovered Robert had cancer. Months later, Kimberly called us and reported her husband was very near death. Arriving at their home in El Cajon, we found Robert to be unresponsive, undergoing labored breathing which we later learned to be a "death rasp." It was near noon, and as other members of the Wilton family were soon to gather, Kimberly asked Mary and me to pick up lunch for all of us. When we arrived back with the lunch, we found family members with expected sad countenances. But when I decided to take a look at Robert, was surprised to discover that he had died only shortly before we came back with the food.

Earlier, on a bright July 12, 1978, I was working on the building of an in-the-ground hot tub behind our La Mesa home. As I pounded nails into its deck, suddenly everything became quiet. I stopped hammering and peered up into the eucalyptus trees stretching high in the lot behind us. They weren't moving, as if any sign of a breeze had ended. I shook my head and continued nailing. Just a few minutes later, the phone in the house rang. Answering it, a woman's voice was on the other side and she said, "Mr. Odendahl?"

"Yes."

"I'm calling from Grossmont Gardens. I'm very sorry to have to tell you this, but your father has expired."

After notifying Mary at the Presbytery, we separately rushed to Grossmont Gardens, where we found Mom sitting despondently in the front room of their apartment. She told us Dad had shot himself. Mary and I went into their bedroom and Dad lay dead on the bed, one side of his face distorted where he had fired a bullet into his ear. A few minutes later, a La Mesa police officer arrived, and soon after a man from the coroner's office. After they completed their investigation, satisfied it was a suicide, the police officer asked about the .38 pistol he held in his hand.

"That gun is mine," I told him, "Loaned it to Dad a while back."

"Okay, it's yours then," and handed it toward me.

"I don't think I want anything more to do with that gun."

He filled out a receipt which read, *"Received from Eric Odendahl, 8273 Vista, La Mesa, CA: 1 Smith & Wesson, Model 36, .38 caliber, 2 and ½ pistol, For destruction."* I've wondered whether it might soon have rested as a second gun in the boot of some La Mesa police officer. I have no idea about that, or whether somewhere it still could remain in operating condition. For what it's worth, I paid $35 for that little, short-barreled .38 pistol in Roswell in the 1950s. It would be worth at least 10 times that to someone if he or she still has it.

I've also only a scant idea about what occurred that morning while nailing on the hot-tub's deck. Yet, it probably is the most spiritual experience which ever has happened to me. Grossmont Gardens was three miles away from our house. I speculate that somehow Dad was relaying through space a message something like, "It's okay. Don't worry about it. Be at peace."

What had happened earlier was that when Dad and Mom lived in their apartment in La Jolla, he enjoyed fishing off a nearby bank and rocks there. One day he slipped on a rock covered with green mossy stuff, fell against the rocks. It apparently broke loose arthritis in his lower back. Dad began to take pain pills, which after a few years Mary and I could tell obviously became very addictive.

One day Dad scratched a match to light the oven in their La Jolla apartment, and the gas – apparently already-turned-on – exploded, mildly searing his face. After that experience, Mary and I had a more difficult time with Dad than Mom in encouraging them to move to Grossmont Gardens. Even though nearer to us in La Mesa, Dad – always a loner – never became a happy camper there.

For example, after eating with others in the common dining area, Dad immediately headed back to their apartment to watch TV. (He also was hooked on newscasts.). Mom would tarry after meals, enjoyed chatting with other Grossmont Gardens residents. Later we found out Dad's particular pain killer had a tendency toward making one suicidal. Yes, actually Mary and I don't know the suicide reason for sure. He was 89 years old, and we also were aware he and Mom had discussed how one of them might live better alone as their somewhat meager retirement income diminished as living prices continued to rise.

Mom and Dad

Obviously, Mom needed to get away from that Grossmont Gardens apartment and she moved into a new retirement place in La Mesa called Regency Park. She became happy there, but the time arrived when she had difficulty finding her way to the dining hall. Mom next lived with three other women, all watched-over, in a private home, until she had deteriorated to the extent she was moved to a nursing home, right back next to Regency Park.

It was one of those units where some patients are tied to wheel chairs, a few of them constantly calling for help. Mom never was tied to a chair, but soon required being fed by someone and Mary helped her with that quite often. Mom became bedridden and soon didn't recognize me, spent her time on her back gazing at the ceiling. She no longer could swallow easily and one day we found her with a tube in her nose. Mom was being fed with food forced through the tube!

We called her sympathetic doctor, who told us he could do nothing about the nursing home's apparent legal inserting of the tube, even though he had been told Mom once had pulled it out. The paper Mom had signed which we thought allowed me to be her guardian and to make near-death decisions wasn't deemed the proper one, was ruled invalid by the nursing home. Oh, how Mom – if able to have been aware of her situation – would have been so angry. About just lying there, about the last of her hard-earned savings being drained through a feeding tube, about no money likely to pass along to her offspring. Finally, with the last of her funds in jeopardy, I applied for California assistance. Before those papers could be processed, Mom died November 16, 1986. She had lived 93 years.

After Mom's death and while searching through family papers, I found a long-ago, undated clipping, probably from the weekly newspaper in Aztec, New Mexico, which read:

"Chas. Johnson returned last week from California to rest up and train this winter before going to Detroit where he has signed for the next year. Chas. is making a success as a baseball pitcher and may someday be with the major leagues."

Mary's father, as the pride of tiny Aztec, pitched his way up to a Triple-A club, just a rung below the major leagues, before "throwing away his arm." That now might be a repairable rotor cuff injury. In those days there were no near-magical operations to mend pitchers' arms, and that ended Chick's pitching career.

It was while he was pitching for a Triple-A team at Little Rock, Arkansas, that Chick met Mary's mother, who was studying nursing. After a romantic, whirlwind courtship, Lula Mae Grigg became Mrs. Charles W. Johnson in 1928. Lula Mae had grown up with a share-cropper's family In Louisiana. Her mother had married at 15, to J. Franklin Grigg, and Lula Mae's father was an older man with one leg.

Chick and Lula Mae's first child Jean arrived, and her full name was Margaret Jeannett as the namesake of Grandma Maggie Johnson — with whom Jean lived several years during Hard Times. The second child, Charles Franklin, died at about a year old. Mary Ethel followed on March 7, 1934 named after her Grandma Mary, Lula Mae's mother with the maiden name of Sumlin. You'll recall it was Grandma Mary who put out those bountiful Sunday "potluck" dinners which I gorged on until barely able to rise from the table.

My wife's middle name Ethel came from Aunt Ethel Utton, the Angel of Aztec, New Mexico. Phyllis Dee was named after Philip, Aunt Ethel's husband whom the family called Uncle Alf. The Dee was after Phyllis's Aunt Lodee, her mother's sister. Greg is Charles Gregory, named after his father "Chick," Charles Wesley Johnson.

300

With it being in the middle of Hard Times, and with his baseball career ended, Chick began working on roads for the New Mexico Highway Department. He later several times served as acting state chief of the department, but demurred from accepting the permanent position because of New Mexico's ever-changing politics. When an opposing Democratic or Republican Party took office, a new chief was named. With a family to raise, Chick preferred keeping a regular, more secure department job, just now-and-again serving as acting chief.

As Mary's father moved around New Mexico from one highway-building job to another, his family went along with him. Mary attended many schools before the Johnsons finally settled in Albuquerque, where she was graduated from the first class of the new Highland High School.

After Chick died as the result of suffering a heart attack at work, just before retiring from the Highway Department, Lula Mae lived on in Santa Fe. As her mother's health began to fail in her 80s, Phyllis drove from Albuquerque to Santa Fe to spend every weekend. After Lula Mae became bedridden, her care giver was Peter Paul Maglione. He took loving round-the-clock care of her for several years before Lula Mae required moving to a nursing home in Albuquerque. Peter and Phyllis had developed a romance, became significant others, and built a home in Cedar Crest, east of Albuquerque. Mary and I later attended, and Ele sang, at their beautiful wedding on a hill above their home.

Lula Mae was 93 when she died in the Albuquerque nursing home in March of 2003. After her memorial service, the family gathered at the Santa Fe cemetery where Lula Mae was being buried next to her husband. Trying to make the sad scene more joyous, someone began to sing *You Are My Sunshine* and the rest of us joined in. Lula Mae had taught her children and grandchildren songs they still remembered.

Sweetly Sings the Donkey soon followed and our group began to dance around the burial hole yelling, "EE, onk, EE, onk." As the braying and laughing continued, a mortician standing nearby gazed at us askance. Looking down at Lula Mae's closed casket, I figured inside she might be raising her right arm and giving us a thumbs up.

I've presented eulogies for three persons. First was for SDSU colleague Frank Holowach, next for Warren Heyer (see below), and last for another SDSU colleague and special friend George Sorensen. Eulogies seem for me very difficult to write and present. Of course, "Never speak ill of the dead," as they say. One wants to joyfully recall good times together, yet realizes some in the audience remain in deep grief. Good fun stories, yes, but no stuff like, "Me and Pete was drunk as skunks one night and started looking over some cute babes…"

In 1995, Mary and I flew to Guatemala as part of a mission team from the La Mesa United Methodist Church led by Carol Conger-Cross. For two weeks we helped complete the building of a medical unit near Chichicastenango. I flew back to Guatemala the next year with friend Warren Heyer, a retired librarian at Mesa Community College. Just a few months earlier, Warren had lost his wife, Roberta — an accomplished artist - to cancer.

While working with the Guatemalan team -building a widow a Jimmy-Carter-like, Habitat-for-Humanity home - I slipped on a downward trail and broke my ankle. My guardian angel was Kaiser Permanente orthopedic nurse practitioner Debbie Palmer, who wrapped my ankle each morning. That made me able to fly with the group to the Tikal pyramid, but of course, was unable to climb it with Warren and the rest.

Also in 1996, Mary and I met Lorna Ross and Linda Mason at JFK airport, headed for a great trip to Spain, Portugal, and Morocco. The next year provided Mary and me with the journey of a lifetime when we traveled to the Holy Land. The trip was led by the Rev. Joe Elmore and his wife, Billye. As an example of their character, trip leaders routinely pay nothing as they are responsible to organize and watch over their traveling flock. Not Joe and Billye. They paid their own way — divided their free trip's price among the rest of us to lower our cost.

We were a Methodist Volunteers in Mission work-and-study team of 19 from California, Texas, North Dakota, and Maine. In the group from La Mesa besides the Elmores were Esther and Tommy Thomas, R.K. and Doty Kelley, Bob and Mary Conger, and the two of us. After those from La Mesa and some others of the group visited Egypt, the whole team gathered in Damascus, Syria.

One morning we became part of a worship service in the Abu Noor Mosque, where Joe Elmore's friend Sheikh Ahmad Kuftara officiated. Joe had been in Damascus years earlier studying Islam when both were young men. Before his retirement, Dr. Elmore was a dean at Earlham College, in Richmond, Indiana, a Quaker institution. Sheikh Kuftara had risen to be the Grand Mufti of the whole Syrian Arab Republic.

The main thrust of the Grand Mufti's message was that Abraham, Moses, Jesus, and Mohammed were prophets for their separate religions, yet believed in the same God and there should be no reason for so much animosity between various faiths. Our fortunate team was invited to his home to a buffet lunch of the best Middle East food I've ever eaten. The Grand Mufti specifically asked our group's women if they had any questions, especially about Islam. They did and he answered them.

Moving on to Palestine, we stayed in Bethlehem on Manager Square next to the Church of the Nativity, the place some credit as the birthplace of Christ. Each morning we first would be awakened by a Muslim cry/call to worship over a loudspeaker in a close-by, tall minaret. Next would come the pealing of bells from the Church of the Nativity. I was struck how the two religions seemed able to meld together in peace there.

I recalled 1948, when the new Jewish state of Israel was formed, even though Mom and Dad and many others worried because it would be surrounded by Arab Muslims. It seemed to me, the general consensus was one of delight at the time, figuring the small Jewish state carved out of Palestine simply would prove a safe and peaceful place of refuge for the mistreated survivors of Hitler's horrible Holocaust. Until we made our 1997 trip, I certainly favored most of Israel's actions—even during several wars and confrontations with Arabs.

During our visit to the Holy Land Mary and I learned that Israelis were continually bulldozing homes of Palestinians and olive trees on their land in order to acquire more territory to build Jewish settlements. Mary's two best friends in high school were Jewish and neither of us felt we were anti-Semitic.

And, as Jewish Michael Bernstein, a historian and father of our granddaughters once pointed out, the word Semitic refers back to Middle East tribes, many of them wandering, and included Muslim Arabs. Technically to be anti-Semitic, Michael told us, one would be against both Israeli Jews and Arab Muslims in the Middle East.

As our team visited Christian villages near Bethlehem, we began to hear disturbing stories from Palestinians. Like how Israeli soldiers appeared at family doors in Palestinian territory in the middle of the night and whisked away young Christian and other men to secret prisons in Israel. Once there, they said they were tortured, often similar to waterboarding. "They tied me to a chair," a young Christian man told us, "leaned me over backwards. I was blind-folded, water was dripped on my forehead. I don't know of any young Palestinian man around here who didn't spend time in prison." He said they were incarcerated for long periods of time, with no charges ever brought against them. Eventually, the lucky ones would be released.

There are, of course, many viewpoints about the Israeli-Palestinian deadlock concerning "Occupied Land" and other impediments to elusive peace in the Middle East. Our team decided then and there not to view it simply as a Jewish and Muslim religious issue. The main dispute appears to be continual arguments about the legality of Israeli expansion and occupation of Palestinian territory.

One of the "highlights" of the 1997 Middle-East trip was visiting the poverty-stricken Gaza-Strip territory of the Palestinians. While in Gaza, our group met with a Roman Catholic priest, who told us that when his mother died in the West Bank, he couldn't attend her funeral because Israelis controlled and blocked his entry to the road between the two Palestine entities. Leading us to Gaza was the Rev. Sandy Olewine, a Methodist Minister from the California Pacific Conference. She was stationed in Jerusalem with the Middle East Council of Churches. Sandy recently was senior minister at a church in Santee and now leads another Methodist church in Pasadena.

While in Bethlehem, my retina became detached in three pieces. Upon returning home, kindly Kaiser Permanente Dr. Howard Cohen reattached the retina during a long operation. I am very thankful to him for having vision in my left eye. After that, I was able to write again, even had a satire about Palestinians and Israelis published by the *San Diego Union-Tribune*.

Earlier in 1997, Mary and I were in New Zealand with Jerry and Norma Bailey, and then on our own to Australia. Jerry, professor of Industrial Studies at SDSU, had retired with the same "Golden Handshake" as I did in 1992. The four of us took two trips to Hawaii, and in 2000 travelled in China while the huge Three Gorges Dam was under construction on the Yangtze River. Among many Chinese sites, we visited the Forbidden City, walked on the Great Wall, and viewed the Terra Cotta Army.

It was a scary time in 2003 when a fire came fairly close to our Highlands Mobile Home Park. As I e-mailed:

"It raced to the north of us on the other side of 52, a freeway. By late afternoon it had made its way west underneath a freeway bridge and was roaring up a hill like a chimney, with flames flickering probably at least a hundred feet into the air, two ridges away from us. Then it began flaring high in the canyon just past the ridge directly west of us . . . at 12:30 a.m. the flames were again glowing in the canyon nearest us. At 3:30 a.m. I could no longer see them, only some fires to the north across the freeway . . . . We count our blessings.

In September of 2005, Jerry and Norma Bailey were to lead us on a stateside trip. At Grant's Pass, Oregon, I became hospitalized for three days with a blocked bowel. With stomach pumped out, Mary drove me home, where at Kaiser's Zion Hospital my gall bladder was removed. Discovered was a stone the size of a pea blocking the gall bladder, but that proved not the sole cause of the problem.

I later had another blockage and hospital stay, this time told about a kinked bowel— probably caused by adhesions from one of my three hernia operations. In January of 2017 there was a third blockage and hospital stay, demanding a six-week, low-fiber diet with plenty of chewing. I also need to continue to consume smaller meals, generally watch my eating Ps and Qs..

In September of 2006, a year after our delayed trip, the Baileys led us to their beloved Northwest of the United States. We began in Park City, Utah, on to Oregon and followed the Columbia River and beautiful sights alongside it. In 2007, Mary and I were at another river, the Colorado in the Grand Canyon with Granddaughter Claire Bernstein at an Inter-Generational Elderhostel. Joining us were my sister Dorothy Voss and her Granddaughter Grace — the daughter of my namesake nephew Eric Voss and his wife Ann. We four, young and old, rafted down the Colorado River through part of the Grand Canyon, including rapids, and exited it by helicopter.

That same year found us in Europe again, this time aboard a small ship on the Danube River, beginning at the Black Sea and visiting Budapest and Prague. Traveling companions were Esther and Tommy Thomas, Sue Berry, and Barbara Sorensen. Mary and I also took a trip to Greece and Turkey one year with Sue Berry and Garnett Foster, both Presbyterian ministers. We had a great time, and Mary and I bought a Turkish rug in Ephesus, where the Paul the Apostle had visited.

In 2008, David Goff was with us for his first trip to the Grand Canyon. We rode the train from Williams, Arizona, and stayed at a motel on the South Rim of the canyon, which in May was covered with light snow. On the way back to Williams, some desperados rode up on horseback, came aboard the train, and attempted to rob us.

David Goff

While poking around the Internet, I discovered a 2010 obituary for Darrell Deane Smith, my best buddy in the U.S. Navy in 1948-49 aboard U.S.S. *Maddox* (DD-731). You'll recall he was the one sailing on that "tin-can" destroyer while writing to two women at the same time in Eads, Colorado. He made the mistake of putting the wrong letters in the wrong envelopes. All apparently ended well, as he married – probably one of his two pen-pals – and they produced five children, including twin boys.

Interestingly, Darrell was a member of the United Methodist Church, although we neither attended church together nor do I recall us talking about religion while in the Navy. His wife had died in 1999, and Darrell, also born as I in 1930, was 80 years old at his death. I simply lost touch with him, may have exchanged a note or two after Navy days. One shouldn't bemoan too much years later what they've neglected to do, but it would have been good to have taken Mary to meet Darrell and his family.

CHAPTER 15 – ODDS AND AN ENDING

As she rode to Mass the morning of May 23, 2014 with her sister Jean and brother-in-law Al Cynova, we almost lost our beloved Mary in an automobile accident.

After waiting for several cars to pass by, Al moved the family Ford Crown Victoria across four-lane State Road 528 toward the newly-built Roman Catholic Church in Rio Rancho, northwest of Albuquerque. But, he didn't notice another vehicle, a Jeep.

The Jeep T-boned the Cynova car, flipped over it, and landed on its own top. Riding as passengers, Mary and Jean were crushed by the Crown Victoria. Luckily for them, and the rest of us, they quickly were ambulanced to the cracker-jack trauma unit at the University of New Mexico hospital.

I received calls from the Cynovas' daughter, our niece Debbie, first advising me of the accident. Then came an ominous second message saying, "Uncle Eric, Mary's heart and liver have been nicked by broken ribs. You better fly out here as quickly as possible."

When I arrived, Pam and Terry already were there and Mary had regained consciousness. With a split-open head pulled together with staples, she suffered nine other fractures, including two to her pelvic area, three to ribs, and others chipping off vertebrae tabs.

Mary remained in the UNM hospital for 10 days until she and I could fly to San Diego by Southwest Airlines accompanied with a nurse. After that came another 10 days' rehab at Stanford Court in Santee. Her stay there was under the careful and watchful eye of good-church-friend Terrie Harrell, nurse practitioner for our health-care provider - Kaiser Permanente at Stanford Court. Mary had visited Terrie's father, Don Steffe, several times in special-care facilities before his death and still helps keep tabs on Donna Steffe, well over 90. Donna lives at the same place, then Regency Park, my Mom did years earlier, now under a different name and management.

Mary still feels periodic pain, probably mostly from arthritis caused by her injuries. Sister Jean suffered fractures of her neck and vertebrae. She and Mary rested in rooms across the hall from one another at UNM's trauma unit. Jean also had a long recovery, forced for months to wear a brace around her neck.

As other sources of insurance were involved, Kaiser didn't automatically assume many of the bills for Mary's care. Paying whom, what, and why seemed over-whelming to us. Our savior appeared in niece Kristen Johnson, daughter of Mary's brother Greg. A graduate of the law school at the University of San Diego, Kristen cheerfully dug into the dozens of bills from UNM, Stanford Court, and Kaiser. Her multiple phone calls and letters amicably resolved all issues. We forever remain grateful to her.

Kristen since married her longtime companion, Jason Bush, at a beautiful wedding Mary and I were privileged to attend. She recently gave birth to a handsome son, James Gregory Bush.

In 2009, Mary had turned 75, meaning at that time she'd resided on this Fine Earth for three-quarters of a century, 58 of them putting up with me. When Mary's Big Five O had come along 25 years earlier, I'd made a reservation at the Bali Hai on Shelter Island, facing San Diego's Bay. Called up as many of her friends as I knew or could remember, mentioned what was going on, and in cheapskate fashion invited them to join us by paying for their own dinner. Can't recall exactly how many arrived (maybe 100), but know several more had to be seated than for the reservation I'd made. We had a great time that night.

Keeping that fun evening in mind, what could I do to make her special birthday even more memorable and pleasant, I hoped. As I moped around about the Big-75, good friend and longtime Methodist-church-member-buddy of Mary's, Linda Mucha, came up with the solution. "Can you reserve the clubhouse in your mobile home park?" she asked, and added, "We could have a nice potluck there for Mary."

That's what we did and Kimberly Wilton sent out the invitations. It at first was supposed to be kept secret from Mary, but it isn't a secret when more than one person knows about something. Linda suggested that her son-in-law, Jim Ybarra, could bring over his band. That part remained a secret, and music greeted Mary when she walked into the door. Wine and beer was provided which, if we'd held the affair at Mary's Methodist church, wouldn't have been kosher.

Always only grape juice for Methodists, even for communion, oddly trying to replicate the story of Biblical wine drinking by Jewish Jesus and his Disciples some 2,000 years earlier. The latest I've read is that, in the days of Jesus, beer may have been the drink. Water way back then wasn't healthy, as it still isn't in many countries of the world. Nor in Flint, Michigan, and lead also recently has been discovered in some of San Diego schools' drinking water.

Linda took over as mistress of ceremonies after the eating and drinking (no heavy quaffing occurred). Accolades came not only from Mary's church friends, but also Soulmates and the Mission Bells RV Club. Mary had been in on the organizing of Soulmates. Five to 10 women friends meet once a month for lunch and to share stories about their lives and spirituality.

I can't recall (took no notes) of all the good things which were said that 75th occasion in praise of Mary. At an earlier United Methodist Women's meeting, Mary had been singled out as a "special person" by her super-special friend, Esther Thomas:

"In her circle she is known for her thoughtful devotions, and sharing which gives a clear picture of her love for her husband, mother, daughters, and grandchildren.

"Church life and outreach would have been a great loss without her. Some of her contributions include leadership and/or membership in the Lay Pastor's Committee, Disciples classes, Companions in Christ, chairing Staff-Parish Relations, heading up the homeless shelter, recruiting, encouraging and training the lay liturgists, and demonstrating outreach through missions and the housing committee. We do love you Mary Odendahl.

It could be that some sort of yet-unknown Methodist-like DNA courses through Mary Ethel's body. Her grandfather, William Marvin Johnson, was a Methodist minister — as were his twin brothers, John G. and Jesse Sykes. (You'll recall that her other grandfather, Franklin Grigg, also was listed as a Methodist — although Mary knew her Grandma Mary as a practicing Baptist.)

Mary's minister Grandfather Johnson's parents were Lydia Carver and William Cannon Johnson. They produced 15 children, of whom five died in a typhus epidemic in Mississippi. Those dying immediately were buried in shallow graves, later exhumed for formal funerals and "proper" burials.

One necessary-early-grave appeared strange. *"When they dug up one of the girls,"* Cousin Kim Johnson, son of Mary's Uncle Marvin wrote, *"they found she had been still alive. She had torn her hair out and scratched the inside of her coffin until her fingernails were off. ....Brrrrr!"*

Among the survivors was Ethel McCoy Johnson, later to become the Angel of Aztec, New Mexico. It was great-"Aunt Ethel" from whom Mary received her middle name. Aunt Ethel had come to Aztec when her brother —Mary's grandfather —arrived there after being assigned as minister of the Aztec Methodist Church.

Mary's grandfather had contracted tuberculosis. Hoping an even-drier climate than Aztec would help him, he was ordered to Alamogordo, New Mexico, where a Methodist minister was needed. Cousin Kim continues about their grandfather:

"He ignored the doctor's advice and kept going out in the middle of nights, cold, wet, dusty.. He died in 1913 - fell so ill after being out one night ministering to someone else who was sick, that he took to bed. The doctor said that he would never get out of bed, and he didn't. They called in the four boys - (who) went in one-at-a-time to say goodbye to their father."

That's the way Mary's compassion works. I'd bet if she were down with influenza, and a friend — especially from her La Mesa United Methodist Church, was in some sort of dire need, she'd rush out, wobbly-driving her car to render aid. Mary's younger sister, Phyllis, who also special-models after their Aunt Ethel, continually tends to the needs of family and friends in the Albuquerque area.

After Mary's grandfather's death from TB in Alamogordo, her Grandmother Maggie (Margaret Julia) moved the family by railroad back to Aztec, near where she had bought a farm. The four sons she raised alone were Grider (Albert Grider — 1900-1976), Brady (William Brady 1902-1952), Mary's father Chick (Charles Wesley, born in Mississippi, 1905-1970), and Marvin (Marvin Jesse 1910-1991).

Grider attempted to follow in his father's footsteps, working toward becoming a Methodist minister. Something happened, and he converted to a dedicated Roman Catholic. Mary's Uncle Grider always greeted her as "Saint Mary," sort'a in jest but at the same time the family was extremely proud of her long work in high school with Job's Daughters in Albuquerque, during which she reigned as one of their queens.

With only meager attendance at the Community Church in Hurley, my first taste of Methodism came in 1953 when attending the Albuquerque church with Mary just before and after we married. Following one service, her father and brother-in-law Tom Hill (Phyllis's first husband) and I smoked cigarettes out on the lawn while waiting for the women to finish chatting inside. It was money-raising time, and the preacher had mentioned tithing, that forking over 10% percent of one's earnings to his church as a pretty good thing to think about doing.

I asked Chick about it and he smiled and said, "Oh, you and Mary shouldn't worry too much about that." He knew we were living on our small salaries that summer, mine as a fill-in at Associated Press and Mary's meager earnings as secretary in the UNM Journalism Department.

"What you and Mary could do, if you wanted to," he added, "is just give the church 10% percent of your net income, not the gross." a single mother's 10% percent net amounts about $2,000. Such a church tithe would place her family in even more dire straits. She might, whenever able to, simply place $1 or $5 into the collection plate on those weeks she attends church.

Over the years, I have mentioned Chick's net-tithing plan to ministers of both Methodist and Presbyterian churches. Most usually roll their eyes in a sort of shocked disbelief. Perhaps in Hebrew-Testament-Biblical Days, pious religiously tithing to Jewish priests amounted to 10% percent of crops or earnings. In this day and age, one is able to "give back" not only through churches but by contributions to many really-needy charities. I think total church/charities giving should be considered as one's "tithe," if you're even kind'a interested in calling your charity-giving as that ancient practice.

Haven't researched it, but wonder how much those ancient Jews in Jesus' time really paid in taxes to their ruling body — the Romans? Mary and I are being assessed at 34% percent by the feds, plus what California demands. We pay the feds, after deductions, what actually amounts to about 10% percent. That money, rightly called "the price of civilization" helps provide for education, for healthy bodies with Medicare and Medicaid, for unemployment benefits, for Social Security in our last years, and so forth - for everyone. Added are sales taxes, and on and on. The bulk totals much more than a 10% percent "tithe" to local, state, and federal governments. As another matter, Mary and I resent helping pay many more billions of dollars than necessary into the "defense" budget, some of it sent overseas to kill thousands each year. Others have other pet peeves about where their tax money goes.

But, "the times they are changing." Me thinks. Sometimes, for the better. During this writing in May of 2017, here is what it was reported Pope Francis had to say:

"It is not necessary to believe in God to be a good person. In a way, the traditional notion of God is outdated. One can be spiritual but not religious. It is not necessary to go to church and give money — for many, nature can be a church. Some of the best people in history did not believe in God, while some of the worst deeds were done in His name."

I've already been accused of too much "preaching" in my two novels and will let it go at that. Of course, one advantage of novel or short-story writing is that you don't necessarily need to defend characters' arguments or beliefs as paralleling personal ones. When cornered, the novelist or short-story writer may reply, "Oh, I guess that's what one of my characters said or maybe might have meant. It's up to you to think about and decide."

Our daughters attended the Methodist church in La Mesa while they were growing up, gradually drifting away. Terry was graduated at age 16 from Helix High School. Mary and I figured she was too young to leave home. She attended San Diego State University, earning her B.A. degree, moved on to be awarded M.A. and PhD degrees in anthropology from the University of Colorado.

"Why didn't you go to Berkeley for your B.A.," Terry often has been asked when applying for jobs. The University of California at Berkeley was thought to have the premier anthropology program in the state.

Pam did go to Berkeley. She first attended several junior (now community) colleges as we began to wonder what the result would be. She transferred to Berkeley and was graduated with honors in psychology. She also was graduated from San Jose State University with a master's in marriage and family counseling.

I'm convinced our daughters retain much of their Johnson mother's Methodist-DNA. The jobs they have taken invariably involve helping other people. Mary and I are more than immensely proud of them, as we are of our socially-conscious and compassionate grandchildren. Just in: Grandson Jeremy Quant has proposed to his significant other, Jaimie Lynne Angeles. Even received a Facebook pic showing the ring on her finger.

Jeremy and Jaimie

In the early years of the 21ˢᵗ Century, Uno came to live with us. When he first arrived in Santee, the plan was to keep the border collie while Terry did a stint teaching at Georgetown University in Washington, D.C. She had acquired Uno as a registered puppy, but as he was to be neutered, his breeding "papers" were of little use. Terry raised him as he grew into a gentle and beautiful black and white dog — with a freckled white face. By the time the year had passed, Mary and I had become quite attached to Uno. It was a very difficult decision for them when Terry, Eleanor, and Claire allowed us to take full custody of him.

Uno

Mary had been doing volunteer work at Sharp's Grossmont Hospital in La Mesa, part of the 11ᵗʰ Hour program led by the Rev. Debbie Timmons, still her fast friend. When someone neared death, the person was able to receive spiritual care. Mary or another compassionate volunteer sat with them — talking to, or more likely gently rubbing and patting arms of comatose patients. It takes special persons to do this sort of charity. I, for example, have a fear of catching something from sick people. And, being around those close to death reminds me too much of my own mortality.

Yet, Mary suggested mild-mannered Uno might make a good therapy dog at Grossmont Hospital. During five-weeks' supervision by Nan Arthur and her Whole Dog Training, Uno worked his way through the hospital's-required American Kennel Club Canine Good Citizen Program. The day arrived for his final test for registration. For an hour before I walked Uno through what might be expected, talking softly to him, reminding how important it all was for both of us.

What I viewed the toughest part of the test was telling your dog to "Stay," then walking away from and not being followed. When that command came up, I ordered "Stay" to Uno and retreated behind a fairly far-away tree. Uno stayed in his seated position, never moving. On August 28, 2006, Uno received his official Canine Good Citizen certificate from the American Kennel Club.

Grossmont Hospital assigned Uno and me to join on walks in the wards with experienced Jean Allen, who had accompanied several other therapy dogs. Uno proved up to the task of putting his nose on beds of those patients who wished to pet him. Some missed their little buddies at home. A few others realized they never would be leaving the hospital alive. Yet quite often Jean, Uno, and I walked away, bowing quietly to the wishes of persons who said things like, "I don't need no damn dog in my room" or simply shook their heads.

Jean Allen and I received a nice note September 14, 2011, from the lady in charge of volunteers at Grossmont Hospital:

"Congratulations on receiving the enclosed Cardgram. Our patients and staff love you and I'm delighted and honored you both are part of our volunteer program!"

Fondly,

Linda Van Fulpen

Jean had a wonderful way with patients, but Uno deserved much of the credit. At one annual volunteers' meeting, when Uno's freckled face flashed on the screen for a few seconds, there were oohs and ahs throughout the large room.

It came very quietly, when obviously Uno was sick. I still see those eyes looking up at us for help, which we were unable to give. A couple of days later, finding no improvement, Mary and I took him to the veterinary clinic, where he was pronounced very ill, advised to stay overnight for observation. When we arrived the next morning, we were told Uno had died during the night.

That was very tough on us, and I believe I probably mourned more for Uno than any dog before him. Perhaps no more than for Skippy, my little dog when maybe I was 10 or 12 years old.

One hot day at 5 Aztec Street in Hurley, I'd carried Skippy with me up a trellis and on to the roof of our house. The metal roof was too hot for Skippy's paws, and I couldn't figure exactly how to carry him back down the trellis. So, I leaned over and dropped him to the ground. Bad News! One of Skippy's back legs broke.

When Dad came home, he gave me one of my well-deserved "don't you have any better sense than that" lectures. But he carefully and gently made a splint for Skippy and my little buddy was able to hop around. A few days later I arrived home from wandering somewhere around Hurley and noticed Skippy lying on our front porch. I went forward, to reach out to pet him. Mom appeared at the screen door and said, "Don't touch Him."

"Why not?"

"He's dead, Max. He's been run over by a car."

There was a 20-mile-per-hour speed limit for Hurley's dirt streets, but cars moving faster often blew dust into our yard. Mom didn't tell me the name of the driver of the car which killed Skippy. There was a lady down the street who routinely raised dust barreling by in her Studebaker Champion. It didn't matter, because I fell into not only grief but extreme guilt for dropping my little buddy off the hot roof. I felt that without his leg in a splint, Skippy would have gotten out of the way of the car.

There is an epilogue to the Skippy story, which I shouldn't repeat, but *of course* I will. A couple of years later another male youngster and I got the idea we ought to dig Skippy out of his grave in the backyard "to see what he looks like." We had just begun digging, not quite reached what might have been left of the dog.

"What are you boys up to?" Mom shouted, this time through the screen of the back door.

"Digging up Skippy," I replied.

"Stop that right away and put all that dirt right back in the hole," she ordered in an exasperated voice.

As for Uno, I especially missed having him along for our morning strolls. One day, weeks later, I received an email from Uno's former trainer, Nan Arthur, telling us about a dog available at the Rancho Coastal Humane Society in Encinitas, just up the coast. I had mentioned thinking about a smaller dog than Uno, and Nan figured this black-and-brown Kelpi — an Australian herding dog — might fit the bill. The pair had become acquainted during some demonstrations at the rescue facility and Nan said Bailey knew all the commands, was smart, and gentle.

I looked up the offerings at Rancho Coastal Humane Society and found a video of Bailey. She ran in a field, doing some fetching. Another sequence was of her being petted in the lap of an attendant. I called David Goff, and he took a gander at the video. We agreed to take a look at Bailey as soon as possible. Mary felt we needed to study more dogs in more places, but the three of us rode to the shelter and I asked to see Bailey. She immediately went to Mary, although my good wife still contends that was because she had a treat in her hand.

Bailey

Nevertheless, after waiting and paying for some dental and other medical work, we fetched the fetcher. Brother-in-law Bill Voss, a veterinarian himself, warned by phone, "Don't judge your new dog against Uno." It was difficult not to. Mary and I have found Bailey to be an especially loving companion, even though overly protective of us. This means we have to keep her away from other dogs when out walking. She is a herder, which sometimes makes her want to nip at strangers, even in our mobile home.

I think one needs to remember that, when you "rescue" a pet, you're often assuming a bad habit or problem. It's somewhat like having the patience to raise a child with special needs. That's all forgotten when Bailey pokes her nose against me each morning as if saying, "It's time to get up." Even after Mary rises and takes him out to pee and search for critters, Bailey comes back in and waits by our bed for me.

Mary, "the girls," and "the grandkids" in 2010 gracefully bestowed upon me a wonderful 80th birthday party at Pinnacle Peak, a now out-of-business steakhouse then only a few blocks away from where we reside at 7467 Mission Gorge Road, Space 165, Highlands Mobile Home Park in western Santee.[75]

I have no idea exactly how many family and friends showed up for the gala steak-chicken-or-salmon Big-Eight-0 event May 28, 2010, but a good guess would be 75. It was "done up right." I hope everyone enjoyed it as much as I did. Naturally, "no gifts, please" were requested from party-goers.

---

[75] Mary and I have lived here after selling our house at 8273 Vista Drive in La Mesa in 2001. We had resided in La Mesa since 1964, on Vista since 1966.

Nevertheless, among the gifts: Mary's nephew Kenny Johnson and wife Karis felt that at my age I needed a bottle of prune juice; her niece Maegan and hubby Chris provided two sets of suspenders to keep my pants from falling down. Another of Mary's nieces, Debbie Talik and husband Stan, handed me a cane with a mirror at the bottom (for dirty old men to check under skirts) and a rubber squeeze horn to get other folks moving out of the way while performing such antics. Along with it came an ear-horn, an "Over-the-Hill-Never-Fail Hearing Enhancer" – to use when hearing aids are out of action.

Terry presented a bright-red Hudson Bay blanket which she had bargained for and picked up at the last minute on eBay[76]. Months before, Mary had bought a comfortable birthday-present office chair in which rests my too-rapidly-aging butt as I "pen" these immortal words. A Christmas or so later, Pam and Sheldon surprised me with a large, flat-screen Samsung TV, on which Mary and I have come to enjoy streaming Netflix, Amazon, and other programs.

Sheldon, Terry, Mary, me and Pam

---

[76] One which I'd wanted for a long time. As brother Alan and I grew up cold nights on cots in a sleeping porch in Hurley, I've wished for heavier bed covers over me than Mary does. This blanket is a single size, so it covers only my side of the bed. *Neat!!!*

The real gifts were the priceless love and affection shown by all whom attended. Two of the night's highlights were singing by granddaughters Claire and Eleanor Bernstein a couple of my Patsy Cline favorites. Claire sang *Crazy,* and Ele sang *I Fall to Pieces.* Both young women captured Patsy's nuances. I know it was difficult work with long practice of what to them must be dorky old Cowboy/Western tunes. For the old guy, it was *special.*

(Incidentally, *Crazy* was written and first sung by Willie Nelson, later made famous by Patsy. At the time, Nelson's gravelly voice wasn't appreciated by the makers of country records. He's still on the road singing and enjoying his pot.)

I gave a little speech, but refrained from sharing what it means to be 80. Sand approaching the bottom of the top portion of a two-tiered timer glass appears to move much faster. Of course, time moves at the same rate while the Earth turns every 24 hours — as each day passes by – and, as the Earth revolves around the sun every 365 days, another year in one's life is gone forever.

One can look back, wonder what more might have been accomplished during those many used-up revolutions of the Earth, but that's a futile exercise. And, there is no way of knowing how long or what lies ahead. Most of us old-timers would prefer to "throw off this mortal coil" during our sleep rather than suffer some long, painful illness or slow erosion of healthy bodily functions. Worse yet, gradually forget everything in some form of serious dementia. That's also out of our hands.

Victor Hugo[77] is supposed to have had this inscription over his study:

To rise at six, to dine at ten,

To sup at six, to sleep at ten,

Makes a man live for ten times ten.

Eight hours is about the amount of sleep I get (sometimes plus an afternoon nap in my stuffed chair — not actually a nap, of course, just resting my eyes), generally sit down for three rather than two meals each day. My druthers would be more like Hugo's, a "brunch" at about nine and "supper" at about five. I certainly should lose more weight to make Hugo's plan work. (Who knows how much food the prodigious writer put away as he dined and supped?)

---

[77] Victor-Marie Hugo was a French poet, playwright, novelist, essayist, statesman, human rights activist, and exponent of the Romantic movement in France. Romanticism emphasized a free form of writing showing strong emotions, experiences of common people, and imaginative expressions and passion.

The fly in the ointment of this theory is that Hugo was born February 26, 1802, and died May 22, 1885. He didn't make his "ten times ten." Yet, with life expectancy much shorter in the 1800s, living to age 83 before modern "miracle drugs" and more complicated operations was uncommon. Perhaps his eating regime did help him.

"You makes your choices and takes your chances," I recall someone saying.

Sometime after 80 seems to be the age that most drivers ease out from behind the steering wheel of their motor-homes. It happened to me after I clipped the passenger mirror of a van in the next lane. Mary and I had "camped" about once a month in motor-homes for nearly 30 years starting in 1986 with the Mission Bells Trailer Club.

She mentioned it was one of the happiest times she had seen me be when in 2013 I self-published my first novel, *The Peeping Tom Murders of Cobre*.[78] The way that came about was that one of Mary's good church friends, Fern Bowen, also attended Lois Knowlton's film discussion group. We separately went to a "picture show" once each month and the group later discussed the film at Lois and Roger Knowlton's home. Fern was in her 90s then, clear-headedly joining the discussions. She died at 103, still alert, but suffering from a severe leg infection.

Somehow, I speculate probably from Mary, Fern learned about my unpublished novel and asked her daughter, Peggy Lang, if she'd help me. An editor, ghostwriter, and writing consultant, Peggy recently was honored for "Best Action/Suspense/ Thriller" at San Diego Book Awards for co-authoring with former Illinois Gov. Dan Walker (1973-1977) *Assassin's Game.*

As Peggy advised me about self-publishing by Amazon's Kindle, she quickly put me in touch with Kimberly Rotter, an editor proficient at preparing manuscripts for Kindle. She also shared the expertise of Robbie Adkins, an artist who produces beautiful book covers.

The fly in the ointment is that Kindle does not accept manuscripts produced in WordPerfect. It does take the Word of Microsoft, but even that process takes someone with the skill of Kimberly Rotter to produce the proper format.

What it meant was that I had to change all of my older WordPerfect format writing into Word. Larger flies in the ointment were messages popping up at random in Word saying "Read Only," which meant constantly forced to save additions and changes to chapters with new titles. If I neglected to delete former "Read Only" chapters or additions to them, it became quite confusing as to what had been added or deleted. Where I was, and still am, in the process. I've lost and/or repeated a great deal of what I wrote over the years

---

[78] There's a link to *Cobre* at the end of this book in case you want to have a look.

because of this dratted "Read Only" process. "Not that it matters very much," you might be saying as you struggle through this over-bloated tome.

Peggy Lang and Kimberly Rotter were on the phone walking me through the whole process, helping right up to just before press-time in 2013. They helped select the title, *The Peeping Tom Murders of Cobre.* (Kimberly even wrote the back cover.) Cobre, meaning copper in Spanish, was a town patterned after Hurley. Besides two young peepers who witnessed a murder, the book introduced State Patrolman Elmer Thornton.

Kimberly and Robbie graciously helped in the production of *Alien Second Comings?*[79], a sequel about now-retired State Police Chief Thornton and his wife, Amy. This time an alien from outer space arrives and gives advice to their friend, Slim Maxwell, the surviving peeping tom as a teenager in the first novel. The Thorntons have taken Slim under their wing.

The second book had been produced with encouragement after a reading of a draft by the Rev. Laurel Gray. (Of course, this doesn't mean he necessarily is in agreement with all of it.) A retired Lutheran minister and former journalist, Laurel was my mentor at one of his Progressive Christianity groups. I am much more at peace now after viewing Christianity as an historical process rather than it being simply judgmental. Nevertheless, life and death still remain a mystery for me.

My last active charity work, besides still joining Mary and others at her church feeding of 30 to 40 homeless persons once a month, was volunteering as a part of Senior Gleaners. With three women, Ann Evans, Lois Pasquale, and Carol Schoenfeld, I rode up early each Tuesday to a Von's supermarket in Poway. We'd collect bakery goods, transport them to a warehouse in Lakeside. Needy churches and organizations in East San Diego County came by and collected the food.

I gave up those neat rides for several years with pleasant women because age had caused irregular early-morning habits with my innards. One interesting aspect was that one of the Senior Gleaners' volunteer women resented competition in food gathering from such groups as Feeding America and Food for the Poor. They are listed as non-profits, but unlike our all-volunteer unit, pay organizers and food gatherers.

"I guess it doesn't matter all that much," I remarked, "if food gets to the needy."

Silence, meaning no agreement on that.

---

[79] There's a link to *Alien*, too, at the end of this book.

Much earlier, when I served on the board of Elderhelp, we found the charity requiring more office space. "Maybe we can take over all the upstairs room that Alpha outfit is using," was one comment. It was stated as if The Alpha Project, which I knew did much for the very needy, wasn't worthwhile.

One of our church friends, Ilene Davis, was working there several days a week.

It was pointed out in a recent San Diego *Reader* story that The Alpha Project "*has been growing from a very small program giving jobs to homeless men and women 30 years ago to now, when we have places and programs all the way up to the Bay Area.*"

Another example, this while representing the La Mesa Methodist church on the board of the San Diego Organizing Project. SDOP is a faith-based group, mainly of Roman Catholic churches throughout the county, seeking added justice while responding to community concerns in their neighborhoods: Catholic Father Joe's name came up.

Father Joe Carroll has, since 1982, run the St. Vincent de Paul Village. In 1976 he had been assigned to St. Pius X Parish in Chula Vista and then to St. Rita Parish. In 1985, Joan Kroc — widow of McDonald's multi-millionaire founder Ray Kroc — contributed $3 million to begin construction of the Village. Father Joe's Village maintains 365 units of affordable housing and 140 units of permanent supportable housing. Hundreds of homeless persons line up each day at Father Joe's to be fed.

"Father Joe doesn't do much to help us," someone on the SDOP board remarked. "He likes to stay in his own territory."

Just three minor examples of how human beings, even those working hard with compassion toward helping others, often appear to find some difficulty existing together. Just another interesting aspect of life of which, overall, I have little understanding.

As I write in late July of 2017, I'm looking down at a brightly-painted rock sitting next to my computer. It was presented to me on my 38th birthday in 1968 by an artist - Myrna Gibson, then wife of colleague Roland Bower teaching Sociology at San Diego State.

Savvy detectives on the TV tube often claim "there are no coincidences" when trying to solve crimes. Maybe not, with Mary and Myrna as they noticed one another in 1964 at a meeting for new - faculty wives at San Diego State College. For Mary and Myrna both had attended Highland High School in Albuquerque, and both of them were in its first graduating class. As our families became good friends, Myrna taught Terry how to play the guitar.

As to the rock Myrna painted white: Printed on it in separate colors are *Who, What, When, Where, and Why*. Of course, in beginning reporting classes, journalism teachers try to drum into students to ask those four questions. And a fifth, if you can or are lucky enough to find out - *How*. That rock rested as a paper weight on my desk for 24 of my 28 years at State.

I've worn behind-the-ear hearing aids for decades, with sounds becoming even more garbled. A couple of days ago at a routine eye exam, my Kaiser optometrist told me I have the beginning of macular degeneration, a progressive ailment with no cure. These are among clear sign things are moving toward the end.

This old reporter doesn't have the answer to any of those routine journalist's questions except *Who*? Natch, that's me. *When*? No idea when I'll die. *Where?* No idea. *What* will happen? No idea. And no idea about *How*?

"You Just Got'ta Keep Right On'a Truckin'," is all I can tell you. Preceding my last-gasp - ending of Looney Tunes travels along twisted crossroads and paths, I imagine the final three signs might read, *"No U-Turn," "No Outlet"* and *"Dead End."* For those Looney-Tunes-age men and women speculating about any sort'a after-life, I figure a reasonable first question they ought'a get set to be a' askin' is, *"What's Up, Doc?"*

The end.

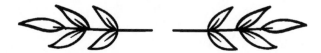

Eric Odendahl's books on Amazon

The Peeping Tom Murders of Cobre (The New Mexico Highway Patrolman Series Book 1)

http://amzn.to/2vp75Tj

Alien Second Comings?? (The New Mexico Highway Patrolman Series Book 2)

http://amzn.to/2voNov7

Praise for Eric Odendahl's novels:

"The book is a page turner."

"This is one of the most interesting reads I've had in years! A roller coaster ride that keeps you on the edge of your seat through a shocking ending. An imagination gone wild! A must read!"

"I felt like I was transported back in time. I couldn't put it down!"

"This story was great for the unexpected resolution to the stories as everything came together at the end."

"This book is so fascinating that I couldn't put it down! It is so well written."

Made in the USA
San Bernardino, CA
17 December 2017